International Free Trade Agreements and Labour Rights

International Studies in Human Rights

VOLUME 151

The titles published in this series are listed at *brill.com/ishr*

International Free Trade Agreements and Labour Rights

New Global Perspectives

Edited by

Jo Carby-Hall and Aneta Tyc

BRILL | NIJHOFF

ISSN 0924-4751
ISBN 978-90-04-76224-4
ISBN 978-90-04-76225-1 (PDF)
DOI https://doi.org/10.1163/9789004762251

Library of Congress Control Number: 2026935325

Brill Nijhoff and Koninklijke Brill BV are part of De Gruyter Brill.
www.degruyterbrill.com

Questions about General Product Safety Regulation: productsafety@degruyterbrill.com

We dedicate this book to the memory of Professor Cornelia Staritz who was to write a chapter

Requiescat in pace

Contents

PART 3
The US's and Canada's approach

PART 4
Australia and New Zealand's approach

Foreword

It is a profound honour for me to write this foreword to International Free Trade Agreements and Labour Rights: New Global Perspectives, edited by Professor Joseph Carby-Hall and Professor Aneta Tyc. This volume is a landmark contribution to the study of international trade and labour law, offering a rich, multidisciplinary, and globally comparative analysis of how free trade agreements (FTAs) intersect with the protection and promotion of labour rights.

I have had the privilege of knowing Professor Carby-Hall for many years – first as my academic tutor and later as a colleague at the University of Hull Law School. His lifelong dedication to the advancement of labour law, combined with his encyclopaedic knowledge and deep humanity, has made him a towering figure in the field. His intellectual generosity, unwavering commitment to justice, and encyclopaedic knowledge of labour law have shaped the work of generations of scholars and practitioners, including my own. Professor Aneta Tyc, a distinguished scholar in her own right, brings a sharp legal mind and a global perspective to this collaboration. Together, they have curated a volume that is both intellectually rigorous and deeply relevant to contemporary global challenges.

This book arrives at a critical moment in the evolution of global trade governance. As FTAs increasingly incorporate labour provisions, questions arise about their effectiveness, enforceability, and real-world impact. The contributors to this volume – drawn from diverse jurisdictions and disciplines – engage with these questions through legal analysis, economic critique, and empirical case studies, offering insights that are both theoretically robust and practically grounded. The volume is structured into four sensible and logical thematic parts, each addressing a distinct dimension of the trade–labour connection:

Part 1: A Policy and Economic Approach

This section lays the foundation for understanding the shifting landscape of trade and labour governance. Sandra Polaski explores the transition from state-level obligations to firm-level accountability, particularly in the context of the USMCA and EU due diligence directives. Christoph Scherrer critically examines the economic debates surrounding labour clauses, contrasting neoclassical and institutional paradigms and highlighting methodological challenges in assessing impact. Martin Myant's case study on Vietnam offers a nuanced view of how trade agreements can influence domestic labour reforms, especially in authoritarian regimes, and the role of international pressure in shaping outcomes.

Part 2: The European Union's Approach

Silvio Bologna provides a legal analysis of the EU's external trade strategy, including the horizontal social clause, the Generalised System of Preferences (GSP Plus), and the role of dispute settlement mechanisms such as ISDS. Axel Marx and Angela María Vanegas Pérez evaluate the use of roadmaps and action plans to strengthen labour rights compliance, drawing on comparative experiences from Bangladesh, Guatemala, and other countries. These chapters highlight the EU's evolving model of "principled globalisation", balancing trade liberalisation with enforceable labour standards and civil society engagement.

Part 3: The US's and Canada's Approach

Jean-Baptiste Velut introduces the concept of "de-FTA-zation", reflecting the shift in US trade policy towards sectoral agreements and autonomous measures. He maps out the implications of this shift for labour rights, including the rise of executive agreements and unilateral enforcement tools such as the Uighur Forced Labour Prevention Act. Vincenzo Ferrante examines the Euro-Canadian CETA, focusing on its social chapter and the legal controversies surrounding investor–state dispute settlement. Professors Carby-Hall and Tyc assess the modernised Canada–Ukraine FTA, exploring its potential to support post-war reconstruction and labour reform through enforceable labour provisions and inclusive development strategies.

Part 4: Australia and New Zealand's Approach

Joo-Cheong Tham critiques Australia's externally driven and inconsistent approach to labour provisions, arguing that its commitments often reflect external pressure rather than internal conviction. Stephen Hoadley traces New Zealand's progressive integration of labour rights into FTAs, while acknowledging the limitations of enforcement and transparency. These chapters underscore the role of domestic political culture and civil society in shaping labour commitments in trade agreements.

Final Reflections and Recommendations

The concluding chapter, co-authored by the editors, synthesises the lessons learned across jurisdictions and offers forward-looking recommendations. It emphasises the need for enforceable mechanisms, transparency, civil society participation, and multilateral cooperation to overcome competitive pressures that hinder labour standards, particularly in developing economies. The editors advocate for a more coherent and principled approach to trade governance – one that places human rights and social justice at its core.

Key Themes and Contributions

This volume is distinguished by its global scope, interdisciplinary methodology, and critical engagement with the trade–labour nexus. Among its key themes are:

- The shift from state-centric to firm-level accountability in labour governance, reflecting the realities of global supply chains.
- The tension between economic liberalisation and social protection, and the need for trade agreements to reconcile these competing imperatives.
- The role of civil society and institutional innovation, including roadmaps, advisory groups, and dispute mechanisms, in monitoring and enforcing labour commitments.
- The fragmentation of traditional FTA frameworks and the emergence of new instruments such as sectoral agreements and autonomous measures.
- The importance of comparative analysis, drawing lessons from diverse jurisdictions to inform future policy design.

This book does not merely document existing practices – it interrogates them, challenges assumptions, and proposes pathways towards more equitable and sustainable trade governance. It reminds us that trade is not merely a technical or economic endeavour, but a profoundly human one, with real consequences for workers, communities, and societies.

For scholars, policymakers, trade negotiators, and labour advocates, this volume offers both a diagnostic and a roadmap. It identifies gaps in current practice and proposes concrete solutions to bridge them. It is a call to action for those committed to building a global trading system that respects and uplifts the dignity of all workers.

I commend Professors Carby-Hall and Tyc for their vision, dedication, and scholarly excellence. Their work stands as a beacon for those seeking to align trade policy with the values of fairness, inclusion, and justice. I hope this volume will inspire further research, dialogue, and action towards a more just and inclusive global economy.

Professor Surya P. Subedi, OBE, KC (Hon)
DPhil and DCL (Oxford)
Professor of International Law, University of Leeds
Honorary Fellow of Exeter College of the University of Oxford
Former UN Special Rapporteur for Human Rights in Cambodia
13 October 2025

Figures and Tables

Figures

Tables

Notes on Contributors

Jo Carby-Hall
Professor/Director: MA, LLB, PhD, D.Litt., LLD (honoris causa) Advocate, is a former editor of "Managerial Law" and Deputy Editor (law) of the "Journal of Legislative Studies", published thirty-two books, numerous chapters in books, encyclopaedia, and articles in five languages, and is a legal adviser to governments/international organisations. He was awarded four State Orders for his advice.

Aneta Tyc
Dr Habil. Iur., Associate Professor at the Department of European, International and Collective Labour Law of the University of Lodz, is an author of numerous publications in the field of labour law, including *Global Trade, Labour Rights and International Law: A Multilevel Approach* (Routledge, 2021).

Sandra Polaski
MA Johns Hopkins School of Advanced International Studies, is an expert on the intersection of trade, labour and social policy. She has published widely on these issues, most recently on the Rapid Response Labor Mechanism of the USMCA.

Christoph Scherrer
is a full professor emeritus of globalisation and politics and an associate of the Kassel Institute for Sustainability; he is a former executive director of the International Center for Development and Decent Work. His research includes the social dimensions of global economic governance.

Martin Myant
is Emeritus Professor at the University of the West of Scotland and Associate Researcher, European Trade Union Institute, Brussels. He has published on eastern European economic development, on European economic policies and on labour provisions in trade agreements.

Silvio Bologna
PhD-Doctor Europaeus (2014), is Professor of Labor law at the University of Palermo and visiting professor of Comparative Labor Law at the University of Paris XII. He has published monographs and articles on international, com-

parative, European, and Italian labour law, including "Le mansioni del lavoratore tra garantismo e liberalizzazione" (2024).

Axel Marx
is Deputy Director of the Leuven Centre for Global Governance Studies (KU Leuven). He has published over 300 papers in journals and books and (co-) edited more than 20 books and special issues, many related to labour rights protection.

Angela María Vanegas Pérez
is Assistant Professor at Universidad EAFIT and a PhD candidate in Administration. Her research examines sustainable development and trade agreements from a management perspective, contributing to global governance debates. She publishes on sustainability, international trade, public policy, and organisational challenges in emerging markets.

Jean-Baptiste Velut
is Professor of American Studies at Sorbonne Nouvelle University of Paris. He has a long record of academic and policy-oriented publications on US and EU trade policies and has coordinated several international research projects on trade governance.

Vincenzo Ferrante
Dr. iur. (1991), PhD (1995), is a professor at the Catholic University of Milan. He has published monographs and articles on nearly every aspect of contemporary labour law and most recently a handbook on Italian social security (Nozioni di diritto della previdenza sociale, WK, 5th ed. 2024).

Joo-Cheong Tham
is a professor at Melbourne Law School. He specialises in labour law and the law of democracy and labour law. Since the 2019 student climate strikes, his research is increasingly orientated towards the climate crisis.

Stephen Hoadley
(PhD Calif) recently retired as a professor of international politics at the University of Auckland. He is author or editor of 14 books, most recently *New Zealand Trade Negotiations*, *New Zealand–United States Relations*, and the Springer Nature *series on International Human Rights*. He is currently editor of the Professional Journal of the Royal New Zealand Navy.

CHAPTER 1

International Free Trade Agreements and Labour Rights: An Introductory Essay

Jo Carby-Hall and Aneta Tyc

Labour provisions in international free trade agreements (FTAs) have proliferated during the last two decades. From only four in 1995, the number of FTAs which include labour provisions increased to 77 in 2016, to 85 in 2019 and to 128 in 2024. Thus, the share of FTAs including labour provisions has increased from 7.3% of the total number of FTAs in 1995 to 28.8% in 2016, to 29% in 2019 and to 40% in 2024.[1] There exist in the world different approaches to labour provisions in FTAs. The aim of this book is to confront the EU's stance on the one hand (the EU still looks for enforcement solutions) with the US's, Canada's, Australia's and New Zealand's approaches on the other hand. If FTAs should constitute a solution for workers, labour provisions included in them have to protect effectively workers' rights. This book shall help answer the research questions of: how to provide not only economic growth but also labour protection through incorporating enforceable labour provisions into FTAs; how to make trade fairer; how to make labour provisions in FTAs more effective, increase their positive impact and make them guarantee effective enforcement of labour rights; how to reduce inequalities between those who own capital and those who carry out work and reduce power imbalances between the global North and the global South; and how to guarantee the effectiveness of international labour standards, in particular fundamental labour rights, including the rights of women and Indigenous Peoples.

The selection of chapters includes most recent and significant advancement in the research field enjoying a worldwide impact. Academics representing different traditions of scholarship and practice, and based in different countries, contributed with their original chapters which have been divided into four parts of this monograph. As a consequence, the book covers a diverse and original range of themes and research questions, *inter alia*: a comparative analysis of existing roadmaps and plans of action, and – consequently – an

1 ILO's LP Hub, https://webapps.ilo.org/LPhub/; ILO, Labour Provisions in G7 Trade Agreements: A comparative perspective (Geneva: ILO 2019) 15.

analysis of the possibilities and limitations, effectiveness and efficiency of using roadmaps to strengthen the implementation of labour rights commitments in the EU FTAs; examining the possible implementation of more effective enforcement mechanisms regarding social obligations in the context of the Comprehensive Economic and Trade Agreement between the EU and Canada; discussing and assessing the modernised 2023 Canada–Ukraine Free Trade Agreement's labour provisions, their potentials and limitations, and formulating possible steps for the future, in particular addressed to countries which would like to follow Canada's footsteps and conclude a FTA with Ukraine; Australia's "puzzling" approach to labour provisions in FTAs; an analysis and assessment of the labour rights protection provisions of New Zealand's most recent FTAs; lesson learned from Vietnam's FTAs concluded with the USA and the EU regarding conditions for the negotiation of meaningful and effective labour provisions, in other words, how Vietnam's experience can serve as a test sample when researching the effectiveness of labour provisions in FTAs. Offering an interdisciplinary perspective (including not only law, but also other disciplines such as policy studies and economics), a critical insight and a problem-solving approach, our book also discusses the economic controversy over the impact of workers' rights clauses in FTAs, as well as a shift in focus of several governments' recent cross-border labour policy approaches from the level of the state to the level of the firm and supply chain. Such a novel and thoughtful view allows even to put forward a hypothesis of "de-FTA-zation" of the US trade policy, which is tested by one of the authors. Thus, a broader perspective proposed by the contributors includes reflections not only on FTAs and the enforcement issues, e.g. the US–Mexico–Canada Agreement (USMCA) with its famous Facility-Specific Rapid Response Labor Mechanism, but also the rise of some other new policy experiments, such as the Uyghur Forced Labor Prevention Act, the EU Corporate Sustainability Due Diligence Directive or the EU Regulation on prohibiting products made with forced labour on the Union market. Furthermore, such a wide outlook embraces remarks of fundamental importance on the "horizontal social clause" under Article 9 TFEU after the Lisbon Treaty, as well as the EU's Generalised System of Preferences with its social clause.

As highlighted in the literature, references to labour rights are included in FTAs for a number of rationales, that is, economic, social and human rights. The economic rationale is based on the assumption that labour provisions should be used as instruments against unfair competition. The social rationale mirrors concerns about guaranteeing social protection. The human rights rationale perceives labour provisions as a measure generally to improve labour standards and to assure respect for human labour rights reflecting values universally accepted by the international community.[2] However, the above-mentioned references to labour rights in FTAs vary extremely in their content and impact on workers.

The choice of topic for this book was dictated by the need to critically evaluate the provisions on labour and their effectiveness in diverse FTAs worldwide. Given President Donald Trump's threats of tariffs and the ongoing World Trade Organization crisis, FTAs seem to be one of the crucial instruments in global trade. This is reflected, e.g. in the actions of the EU, which is looking for new trading partners and is constantly negotiating new FTAs (at the time of writing, e.g. with India, Indonesia, Malaysia, Philippines, United Arab Emirates[3]). One might wonder if there are FTAs models in the world that ensure better effectiveness of fundamental labour rights than the EU framework. For instance, the US's model involves FTAs that use a conditional approach. This amounts to the fact that FTAs contain labour provisions that make the conclusion of a FTA conditional upon respect for particular labour standards (pre-ratification conditionality) and/or provisions in the concluded FTAs that authorise sanctions if labour standards are infringed (post-ratification conditionality).[4] On the other hand, e.g. the EU model generally involves a promotional approach. It means that labour provisions included in FTAs do not link compliance to economic consequences (with the exception of the 2022 EU–New Zealand FTA) and focus on dialogue and cooperation. It may seem that the conditionality-based model in place in the USA ensures better effectiveness of fundamental labour rights than the EU model. The US–Mexico–Canada Agreement may serve as an example. It effectively required Mexico to carry out very serious reforms of labour law (in 2019) and to ratify all the fundamental ILO Conventions. Moreover, after the analysis of the USMCA cases (e.g. GM Silao, Tridonex, Panasonic, Teksid, Saint Gobain[5]), one may note that the above-mentioned recent USMCA's Facility-Specific Rapid Response Labor Mechanism has proved to be effective in ensuring remediation of a "Denial of Rights" of free association and collective bargaining for workers

2 Samantha Velluti, "The EU's Social Dimension and Its External Trade Relations" in Axel Marx, Jan Wouters, Glenn Rayp, Laura Beke (eds), Global Governance of Labour Rights: Assessing the Effectiveness of Transnational Public and Private Policy Initiatives (Cheltenham, Northampton: Edward Elgar Publishing 2015) 43–44.

3 https://policy.trade.ec.europa.eu/eu-trade-relationships-country-and-region/negotiations-and-agreements_en.

4 ILO, Social Dimensions of Free Trade Agreements: Studies on Growth with Equity (Geneva: ILO 2013) 1.

5 For the full and up-to-date list, see: https://ustr.gov/trade-topics/enforcement/dispute-settlement-proceedings/fta-dispute-settlement/usmca/chapter-31-annex-facility-specific-rapid-response-labor-mechanism.

(including due to its great deterrence effect), and has significantly contributed to the emergence of the trade union movement in Mexico. New, independent trade unions have been extremely active, e.g. Sindicato Independiente Nacional de Trabajadores Trabajadoras de la Industria Automotriz, Sindicato Nacional Independiente de Trabajadores de Industrias y de Servicios, Los Mineros or Liga Sindical Obrera Mexicana. The EU, which still seems to be looking for enforcement solutions, should look at tools that work in other countries. Of course, one should remember that any provisions cannot be just blindly and uncritically copied into another trade agreement because it may simply bring unexpected results. Instead, when taking into account a "copying" method, one shall first assess all contextual differences.[6]

As mentioned above, in 2022, the EU concluded negotiations for a FTA with New Zealand. This FTA includes some groundbreaking solutions, *inter alia* the possibility of using trade sanctions as a matter of last resort in cases of serious infringements of the ILO core labour conventions. Such a mechanism should help make the commitments on workers' rights protection enforceable. However, this is not a rule in the current generation of the EU FTAs that is characterised rather by the so-called "promotional approach". Deficiency of the latter could be observed on the example of the EU–South Korea FTA which resulted in convening a Panel of Experts. The Panel concluded that Korea's efforts are less than optimal, and that there is still much to be done. However, the less-than-optimal effort of Korea does not fall below the legal standard set out in the last sentence of Article 13.4.3 of the EU–Korea FTA, namely "The Parties will make continued and sustained efforts towards ratifying the fundamental ILO Conventions as well as the other Conventions that are classified as "up-to-date" by the ILO". Later, admittedly Korea ratified Conventions Nos. 29, 87 and 98, but according to the opinion of the European Economic and Social Committee entitled "Next Generation Trade and Sustainable Development – Reviewing the 15-point action plan" (2021): "The vague terminology 'continued and sustained efforts' grants Parties too much margin for manoeuvre. While Korea did ratify three out of four missing ILO Conventions (not C105 on abolition of forced labour), questions do remain on whether the Korean legislation amendments fully implement the provisions of C29, C87 and C98". This contributed to a breakthrough in the EU's thinking about trade policy. It seemed that all this would permanently influence the shape of the new generation of the EU FTAs and that the sanction-based mechanism – as adopted in the EU–New Zealand FTA – would stay with us. However, it is not being contin-

6 See: Christoph Scherrer, "Novel Labour-related Clauses in a Trade Agreement: From NAFTA to USMCA" (2020) 11(3) Global Labour Journal 291, passim.

ued at the moment. For example, as regards the violations of fundamental labour rights, no reference to sanctions has been made in the EU–Kenya Economic Partnership Agreement concluded on 19 June 2023. The parties have only adopted a "Joint Statement on Trade and Sustainable Development" according to which they "commit…to further explore strengthening mutual mechanisms for the effective implementation and application of commitments on trade and sustainable development…". Obviously, this outcome is related to a targeted and country-specific approach (one could say understandable in the case of Kenya), but the lack of sanctions for violations of labour rights continues to be visible in other new agreements, such as the modernised global agreement between the EU and Mexico and the EU–Mercosur agreement. One may put forward the thesis that this is a step backwards for sanctions for non-compliance with the ILO core labour conventions. It is extremely important to formulate de lege ferenda postulates in this regard. The above issues, mentioned only by way of example, are intended to indicate the importance of confronting different approaches to labour provisions in FTAs.

Regarding the content and the more detailed chapters' outlines, we open the first part of our edited volume with a contribution by *Sandra Polaski* (Boston University) entitled "Trade and Labour Rights: An Evaluation of Recent Policy Initiatives that Create Cross-Border Labour Obligations for Firms as well as States". In her chapter, the author identifies and discusses a shift of the focus of diverse governments' recent cross-border labour policy approaches from the level of the state to the level of the firm and supply chain. This trend is viewed as an answer to the dissatisfaction of public opinion against the impact of trade and offshoring on workers and communities in high-income countries and simultaneously against the perceived failure of the labour provisions included in FTAs to improve wages and labour conditions in developing countries. In her engaging chapter, Sandra Polaski offers a scientific and comprehensive analysis of the current policy approaches of the USA and the EU, including not only the US–Mexico–Canada Agreement with its Facility-Specific Rapid Response Labor Mechanism, and the 2021 Uyghur Forced Labor Prevention Act, but also the EU Corporate Sustainability Due Diligence Directive, and the Regulation of the European Parliament and of the Council on prohibiting products made with forced labour on the Union market. The author goes a step further and refers to important national laws, namely the French Duty of Vigilance Law, as well as the German Act on Corporate Due Diligence in Supply Chains.

The second chapter in this part, entitled "The Impact of Labor Clauses in Trade Agreements: The Economic Controversy", is by *Christoph Scherrer* based at the University of Kassel. The author highlights that the enforcement of international workers' rights and labour standards through the international trade regime is a highly controversial issue in the field of economics. He starts with explaining to the readers that mainstream international trade scholars contend that any increase in labour costs will allegedly jeopardise developing countries' key comparative advantage of abundant labour. On the other hand, heterodox economists see better enforcement through FTAs as an important contribution to sustainable development. Christoph Scherrer adds to the debate a further layer, namely he makes an assumption that the lack of compliance with the ILO international standards is a collective action problem. It results from fierce competition among countries characterised by similar labour skills and technologies and by a labor force expansion that is not matched by sufficient job creation. The author tries to convey that the problem of competitiveness is not a North–South issue, but a South–South issue. He points out that even small cost increases resulting from higher standards will give countries a competitive advantage over their competitors at similar levels of industrial development. Mentioning policy implications, he suggests that developing countries are limited in their ability to raise labour standards on their own and that labour rights must be negotiated internationally. In this context, Christoph Scherrer sheds new light on multilateral trade agreements and answers the questions whether or not could they be perceived as a tool appropriate to raise standards concomitantly with other countries, and whether or not could they be an adequate instrument for the enforcement on a binding basis of core labour standards at the international level (if equipped with sanctionable labour clauses).

The last chapter in this part written by *Martin Myant* from the University of the West of Scotland and the European Trade Union Institute is entitled "Vietnam: From Labour Provisions to Independent Trade Unions?". In his absorbing contribution, the author meticulously presents a panorama of Vietnam's relations with the EU and the USA and the impact of FTAs concluded by Vietnam with these two actors, namely the Trans-Pacific Partnership (negotiated between 12 countries, including the USA and Vietnam), a separate US–Vietnam Plan for the Enhancement of Trade and Labour Relations, as well as the EU–Vietnam Free Trade Agreement. The author shows how Vietnam's experience can be used as a test of the effectiveness of labour provisions included in FTAs. Analysing the situation in this country, he pays attention to clarifying to what extent economic development could benefit from improved access to the EU and US markets, and what is the degree of effectiveness of the pre-ratification and post-ratification conditionality in the case of Vietnam. As the title of the chapter suggests, the discussion is diverted towards trade unions, and the question whether or not labour provisions in FTAs are able to help ensuring their genuine independence. Interestingly, the author indicates – in a revealing and original way – the determinants of concluding meaningful labour provisions in FTAs.

The second part of the book is intended to present the EU's approach to trade and FTAs. It includes two contributions: first, by *Silvio Bologna* based at the University of Palermo (chapter entitled "Global Trade and Social Fundamental Rights: The Perspective of the European Union"), and second, co-authored by *Axel Marx* from the University of Leuven and *Angela María Vanegas Pérez* – visiting scholar at the University of Leuven from the EAFIT University (chapter entitled "Strengthening the Implementation and Monitoring of Labour Rights Commitments in EU Free Trade Agreements: What Role for Roadmaps?"). The main emphasis of the former is the EU's vision of how to promote respect for human labour rights in its external action. The theoretical focus concerns, in particular, the "horizontal social clause" under Article 9 TFEU in conjunction with Articles 2 and 3 of the TEU, the EU's Generalised System of Preferences with its social clause, as well as the complaint and dispute settlement mechanisms, including the Investor–State Dispute Settlement Clause and the risks it poses. Silvio Bologna puts forward a number of interesting hypotheses, observations, arguments and proposals, embedding the research within the context of labour provisions in FTAs. The author's broad perspective and rational approach – not overstating the importance of the nexus between global trade and labour rights in the EU's policy – enable him to make accurate conclusions regarding the real scope of the social clause in FTAs, in particular considering "the sanction as part of a legal system".

The chapter written by Axel Marx and Angela María Vanegas Pérez presents a scholarly overview of seven roadmaps or action plans aimed at addressing non-compliance with the ILO core conventions included in FTAs.[7] The chapter conveys an instructive lesson on both pre-ratification and post-ratification conditionality given that the authors refer not only to ex-ante roadmaps which are developed to fulfill specific commitments in advance of concluding a FTA, but also to ex-post roadmaps aimed at addressing non-compliance with international conventions. As for roadmaps the authors discuss: Sustainability Compact for Bangladesh; Bangladesh Roadmap for Labour Inspection Convention, ILO No. 81, 87, 98; Bangladesh National Action Plan on the Labour Sector,

7 As clarified by the authors, adopting a roadmap or action plan means that countries are requested to submit a Plan of Action (or roadmap) on the implementation of the ILO core conventions, among other things. Such a plan details the measures that a country shall take to implement the conventions. In order to make the implementation as effective as possible, it shall include clear benchmarks and deadlines for each measure and action.

2021–2026; ILO-Guatemala Roadmap. With regard to action plans, they focus on: the US–Colombia Labour Action Plan; Enforcement Plans for Guatemala and Honduras under US-CAFTA-DR; and Canada–Colombia Action Plan under Labour Cooperation Agreement. Axel Marx and Angela María Vanegas Pérez use a comparative case study method to discover the capabilities and limitations of these instruments in strengthening implementation and monitoring of labour rights in the EU's FTAs. They present to the readers the findings of international practice and different approaches adopted in roadmaps and – in a visionary way – draw valuable implications for the use of these tools in the context of the EU FTAs.

The chapter entitled "Adieu International Labor Rights? US Trade and Labor Linkages in a Post-FTA Era" by *Jean-Baptiste Velut* from the Sorbonne Nouvelle University is the first in a cluster of chapters forming Part 3 of the book entitled "The US's and Canada's Approach". In his instructive contribution, the author tests a hypothesis of "de-FTA-zation" of the US trade policy resulting from "the search for a new balance between domestic and international objectives, the geopoliticization of trade and, to a lesser extent, the deepening of trade and sustainability linkages". Against the background of an evaluation of the "contribution that US FTAs have made to the promotion of international labor rights", the author highlights the existence of a new political economic paradigm and takes stock of some new trends in order to analyse "the present and future" of trade and labour nexus and to answer the question of "how the de-FTA-zation of US trade policy threatens the institutionalization of labor rights in trade policymaking". The study contains a thought-provoking discussion not only of the diversification of trade policy instruments, but also of the shift of focus from economic globalisation to new "intermestic compromises" favouring industrial policies and sectoral agreements and paving the way for economic nationalism, such as in Donald Trump's version in his second tenure as the president of the USA. Following a trail similar to the one adopted by Sandra Polaski, Jean-Baptiste Velut also stresses the rise of new policy experiments, namely less visible forms of trade and regulatory cooperation, e.g. the so-called "mini-deals" such as "memoranda of understanding and sectoral agreements" and "autonomous measures on behalf of labor rights or the environment (e.g. Uighur Forced Labor Prevention Act)".

Vincenzo Ferrante from the Catholic University of the Sacred Heart in Milan is the author of the next chapter entitled "The EU–Canada Comprehensive Free Trade Agreement (CETA): An Opportunity for a Fairer Trade Alliance". The author explains that signed in August 2014 between Canada and the EU, the Comprehensive Economic and Trade Agreement includes not only a general set of rules to increase transnational trade, but also a regulatory framework aimed at promoting further developments in environment, sustainable development and social rights fields. The author reminds us that with the aim of addressing concerns regarding the original text of the agreement, the European Commission and the Canadian federal government have changed the final text and have deleted the ISDS clause, in order to "move to a permanent, transparent, and institutionalized dispute settlement tribunal" and to "revise the process for the selection of tribunal members, who will adjudicate investor claims; set out more detailed commitments on ethics for all tribunal members; and agree to an appeal system". Nevertheless, he highlights that a bilateral settlement system has remained for matters relating to the resolution of disputes concerning the application of labour law. Given this and starting from the analysis of the Canadian legal system for the protection of workers' rights, Vincenzo Ferrante offers an in-depth and careful scrutiny of the "social chapter" included in the CETA. In his comprehensive study, he examines the effect that CETA has exerted on the Canadian Constitutional Court and the federal Parliament in implementing the ILO's core labour conventions needed to ratify CETA. Moreover, the author transmits to the reader a broader reflection on criticism regarding the question of the arbitration system for the protection of foreign investments. All this detailed analysis serves to delve into the question of the possible implementation of more effective enforcement mechanisms concerning social commitments, including the use of trade sanctions.

The last chapter in Part 3, entitled "Trying to Build a Better Future: The Modernised 2023 Canada–Ukraine Free Trade Agreement and Labour Rights", was written by *Aneta Tyc* (University of Lodz) and *Jo Carby-Hall* (University of Hull). The aim of this contribution is to focus on the development of Ukrainian trade relations with Canada, paying particular attention to the modernised 2023 CUFTA (which entered into force on 1 July 2024) and assessing its labour and temporary entry for business persons provisions, as well as chapters on Indigenous Peoples and gender through the prism of labour and employment laws in Ukraine. The authors also try to answer the questions whether the modernised CUFTA may contribute to the development of Ukraine after the war with Russia in order to expand businesses, create jobs, improve working and wage conditions and protect employment. They highlight that Ukrainian employment law was already weak before the war, but the war weakened it even more. A new labour chapter in the modernised CUFTA, subject to the dispute settlement provisions, is designed so that it could "improve labour standards and working conditions in the two countries by building on international labour principles and rights". The authors argue that a new labour chapter alone cannot guarantee the introduction of high labour standards in Ukraine, but is a good step forward and in conjunction with other chapters may be beneficial to workers, including women and Indigenous Peoples, as well as enterprises. Importantly, Jo Carby-Hall and Aneta Tyc assess the fact that labour chapter is subject to the dispute settlement mechanism and reflects a "sanctions-based" approach. They also attempt to answer the question whether or not the modernised CUFTA with its crucial solutions such as the provisions on "temporary entry for business persons" can exert a major impact on fostering the future participation of Canadian businesses in the process of the recovery – including the economic recovery – of Ukraine after the war. Finally, the authors propose some recommendations for a strategic investment policy of Ukraine after the war.

Last but not least, the selection of chapters includes most recent and significant research in the field of FTAs concluded by Australia and New Zealand. Thus, Part 4 of the book contains two contributions entitled: "Labour Provisions in Trade Agreements: The Curious Case of Australia" by *Joo-Cheong Tham* from the University of Melbourne and "New Zealand's trade agreements and labour rights" by Stephen Hoadley based at the University of Auckland. In his illuminating chapter, Joo-Cheong Tham discusses "the puzzling stance taken by Australia to the linking of trade and labour". Reminding the reader that it was, *inter alia*, Australia that opposed the trade and labour nexus during the first Ministerial Conference of the World Trade Organization in 1996, the author explains the astonishing fact that Australia has nonetheless accepted such a linkage in its labour clauses in FTAs. In his complex picture of Australia's approach to FTAs, Joo-Cheong Tham proposes three steps in order to better understand its intricacies. He not only suggests the mixed picture of Australia's FTAs with and without labour provisions, but also analyses the labour provisions in Australian FTAs, "distinguishing between provisions that include insubstantial obligations, and others that are more substantial, being largely based on the United States' approach". The last step is to try to "make sense of Australia's approach to labour provisions which can be summed up as labour provisions being viewed as both protectionist and protection-lite". Indeed, a certain split is suggested by the author, namely on the one hand Australia makes commitments to labour provisions (e.g. the ILO conventions nos. 87 and 98), but on the other hand, weak clauses adopted by this country – in terms of both their substantive obligations and enforcement – facilitate being in breach of the ILO conventions on freedom of association and collective bargaining.

In the last chapter of this final part of the book, *Stephen Hoadley* in a factual and informative way presents the history of protection of labour rights at home and labour provisions in FTAs concluded by New Zealand, while stressing how the former has influenced the latter. Viewing it from inside, the author emphasises the importance of a government's document entitled "Frameworks for Integrating Labour and Environment Standards in Trade Agreements" and its considerable influence on the drafting of labour chapters included in FTAs with Thailand, China, Philippines, Korea, the UK and the EU, as well as plurilateral agreements such as the Comprehensive and Progressive Trans Pacific Partnership. Viewing from outside, Stephen Hoadley expresses concern about the lack of capacity on the part of the government to monitor and enforce labour rights within the borders of New Zealand's trade partners. What is proposed instead is that New Zealand's FTAs mandate "joint liaison committees, periodic reports on labour conditions in partner countries, and dispute resolution procedures", namely tools that are "vague in terms of reference, rely on voluntary reporting, and specify no enforcement remedies". The author's analysis and evaluation of labour clauses included in New Zealand's most recent FTAs lead to conclusions regarding not only progressive initiatives in aspirations, but also shortfalls and gaps in implementation and monitoring. Following this, some fresh ideas and policy recommendations are provided on how to bring New Zealand's FTAs up to international best practice when it comes to the protection of labour rights.

The two editors of this book had the privilege of working with a group of excellent researchers from different world universities who contributed to the subject with highly enriching and diverse perspectives. We truly hope that the book manages to pass that interesting experience on to its readers. A special thanks is addressed to our wonderful team of scholars who made this project possible.

Bibliography

ILO, Labour Provisions in G7 Trade Agreements: A comparative perspective (Geneva: ILO 2019).

ILO, Social Dimensions of Free Trade Agreements: Studies on Growth with Equity (Geneva: ILO 2013).

Scherrer Christoph, "Novel Labour-related Clauses in a Trade Agreement: From NAFTA to USMCA" (2020) 11(3) Global Labour Journal.

Velluti Samantha, "The Eu's Social Dimension and Its External Trade Relations" in Axel Marx, Jan Wouters, Glenn Rayp, Laura Beke (eds), Global Governance of Labour Rights: Assessing the Effectiveness of Transnational Public and Private Policy Initiatives (Cheltenham, Northampton: Edward Elgar Publishing 2015).

PART 1

A Policy and Economic Approach

CHAPTER 2

Trade and Labour Rights: An Evaluation of Recent Policy Initiatives That Create Cross-border Labour Obligations for Firms as well as States

Sandra Polaski

1 Introduction and Historical Background

During the period of rapid globalization beginning in the 1990s, the United States (US), European Union (EU) and eventually other countries began to include labour and social clauses in their trade agreements. They imposed obligations on states that are party to the agreements to enforce their labour laws and/or to adopt international labour standards. The *demandeurs* did this in response to fears in their own countries that trade opening would encourage corporations to offshore production from the industrialized economies to lower-wage countries, leading to job loss and creating a global race to the bottom in wages and labour rights.

To put the link between trade and labour in historical context, governments had recognized the impact of poor labour conditions in one country on workers in other countries for over a century, dating back to the first wave of globalization in the nineteenth century. In the USA the McKinley Tariff Act of 1890 included a provision banning imports of products made by convicts and the United Kingdom adopted a similar ban in 1897.[1] The 1919 Treaty of Versailles, which ended the first World War, included a formal international acknowledgement of the negative cross-border impacts of labour abuse.[2] The Treaty created the International Labour Organization (ILO), explaining that 'the failure of any nation to adopt humane conditions of labour is an obstacle in the way of other nations which desire to improve the conditions in their own countries'.[3] The ILO was assigned authority to create international stand-

1 The McKinley Tariff of 1890. https://history.house.gov/Historical-Highlights/1851-1900/The-McKinley-Tariff-of-1890/.

2 Treaty of Versailles, Versailles, 28 June 1919, Part 1, Article 23.

3 The original ILO Constitution formed Part 13 of the Treaty of Versailles. International Labour Organization Constitution, preamble. NORMLEX. https://normlex.ilo.org/dyn/nrmlx_en/f?p=1000:62:0::NO:62:P62_LIST_ENTRIE_ID:2453907:NO.

 | HTTPS://DOI.ORG/10.1163/9789004762251-003

ards setting minimum conditions for treatment of workers, although it was not given authority to enforce these labour standards.

At the end of World War II, global policy makers again turned attention to the link between labour standards and trade. The United Nations Conference on Trade and Employment, convened in Havana in 1947–48 to develop a post-war global trade architecture, declared that full employment was central to achieving a stable and inclusive world economy and that policy space to pursue employment and social welfare goals should be part of global trade rules.[4] The Conference was meant to launch an International Trade Organization (ITO) on a par with the International Monetary Fund (IMF) and the World Bank (WB).[5] However, after a rightward shift in US politics as the Cold War began, the US Congress declined to ratify the agreement and the ITO was not launched.[6] Instead, a narrower General Agreement on Tariffs and Trade (GATT) was negotiated in 1947, with only one labour provision: a right for countries to ban products made with prison labour, echoing the long-standing ban on such imports by the USA and UK.[7]

During negotiations that began in 1986 to replace the GATT with the more institutionalized World Trade Organization (WTO), the USA and some European countries proposed various ways to address labour issues in the new body, but failed to win broad support.[8] At a ministerial meeting in Singapore in 1996, many countries opposed any linkage of trade with labour standards and the ministerial declaration stated that 'the International Labour Organization (ILO) is the competent body to set and deal with these standards'.[9] Thirty years later, the issue is still excluded from the WTO agenda.

As the new wave of globalization accelerated in the 1990s, and in the absence of enforceable multilateral rules to address the impact of trade on labour, the USA and EU began to fashion labour clauses in bilateral and regional trade pacts. This chapter discusses the evolution of those policies

---

4 UN Trade and Development (UNCTAD), *Trade and Development Report 2017 – Beyond Austerity: Towards a Global New Deal* (Geneva: UNCTAD, 2017), pp. 149–151. https://unctad.org/publication/trade-and-development-report-2017.

5 Jean-Christophe Graz, 'The Havana Charter: when state and market shake hands', in Rainer Kattel, Jayati Ghosh and Erik Reinert (eds.), *Handbook of Alternative Theories of Economic Development* (Cheltenham, UK: Edward Elgar Publishing, 2016), pp. 281–290.

6 Kevin J. Middlebrook, *The International Defense of Workers: Labor Rights, U.S. Trade Agreements, and State Sovereignty* (New York: Columbia University Press, 2024), pp. 81–83.

7 General Agreement on Tariffs and Trade (GATT 1947) Article XX, Geneva, 30 October 1947, in force 1 January 1948. https://www.wto.org/english/docs_e/legal_e/gatt47_e.htm.

8 Middlebrook, International Defense of Workers, pp. 94–95.

9 World Trade Organization, 'Singapore Ministerial Declaration' para. 4, 1996. https://www.wto.org/english/news_e/pres96_e/wtodec.htm

over the subsequent decades, proceeding as follows. Section 2.2 looks at the origins of the first generation of labour clauses in USA and EU trade agreements and assesses their impact. Section 2.3 discusses the development of a backlash against globalization in high-income countries and the political consequences for trade policy, particularly in the USA. It identifies a break in the US policy path on trade–labour linkage, as policy makers added a new focus on the role of firms in protecting labour rights. It describes the evolution of policy instruments in the USA and EU after 2017. Section 2.4 discusses the logic of the firm-level approach, the diverging instruments designed by the USA and Europe to require firms to respect labour rights outside of their national borders and the early performance of the new tools. Section 2.5 concludes.

2 First-Generation Labour and Social Clauses in US and EU Trade Agreements

Technological breakthroughs in communications and shipping led to the growth of international trade beginning in the 1970s, which then accelerated in the 1990s as the Soviet Union and its separate socialist trading bloc collapsed and those countries and China joined what became a single global production system.[10] The USA and EU sought to manage the increasing global integration on terms favourable to their own economies and corporations by negotiating bilateral and regional trade agreements, as well as creating the WTO. However, along with the economic opportunities, the integration of China and the former socialist bloc brought a huge surge of labour supply into the capitalist production system, threatening to put strong downward pressure on wages in the high-income economies.[11] The new trade agreements reinforced that risk by providing USA and EU capital with new protections for overseas investments and offshoring of production, while guaranteeing access back into their markets at low or no tariffs.

10 UN Trade and Development, 'Key evolutions in trade and development over the decades', (Geneva: UNCTAD, 2024). https://unctad.org/news/key-evolutions-trade-and-development-over-decades.

11 Sandra Polaski, 'Job Anxiety Is Real – and It's Global', Policy Brief No. 30 (Washington: Carnegie Endowment for International Peace). https://carnegieendowment.org/posts/2004/04/job-anxiety-is-real-and-its-global?lang=en.

2.1 US Labour Chapters in Free Trade Agreements, 1993–2017

The domestic political implications of this shift in the balance between labour and capital in the new global economy first emerged in the USA, in the context of negotiations of the North American Free Trade Agreement (NAFTA).[12] This was the first US trade agreement to include a low-wage developing country, Mexico, in a full free trade area. Opposition to the agreement was an important issue in the 1992 presidential and congressional elections and, to achieve ratification of the agreement, the administration of President Bill Clinton negotiated a side agreement on labour.[13] The North American Agreement on Labor Cooperation (NAALC) created obligations on the states party to the agreement to enforce their labour laws and created consultation mechanisms to address disputes over labour issues.[14] The agreement was seen as weak, given widespread critiques of existing labour law and practice in Mexico, and the enforcement provisions were convoluted and were never fully used.[15]

In subsequent free trade agreements (FTAs), US negotiators gradually strengthened the labour obligations.[16] The evolution towards stronger labour provisions reflected the interplay of divided constitutional authority over trade between the executive branch, which holds the power to negotiate international agreements, and the legislature, which holds the power to control income (including tariffs) and spending. Under the US system, the Congress must grant authority to the executive to change tariffs and they have periodically done so, while establishing key negotiating objectives that must be included if a proposed trade agreement is to be eligible for ratification without amendment.[17] In the political economy of the USA, the president is

---

12 North American Free Trade Agreement, 17 December 1992, in force 1 January 1994–30 June 2020. P.L. 103–182 https://www.congress.gov/bill/103rd-congress/house-bill/3450/text.

13 Alisa DiCaprio, 'Are Labor Provisions Protectionist?: Evidence from Nine Labor Augmented U.S. Trade Arrangements' (2004) 26 *Comparative Labor Law and Policy Journal* 1, 12.

14 North American Agreement on Labour Cooperation, 13 September 1993. https://www.dol.gov/agencies/ilab/reports/pdf/naalc.

15 Lance Compa and Tequila Brooks, *NAFTA and NAALC: Twenty-five Years of North American Trade* (Philadelphia, PA: Kluwer Law International, 2019).

16 Middlebrook, International Defense of Workers, pp. 332–344.

17 Sandra Polaski, 'The strategy and politics of linking trade and labor standards: an overview of issues and approaches', in Kimberly Ann Elliott (ed.), *Handbook on Globalisation and Labour Standards* (Cheltenham, UK: Edward Elgar, 2022), pp. 206–207.

elected by a coalition of interests across the states; once elected, the executive is relatively free to act on its political philosophy during its four-year term. However, members of Congress are elected more frequently and are linked to a particular geography and sectoral pattern of employment that can make them more sensitive to the impact of trade on jobs and wages, regardless of ideology. Over recent decades, there has been a significant bloc of legislators that have prevented ratification of trade agreements that do not contain labour chapters they deem to be sufficiently ambitious. The result of this interplay between branches of government has been to make labour rights a key objective in US trade negotiations over recent decades. All US free trade agreements post-NAFTA include the obligation of trading partners to effectively enforce their labour laws and since 2007 have required upward convergence to protect the foundational rights described in the ILO's Declaration on Fundamental Principles and Rights at Work.[18]

Beyond the definition of obligations, the efficacy of a labour clause depends on the enforcement mechanisms that are available to ensure compliance and whether they are used.[19] After NAFTA, the USA incorporated labour provisions into the body of subsequent FTAs and made them subject to enforcement through the dispute settlement procedures applicable to other provisions of the agreements. However, in the case of labour disputes, threshold criteria were included that required that a failure by a party to enforce its labour laws must occur 'in a manner affecting trade or investment between the Parties' and through a 'sustained or recurring course of action or inaction' to be subject to enforcement.[20] These restrictive criteria did not apply to disputes over other obligations of the agreement, for example, the protection of investors' rights or intellectual property.

The USA took only one labour case to a dispute settlement panel during the twenty-five years from 1994 to 2019. The case involved violations of Guatemalan workers' rights and the USA lost, due to a ruling by the panel that the violations had occurred, but not 'in a manner affecting trade or investment

18 International Labour Organization, Declaration on Fundamental Principles and Rights at Work, 1998. https://www.ilo.org/declaration/lang–en/index.htm.

19 Sandra Polaski, 'Protecting Labor Rights through Trade Agreements: An Analytical Guide', (2004) 10 *Journal of International Law and Policy* 17–20.

20 See, for example, United States-Colombia Trade Promotion Agreement Article 17(3)(1)(a). https://ustr.gov/sites/default/files/uploads/agreements/fta/colombia/asset_upload_file993_10146.pdf

between the Parties'.[21] The USA has not imposed sanctions for labour violations on trading partners under any of its free trade agreements.[22]

2.2 EU Social Clauses in Preferential Trade Agreements, 1999–2022

The first EU trade agreement to include labour commitments was an agreement with South Africa signed in 1999. This and other bilateral EU pacts negotiated before 2010 included declaratory commitments to respect international labour standards but did not include binding obligations or enforcement provisions.[23] Beginning in 2010 with the EU–Korea Preferential Trade Agreement, all subsequent EU preferential trade agreements (PTAs) include trade and sustainable development chapters that commit the parties to improve their labour standards in line with the ILO 1998 Declaration on Fundamental Principles and Rights at Work as well as the ILO conventions that all parties to the agreements have ratified.[24] They provide for consultations between the parties on labour matters at the initiative of party governments or based on submissions made by domestic advisory groups (DAGs).[25] If the problems are not resolved, a government party can request the establishment of a labour expert panel to investigate and make recommendations.[26] There is no provision for enforcement of the panel's recommendations.

The less binding approach chosen by EU negotiators compared to that of the USA can be partly explained by their different institutional structures. In the EU, the executive (the European Commission) is not directly elected and in effect is a coalition reflecting the political and economic variations across the twenty-seven member states, each with its own relations of power, gov-

21 Tequila J. Brooks, 'U.S.-Guatemala Arbitration Panel Clarifies Effective Enforcement Under Labor Provisions of Free Trade Agreement International Labor Rights Case Law' (2018) 4 *International Labor Rights Case Law*, 1, 45–51.

22 The USA has occasionally imposed sanctions for violations of labour rights under its unilateral trade preference programmes for developing countries authorized by the Trade and Tariff Act of 1984. Middlebrook, International Defense of Workers, pp. 97–126.

23 Evgeny Postnikov, 'Labor standards in EU and US preferential trade agreements mainstreaming the trade-labor linkage', in Kimberly Ann Elliott (ed.), *Handbook on Globalisation and Labour Standards* (Cheltenham, UK: Edward Elgar, 2022), pp. 244–257.

24 It should be noted that US FTAs do not include obligations to respect ratified ILO conventions because the USA has ratified few of them.

25 The DAGs are created by the agreements and are made up of business, labour and non-government group representatives from the parties to the agreement.

26 Marva Corley-Coulibaly, Gaia Grasselli and Ira Postolachi, *Promoting and enforcing compliance with labour provisions in trade agreements: Comparative analysis of Canada, European Union and United States approaches and practices* (Geneva: ILO, 2023), pp. 76–82.

erning philosophy and sectoral trade interests. Until 2009 the Commission had a relatively free hand in designing EU trade policy with limited democratic accountability.[27] The Treaty of Lisbon then gave the European Parliament shared authority over trade policy. The parliamentarians are directly elected in particular regions with their own mix of labour and product markets, somewhat analogous to US members of Congress. From 2010 the Parliament insisted on the inclusion of a social clause in all trade agreements, as reflected in the EU–Korea PTA and subsequent trade pacts.[28]

The first labour expert panel requested by the EU arose under the EU–Korea PTA in 2019.[29] The case involved a claim of violation of trade union rights by the Republic of Korea, with the panel finding that the country's trade union law violated fundamental aspects of the right to freedom of association. Notably, the panel dismissed claims by the Korean government that the violation must be related to trade, stating that the ILO Constitution and 1998 Declaration establish the universality of freedom of association rights that cannot be limited by requirements such as the relationship to trade.[30] The panel also noted that ILO conventions cannot be ratified with reservations, such as excluding workers who are not in trade-related sectors. Although the PTA does not include possible sanctions, Korea did ratify ILO conventions 87 and 98 on freedom of association and collective bargaining after the panel's finding.[31]

---

27 Lore Van den Putte, Ferdi De Ville and Jan Orbie, 'The European Parliament's New Role in Trade Policy: Turning Power into Impact', (2014), Centre for European Policy Studies: CEPS Special Reports No. 89. https://ssrn.com/abstract=2445899.

28 European Parliament, 'External Dimension of Social Policy, Promoting Labour and Social Standards and European Corporate Social Responsibility', 2010/2205. http://www.europarl.europa.eu/sides/getDoc.do?type=REPORT&reference=A7-2011-0172&language=EN; James Harrison, Mirela Barbu, Liam Campling, Franz Christian Ebert, Deborah Martens, Axel Marx, Jan Orbie, Ben Richardson and Adrian Smith, 'Labour Standards Provisions in EU Free Trade Agreements: Reflections on the European Commission's Reform Agenda' (2018) 18 *World Trade Review*, 4, pp. 635–657.

29 European Commission, 'EU moves ahead with dispute settlement over workers' rights in Republic of Korea', EU News, 5 July 2019. https://policy.trade.ec.europa.eu/news/eu-moves-ahead-dispute-settlement-over-workers-rights-republic-korea-2019-07-05_en.

30 María J García, 'Sanctioning Capacity in Trade and Sustainability Chapters in EU Trade Agreements: The EU-Korea Case' (2022) 10 *Politics and Governance*, 1, 58–67. https://doi.org/10.17645/pag.v10i1.4782.

31 Tonia Novitz, 'Enforceable social clauses in trade agreements with 'bite'? Implications of the EU–South Korea Panel of Experts Report of 20 January 2021' (2021), European Trade Union Institute. https://www.etui.org/publications/enforceable-social-clauses-trade-agreements-bite.

The European provisions are often considered to be 'soft law' based on consultation, while the US provisions are considered 'hard law' based on the ability to withdraw trade benefits as a sanction for labour violations.[32] However, this distinction is not so clear in practice. Both the USA and EU engage in extensive consultations over labour issues before moving to dispute settlement or expert panels.[33] Each has taken only one case to expert or dispute settlement panels over the two decades such options have existed. And, as noted above, the USA has not imposed trade sanctions on any FTA partner countries for labour violations under any of its existing agreements.

3 Growing Backlash against Globalization Shifts the Approach to Trade and Labour

The fears of job loss and downward pressure on wages in high-income countries were borne out over time. As production and jobs were shifted from high-income economies to low-wage developing countries, there was a significant shift in the distribution of global income growth. A famous graph called the 'elephant curve' because of its shape showed that between 1988 and 2008, most of the growth in global income accrued to households between the tenth and seventieth deciles of income and to those in the top one per cent.[34] The fortunate households were those in developing countries, especially in China and developing Asia, where millions of people were able to move out of agriculture and low-productivity services into higher-paid manufacturing jobs. The highest income households enjoyed strong growth of already high incomes. However, the households in the seventieth to eightieth deciles of global income saw little income growth over those decades. In terms of global income distribution, these are the working and lower middle classes of the richer countries.

---

32 Kimberly Ann Elliott, 'Hard and soft law approaches to protecting worker rights', in Kimberly Ann Elliott (ed.), *Handbook on Globalisation and Labour Standards* (Cheltenham, UK: Edward Elgar, 2022), pp. 326–338.

33 Corley-Coulibaly et al, 'Promoting and enforcing compliance with labour provisions', pp. 77–84.

34 Christoph Lakner, and Branko Milanovic, 'Global income distribution: From the Fall of the Berlin Wall to the Great Recession' Policy Research Working Paper No. 6719 (Washington: World Bank, 2013). https://openknowledge.worldbank.org/search?spc.page=1&query=Global%20income%20distribution:%20From%20the%20Fall%20of%20the%20Berlin%20Wall%20to%20the%20Great%20Recession.

This global picture could be seen at the local level in communities in the USA and parts of Europe, where offshoring of jobs led to sharp declines in living standards. A series of studies in the 2010s used microdata sources that showed reductions in employment, wages, health and public goods in the most affected localities and industries in the USA.[35] The lived experience in these communities hardened into an anti-globalization narrative that was weaponized by candidate Donald Trump to win the 2016 presidential election.[36] The evident public discontent led to a significant shift in the US approach to trade policy and trade–labour linkage.

3.1 US Firm-Level Labour Obligations and Enforcement Mechanisms, 2017–2025

Once in office, President Donald Trump launched a renegotiation of NAFTA, which he denounced as the worst trade agreement ever.[37] While his administration was anti-union on domestic labour issues, his negotiators recognized that it would be difficult to win congressional ratification for a new North American trade pact, given public anti-trade sentiment.[38] They focused on the specific complaint that Mexican wages had not converged upwards over the quarter century that NAFTA was in effect.[39] Critics of the agreement

35 Leo Feler and Mine Zeynep Senses, 'Trade Shocks and the Provision of Local Public Goods' IZA Discussion Paper No. 10231 (2016) (Bonn, Germany: Institute for the Study of Labor). https://ssrn.com/abstract=2846322; David H. Autor, David Dorn, and Gordon H. Hanson, 'The China Shock: Learning from labor market adjustment to large changes in trade' NBER Working Paper No. 21906, (2016) (Cambridge, MA: National Bureau of Economic Research). https://www.nber.org/papers/w21906.pdf.

36 Andrea Cerrato, Francesco Ruggieri and Federico M. Ferrara, 'Trump won in counties that lost jobs to China and Mexico', Washington Post, 2 December 2016. https://www.washingtonpost.com/news/monkey-cage/wp/2016/12/02/trump-won-where-import-shocks-from-china-and-mexico-were-strongest/; Nick Corasaniti, Alexander Burns and Binyamin Appelbaum, 'Donald Trump vows to rip up trade deals and confront China', New York Times, 28 June 2016. https://www.nytimes.com/2016/06/29/us/politics/donald-trump-trade-speech.html?searchResultPosition=1.

37 Maggie Severns, 'Trump pins NAFTA, "worst trade deal ever," on Clinton', Politico, 26 September 2016. https://www.politico.com/story/2016/09/trump-clinton-come-out-swinging-over-nafta-228712.

38 Robert Lighthizer, *No Trade Is Free: Changing Course, Taking on China, and Helping America's Workers* (New York: Broadside/HarperCollins, 2023), pp. 215–243.

39 For example, in the increasingly integrated automobile industry, the average hourly wage dropped in all three countries. In Canada the wage dropped from US$34.09 to US$26.34 per hour between 1994 and 2016. In the same period, wages dropped from US$35.91 to US$28.60 per hour in the United States and from US$6.65 to US$3.14 per hour in Mexico (data from Mexican National Institute of Statistics and Geography

pointed to a Mexican government policy of repressing wages that began in the 1980s, when the government adopted a neoliberal, export-oriented development strategy that was based on maintaining low wages.[40] One of the policy instruments used was to lower minimum wages set by government. By 2015 the real value of the Mexican minimum wage stood at only 25 per cent of its real value in 1982.[41] Another important instrument of wage repression was based on a corporatist system of industrial relations involving employers, unions and the government. The system had become corrupted, with widespread collusion between the three parties to repress labour costs.[42] In response, Trump's negotiators included strong requirements for Mexico to reform its labour relations law to eliminate collusion between corrupt 'protection unions' and employers to repress wages.[43] The agreement, now called the US–Mexico Canada Agreement (USMCA), also strengthened protections for migrant workers, women workers and the right to strike. It included a provision requiring the three governments to prohibit the importation into their territories of goods produced by forced or compulsory labour, building on an existing US prohibition discussed in Section 4.3.1 below.[44]

(INEGI), the US Bureau of Labor Statistics and Statistics Canada. In percentage terms, at 52 percent the drop in Mexico was the largest. Graciela Bensusán, 'Empleos bajo presión: con o sin TLCAN', in Oscar Fernando Contreras, Gustavo Vega, Eduardo Mendoza, Clemente Ruiz Durán and Jorge Carrillo (eds.), *La renegociación del Tratado de Libre Comercio en Norteamérica: Desafíos para México y sus Regiones* (Baja California: El Colegio de la Frontera Norte, 2019).

40 Robert A. Blecker, Juan Carlos Moreno-Brid and Isabel Salat, 'Trumping the NAFTA renegotiation: An alternative policy framework for Mexican-United States cooperation and economic convergence' (2017). Economic Commission for Latin America and the Caribbean (ECLAC), Sub-regional Headquarters in Mexico. https://www.cepal.org/en/publications/42579-trumping-nafta-renegotiation-alternative-policy-framework-mexican-united-states.

41 Juan Moreno-Brid and Stefanie Garry, 'El salario mínimo en México: en falta con la Constitución mexicana y una aberración en América latina' in Miguel Ángel Mancera (ed.), *Del salario mínimo al salario digno, 105–121* (Mexico City: Mexico City Economic and Social Council). https://www.researchgate.net/publication/292175585_El_salario_minimo_en_Mexico_en_falta_con_La_Constitucion_mexicana_y_una_aberracion_en_America_Latina.

42 Graciela Bensusán, 'The Transformation of the Mexican Labour Regulation Model and its link to North American Economic Integration', Working Paper No. 15 (Geneva: International Labour Organization, 2020). https://www.ilo.org/static/english/intserv/working-papers/wp015/index.html.

43 United States–Mexico–Canada Agreement, Mexico City, Mexico, 19 December 2019 (revised version), in force 1 July 2020. Chapter 23 and Annex 23. https://ustr.gov/sites/default/files/files/agreements/FTA/USMCA/Text/23-Labor.pdf

44 USMCA Article 23 (6) Forced or Compulsory Labor.

Two years into Trump's term, as the USMCA was being finalized, the Democrats won elections to retake control of the House of Representatives, the legislative body with control of the ratification process. Despite the gains in the *de jure* labour obligations of the tentative agreement, they refused to ratify it because of what they considered to be inadequate enforcement provisions. An internal negotiation between the executive and congressional branches ensued, during which the Democrats insisted on creating a new enforcement mechanism to hold individual firms and facilities accountable for their violations of labour rights, in addition to the state-to-state dispute settlement mechanism.[45] The logic behind the approach reflected the role of Mexican firms and corrupt unions in wage repression over the previous decades. The result was the Facility-Specific Rapid Response Labor Mechanism (RRM). The US negotiators then presented this proposal to the newly elected Mexican President Andrés Manuel López Obrador, who reacted positively based on his own electoral commitment to increase Mexican wages.[46] A bilateral agreement on the new enforcement mechanism was reached as part of a Protocol of Amendment to the USMCA.[47] A bilateral agreement between Mexico and Canada with the same provisions followed shortly.

In terms of substance, the RRM establishes a process to act directly and expeditiously in cases where a firm is accused of violating workers' rights to freedom of association and collective bargaining at a specific workplace. The facility-specific approach acknowledges that, while governments are responsible for enforcing labour laws, in the private sector it is the employing firm that directly denies the workers' rights and benefits from the denial of rights. Workers who believe their rights have been denied can file a petition with one of the governments requesting review of the situation. It can also be initiated directly by one of the governments when that party has a good faith basis to believe that workers are being denied their rights. That government then requests the government of the country where the alleged denial has occurred to conduct its own review and, if the responding government agrees that there has been a

45 Sandra Polaski, 'USMCA and the Rapid Response Labor Mechanism: A new approach to cross-border governance of labor rights', Social Science Research Network, 2023. http://dx.doi.org/10.2139/ssrn.4639948.

46 Graciela Bensusán and Kevin J. Middlebrook, 'Democratic Labor Reform in Mexico'(Washington: Wilson Center Mexico Institute, 2020). https://www.wilsoncenter.org/sites/default/files/media/uploads/documents/Bensus%C3%A1n%20%26%20Middlebrook%20-%20Democratic%20Labor%20Reform%20in%20Mexico.pdf.

47 Protocol of Amendment to the United States–Mexico–Canada Agreement, 19 December 2019, Chapter 31, Annex 31-A Facility-Specific Rapid-Response Labor Mechanism. https://ustr.gov/trade-agreements/free-trade-agreements/united-states-mexico-canada-agreement/protocol-amendments.

denial of rights, the two parties can then fashion a course of remediation for the firm. If the responding government fails to review the complaint or believes that there is no denial of rights, the complaining government can request formation of a labour panel composed of three panellists independent of the parties with expertise in labour law. The panel's purpose is to verify whether there has been a denial of rights. The RRM establishes relatively short timelines at each step of the procedure and provides each government with the right to call for labour panel review at various stages of the process. After determination by a panel that there has been a denial of rights, a complaining government may suspend the preferential tariff treatment provided by USMCA for goods manufactured at the relevant facility or impose other penalties on goods or services provided by the facility. In cases where a firm had denied rights on two or more prior occasions, the remedies may include denial of entry of goods manufactured by that firm into the complaining government's territory.[48]

In effect, this means that access to the US or Canadian market is now available as a source of leverage to support Mexican workers' labour rights in the face of resistance by employers. The RRM offers a quid pro quo or incentive to the firm: respect the labour rights protected by the agreement or lose the benefits of the agreement.

3.2 European Trade–Labour Linkage and Due Diligence Obligations, 2017–2025

In the EU, where most trade occurs within the bloc itself, the negative impact on labour incomes shown in the 'elephant curve' was largely a result of the accession to the EU of eastern European countries that had been part of the socialist bloc.[49] The addition of a large cohort of skilled labour to the EU single market had the effect of driving down wages in western Europe. Thus the domestic political impact of *global* trade was not as intense in Europe as in the USA. Nonetheless, sectors of the European Parliament and publics sought to improve the protection of labour rights and social standards in trading partner countries and the European Commission's negotiators recognized that the

48 Article 31-A.10.

49 Wolfgang Dauth, Sebastian Findeisen and Jens Suedekum, 'The Rise of the east and the far east: German labor markets and trade integration' (2014) 12 *Journal of the European Economic Association*, 1643–1675; Dalia Marin, 'The opening-up of Eastern Europe at 20: Jobs, skills, and reverse Maquiladoras in Austria and Germany' Working Paper No. 2010/02 (Brussels: Bruegel, 2010). https://www.bruegel.org/wp-content/uploads/imported/publications/wp_2010_02_maquiladoras_.pdf.

public concerns required a response.[50] After a series of public debates, it gradually strengthened provisions in the template of trade and sustainable development chapters and in 2022 included the possibility of trade sanctions in instances of serious violations of the core ILO standards.[51] The new approach was first applied in negotiations with New Zealand. Under the resulting PTA a finding by a dispute settlement panel of a violation of a core ILO labour standard can lead to suspension of the agreement's benefits.[52] The agreement includes high thresholds for proving a violation, namely that a country 'through a sustained or recurring course of action or inaction, fail[s] to effectively enforce its environmental or labour law in a manner affecting trade or investment', the same language that led to the US loss in the Guatemala case.[53]

The EU has not taken a firm-level approach to enforcement of labour rights in its free trade agreements to date. However, a European response to concerns about labour conditions in global supply chains has emerged through a different policy channel. France and Germany adopted laws holding firms responsible to identify and mitigate risks to labour, human rights, and the environment throughout their supply chains.[54] More recently, at the initiative of the European Parliament, the EU adopted a directive on Corporate Sustainability Due Diligence (CSDDD) and a regulation to prohibit products made with forced labour from entering the EU market.[55] These policy instruments are discussed in Sections 4.2 and 4.3.2 below.

---

50 James Harrison, Mirela Barbu, Liam Campling, Franz Christian Ebert, Deborah Martens, Axel Marx, Jan Orbie, Ben Richardson and Adrian Smith, 'Labour Standards Provisions in EU Free Trade Agreements: Reflections on the European Commission's Reform Agenda' (2019) 18 *World Trade Review*, 4, 635–657. doi:10.1017/.

51 European Commission, 'Communication from the Commission to the European Parliament, the Council, the European Economic and Social Committee and the Committee of the Region, The power of trade partnerships: together for green and just economic growth' (2022). https://eur-lex.europa.eu/legal-content/EN/TXT/PDF/?uri=CELEX:52022DC0409.

52 Free Trade Agreement between the European Union and New Zealand, 9 July 2023, in force 1 May 2024 Chapters 19 and 26. https://policy.trade.ec.europa.eu/eu-trade-relationships-country-and-region/countries-and-regions/new-zealand/eu-new-zealand-agreement/text-agreement_en.

53 Article 19(2)(6).

54 Government of France, LAW No. 2017-399 of 27 March 2017 relating to the duty of care of parent companies and contracting companies. https://www.legifrance.gouv.fr/jorf/id/JORFTEXT000034290626/; German Act on Corporate Due Diligence Obligations in Supply Chains (Gesetz über die unternehmerischen Sorgfaltspflichten in Lieferketten), in force 1 January 2023. https://www.csr-in-deutschland.de/SharedDocs/Downloads/EN/act-corporate-due-diligence-obligations-supply-chains.pdf?__blob=publicationFile#linkicon.

55 European Union, 'Directive (EU) 2024/1760 of the European Parliament and of the Council of 13 June 2024 on corporate sustainability due diligence and amending Direc-

4 The Logic of Firm-Level Labour Obligations and Assessment of Early Applications

The USMCA RRM, the CSDDD and national European due diligence laws, and forced labour import prohibitions operate according to the same foundational logic. They reflect the conviction that, in addition to governments, firms must also be held accountable for respecting labour and human rights if meaningful progress is to be achieved at the global level.[56] As global supply chains were articulated over recent decades, it became clear that firms, especially lead firms, often had more control over decisions that affected labour and other human rights than governments of host countries, particularly in low-income, export-oriented countries.[57] Voluntary corporate programmes to encourage compliance with international labour rights norms proliferated in the late 1990s and early 2000s, but accumulating experience showed that they did not effectively protect those rights.[58] A dramatic illustration of the problems in global supply chains occurred in April 2013, when the Rana Plaza building in Dhaka, Bangladesh collapsed, killing more than 1100 Bangladeshi garment workers employed in the multiple clothing factories in the building.[59] This contributed to various initiatives to strengthen corporate responsibility obligations, including establishment of a United Nations (UN) intergovernmental working group in 2014 with the mandate 'to elaborate an international legally binding instrument to regulate, in international human rights law, the activi-

---

tive (EU) 2019/1937 and Regulation (EU) 2023/2859' (2024). https://eur-lex.europa.eu/legal-content/EN/TXT/PDF/?uri=OJ:L_202401760; Regulation (EU) 2024/3015 of the European Parliament and of the Council of 27 November 2024 on prohibiting products made with forced labour on the Union market and amending Directive (EU) 2019/1937. https://eur-lex.europa.eu/eli/reg/2024/3015/oj/eng.

56 Maria-Therese Gustafsson, Almut Schilling-Vacaflor and Andrea Lenschow, 'The politics of supply chain regulations: Towards foreign corporate accountability in the area of human rights and the environment?' (2023) 17 *Regulation & Governance*, 853–869.

57 Frederick Mayer and Gary Gereffi, 'Regulation and Economic Globalization: Prospects and Limits of Private Governance' (2010) 12 *Business and Politics*, 3, 1–25; Frederick Mayer and Nicola Phillips, 'Outsourcing governance: states and the politics of a "global value chain world"' (2017) 22 *New Political Economy*, 2, 134–152.

58 Mark Anner, Jennifer Bair, and Jeremy Blasi, 'Towards Joint Liability in Global Supply Chains: Addressing the Root Causes of Labor Violations in International Subcontracting Networks' (2013) 35 *Comparative Labor Law and Policy Journal*, 1, 1–43.

59 John A. Quelch and Margaret L. Rodriguez, 'Rana Plaza: Workplace Safety in Bangladesh (A)' (2014) Harvard Business School Supplement 514–035, September 2013, revised June 2014. https://www.hbs.edu/faculty/Pages/item.aspx?num=45540.

ties of transnational corporations and other business enterprises'.[60] After more than a decade, those negotiations are still underway without agreement on a binding instrument.

The limited impact of voluntary compliance programmes and the difficulty of reaching a global agreement contributed to the pressure from European civil society to launch mandatory due diligence legislation, first at national levels and then EU-wide.[61] The RRM, on the other hand, arose from the more specific experience of labour rights violations in North America under the NAFTA.[62] Despite the different genesis, the underlying logic was the same in both cases. Corporations have direct control over treatment of labour in their workplaces. While governments are responsible for enforcing labour laws, in the private sector it is the employing firm that directly denies workers' rights and benefits from the denial through lower wages and poor working conditions that lower labour costs. It is also the firm that benefits from globalization by offshoring production to low-cost countries and then enjoying guaranteed access to high-income markets on the preferential terms provided by trade agreements.[63] Thus, the direct private sector beneficiaries of free trade should also be held accountable for compliance with the labour obligations imposed by the FTAs, as well as by internationally recognized labour standards and due diligence laws. State-to-state dispute settlement provisions are appropriate to address a derogation by a government, for example, when the laws of a state do not conform to the obligations or when it fails to enforce its laws due to regulatory capture. However, in the case of low-income countries in particular, the government might lack the resources or capacity to effectively enforce labour rights, even if it has the political will to do so. When labour violations are carried out by a specific firm, standard principles of regulation suggest that the investigation, liability and remedy should be

60 United Nations Human Rights Council, 'Open-ended intergovernmental working group on transnational corporations and other business enterprises with respect to human rights' (2024). https://www.ohchr.org/en/hr-bodies/hrc/wg-trans-corp/igwg-on-tnc.

61 David Weihrauch, Sophia Carodenuto and Sina Leipold, 'From voluntary to mandatory corporate accountability: The politics of the German supply chain due diligence act' (2023) 17 *Regulation & Governance*, 909–926; Gustafsson et al, 'Politics of supply chain regulations'.

62 Sandra Polaski, 'USMCA and the Rapid Response Labor Mechanism: A new approach to cross-border governance of labor rights' (2023), Social Science Research Network http://dx.doi.org/10.2139/ssrn.4639948.

63 James Harrison, 'Trade Agreements and Sustainability: Exploring the Potential of Global Value Chain (GVC) Obligations' (2023) 26 *Journal of International Economic Law* 199–215.

targeted as directly as possible on the violator.[64] This avoids escalation from the firm to the national government and avoids spillover to compliant firms. It can also change the firm's calculation of the cost of violations and thus better align the incentives facing the firm with the public interest in respect for workers' rights.

The microeconomic tool of withdrawal of trade benefits in the case of the RRM, or administrative sanctions and civil liability in the case of due diligence laws, are scaled and targeted to the specific corporate agent responsible for a violation. The following sections assess these new firm-level policy instruments based on their early application. There is also a brief discussion of separate US and EU instruments that seek to exclude products made with forced labour, which are also targeted at the level of the firm.

4.1 The RRM in Practice

The Mexican labour law reform and the labour provisions of the USMCA established a four-year transition, during which Mexican workers were given the opportunity to vote on all existing collective bargaining agreements (CBAs) to determine whether they would accept them and allow the incumbent union to continue to represent them. Of the CBAs put to a vote, 30,520 were accepted and 663 were rejected.[65] A number of observers consider the high proportion of CBAs accepted to reflect a weakness of the transition process, in which the votes were run by the incumbent union with limited oversight by the government, giving rise to concerns about the inherent conflict of interest and amid reports of misinformation, bribery or harassment of workers.[66]

The first RRM cases arose in the context of such votes. Once the transition period ended, new petitions have been filed alleging other violations of the

64 Polaski, 'USMCA and the Rapid Response Labor Mechanism', pp. 13–18.

65 Federal de Conciliación y Registro Laboral, '30,529 Legitimized collective contracts' (2023). https://legitimacion.centrolaboral.gob.mx/.

66 Independent Mexico Labor Expert Board, 'IMLEB Report and Separate Statement of Members Fortson et al' (2021). https://www.researchgate.net/publication/359529197_IMLEB_Report_and_Separate_Statem ent_of_Members_Fortson_et_al_2021077; Independent Mexico Labor Expert Board, 'Report to the Interagency Labor Committee (ILC) and the United States Congress pursuant to Section 734 of the United States-Mexico-Canada Agreement Implementation Act, P.L. 116–113' (2023), pp. 8–12. https://www.researchgate.net/publication/369383619_IMLEB_Report-2023_03_20_FINAL; Alex Covarrubias V., 'Cuatro años de reforma laboral… y el dinosaurio todavía sigue ahí (parte I)', El Economista, 4 May 2023; CILAS (Centro de Investigación Laboral y Asesoria Sindical), 'The change that never comes: The Labor Reform in four years' (Mexico City: CILAS, 2023). https://calisnacional.com/?p=26483.

rights to organize and bargain collectively without employer interference or collusion with corrupt unions. As of mid-2025, the RRM had been invoked thirty-eight times: thirty-seven times by the USA and once by Canada.[67] Twenty-five of the cases had been resolved by mid-2025, through remediation plans or Mexican, US or Canadian government actions that allowed workers to vote freely for unions or ratification of CBAs, with independent unions winning against incumbent unions in most cases and then negotiating improved wages. The remediation plans also involved reinstatement with back pay of workers fired for union activity and pledges by the firms of future neutrality in labour relations matters. Five cases were before labour panels at the time of publication and in other cases the investigation or remediation processes were still underway. One factor contributing to the frequent use of the RRM is the significant weaknesses in the domestic enforcement of the reformed Mexican labour law. The RRM provides a backstop to fill gaps in enforcement by Mexico.[68]

The three governments have publicly evaluated the early experience with the USMCA labour provisions and RRM as successful.[69] The true test of the RRM rests on whether it creates deterrence, effectively discouraging firms

67 USMCA Chapter 31 and Annex A Fact Sheets. https://ustr.gov/sites/default/files/files/agreements/FTA/USMCA/Text/31%20Dispute%20Settlement.pdf; Reuters, 'Canada closes labor complaint in Mexico at German manufacturer Fraenkische', Reuters 25 July 2023. https://www.reuters.com/world/americas/canada-closes-labor-complaint-mexico-german-manufacturer-fraenkische-2023-07-25/2023).

68 Independent Mexico Labor Expert Board, 'Report to the Interagency Labor Committee', pp. 33–47.

69 Jamieson Greer, 'Hearing to Consider the Nomination of Jamieson Greer, of Maryland, to be United States Trade Representative, with the rank of Ambassador Extraordinary and Plenipotentiary', 6 February 2025, United States Senate Committee on Finance (at 1 hour 34 minutes and following). https://www.finance.senate.gov/hearings/hearing-to-consider-the-nomination-of-jamieson-greer-of-maryland-to-be-united-states-trade-representative-with-the-rank-of-ambassador-extraordinary-and-plenipotentiary; United States Trade Representative, 'Remarks by Ambassador Tai to Discuss Updates on Biden-Harris Administration's Worker-Centered Trade Agenda at the Center for American Progress', 4 October 2023. https://ustr.gov/about-us/policy-offices/press-office/speeches-and-remarks/2023/october/remarks-ambassador-katherine-tai-discuss-updates-biden-harris-administrations-worker-centered-trade; Government of México, 'Mexico receives the trade authorities of the United States and Canada to celebrate the T-MEC Free Trade Commission' (6 July 2023). https://www.gob.mx/se/prensa/mexico-recibe-a-las-autoridades-comerciales-de-estados- unidos-y-canada-para-celebrar-la-comision-de-libre-comercio-del-t-mec?idiom=es; Dylan Robertson, 'Left-leaning Mexico seeks closer Canada ties in labour and business amid mining spat', The Canadian Press, 11 June 2023. https://nationalpost.com/news/left-leaning-mexico-seeks-closer-canada-ties-in-labour-and- business-amid-mining-spat)

from violating labour rights, and whether it provides meaningful remedy for victims. With respect to deterrence, twenty-three of the firms in resolved RRM cases were deterred from continued violations.[70] In those cases, the violations of victims' rights were directly remedied through new union elections, reinstatement with back pay, pledges of future neutrality by the firms and other measures. With respect to broader deterrence, the weakness of Mexican government enforcement of the labour reforms contributes to a continued sense of impunity among many firms.[71] The thirty-eight RRM cases to date are not yet enough to meaningfully deter the thousands of firms covered by the USMCA.

The USA and Mexico held presidential and legislative elections in 2024 and Canada did so in 2025 and the ideological orientations of the new administrations may affect the future use of the RRM. Five new cases were filed by the incoming Trump administration as of mid-2025, indicating continuity in use of the tool, although the overall trade relationship between the three USMCA parties was uncertain due to the US announcement of new tariffs. The parties will conduct a joint review of the USMCA in 2026, which could lead to amendments.[72]

4.2 European Due Diligence Obligations

France and Germany were the first countries to adopt cross-sectoral, mandatory due diligence laws covering a broad range of labour and human rights.[73] The EU adopted a directive in 2024 that requires all EU member states to

70 Two of the firms involved ceased operations due to tenuous finances beyond the labour violations. Maria del Pilar Martinez, 'Factory closes and labor remediation is truncated', El Economista 11 September 2023. https://www.eleconomista.com.mx/empresas/Cierra-fabrica-y-trunca-remediacion-laboral-20231109-0141.html.

71 Fuentes, Manuel, 'La niña obrera cumplió 6 años' [The working girl turned 6 years old], La Silla Rota, 13 May 2025. https://lasillarota.com/opinion/columnas/2025/5/13/la-nina-obrera-cumplio-anos-536043.html; Maria del Pilar Martínez, 'Persiste simulación en corporativismo sindical: CFCRL' [Simulation persists in corporatist unions: Federal Center for Labor Conciliation and Registration], El Economista, 27 January 2025. https://www.eleconomista.com.mx/empresas/hay-practicas-han-reinventado-corporativismo-sindical-cfcrl-20250127-743794.html; Maria del Pilar Martínez, 'Plantean retos del CFCRL a diputados; persiste la injerencia patronal' [CFCRL challenges deputies; employer interference persists], El Economista, 4 May 2025. https://www.eleconomista.com.mx/empresas/plantean-retos-cfcrl-diputados-persiste-injerencia-patronal-20250504-757544.html?fbclid=IwY2xjawKHHDZleHRuA2FlbQIxMAABHoF_YtF8Sis47tGCLO50kmSyER_VN8zFvH5BoQzlVTU57nkl74mgNg0OYkOI_aem_pVcS9mRflA078K9-CmEjIw.

72 Article 34(7) Review and Term Extension.

73 Gustafsson et al, 'Politics of supply chain regulations'.

adopt national laws to 'ensure that companies conduct risk-based human rights and environmental due diligence' in accordance with specific provisions.[74] The EU also adopted a regulation designed to prevent goods produced with forced labour from entering the EU market.[75] The following subsections summarize those legal instruments, their current status and their early application.

4.2.1 French Duty of Vigilance Law

Adopted in 2017, the Law created new human rights and environmental due diligence obligations for companies with head offices in France and with at least 5,000 employees in France or 10,000 employees globally.[76] Companies are required to establish and implement a due diligence plan that contains measures sufficient to identify risks and to prevent serious human rights violations, serious bodily injury, and environmental damage. The Law provides for a civil liability proceeding in which companies failing to comply can be sued and ordered to compensate a loss that could have been avoided if the due diligence obligations had been fulfilled. The Law also provides for injunctive relief, whereby the Paris Civil Court can order companies to comply with their duties.

Several claims have been brought by municipalities or civil society organizations based on environmental or climate harms and by trade unions based on worker and trade union rights violations. Early court decisions adopted strict interpretations of threshold questions such as admissibility of claims and standing of claimants to deny relief. Recent decisions on appeal of those rulings have clarified questions of admissibility, standing of claimants and other procedural matters that now make it easier to pursue claims.[77] In terms of substance, the first decision on the merits in a duty of vigilance case resulted in an order to the firm involved, the French postal company La Poste,

---

74 European Union, 'Directive (EU) 2024/1760 of the European Parliament and of the Council of 13 June 2024 on corporate sustainability due diligence and amending Directive (EU) 2019/1937 and Regulation (EU) 2023/2859'.

75 European Union, Regulation 2024/3015 of the European Parliament and of the Council of 27 November 2024 on prohibiting products made with forced labour on the Union market and amending Directive (EU) 2019/1937.

76 Government of France, LAW No. 2017-399 of 27 March 2017 relating to the duty of care of parent companies and contracting companies.

77 Business and Human Rights Resource Center, 'France's Duty of Vigilance Law' (2024). https://www.business-humanrights.org/en/big-issues/corporate-legal-accountability/frances-duty-of-vigilance-law/

to make substantial changes to its vigilance plan.[78] In terms of deterrence and remedy, the provisions that expose firms to civil liability for harms that could have been prevented through adequate due diligence appear strong enough to create deterrent effects and they explicitly provide for remedy. However, at the time of writing the *de jure* provisions have not yet been applied in practice.

4.2.2 German Act on Corporate Due Diligence in Supply Chains

The Act came into force in 2023 and applies to companies with more than 1,000 employees in Germany.[79] It requires covered firms to perform risk analysis, to develop policies to prevent harms to human rights or the environment, and to remedy any violations. The obligation covers the direct actions of the firm and also extends to the actions of its direct and indirect suppliers. Oversight of compliance with the due diligence requirements is carried out by the Federal Office of Economics and Export Control (BAFA by its German acronym) through 'risk-based inspections' and audits of the mandatory reports submitted by companies.[80] If companies are found to have violated the obligations, fines of up to eight million euros, or up to two per cent of annual global sales for firms with an annual turnover of more than 400 million euros may be imposed, and they can be excluded from eligibility for public contracts.

The first complaint to be filed under the Act was brought by Bangladeshi unions and German civil society organizations, claiming that Amazon, IKEA and other firms endangered the workplace safety of Bangladeshi workers through their failure to monitor and prevent harms.[81] The results of BAFA's investigation of the complaint had not been published at the time of writing. A pilot project related to the Act's requirement that firms establish complaint mechanisms was launched by German auto firms operating in Mexico. The project establishes a cross-company grievance mechanism for workers' com-

78 Paris Civil Court, 5 December 2023, RG no. 21/15827. https://web.lexisnexis.fr/LexisActu/laposte.pdf.

79 German Act on Corporate Due Diligence Obligations in Supply Chains (Gesetz über die unternehmerischen Sorgfaltspflichten in Lieferketten), in force 1 January 2023.

80 In October 2024, BAFA announced it would delay its initial review of company reports under the Act to January 2026.

81 Libby Annat, 'First case filed under the German Supply Chain Due Diligence Act against Tom Tailor, Amazon, and IKEA by Bangladeshi workers'. Due Diligence Design (2023). https://duediligence.design/first-case-filed-under-the-german-supply-chain-due-diligence-act-against-tom-tailor-amazon-and-ikea-by-bangladeshi-workers/.

plaints. A first use of the procedure was initiated in October 2024 by workers claiming their right to freedom of association was violated by the German auto parts firm Contitech Mexico and was underway at the time of writing.[82] It is too early to know if the Act will achieve deterrence and provide remedy.

4.2.3 EU Corporate Sustainability Due Diligence Directive

In order to establish a single EU-wide due diligence standard rather than competing national level approaches, the EU's Commission, Parliament and Council reached agreement on the Corporate Sustainability Due Diligence Directive (CSDDD) in April 2024, although the Commission and Council are attempting to renegotiate the terms as of mid-2025. The Directive as adopted in 2024 requires all EU member states to adopt national laws to 'ensure that companies conduct risk-based human rights and environmental due diligence' in accordance with the specific provisions of the Directive.[83] The due diligence measures must apply to the firms' 'own operations, those of their subsidiaries, as well as those of their direct and indirect business partners throughout their chains of activities'. The member states' legislation must 'ensure that companies take appropriate measures to bring actual adverse impacts that have been, or should have been, identified' to an end, and must provide remediation. The member states must create penalties that are 'effective, proportionate and dissuasive' for firms that do not comply, including fines and civil liability. Member states have up to two years to transpose the terms of the Directive into national law and must take effect in 2027, 2028, or 2029, depending on the size of the firm. The CSDDD as adopted in April 2024 is stronger than the French or German laws, in that it includes *both* administrative fines for corporate violations *and* requires that member states create civil liability for firms for harm that results from their failure to conduct due diligence.[84]

---

82 Maria del Pilar Martinez, 'Germany admits for the first time labor complaint from Contitech Mexico workers', El Economista, 24 October 2024). https://www.eleconomista.com.mx/empresas/alemania-admite-primera-vez-queja-laboral-trabajadores-contitech-mexico-20241024-731450.html.

83 European Union, 'Directive (EU) 2024/1760 of the European Parliament and of the Council of 13 June 2024 on corporate sustainability due diligence and amending Directive (EU) 2019/1937 and Regulation (EU) 2023/2859'.

84 European Parliament, 'Due diligence: MEPs adopt rules for firms on human rights and environment' (2024). https://www.europarl.europa.eu/news/en/press-room/20240419IPR20585/due-diligence-meps-adopt-rules-for-firms-on-human-rights-and-environment.

The potentially powerful directive was adopted after a process that was highly contested by some firms and corporate lobby groups and it continues to be contested. In February 2025 the European Commission introduced a proposal to amend the terms of the CSDDD, along with amendments to the Corporate Sustainability Reporting Directive and other related rules, in the 'Simplification Omnibus package'.[85] Among the many significant changes, the amendments would limit the Directive's applicability to medium-sized firms, narrow the obligations with respect to indirect business partners in the value chain, reduce the required frequency of monitoring and narrow the definition of stakeholders who have a right to be consulted.[86] Notably, the proposal removes the requirement for a civil liability regime across the EU. The proposal was taken up by the Council of the EU in June 2025, which called for further weakening of the CSDDD. The debate will now move through the EU legislative process in which the European Parliament will debate the proposed changes and the three institutions will negotiate over potential amendments.

4.3 US and EU Instruments that Seek to Exclude Products Made with Forced Labour

As noted in the introduction, the earliest government policies addressing the linkage between trade and labour attempted to exclude products made with prison labour. The underlying logic was that because such labour was not freely chosen, wages and working conditions could be so adverse that producers and workers in other countries could not compete. The USA incorporated a ban on importation of products made with forced labour into its basic trade law in 1930 and, with subsequent modifications, the law is still in effect.[87] The EU created its first instrument to ban products made with forced labour in

85 European Commission, 'Proposal for a Directive of the European Parliament and of the Council amending Directives 2006/43/EC, 2013/34/EU, (EU) 2022/2464 and (EU) 2024/1760 as regards certain corporate sustainability reporting and due diligence requirements' (2025). https://finance.ec.europa.eu/document/download/161070f0-aca7-4b44-b20a-52bd879575bc_en?filename=proposal-directive-amending-accounting-audit-csrd-csddd-directives_en.pdf.

86 Business and Human Rights Resource Center, 'EU: Experts analyse key implications of Omnibus package for CSDDD, CSRD, and EU Taxonomy' 2025. https://www.business-humanrights.org/en/latest-news/eu-experts-analyse-the-key-implications-of-the-omnibus-package-for-csddd-csrd-and-eu-taxonomy/.

87 United States Code Title 19 – Chapter 4 – Tariff Act of 1930. 19 U.S.C. 1307. https://www.govinfo.gov/app/details/USCODE-2011-title19/USCODE-2011-title19-chap4-subtitleII-partI-sec1307.

2024, with full implementation scheduled for 2027.[88] Both of these approaches are targeted at the level of the firm. The focus on the firm is appropriate given the pattern of forced labour: the ILO and others estimate that of the 27.6 million people in forced labour in 2021, 23.6 million worked in the private sector.[89] The ILO further estimated that the private sector generates $63.9 billion annually in profits from forced labour within supply chains.[90] The following sections briefly summarize the US and EU instruments and their application.

4.3.1 US Instruments to Exclude Products Made with Forced Labour

The US Customs and Border Protection (CBP) agency is charged with enforcing the long-standing ban on importation of products made with forced labour. Until 2015 the law provided a broad exception that such products could be blocked only if US producers could meet domestic consumption demand for those goods; if not, they were permitted to enter the United States even if made with forced labour. As evidence of forced labour in global supply chains was increasingly documented, Congress amended the law in 2015 to remove the exception related to consumptive demand and the law has been used much more extensively since then.[91]

Any person or organization that has reason to believe merchandise produced in whole or in part with forced labour is being imported into the United States can submit the allegation to the CBP, which then investigates. If the CBP finds information indicating that forced labour is involved, it issues a withhold release order (WRO) that prevents the product from being released into the USA unless the importing firm can prove the absence of forced labour in the product's supply chain. If CBP conclusively finds that forced labour was used in production of a good that seeks to enter the US market, it issues a finding that allows it to seize and destroy the products. As of 2025, fifty-two

---

88 European Union, 'Regulation of the European Parliament and of the Council on prohibiting products made with forced labour on the Union market and amending Directive (EU) 2019/1937'. https://data.consilium.europa.eu/doc/document/PE-67-2024-INIT/en/pdf.

89 International Labour Organization, Walk Free and International Organization for Migration, 'Global Estimates of Modern Slavery: Forced Labour and Forced Marriage' (2022). https://www.ilo.org/sites/default/files/wcmsp5/groups/public/%40ed_norm/%40ipec/documents/publication/wcms_854733.pdf.

90 International Labour Organization, 'Profits and poverty: The economics of forced labour' (2024). https://www.ilo.org/sites/default/files/2024-10/Profits%20and%20poverty%20-%20The%20economics%20of%20forced%20labour_WEB_20241017.pdf.

91 Congressional Research Service, 'Section 307 and Imports Produced by Forced Labor'. https://www.congress.gov/crs-product/IF11360.

WROs and nine findings were in force involving firms from fifteen countries.[92] The products involved were concentrated in agriculture, fishing, mining, and garments.

While the US forced labour law has mainly been applied with respect to specific products where there is a reasonable basis to believe that forced labour was used, the law has occasionally been applied to broader categories of goods emanating from regions of countries where there are suspicions of more systemic forced labour, for example, artisanal mining from certain regions in some countries. The broader approach has now been applied to all products mined, produced or manufactured wholly or in part in the Xinjiang Uyghur Autonomous Region (XUAR) of China based on the 2021 Uyghur Forced Labor Prevention Act.[93] The act creates a rebuttable presumption that all goods from the region involve forced labour. The law created a Forced Labor Enforcement Task Force that is charged with preparing an 'Entity List' of firms assumed to use forced labour, which now numbers 150 firms. The foundation for the expansive approach is the US view that Uyghurs are subject to state-imposed forced labour, an accusation that China denies.[94] China maintains that the purpose of the UFLPA is to constrain China's development by 'containing China with Xinjiang'.[95]

Both the ban on products made with forced labour in the Tariff Act of 1930 and the UFLPA can create substantial deterrent effects. Where products are already subject to WROs or findings under the Tariff Act or are on the Entity List associated with the UFLPA, lead firms and importers will be discouraged from attempting to bring such products into the US market and will typically seek other suppliers. However, in terms of remedy, neither law provides any form of relief to workers subjected to forced labour.

92 Customs and Border Protection Withhold Release Orders and Findings Dashboard. https://www.cbp.gov/trade/forced-labor/withhold-release-orders-and-findings.

93 Public Law 117–78 – An act to ensure that goods made with forced labor in the Xinjiang Uyghur Autonomous Region of the People's Republic of China do not enter the United States market, and for other purposes. https://www.govinfo.gov/app/details/PLAW-117publ78.

94 International Labour Organization, 'Report of the Committee of Experts on the Application of Conventions and Recommendations' (2025), pp. 362–365. https://www.ilo.org/sites/default/files/2025-02/Report%20III%28A%29-2025-%5BNORMES-241219-002%5D-EN.pdf.

95 Xinhua, 'Chinese top legislature opposes U.S. signing of so-called "Uyghur Forced Labor Prevention Act"', 24 December 2021. https://english.news.cn/northamerica/20211224/debcd2faa15b4994a95ab5afdcc9a31d/c.html.

4.3.2 The EU Forced Labour Regulation

In November 2024 the European Union adopted a regulation prohibiting products made with forced labour from entering the EU market.[96] The regulation covers goods and their components that involve forced labour – as defined by the ILO – which are made in the EU or imported into or exported from that market. The regulation covers all products of firms of all sizes. It will be implemented from November 2027.

The responsibility for implementation is shared between the European Commission, which will act as the lead authority when the suspected forced labour takes place outside the EU, while a member state will act as the lead authority when the suspected forced labour takes place in its territory. The Commission will establish and maintain an up-to-date database that indicates forced labour risks in specific geographic areas or with respect to specific products or product groups 'based on independent and verifiable information from international organisations, in particular the ILO and the UN, or institutional, research or academic organisations'.[97] By May 2026 the Commission will issue guidelines for firms (called 'economic operators' in the regulation) setting out due diligence requirements with respect to forced labour and best practices for ending and remediating different types of forced labour.[98] The Commission will establish a centralized mechanism for the submission of information about suspected forced labour by members of the public.[99] The regulation sets out the steps for investigation of allegations.[100] When an investigation confirms the use of forced labour, the lead authority can order the product to be withheld for the time necessary to eliminate the forced labour at the cost of the economic operator or may order that the product be disposed to prevent it from being exported elsewhere.[101] The regulation further directs the member states to establish and apply penalties that are 'effective, proportionate and dissuasive' to firms that do not comply with such orders.[102]

Since the regulation has not yet been implemented there is no empirical evidence on which to evaluate it. There is no indication at the time of writing

96 Regulation of the European Parliament and of the Council on prohibiting products made with forced labour on the Union market and amending Directive (EU) 2019/1937. https://data.consilium.europa.eu/doc/document/PE-67-2024-INIT/en/pdf.

97 Article 8.

98 Article 11.

99 Article 9.

100 Articles 14–18.

101 Article 20.

102 Article 37.

that the EU institutions will attempt to renegotiate this regulation as they are currently doing with respect to the due diligence regulation, the CSDDD, approved in 2024. However, the forced labour regulation explicitly states that it 'does not create additional due diligence obligations for economic operators other than those already provided for in Union or national law'.[103] If the CSDDD is weakened, it could potentially weaken the implementation of the forced labour regulation as well.

5 Conclusion

The policies discussed in this chapter show that labour rights have been increasingly subject to cross-border enforcement through free trade agreements, corporate due diligence laws and import bans on products made with forced labour. After a period when trade agreements' labour rights obligations and enforcement mechanisms were applicable mainly to actions or failures by governments, recent innovations have extended the scope and focus to target violations at the level of the firm as well as the state. Instruments such as the Rapid Response Mechanism in the USMCA and due diligence laws in France and Germany create direct liability for firms that violate labour rights.

These policy innovations arose as a result of advocacy by trade unions, civil society and pro-worker legislators to address labour violations in global supply chains. They recognize the inherent power imbalance between workers and firms at both local and cross-border levels and can offer victims who are denied their rights new avenues for recourse. The rigor of the obligations as well as the available remedies differs widely among trade agreements and due diligence laws. Many of the enforcement tools are very recent or in the case of the EU are still contested. Additional experience will be required to judge their effectiveness and substantive impacts.

Cross-border enforcement of labour rights is currently playing out against a backdrop of heightened geopolitical tensions and recent shifts in trade and economic policies in both the USA and EU. The multilateral and bilateral trade agreements and rules developed during the period of rapid globalization are increasingly ignored in favour of nationalist policies or competitive advantage. Labour rights provisions that are embedded in those agreements are vulnerable to the broader disruptions. Recent tools to create liability for firms for labour violations that occur in their supply chains are currently being relitigated. It remains to be seen whether policy makers will continue to advance

103 Article 1(3).

the hundred-year-old effort to protect labour rights across borders or will sacrifice workers' rights in the pursuit of geopolitical or other advantage.

Bibliography

Annat, Libby, 'First case filed under the German Supply Chain Due Diligence Act against Tom Tailor, Amazon, and IKEA by Bangladeshi workers' (Due Diligence Design, 2023) https://duediligence.design/first-case-filed-under-the-german-supply-chain-due-diligence-act-against-tom-tailor-amazon-and-ikea-by-bangladeshi-workers/.

Anner, Mark, Bair, Jennifer and Blasi, Jeremy, 'Towards Joint Liability in Global Supply Chains: Addressing the Root Causes of Labor Violations in International Subcontracting Networks'. *Comparative Labor Law and Policy Journal*, 35 (1) https://www.academia.edu/17960500/Towards_Joint_Liability_in_Global_Supply_Chains_Addressing_the_Root_Causes_of_Labor_Violations_in_International_Subcontracting_Networks.

Autor, David H., Dorn, David, & Hanson, Gordon H., 'The China Shock: Learning from labor market adjustment to large changes in trade' NBER Working Paper No. 21906 (Cambridge, MA. National Bureau of Economic Research, 2016) https://www.nber.org/papers/w21906.pdf.

Bensusán, Graciela, 'Empleos Bajo Presión: Con O Sin Tlcan', in Oscar Fernando Contreras, Gustavo Vega, Eduardo Mendoza, Clemente Ruiz Durán and Jorge Carrillo (eds), *La renegociación del Tratado de Libre Comercio en Norteamérica: Desafíos para México y sus Regiones*, (Baja California: El Colegio de la Frontera Norte, 2019)

Bensusán, Graciela, 'The Transformation of the Mexican Labour Regulation Model and its link to North American Economic Integration', Working Paper No. 15 (Geneva: International Labour Organization, 2020) https://www.ilo.org/static/english/intserv/working-papers/wp015/index.html.

Bensusán, Graciela and Kevin J. Middlebrook, 'Democratic Labor Reform in Mexico', (Washington: Wilson Center Mexico Institute, 2020) https://www.wilsoncenter.org/sites/default/files/media/uploads/documents/Bensus%C3%A1n%20%26%20Middlebrook%20-%20Democratic%20Labor%20Reform%20in%20Mexico.pdf.

Blecker, Robert A., Juan Carlos Moreno-Brid and Isabel Salat, 'Trumping the NAFTA renegotiation: An alternative policy framework for Mexican-United States cooperation and economic convergence'. (Economic Commission for Latin America and the Caribbean (ECLAC), Sub-regional Headquarters in Mexico, 2017) https://www.cepal.org/en/publications/42579-trumping-nafta-renegotiation-alternative-policy-framework-mexican-united-states.

Brooks, Tequila J., 'U.S.-Guatemala Arbitration Panel Clarifies Effective Enforcement Under Labor Provisions of Free Trade Agreement International Labor Rights Case Law', *International Labor Rights Case Law*, 4(1), 45–51. https://brill.com/view/journals/ilrc/4/1/article-p45_45.xml.

Business and Human Rights Resource Center, 'Complaints under the German Supply Chain Act', Business and Human Rights Resource Center, 2023 https://www.business-humanrights.org/en/latest-news/beschwerden-bafa-lksg/.

Business and Human Rights Resource Center, 'France's Duty of Vigilance Law', Business and Human Rights Resource Center, 2024 https://www.business-humanrights.org/en/big-issues/corporate-legal-accountability/frances-duty-of-vigilance-law/.

Business and Human Rights Resource Center, 'EU: Experts analyse key implications of Omnibus package for CSDDD, CSRD, and EU Taxonomy', Business and Human Rights Resource Center, 2025. https://www.business-humanrights.org/en/latest-news/eu-experts-analyse-the-key-implications-of-the-omnibus-package-for-csddd-csrd-and-eu-taxonomy/.

Centro Federal de Conciliación y Registro Laboral, '30,529 Legitimized collective contracts' https://legitimacion.centrolaboral.gob.mx/.

Cerrato, Andrea, Ruggieri, Francesco, & Ferrara, Federico M., 'Trump won in counties that lost jobs to China and Mexico'. The Washington Post, 2 December 2016. https://www.washingtonpost.com/news/monkey-cage/wp/2016/12/02/trump-won-where-import-shocks-from-china-and-mexico-were-strongest/.

CILAS (Centro de Investigación Laboral y Asesoria Sindical), 'The change that never comes: The Labor Reform in four years' (Mexico City: CILAS, 2023) https://calisnacional.com/?p=26483.

Compa, Lance and Tequila Brooks, *NAFTA and NAALC: Twenty-five Years of North American Trade* (Philadelphia, PA: Kluwer Law International, 2019).

Congressional Research Service, 'Section 307 and Imports Produced by Forced Labor'. https://www.congress.gov/crs-product/IF11360.

Corasaniti, Nick, Burns, Alexander, & Appelbaum, Binyamin, 'Donald Trump vows to rip up trade deals and confront China', The New York Times, 28 June 2016. https://www.nytimes.com/2016/06/29/us/politics/donald-trump-trade-speech.html?searchResultPosition=1.

Corley-Coulibaly, Marva, Gaia Grasselli and Ira Postolachi, *Promoting and enforcing compliance with labour provisions in trade agreements: Comparative analysis of Canada, European Union and United States approaches and practices* (Geneva: ILO, 2023) https://www.ilo.org/wcmsp5/groups/public/---dgreports/---inst/documents/publication/wcms_885151.pdf.

Covarrubias V., Alex, 'Cuatro años de reforma laboral… y el dinosaurio todavía sigue ahí (parte I)', El Economista, 4 May 2023. https://www.eleconomista.com.mx/cap

italhumano/Cuatro-anos-de-reforma-laboral-y-el-dinosaurio-todavia-sigue-ahi-20230504-0077.html.
Customs and Border Protection Withhold Release Orders and Findings Dashboard. https://www.cbp.gov/trade/forced-labor/withhold-release-orders-and-findings.
Dauth, Wolfgang, Sebastian Findeisen and Jens Suedekum, 'The Rise of the east and the far east: German labor markets and trade integration' 12 *Journal of the European Economic Association*, 1643–1675.
Elliott, Kimberly Ann, 'Hard and Soft Law Approaches to Protecting Worker Rights', in Kimberly Ann Elliott (ed.), *Handbook on Globalisation and Labour Standards*, (Cheltenham, UK: Edward Elgar, 2022).
European Commission, 'EU moves ahead with dispute settlement over workers' rights in Republic of Korea', 2019. https://policy.trade.ec.europa.eu/news/eu-moves-ahead-dispute-settlement-over-workers-rights-republic-korea-2019-07-05_en.
European Commission, 'Communication from the Commission to the European Parliament, the Council, the European Economic and Social Committee and the Committee of the Region, The power of trade partnerships: together for green and just economic growth' 2022. https://eur-lex.europa.eu/legal-content/EN/TXT/PDF/?uri=CELEX:52022DC0409.
European Commission, Free Trade Agreement between the European Union and New Zealand, 9 July 2023, in force 1 May 2024, Chapters 19 and 26. https://policy.trade.ec.europa.eu/eu-trade-relationships-country-and-region/countries-and-regions/new-zealand/eu-new-zealand-agreement/text-agreement_en.
European Commission, 'Proposal for a Directive of the European Parliament and of the Council amending Directives 2006/43/EC, 2013/34/EU, (EU) 2022/2464 and (EU) 2024/1760 as regards certain corporate sustainability reporting and due diligence requirements' 2025. https://finance.ec.europa.eu/document/download/161070f0-aca7-4b44-b20a-52bd879575bc_en?filename=proposal-directive-amending-accounting-audit-csrd-csddd-directives_en.pdf.
European Parliament, 'External Dimension of Social Policy, Promoting Labour and Social Standards and European Corporate Social Responsibility' 2010/2205. http://www.europarl.europa.eu/sides/getDoc.do?type=REPORT&reference=A7-2011-0172&language=EN.
European Parliament, 'Due diligence: MEPs adopt rules for firms on human rights and environment' 2024. https://www.europarl.europa.eu/news/en/press-room/20240419IPR20585/due-diligence-meps-adopt-rules-for-firms-on-human-rights-and-environment.
European Union, 'Directive (EU) 2024/1760 of the European Parliament and of the Council of 13 June 2024 on corporate sustainability due diligence and amending Directive (EU) 2019/1937 and Regulation (EU) 2023/2859'. https://eur-lex.europa.eu/legal-content/EN/TXT/PDF/?uri=OJ:L_202401760.

European Union, 'Regulation (EU) 2024/3015 of the European Parliament and of the Council of 27 November 2024 on prohibiting products made with forced labour on the Union market and amending Directive (EU) 2019/1937'. https://eur-lex.europa.eu/eli/reg/2024/3015/oj/eng.

Feler, Leo and Senses, Mine Zeynep, 'Trade Shocks and the Provision of Local Public Goods' IZA Discussion Paper No. 10231 (Bonn, Germany: Institute for the Study of Labor, 2016). https://ssrn.com/abstract=2846322.

García, María J., 'Sanctioning Capacity in Trade and Sustainability Chapters in EU Trade Agreements: The EU-Korea Case'. *Politics and Governance*, 10(1), 58–67.

General Agreement on Tariffs and Trade, Article XX General Exceptions. https://www.wto.org/english/res_e/booksp_e/gatt_ai_e/art20_e.pdf.

German Federal Ministry of Economic Cooperation and Development, 'The German Act on Corporate Due Diligence in Supply Chains', 2021. https://www.bmas.de/SharedDocs/Downloads/DE/Internationales/act-corporate-due-diligence-obligations-supply-chains.pdf?__blob=publicationFile&v=3.

Government of France, 'LAW No. 2017-399 of 27 March 2017 relating to the duty of care of parent companies and contracting companies'. https://www.legifrance.gouv.fr/jorf/id/JORFTEXT000034290626.

Government of México, 'Mexico receives the trade authorities of the United States and Canada to celebrate the T-MEC Free Trade Commission', 6 July 2023. https://www.gob.mx/se/prensa/mexico-recibe-a-las-autoridades-comerciales-de-estados-unidos-y-canada-para-celebrar-la-comision-de-libre-comercio-del-t-mec?idiom=es.

Graz, Jean-Christophe, 'The Havana Charter: When State and Market Shake Hands', in Rainer Kattel, Jayati Ghosh and Erik Reinert (eds.), *Handbook of Alternative Theories of Economic Development* (Cheltenham, UK: Edward Elgar Publishing, 2016), pp. 281–290.

Greer, Jamieson, 'Hearing to Consider the Nomination of Jamieson Greer, of Maryland, to be United States Trade Representative, with the rank of Ambassador Extraordinary and Plenipotentiary'. United States Senate Committee on Finance, 6 February 2025 (at 1 hour 34 minutes and following). https://www.finance.senate.gov/hearings/hearing-to-consider-the-nomination-of-jamieson-greer-of-maryland-to-be-united-states-trade-representative-with-the-rank-of-ambassador-extraordinary-and-plenipotentiary.

Gustafsson, Maria-Therese, Almut Schilling-Vacaflor and Andrea Lenschow, 'The politics of supply chain regulations: Towards foreign corporate accountability in the area of human rights and the environment?' 17 *Regulation & Governance*, 853–869.

Harrison, James, 'Trade Agreements and Sustainability: Exploring the Potential of Global Value Chain (GVC) Obligations', 26 *Journal of International Economic Law*, 199–215.

Harrison, James, Mirela Barbu, Liam Campling, Franz Christian Ebert, Deborah Martens, Axel Marx, Jan Orbie, Ben Richardson and Adrian Smith, 'Labour Standards Provisions in EU Free Trade Agreements: Reflections on the European Commission's Reform Agenda'. *World Trade Review*, 1–23.

Independent Mexico Labor Expert Board, 'IMLEB Report and Separate Statement of Members Fortson et al', 2021. https://www.researchgate.net/publication/359529197_IMLEB_Report_and_Separate_Statement_of_Members_Fortson_et_al_2021077.

Independent Mexico Labor Expert Board, 'Report to the Interagency Labor Committee (ILC) and the United States Congress pursuant to Section 734 of the United States-Mexico-Canada Agreement Implementation Act, P.L. 116–113', 2023. https://www.researchgate.net/publication/369383619_IMLEB_Report-2023_03_20_FINAL.

International Labour Organization, Constitution. NORMLEX.

International Labour Organization, Declaration on Fundamental Principles and Rights at Work, 1998. https://www.ilo.org/declaration/lang–en/index.htm.

International Labour Organization, 'Profits and poverty: The economics of forced labour' (Geneva: ILO, 2024). https://www.ilo.org/sites/default/files/2024-10/Profits%20and%20poverty%20-%20The%20economics%20of%20forced%20labour_WEB_20241017.pdf.

International Labour Organization, Report of the Committee of Experts on the Application of Conventions and Recommendations, 2025, pp. 362–365.https://www.ilo.org/sites/default/files/2025-02/Report%20III%28A%29-2025-%5BNORMES-241219-002%5D-EN.pdf.

International Labour Organization, Walk Free and International Organization for Migration, 'Global Estimates of Modern Slavery: Forced Labour and Forced Marriage' (Geneva: ILO, 2022).https://www.ilo.org/sites/default/files/wcmsp5/groups/public/%40ed_norm/%40ipec/documents/publication/wcms_854733.pdf.

Lakner, Christoph and Branko Milanovic, 'Global income distribution: From the Fall of the Berlin Wall to the Great Recession' Policy Research Working Paper No. 6719 (Washington: World Bank, 2013). https://openknowledge.worldbank.org/search?spc.page=1&query=Global%20income%20distribution:%20From%20the%20Fall%20of%20the%20Berlin%20Wall%20to%20the%20Great%20Recession.

Lighthizer, Robert, *No Trade Is Free: Changing Course, Taking on China, and Helping America's Workers* (New York: Broadside/HarperCollins, 2023).

Marin, Dalia, 'The opening-up of Eastern Europe at 20: Jobs, skills, and reverse Maquiladoras in Austria and Germany' Working Paper No. 2010/02 (Brussels: Bruegel, 2010). https://www.bruegel.org/wpcontent/uploads/imported/publications/wp_2010_02_maquiladoras_.pdf.

Mayer Frederick and Gary Gereffi, 'Regulation and Economic Globalization: Prospects and Limits of Private Governance' (2010) 12 *Business and Politics*, 3, 1–25.

Mayer, Frederick and Nicola Phillips, 'Outsourcing governance: states and the politics of a 'global value chain world" (2017) 22 *New Political Economy*, 2, 134–152.

Middlebrook, Kevin J., *The International Defense of Workers: Labor Rights, U.S. Trade Agreements, and State Sovereignty* (New York: Columbia University Press, 2024).

Moreno-Brid, Juan, and Stefanie Garry, 'El Salario Mínimo En México: En Falta Con La Constitución Mexicana Y Una Aberración En América Latina', in Miguel Ángel Mancera (ed.), *Del salario mínimo al salario digno*, 105–121. (Mexico: Mexico City Economic and Social Council, 2015). https://www.researchgate.net/publication/292175585_El_salario_minimo_en_Mexico_en_falta_con_La_Constitucion_mexicana_y_una_aberracion_en_America_Latina.

North American Agreement on Labor Cooperation, 13 September 1993. https://www.dol.gov/agencies/ilab/naalc.

Novitz, Tonia, 'Enforceable social clauses in trade agreements with 'bite'? Implications of the EU–South Korea Panel of Experts Report of 20 January 2021'. European Trade Union Institute. https://www.etui.org/publications/enforceable-social-clauses-trade-agreements-bite.

Paris Civil Court, 5 December 2023, RG no. 21/15827. https://web.lexisnexis.fr/LexisActu/laposte.pdf.

Pilar Martinez, Maria del, 'Germany admits for the first time labor complaint from Contitech Mexico workers', El Economista, 24 October 2024. https://www.eleconomista.com.mx/empresas/alemania-admite-primera-vez-queja-laboral-trabajadores-contitech-mexico-20241024-731450.html.

Polaski, Sandra, 'Job Anxiety Is Real – and It's Global' Policy Brief No. 30 (Washington: Carnegie Endowment for International Peace, 2004). https://carnegieendowment.org/posts/2004/04/job-anxiety-is-real-and-its-global?lang=en.

Polaski, Sandra, 'Protecting Labor Rights through Trade Agreements: An Analytical Guide' (2004) 10 *Journal of International Law and Policy*, 17–20. https://www.researchgate.net/publication/247288022_Protecting_Labor_Rights_through_Trade_Agreements_An_Analytical_Guide.

Polaski, Sandra, 'the Strategy and Politics of Linking Trade and Labor Standards: an Overview of Issues and Approaches', in Kimberly Ann Elliott (ed.), *Handbook on Globalisation and Labour Standards* (Cheltenham, UK: Edward Elgar, 2022).

Polaski, Sandra, 'USMCA and the Rapid Response Labor Mechanism: A new approach to cross-border governance of labor rights', Social Science Research Network, 2023. http://dx.doi.org/10.2139/ssrn.4639948

Postnikov, Evgeny, 'Labor Standards in Eu and Us Preferential Trade Agreements Mainstreaming the Trade-Labor Linkage', in Kimberly Ann Elliott (ed.), *Handbook on Globalisation and Labour Standards* (Cheltenham, UK: Edward Elgar, 2022).

Quelch, John A., and Margaret L. Rodriguez, 'Rana Plaza: Workplace Safety in Bangladesh (A)'. Harvard Business School Supplement 514–035, September 2013, revised June 2014. https://www.hbs.edu/faculty/Pages/item.aspx?num=45540.

Reuters, 'Canada closes labor complaint in Mexico at German manufacturer Fraenkische', Reuters, 25 July 2023. https://www.reuters.com/world/americas/canada-closes-labor-complaint-mexico-german-manufacturer-fraenkische-2023-07-25/.

Robertson, Dylan, 'Left-leaning Mexico seeks closer Canada ties in labour and business amid mining spat', The Canadian Press, 11 June 2023. https://nationalpost.com/news/left-leaning-mexico-seeks-closer-canada-ties-in-labour-and-business-amid-mining-spat.

Severns, Maggie, 'Trump pins NAFTA, "worst trade deal ever," on Clinton', Politico, 26 September 2016. https://www.politico.com/story/2016/09/trump-clinton-come-out-swinging-over-nafta-228712.

Tai, Katherine, 'USMCA Priorities for the United States in 2022', in *USMCA Forward* (Washington: The Brookings Institution, 2022). https://www.brookings.edu/articles/usmca-priorities-for-the-united-states-in-2022/.

United Nations Human Rights Council, 'Open-ended intergovernmental working group on transnational corporations and other business enterprises with respect to human rights' (2024) https://www.ohchr.org/en/hr-bodies/hrc/wg-trans-corp/igwg-on-tnc.

UN Trade and Development (UNCTAD), *Trade and Development Report 2017* (Geneva: UNCTAD, 2017). https://unctad.org/publication/trade-and-development-report-2017.

UN Trade and Development (UNCTAD), 'Key evolutions in trade and development over the decades' (Geneva: UNCTAD, 2024). https://unctad.org/news/key-evolutions-trade-and-development-over-decades.

United States–Mexico–Canada Agreement, Mexico City, Mexico, 19 December 2019 (revised version), in force 1 July 2020. https://ustr.gov/trade-agreements/free-trade-agreements/united-states-mexico-canada-agreement.

United States Trade Representative, 'Chapter 31 Annex – Facility-Specific Rapid-Response Labor Mechanism Fact Sheets'. https://ustr.gov/issue-areas/enforcement/dispute-settlement-proceedings/fta-dispute-settlement/usmca/chapter-31-annex-facility-specific-rapid-response-labor-mechanism.

United States Trade Representative, 'Remarks by Ambassador Tai to Discuss Updates on Biden-Harris Administration's Worker-Centered Trade Agenda at the Center for American Progress', 4 October 2023. https://ustr.gov/about-us/policy-offices/press-office/speeches-and-remarks/2023/october/remarks-ambassador-katherine-tai-discuss-updates-biden-harris-administrations-worker-centered-trade.

Van den Putte, Lore, Ferdi De Ville and Jan Orbie, 'the European Parliament's New Role in Trade Policy: Turning Power into Impact' CEPS Special Reports No. 89. (Brussels: Centre for European Policy, 2014).

Weihrauch, David, Sophia Carodenuto and Sina Leipold, 'From voluntary to mandatory corporate accountability: The politics of the German supply chain due diligence act' (2023) 17 *Regulation & Governance*, 909–926.

World Trade Organization, 'Singapore Ministerial Declaration', 1996. https://www.wto.org/english/news_e/pres96_e/wtodec.htm.

Xinhua, 'Chinese top legislature opposes U.S. signing of so-called 'Uyghur Forced Labor Prevention Act'', Xinjua, 24 December 2021. https://english.news.cn/northamerica/20211224/debcd2faa15b4994a95ab5afdcc9a31d/c.html.

CHAPTER 3

The Impact of Labour Clauses in Trade Agreements: The Economic Controversy

Christoph Scherrer

1 Introduction

The use of the international trade regime to enforce international workers' rights and labour standards is highly controversial in the field of economics. Mainstream international trade scholars contend that any increase in labour costs will allegedly jeopardize poor countries' key comparative advantage of abundant labour. Heterodox economists see better enforcement through trade agreements as an important contribution to sustainable development.

Efforts to enforce core labour rights are primarily aimed at low- and middle-income countries. For this reason, the justification for internationally binding labour rights is also derived from their contribution to the industrialization opportunities of so-called developing and emerging countries.[1] Since the economic literature usually refers to labour standards rather than labour rights, even though the labour clauses in preferential trade agreements (PTAs) mostly refer to the core International Labour Organization (ILO) conventions that entail workers' rights, the term labour standards will also be used in this chapter, assuming that rights are used to upgrade labour standards.

Opponents of international labour standards see them as superfluous or even detrimental to the industrial catch-up process. The first step is therefore to examine the extent to which previous empirical studies suggest that better labour standards can be achieved through trade liberalization alone. In a second step, the validity of the more severe criticism of international labour standards, namely that higher standards undermine the competitiveness of catching-up economies, is measured against the empirical evidence to date. The ambiguous results of previous studies invite a theoretical reflection on the relationship between standards and catching-up. For the dominant neoclassical paradigm of economics, it can be shown that although it is mostly used to

1 Since some of these countries are older than 'my' country, I do not consider 'developing' and 'emerging' to be appropriate terms for them. I prefer the distinction between capitalist centres and capitalist peripheries.

 | HTTPS://DOI.ORG/10.1163/9789004762251-004

reject internationally enforced standards, compliance with core labour standards can be brought into line with central assumptions of the paradigm. The neo-institutional paradigm also explains why higher standards promote economic development in the long run. Why, however, these standards are often not met needs further explanation. My contribution to this debate is the following argument. Beyond the fear of a strengthened opposition in autocratic states, the lack of compliance with ILO conventions is a collective action problem. It results from fierce competition among countries that rely on similar labour skills and technologies, and that experience a labour force expansion that is not matched by sufficient job creation. The collective action problem can be overcome through effective enforcement of ILO Conventions.

2 Better Standards through Trade?

According to the neoclassical paradigm of economics, prosperity-enhancing efficiency gains in foreign trade can only be achieved if the unimpeded movement of goods allows production to specialize on the basis of comparative cost advantages. Any compulsory increase in production costs would impair sales opportunities on the world market and thus the development opportunities of the countries concerned. Any increase in labour costs would jeopardize the essential comparative advantage of poor countries. Thus, better working conditions cannot be mandated by law or international agreement, but will emerge in the course of industrialization. Economic development is most likely to be promoted by a trade regime that is as free as possible.[2]

Do economic development and expansion of the export economy necessarily lead to greater respect for core labour standards?

Mainstream assessments of the impact of trade liberalization use computable general equilibrium and partial equilibrium models (CGE and CPE) based on the typical neoclassical assumptions of perfect competition, optimizing agents, and full employment, among others. These econometric analyses predict increased employment and welfare. While unequal distributional effects are acknowledged, adjustment costs and time are considered negligible. In recent decades, deep integration preferential trade agreements (PTAs) have

2 J. Bhagwati, 'A View from Academia', in U.S. Department of Labor, Bureau of International Labor Affairs (eds.), International Labor Standards and Global Economic Integration (Washington, 1994). P.K. Goldberg and T. Reed 'Is the Global Economy Deglobalizing?' Policy Research Working Paper 10392 (Washington: World Bank Group, 2023), p. 41. P. Krugman, 'Does Third World Growth Hurt First World Prosperity?' (1994) Harvard Business Review, 72(4).

become the norm. These PTAs go beyond tariff reduction and address so-called behind-the-border discriminatory practices, also known as non-tariff barriers (NTBs). NTBs pose a challenge to CGE/CPE models because, unlike tariffs, their costs are not easily determined, opening the door to subjective estimates.[3] In other words, these more general assessments of liberalized trade are not informative with respect to our question, as these PTAs increasingly include labour clauses.

The studies that focused on trade liberalization and the observance of labour rights were initially unable to find a correlation between the two.[4] Later econometric analyses found a positive correlation between trade liberalization and labour rights: A higher share of trade in GDP is associated with a higher number of ratifications of ILO conventions or lower levels of child labour.[5] However, these cross-sectional studies do not allow us to determine the direction of causality; they allow both the conclusion that trade liberalization leads to higher standards and, conversely, that higher standards will promote foreign trade.

The limitations of the cross-sectional analysis become clear in a study by Matthias Busse (2004), who also conducts a longitudinal analysis. While he shows in the cross-section that trade liberalization is correlated with better compliance with core labour standards, the longitudinal analysis (1970–2000) shows that the actual extent of discrimination against women and the incidence of child labour increases with greater trade dependence. Moreover, in Southeast Asia, with its high export volumes, the increase in trade volume is not followed by a significant improvement in compliance with core labour standards.[6] However, it was the disregard for workers' rights in this region in particular that triggered the social clause debate in the early 1990s. As with many other studies (see below), the validity of the econometric country comparison studies is limited by the statistically equal treatment of China and other Southeast Asian exporting countries. The studies are not weighted

3 For a detailed explanation of CGE/CPE models plus critique, see M. Hernandez, 'Impacts of international trade on the labour market: Common methodological approaches for macro- and meso-level assessments', in M. Corley-Coulibaly, P.S. Richiardi and F.C. Ebert (eds.), Integrating trade and decent work Volume 1 (Geneva: International Labour Office, 2023), pp. 43–77.

4 OECD 'Trade, Employment and Labour Standards' (Paris: OECD, 1996).

5 E.V. Edmonds and N. Pavcnik 'International Trade and Child Labor' (2006) Journal of International Economics, 68(1), p. 115.

D.K. Brown 'International Trade and Core Labour Standards' OECD Labour Market and Social Policy Occasional Papers 43 (Paris: OECD, 2000).

6 M. Busse 'On the Determinants of Core Labour Standards' (2004) Economic Letters 83(2), p. 211.

according to world trade shares, let alone growth in world trade shares; they are always concerned only with the country-specific degree of openness to the world market (which is relatively low for China, for example, because of its large domestic market).

Country studies are sometimes more revealing. Nina Pavnik, with several co-authors, studied the impact of US tariff cuts on Vietnam and found a small increase in formal employment.[7] In contrast, domestic tariff cuts may be less beneficial. Studies have highlighted displacement effects in import-substituting industries that are not always offset by improved export opportunities due to tariff reductions in export destinations.[8] Moreover, in some countries, such as Brazil, displaced workers often suffered from a long search for new jobs, often at lower wages.

A study by Mosley and Uno[9] comes to the opposite conclusion, namely that economic development does not automatically lead to better compliance with workers' rights. The study is notable not only for its longitudinal design (1986–2002), but also for its very well thought-out construction of indicators of the actual degree of compliance with workers' rights and its consideration of many possible influencing factors. The study shows that countries with a higher share of imports and exports in their gross domestic product treat their wage earners worse. They attribute this to competitive pressures at the various stages of the value chain, which they try to capture by considering countries with a similar specialization profile and belonging to the same world region. However, only the 'regional' variable is statistically significant, suggesting that political-mimetic influences, e.g. value diffusion, could also play a role.

The fact that not only neighbouring countries, but also major buyer countries, have an influence on labour standards is demonstrated by another longitudinal study in which Mosley participated. However, the correlation only exists with respect to formal legislation, not actual practice.[10] While this study identifies the prevailing standards in the main buyer country as the cause, a

7 Edmond and Pavcnik 'International Trade and Child Labor'.

8 N. Pavcnik 'The impact of trade on inequality in developing countries' No. w23878 (Washington: National Bureau of Economic Research, 2017). B. Aleman-Castilla 'Trade and decent work in Mexico's manufacturing sector', in M. Corley-Coulibaly, P. Sekerler Richiardi and F.C. Ebert (eds.) Integrating trade and decent work Volume 1 (Geneva: International Labour Office, 2023), pp. 151–181.

9 L. Mosley and S. Uno, 'Racing to the Bottom or Climbing to the Top?' (2007) Comparative Political Studies 40(8), p. 923.

10 B. Greenhill, L. Mosley and A. Prakash 'Trade-based Diffusion of Labor Rights' (2009) American Political Science Review 103(4), p. 669.

study on Indonesia speculates that the observable improvement in compliance with workers' rights in the Indonesian export industry can be attributed to the social clause in the US tariff preference programme and its politicization.[11] The same has been identified for Cambodia.[12] A more recent study, based on sophisticated regression analysis, shows a decline in labour rights for African countries after a switch from exporting to high-standard countries to exporting to a low-standard country, i.e. the People's Republic of China.[13]

Drusilla Brown, in a 2009 review of several studies, concluded that these studies had underestimated the impact of outsourcing. The assumption of the Stolper–Samuelson theorem that wages for low-skilled workers in the capitalist periphery rise because they become scarce due to increased demand caused by globalization proved to be incorrect. Multinational firms do not necessarily pay more than local firms. In particular, the increased bargaining power of these companies should be taken into account. They use their monopsonistic market power to find the most cost-effective locations. This is compounded by state repression of trade union activity and high levels of unemployment or underemployment in many countries.[14] The pressure exerted by international clothing brands on suppliers in Vietnam and India has been well documented by Mark Anner.[15]

The need to take into account sector-specific conditions of competition is impressively demonstrated by Berik et al. with respect to the prohibition of discrimination, using the examples of South Korea and Taiwan. Trade liberalization led to a widening of the gender wage gap. Firms exploited the weak position of women in segregated labour markets.[16] This observation is underscored by a study of the impact of trade liberalization in Indonesia. Hariati

---

11 A. Harrison and J. Scorse 'The Impact of Globalization on Compliance with Labor Standards' (Washington: Brookings Trade Forum, 2003).

12 G. Berik and Y. van der Meulen Rodgers 'Options for Enforcing Labour Standards: Lessons from Bangladesh and Cambodia', (2010) Journal of International Development 22(1), p. 56.
R. Robertson, 'Lights On: Transparency and Compliance Evidence from Cambodia', Better Work Discussion paper 29 (Geneva: International Labour Office, 2019).

13 C. Adolph, V. Quince and A. Prakash 'The Shanghai Effect: Do Exports to China Affect Labor Practices in Africa?' (2017) World Development 89, pp. 1–18.

14 D.K. Brown, 'A Review of the Globalization Literature: Implications for Employment, Wages, and Labor Standards', in R. Robertson et al. (eds.), Globalization, Wages, and the Quality of Jobs (Washington DC, 2017), p. 21.

15 M. Anner, 'Predatory purchasing practices in global apparel supply chains and the employment relations squeeze in the Indian garment export industry', (2019) International labour review 158.4, pp. 705–727.

16 G. Berik et al., 'International Trade and Wage Discrimination: Evidence from East Asia', World Bank Policy Research Working Paper 3111 (Washington: World Bank, 2003).

Sinaga shows that the degree of compliance with labour rights depends on skill requirements and entry barriers. When both are high, as in the automotive industry, working conditions are better than in the garment industry. In addition, the gender composition of the workforce differs in the two sectors.[17]

Since world trade has been substantially liberalized on a broad basis in recent decades, violations of fundamental labour rights should have declined worldwide to confirm the export success thesis. This is not the case, however, according to the annual reports of the International Trade Union Confederation.[18] Where workers' rights have been strengthened with increasing success on the global market, as in South Korea, this has been preceded by fierce social conflicts.[19]

In sum, the various studies reviewed in this section question whether trade-driven growth is sufficient to improve labour standards. The more skilled and mobile workers seem to benefit most from export opportunities, but other workers mostly do not.

3 Do Higher Standards Undermine the Competitiveness of Countries in the Capitalist Periphery?

As mentioned in the introduction, from a neoclassical perspective, it is usually argued that any mandated increase in production costs hurts sales opportunities on the world market and thus the development opportunities of the countries concerned. What is the empirical evidence for this claim?

A cross-sectional study by Busse and Braun[20] provides partial evidence: The extent of forced labour is positively correlated with competitiveness in labour-intensive sectors without special skill requirements. However, a large number of studies actually show that there is no competitive advantage from workers' rights violations.[21] A study by David Kucera and Ritasch Sarna inadvertently casts doubt on this consensus. It shows that weak trade union rights do not

17 H. Sinaga, 'Intersectional perspectives on land relations of oil palm plantations' (2024) Forest Policy and Economics 159, 103124.

18 ITUC, '2024 Global Rights Index' (Geneva: International Trade Union Confederation, 2024).

19 A. Irwan 'Real wages and class struggle in South Korea' (1987) Journal of Contemporary Asia, 17(4) pp. 385–408.

20 M. Busse and S. Braun 'Trade and Investment Effects of Forced Labour', (2003) International Labour Review 142(1) pp. 49.

21 V. Dehejiaand Y. Samy 'Trade and Labour Standards', in R. Kanburand J. Svejnar (eds.) Labour Markets and Economic Development (Abingdon: Oxon, 2009).

correlate with strong export activity. There is, however, one exception: East Asia. The authors classify these East Asian countries as unrepresentative: '[...] the East Asian experience is anomalous in the broader global context'.[22] While the above studies minimize China's importance in world trade by not weighting it by market share, Kucera and Sarna explicitly declare the East Asian countries, including China, to be a special case that should be neglected. This seems odd, given that global competitive pressures emanate from this very region.[23]

Qualitative comparative studies with a smaller number of countries appear to be more informative.[24] Berik and van der Meulen's comparison of the textile and garment industries in Bangladesh and Cambodia is instructive. While working conditions in Bangladesh deteriorated due to strong competitive pressure from China after the end of export quotas for textile products (MFA), Cambodia was able to improve its reputation through higher labour standards, which protected it from a slump in demand.[25] Of course, the foundation for this reputational gain was laid by the requirements of the US–Cambodia textile agreement. Therefore, the Cambodian experience cannot be generalized.

Improved data on trade flows and a refined classification of the content of labour clauses have motivated new econometric studies of the impact of labour clauses on trade flows. For example, the group of Céline Carrère, Marcelo Olarreaga, and Damian Raess compares bilateral trade relations between countries that have signed trade agreements with a labour clause and those that have not. Controlling for gravity (distance, sharing a border, a language, colonial ties, etc.), they find, on average, no statistically significant effect of a labour clause. However, they do notice a significant increase in exports from countries with weak labour standards to high-income countries with strong labour standards after the inclusion of a labour clause. Among the different types of labour clauses, those that seek deep cooperation on labour issues are most closely associated with export success, as opposed to shallow clauses or clauses with strong enforcement language.[26] Desiree LeClercq, Raymond Robertson, and Daniel Samaan, also using a gravity model but with a narrower definition of labour clauses (only those that 'refer to "labour", specify labour

22 D. Kucera and R. Sarna 'How Do Trade Union Rights Affect Trade Competitiveness?' Working Paper No. 39 Policy Integration Department (Geneva: ILO, 2004).

23 G. Berik and Y. van der Meulen Rodgers 'Options for Enforcing Labour Standards' p. 56.

24 R. Robertson et al. (eds.) Globalization, Wages, and the Quality of Jobs (Washington: World Bank Group, 2009).

25 G. Berik and Y. van der Meulen Rodgers 'Options for Enforcing Labour Standards'

26 C. Carrère, M. Olarreaga and D. Raess 'Labor clauses in trade agreements: Hidden protectionism?' (2022) The Review of International Organizations (17) pp. 453–483.

standards, and are legally binding'), find neither a positive nor a negative impact of a labour clause in an PTA on bilateral trade flows for the period 1990–2014.[27]

While these recent studies on trade flows suggest that a labour clause at least does not limit the export opportunities of low-income countries and may even improve their access to high-standard markets, the study by Timini et al. comes to the opposite conclusion. Again, using a gravity model, their comparison of weak and strong labour clauses in PTAs finds a significant increase in exports of labour-intensive goods from poor countries to rich countries when the PTA contains no or unenforceable labour clauses, but not for an PTA with strong labour provisions.[28]

Overall, it cannot be empirically ruled out that in labour-intensive industries, compliance with standards may lead to competitive disadvantages under given competitive conditions. However, it has also become clear that today's global marketplace allows for a very wide range of behaviour. In particular, when consumers or their political representatives express ethical concerns about goods produced in violation of international core labour standards, compliance with standards may prove to be a competitive advantage.

4 Neoclassical Economics Can Also Justify Core Labour Standards

The question of the justification of labour standards touches on the fundamental understanding of the market as a social governance mechanism. The different views of the market can be simplified to two paradigmatic approaches: the neoclassical and the neo-institutional 'school'.[29]

As mentioned above, the neoclassical perspective usually argues that any mandated increase in labour costs will reduce the sales opportunities on the world market and thus the development opportunities of the countries concerned.[30] This argument presupposes that the markets found in reality actually function according to the ideal of the neoclassical market model. How-

27 D. LeClercq, R. Robertson and D. Samaan 'Labor provisions in trade agreements: recasting the protectionist debate', (2024) The Journal of Law, Economics, and Organization 40(3) pp. 673–693.

28 J. Timini, N. Cortinovis and F. López Vicente 'The heterogeneous effects of trade agreements with labour provisions', (2022) The World Economy 45(9) pp. 2820–2853.

29 T.A. Kochan and W. Nordlund 'Reconciling Labor Standards and Economic Goals', (U.S. Department of Labor, Washington DC.: U.S. Government Printing Office).

30 J. Bhagwati, 'A View from Academia' p. 60.

ever, market failures are not unknown to neoclassicism. According to Arthur Pigou, the founder of neoclassical welfare theory, political corrections to market outcomes are justified when the values of private and social marginal net product deviate from each other. To correct these deviations, Pigou recommended government measures such as prohibitions, social legislation, and, above all, taxation of firms that produce externalities.[31] In the case of basic workers' rights, it can be shown that, on the one hand, there are deficits in the respective national labour markets and, on the other hand, there is an international market failure for these rights.

Freedom of association, for example, is a response to the ability of employers to wait, while wage earners are generally forced to constantly offer their labour in order to survive. This power imbalance is further exacerbated by monopsonistic demand, as demand in the labour market is shaped not by independent entrepreneurs, but by large corporations and the public sector. Collective actors, i.e. legal persons, encounter natural persons. Associations of these 'natural' workers, i.e. trade unions, could reduce this market distortion.[32] Of course, under certain conditions, unions can create new distortions.[33]

The prohibition of forced and child labour is one of the basic principles of a neoclassical market order, since the market is defined as the exchange of goods among free subjects. Moreover, respect for rights can contribute to both economic and corporate efficiency. Trade unions contribute to efficiency gains primarily by giving workers a voice.[34]

Since discrimination is a form of restriction of competition, the full functioning of the market as an efficient allocation mechanism requires a prohibition of discrimination. Discrimination is also detrimental to production efficiency because it can result in a person not being employed in the job for which he or she is best suited.[35]

Market failures can also be observed in the global market. Through the competitive mechanism of the world market, violations of basic workers'

---

31 A.C. Pigou 'The Economics of Welfare', 4th ed. (London: St. Martins, 1962), pp. 134–196.

32 R.B. Freeman and J.L. Medoff, 'What Do Unions Do?' (1985) ILR Review 38(2) pp. 244–263.

33 K.E. Maskus, 'Should Core Labor Standards Be Imposed Through International Trade Policy?' World Bank Policy Research Working Paper No. 1817 (Washington: The World Bank Group, 1997).

34 Ö. Onaran, A. Guschanski, J. Meadway and A.Martin 'Working for the economy: The economic case for trade unions', (Greenwich: Greenwich Political Economy Research Centre, 2015).
R.B. Freeman and J.L. Medoff. 'What Do Unions Do?'.

35 K. Basu, 'Child Labor: Cause, Consequence and Cure' World Bank Policy Research Working Paper 2027, (Washington: The World Bank Group, 1998).

rights in some countries can lead to non-compliance with these rights in other countries.[36] In extreme cases, this can lead to 'ruinous competition' that drives down social standards in trading countries to the lowest level. The displacement of good standards by poor standards is disputed by critics of international labour standards (see above). However, the concept of ruinous competition also has its place in the neoclassical paradigm.[37] This can lead to the abnormal market reaction that the quantity supplied is not adjusted downwards when the price falls and, in extreme cases, is even expanded. This phenomenon occurs especially when it is difficult to exit the market.[38]

High population growth often contributes to the structural oversupply of labour in the capitalist periphery. The displacement of subsistence agriculture or inefficient industry frees labour faster than the much more productive world market-oriented agriculture or industry can absorb in many regions, even with strong market expansion.[39] But the oversupply of labour is also caused by the difficulty of exiting the market. Workers lack alternatives to wage labour. Once the subsistence economy has been abandoned, a return is rarely possible, partly because subsistence households are displaced from productive land in favour of less labour-intensive, market-oriented farms. On the other hand, the horizon of expectations has shifted. Hard work in traditional agriculture often seems less attractive than even life in urban slums.

A lack of social security and falling real wages exacerbate the pressure on labour supply, so that without corrective intervention, the impoverishment of broad segments of the wage-earning population can become a self-sustaining process: When an expansion of the labour supply causes real wages to fall, maintaining household income requires working more. In extreme cases, the supply of child labour becomes necessary to secure household income. Furthermore, if spending on educational institutions is cut, for example as a result of the debt crisis, the number of working children will increase even more.[40]

---

36 D.W. Leebron, 'Lying Down with Procrustes: An Analysis of Harmonization Claims', in: J. Bhagwati and R.E. Hudec (eds.), Fair Trade and Harmonization. Prerequisites for Free Trade? (Cambridge, MA: MIT Press, 1996) p. 41.

37 F.M. Bator, 'The Anatomy of Market Failure', (1958) Quarterly Journal of Economics 72(3) p. 351. in the context of the labour clause debate, see A.B. Krueger, 'Observations on International Labor Standards and Trade', NBER Working Paper Series No. 5632, (Cambridge: NBER, 1996).

38 W. Semmler, 'Competition, Monopoly, and Differential Profit Rates', (New York: Columbia University Press, 1987).

39 C. Scherrer, 'Labour surplus is here to stay', (2018) Journal of Social and Economic Development 20(2) pp. 293–307.

40 J. Kane, 'What the Economic Crisis Means for Child Labour', (2009) Global Social Policy 9 (1_suppl) pp. 175–196.

In order to restore economic equilibrium, the accelerated exit of suppliers from the market is necessary according to the logic of the market economy. For the mass of wage earners, market exit is not an alternative for the reasons mentioned above. Historically, the answer to the oversupply of labour during the industrialization process was to limit the supply of labour: the fight for the eight-hour day, the ban on child labour, and (from today's perspective, no longer viewed positively) the exclusion of women from certain professions and trades.[41]

In the absence of such collective solutions, destructive competition can cross borders through trade and investment. Firms can engage in arbitrage between individual labour markets, so that oversupply in some labour markets spreads to an increasing number of labour markets.

Most critics of international labour rights, however, believe that the lower level of regulation enforced by competition is justified. In doing so, however, they engage in a circular argument: the market is declared to be the mechanism for determining the regulatory scope of the market.[42]

5 Securing Long-Term Advantages over Short-Term Calculations

In contrast to neoclassic economics, the neo-institutional approach points to the destructive potential of market mechanisms, which can unfold precisely in trade between nations because the international arena lacks a central regulatory authority. Foreign trade would therefore have to be socially flanked by domestic policy and regulated by multilateral agreements in foreign policy.[43]

From a neo-institutional perspective, ILO standards are seen as particularly necessary for the development of human capital.[44] Moreover, the enforce-

41 G. Holloway, 'Women and Work in Britain since 1840' (1st ed.) (London: Routledge, 2005) chpt. 4.

42 B.A. Langille, 'General Reflections on the Relationship of Trade and Labor', in J. Bhagwati and R.E. Hudec (eds.), Fair Trade and Harmonization. Vol. 2: Legal Analysis (Cambridge, MA: MIT Press, 1996) p. 231.

43 OECD-ILO 'Building trust in a changing world of work' (Paris: OECD, 2018). cf. M.J. Piore 'International Labor Standards and Business Strategies', (U.S. Department of Labor, Washington DC.: U.S. Government Printing Office, 1994) p. 21.

44 W. Sengenberger, 'Globalization and Social Progress: The Role and Impact of International Labor Standards', 2nd ed. (Bonn: Friedrich Ebert Stiftung, 2007).

ment of higher standards encourages firms to use their workers more efficiently, thereby increasing overall labour productivity.[45] Drawing on the efficiency wage theory,[46] Vivek Dehejia and Yiagadeesen Samy argue that the costs of complying with labour standards can be offset by productivity gains. The direction and magnitude of these effects depend on the context.[47]

If workers' rights really promote development, shouldn't their observance be in the interest of the countries concerned and therefore voluntary? In fact, almost all countries have voluntarily ratified ILO Conventions. However, many of them are not particularly vigilant in enforcing these conventions, and some of the new exporting nations in particular have signed only a few conventions. Power political interests are one of the main reasons for this attitude. Where trade unions (and usually criticism of the government) are banned, there is a not unjustified fear that trade unions could become a refuge for the political opposition, such as Solidarnosc in Poland. Another is uncertainty about whether the long-term benefits will materialize in the short term. Similar to investments in physical infrastructure, compliance with workers' rights may incur initial costs that pay off only in the long run.[48] For example, an ILO industry study found that child labour saves five to ten per cent of total labour costs.[49] For importers and the purchasing departments of international companies, relatively small differences in wage costs between suppliers in the same market segment can play a decisive role.

Competition is fiercest where comparable products are offered using similar production techniques.[50] The fierceness of competition in the capitalist periphery is intensified by the following factors: (a) simple production techniques that facilitate the entry of new competitors, (b) a rapidly growing labour force due to the displacement of subsistence economies, (c) the debt crisis that increases the need to earn foreign exchange, and (d) the ability of transnational corporations to relocate production facilities. Consequently, it is the workers of the populous countries of the capitalist periphery who are in com-

---

45 R. Robertson (eds.) 'Globalization, Wages, and the Quality of Jobs', pp. 9–14.
D. Card and A.B. Krueger, 'Myth and Measurement. The New Economics of the Minimum Wage', (Princeton: Princeton University Press, 1995).

46 see G. Akerlof and J. Yellen, 'Efficiency Wage Models of the Labor Market', (Cambridge: Cambridge University Press, 1986).

47 V. Dehejia and Y. Samy, 'Trade and Labour Standards: Theory and New Empirical Evidence' (2004) Journal of International Trade and Economic Development 13(2) p. 179.

48 V. Dehejia and Y. Samy 'Trade and Labour Standards'.

49 R. Anker, S. Barge, S. Rajagopal, M.P. Joseph (eds.) 'Economics of child labour in hazardous industries of India', (Baroda, India: Centre for Operations Research and Training, 1998).

50 L. Mosley, Layna and S. Uno, 'Racing to the Bottom or Climbing to the Top?' p. 923.

petition with each other. A case in point is the above-mentioned empirical evidence for the garment industry.

6 Effective Enforcement of Core Labour Standards Creates a Level Playing Field

The objections to social standards are ultimately based on the argument that social standards that drive the price of the wage factor above the market-clearing price make the companies concerned uncompetitive on the market. The cost considerations above would seem to confirm this position.

However, this argument can also be used to justify internationally negotiated social standards. As long as it is possible for one economic region to gain a competitive advantage by undercutting the social standards prevailing in other regions, these other regions run the risk of losing market share and thus employment opportunities. This danger is all the greater the more similar the factor endowments (capital, labour, land) and previous market positions of the regions are. It is particularly pronounced when market success is based on only one factor, namely low-skilled labour. In such a case, the threat of lower standards cannot be offset by other factors. For these reasons, countries in the capitalist periphery face competitive pressures if they raise their social standards alone.

If fundamental labour rights can be made internationally binding, the competitive situation will change. Individual competitors will no longer have to fear that compliance with these rights will put them at a disadvantage vis-à-vis their competitors. Rather, they can expect their competitors to compete on a level playing field.

The need for internationally binding minimum standards can be drastically illustrated by the example of child labour. For children in economically problematic areas, the only alternative is often seen to be between work and starvation, which is why there are arguments against a ban on child labour.[51] However, such an inhumane alternative only arises if the conditions of competition remain unchanged. For example, if child labour in carpet weaving is banned in only one region, there is a risk that carpet companies in that region will lose market share. However, if all regions ban child labour, market shares

---

51 H. Grossmann and J. Michaelis, 'Trade Sanctions and the Incidence of Child Labor', (2007) Review of Development Economics 11(1) p. 49.
B. White, 'Child Workers' in M. Moore, C. Scherrer and M. van den Linden (eds.) 'The Elgar Companion to Decent Work and the Sustainable Development Goals', (Cheltenham: Edward Elgar, 2025) pp. 213–224.

are less likely to change. Family wages could then be paid to adults. However, the question is whether the higher prices that all carpet weavers could then charge would not lead to a decline in overall demand.

The answer to this question depends on the extent to which a price increase leads to less demand (elasticity of demand) or to switching to other products with similar characteristics (elasticity of substitution). Estimating these elasticities is fraught with uncertainty.[52] The elasticities of substitution and demand also vary considerably from product to product. Hand-knotted carpets, handicrafts, and tropical agricultural products are only slightly substitutable for goods produced in rich consumer countries. Their demand depends more on income growth in the consuming countries. The same is true for labour-intensive, simple manufacturing processes, such as in the garment industry, which have largely left the rich countries.[53] Moreover, the production costs of some branded goods bear no relation to the retail price. The median mark-up has increased significantly over the last decade.[54] Higher production costs can thus be absorbed by intermediaries and retailers.[55]

A much higher elasticity of substitution can be expected for complex industrial products from the capitalist periphery. However, even for these products, higher wages do not lead to rising selling prices to the same extent because the higher capital intensity of their production keeps the share of labour costs in total production costs lower than for the products in the example above.

As long as labour standards that do not go beyond the ILO conventions are observed, labour costs will remain significantly lower than in the capitalist centres.[56] According to a calculation by Barry and Reddy using UNIDO data, in their most conservative scenario, wages would have to increase threefold before the cost advantage over rich countries would be lost (taking into account managerial salaries and a high proportion of indirect labour costs

---

52 M. Hernandez, 'Impacts of international trade on the labour market' p. 49.

53 A. Wood, 'North-South Trade, Employment, and Inequality', (Oxford: Oxford University Press, 1994).

54 F. Boissay, F. De Fiore, D. Igan, A. Pierres-Tejada and D. Rees, 'Are major advanced economies on the verge of a wage-price spiral?' (2022) BIS Bulletin, 53(4), Bank for International Settlements, p. 3.

55 R. Pollin, J. Burns and J. Heintz, 'Global apparel production and sweatshop labour: can raising retail prices finance living wages?', (2004) Cambridge Journal of Economics 28(2) pp. 153–171.

56 P. Krugman, 'Divided over trade', (2007) New York Times, 14 May.

due to many preliminary processing stages). The sixteen-fold increase represents the other pole of their calculations.[57]

The above considerations can be summarized as follows:

- The controversy in economics over the impact of a labour rights clause in a trade agreement is part of the general paradigmatic difference in economics. Although adherents of neoclassical economics are sceptical of these clauses, it can be shown that international labour rights are in fact consistent with the central assumptions of this paradigm: welfare losses due to monopsony, monopoly, and discrimination.
- Empirical methods for assessing the impact of workers' rights clauses have improved over time. However, their results remain rather inconclusive, not least because they do not sufficiently take into account competition between production locations with similar factor endowments. It cannot be empirically ruled out that in labour-intensive industries, compliance with standards may lead to competitive disadvantages under given competitive conditions.
- Neo-institutionalism provides compelling arguments that respect for workers' rights secures a country's industrial development in the long run: development of human capital and more efficient use of workers. In the short run, disregarding workers' rights promises competitive advantages, so that in addition to power-political motives, economic calculations lead to their violation.
- As long as it is possible for one country to gain a competitive advantage in this way, other countries risk losing market share and thus employment opportunities. Accordingly, they will be less willing to uphold workers' rights.
- It is therefore important that core labour rights be enforced on a binding basis at the international level, for example by means of a sanctionable labour clause in multilateral trade agreements. Individual competitors need not fear that compliance with these rights will put them at a competitive disadvantage. Instead, they can assume that their competitors are competing on a level playing field.
- In view of the significant differences in labour costs, there is no reason to fear a decline in demand for products from the capitalist periphery.

57 C. Barry and S.G. Reddy 'International Trade and Labor Standards: A Proposal for Linkage', (2006) Cornell International Law Journal (39)3, pp. 629–639.

Bibliography

Adolph, C., V. Quince and A. Prakash 'The Shanghai Effect: Do Exports to China Affect Labor Practices in Africa?' (2017) World Development 89, pp. 1–18.

Akerlof, G. and J. Yellen, 'Efficiency Wage Models of the Labor Market', (Cambridge: Cambridge University Press, 1986).

Aleman-Castilla, B. 'Trade and Decent Work in Mexico's Manufacturing Sector', in M. Corley-Coulibaly, P.S. Richiardi and F.C. Ebert (eds.) Integrating trade and decent work Volume 1 (Geneva: International Labour Office, 2023), pp. 151–181.

Anker, R., S. Barge, S. Rajagopal, M.P. Joseph (eds.) 'Economics of child labour in hazardous industries of India', (Baroda, India: Centre for Operations Research and Training, 1998).

Anner, M. 'Predatory Purchasing Practices in Global Apparel Supply Chains and the Employment Relations Squeeze in the Indian Garment Export Industry', (2019) International Labour Review 158.4, pp. 705–727.

Barry, C. and S.G. Reddy 'International Trade and Labor Standards: A Proposal for Linkage', (2006) Cornell International Law Journal (39)3, pp. 629–639.

Basu, K. 'Child Labor: Cause, Consequence and Cure' World Bank Policy Research Working Paper 2027, (Washington: The World Bank Group, 1998).

Bator, F.M. 'The Anatomy of Market Failure', (1958) Quarterly Journal of Economics 72 (3) pp. 351–379.

Berik, G. and Y. van der Meulen Rodgers 'Options for Enforcing Labour Standards: Lessons from Bangladesh and Cambodia', (2010) Journal of International Development 22(1) pp. 56–85.

Berik, G. et al., 'International Trade and Wage Discrimination: Evidence from East Asia', World Bank Policy Research Working Paper 3111 (Washington: World Bank, 2003).

Bhagwati, J. 'A View from Academia', in U.S. Department of Labor, Bureau of International Labor Affairs (eds.), International Labor Standards and Global Economic Integration (Washington, 1994).

Boissay, F., F. De Fiore, D. Igan, A. Pierres-Tejada and D. Rees, 'Are Major Advanced Economies on the Verge of a Wage-Price Spiral?' (2022) BIS Bulletin, 53(4), Bank for International Settlements.

Brown, D.K. 'A Review of the Globalization Literature: Implications for Employment, Wages, and Labor Standards', in R. Robertson et al. (eds.), Globalization, Wages, and the Quality of Jobs (Washington DC, 2017).

Brown, D.K. 'International Trade and Core Labour Standards' OECD Labour Market and Social Policy Occasional Papers 43 (Paris: OECD, 2000).

Busse, M. and S. Braun 'Trade and Investment Effects of Forced Labour', (2003) International Labour Review 142(1) pp. 49–71.

Busse, M. 'On the Determinants of Core Labour Standards' (2004) Economic Letters 83(2), pp. 211–217.

Carrère, C., M. Olarreaga and D. Raess 'Labor Clauses in Trade Agreements: Hidden Protectionism?' (2022) The Review of International Organizations (17) pp. 453–483.

Card, D. and A.B. Krueger, 'Myth and Measurement: The New Economics of the Minimum Wage', (Princeton: Princeton University Press, 1995).

Dehejia, V. and Y. Samy, 'Trade and Labour Standards: Theory and New Empirical Evidence' (2004) Journal of International Trade and Economic Development 13(2) pp. 177–196.

Dehejia, V. and Y. Samy 'Trade and Labour Standards', in R. Kanburand J. Svejnar (eds.) Labour Markets and Economic Development (Abingdon: Oxon, 2009).

Edmonds, E.V. and N. Pavcnik 'International Trade and Child Labor' (2006) Journal of International Economics, 68(1).

Freeman, R.B. and J.L. Medoff, 'What Do Unions Do?' (1985) ILR Review 38(2) pp. 244–263.

Goldberg, P.K. and T. Reed 'Is the Global Economy Deglobalizing?' Policy Research Working Paper 10392 (Washington: World Bank Group, 2023).

Greenhill, B., L. Mosley and A. Prakash 'Trade-based Diffusion of Labor Rights' (2009) American Political Science Review 103(4) pp. 669–690.

Grossmann, H. and J. Michaelis, 'Trade Sanctions and the Incidence of Child Labor', (2007) Review of Development Economics 11(1), pp. 49–62.

Harrison, A. and J. Scorse 'The Impact of Globalization on Compliance with Labor Standards' (Washington: Brookings Trade Forum, 2003).

Hernandez, M. 'Impacts of International Trade on the Labour Market: Common Methodological Approaches for Macro- and Meso-Level Assessments', in M. Corley-Coulibaly, P.S. Richiardi and F.C. Ebert (eds.), Integrating trade and decent work Volume 1 (Geneva: International Labour Office, 2023), pp. 43–77.

Holloway, G. 'Women and Work in Britain since 1840' (1st ed.) (London: Routledge, 2005) chpt. 4.

Irwan, A. 'Real wages and class struggle in South Korea' (1987) Journal of Contemporary Asia, 17(4) pp. 385–408.

ITUC, '2024 Global Rights Index' (Geneva: International Trade Union Confederation, 2024).

Kane, J. 'What the Economic Crisis Means for Child Labour', (2009) Global Social Policy 9(1_suppl) pp. 175–196.

Kochan, T.A. and W. Nordlund 'Reconciling Labor Standards and Economic Goals', (U.S. Department of Labor, Washington DC.: U.S. Government Printing Office, 1989).

Krueger, A.B. 'Observations on International Labor Standards and Trade', NBER Working Paper Series No. 5632, (Cambridge: NBER, 1996).

Krugman, P. 'Does Third World Growth Hurt First World Prosperity?', (1994) Harvard Business Review, 72(4), pp. 113–122.
Krugman, P. 'Divided over trade', (2007) New York Times, 14 May.
Kucera, D. and R. Sarna 'How Do Trade Union Rights Affect Trade Competitiveness?' Working Paper No. 39 Policy Integration Department (Geneva: ILO, 2004).
Langille, B.A. 'General Reflections on the Relationship of Trade and Labor', in J. Bhagwati and R.E. Hudec (eds.), Fair Trade and Harmonization. Vol. 2: Legal Analysis (Cambridge, MA: MIT Press, 1996).
LeClercq, D., R. Robertson and D. Samaan 'Labor Provisions in Trade Agreements: Recasting the Protectionist Debate', (2024) The Journal of Law, Economics, and Organization 40(3) pp. 673–693.
Leebron, D.W. 'Lying down with Procrustes: An Analysis of Harmonization Claims', in: J. Bhagwati and R.E. Hudec (eds.), Fair Trade and Harmonization. Prerequisites for Free Trade? (Cambridge, MA: MIT Press, 1996).
Maskus, K.E. 'Should Core Labor Standards Be Imposed through International Trade Policy?' World Bank Policy Research Working Paper No. 1817 (Washington: The World Bank Group, 1997).
Mosley, L., Layna and S. Uno, 'Racing to the Bottom or Climbing to the Top?' (2007) Comparative Political Studies 40(8) pp. 923–948.
OECD 'Trade, Employment and Labour Standards' (Paris: OECD, 1996).
OECD-ILO 'Building Trust in a Changing World of Work' (Paris: OECD, 2018).
Onaran, Ö., A. Guschanski, J. Meadway and A. Martin 'Working for the Economy: The Economic Case for Trade Unions', (Greenwich: Greenwich Political Economy Research Centre, 2015).
Pavcnik, N. 'The Impact of Trade on Inequality in Developing Countries' No. w23878 (Washington: National Bureau of Economic Research, 2017).
Pigou, A.C. 'The Economics of Welfare', 4th ed. (London: St. Martins, 1962), pp. 134–196.
Piore, M.J. 'International Labor Standards and Business Strategies', (U.S. Department of Labor, Washington DC.: U.S. Government Printing Office, 1994).
Pollin, R., J. Burns and J. Heintz, 'Global Apparel Production and Sweatshop Labour: Can Raising Retail Prices Finance Living Wages?', (2004) Cambridge Journal of Economics 28(2) pp. 153–171.
Robertson, R. (eds.) 'Globalization, Wages, and the Quality of Jobs', (Washington: The World Bank Group, 2009) pp. 9–14.
Robertson, R. 'Lights On: Transparency and Compliance Evidence from Cambodia', Better Work Discussion paper 29 (Geneva: International Labour Office, 2019).
Scherrer, C. 'Labour Surplus Is Here to Stay', (2018) Journal of Social and Economic Development 20(2) pp. 293–307.

Semmler, W. 'Competition, Monopoly, and Differential Profit Rates', (New York: Columbia University Press, 1987).

Sengenberger, W. 'Globalization and Social Progress: The Role and Impact of International Labor Standards', 2nd ed. (Bonn: Friedrich Ebert Stiftung, 2007).

Sinaga, H. 'Intersectional Perspectives on Land Relations of Oil Palm Plantations' (2024) Forest Policy and Economics 159, pp. 103–124.

Timini, J., N. Cortinovis and F. López Vicente 'The Heterogeneous Effects of Trade Agreements with Labour Provisions', (2022) The World Economy 45(9) pp. 2820–2853.

White, B. 'Child Workers' in M. Moore, C. Scherrer and M. van den Linden (eds.) 'The Elgar Companion to Decent Work and the Sustainable Development Goals', (Cheltenham: Edward Elgar, 2025) pp. 213–224.

Wood, A. 'North-South Trade, Employment, and Inequality', (Oxford: Oxford University Press, 1994).

CHAPTER 4

Vietnam: From Labour Provisions to Independent Trade Unions?

Martin Myant

Labour provisions in trade agreements, pressed for particularly by the USA and EU, are widely judged to have made little or no difference. Labour issues have been a much lower priority than commerce and the demands of business during negotiations and after agreements have been signed.[1] However, labour's advocates have learned from experience and sought improvements, making commitments clearer, linking them to the internationally recognised labour standards formulated by the ILO and, above all, pressing for fulfilment of key conditions from the partner countries before an agreement is ratified. Vietnam appears as a case of significant positive changes in its employment relations following the negotiation of two important trade agreements.

The first was the Trans-Pacific Partnership (TPP), originally to be the Comprehensive and Progressive Agreement for Trans-Pacific Partnership (CPTPP) until the withdrawal of the USA in January 2017 and ratified by Vietnam on 12 November 2018. The second was the EU–Vietnam Free Trade Agreement (EVFTA), ratified by Vietnam on 8 June 2020. As negotiations were conducted with the USA and the EU in overlapping periods, Vietnam's experience provides a comparison of their different methods and priorities. Vietnam's experience is also of interest because, as a country ruled by a Communist Party, it had established trade unions with substantial membership but unable to play a traditional trade-union role. Unlike countries with more explicitly anti-union traditions, the key question is not the right of trade unions to function at all, but rather the role they can play and how far they are independent of the state.

By the start of 2025, it was clear that some changes had taken place, at least in terms of ratifying some key ILO conventions and incorporating them into Vietnamese law. Negotiating the trade agreements had undeniably contrib-

1 For summary discussions, see A. Smith, J. Harrison, L. Campling, B. Richardson and M. Barbu, *Free Trade Agreements and Global Labour Governance: The European Union's Trade-Labour Linkage in a Value Chain World* (London: Routledge, 2020); M. Myant, *The Impact of Trade and Investment Agreements on Decent Work and Sustainable Development* (Brussels: ETUI, 2017); M. Myant, *Labour Rights in Trade Agreements: Five New Stories* (Brussels: ETUI, 2017).

 | HTTPS://DOI.ORG/10.1163/9789004762251-005

uted to that process. However, the depth and full significance of changes remained unclear in view of the constraints imposed by the authoritarian political system. The following sections pursue this, starting with a discussion of economic development and Vietnam's resulting bargaining strength. The second and third sections cover the role of, and attempts to change, the existing trade unions. The fourth and fifth sections cover, respectively, trade negotiations involving the USA and EU, while the last section covers developments with agreements in operation.

1 Vietnam's Economic Development

Vietnam, a country with a population of over 100 million in 2023, experienced rapid economic development after the so-called *Doi Moi* (renovation/innovation) reforms initiated in 1986. The stated aim was the creation of a 'socialist-oriented market economy'. The reality was an economy increasingly dominated by private enterprise, albeit alongside substantial state investment in infrastructure (7 per cent of GDP in 2023), education and health. Growth was very rapid with a fivefold increase in per capita GDP between 1986 and 2023, and Vietnam won praise from international agencies as 'the envy of developing countries around the world'.[2] Despite this, it remained a low-income and low-wage country in world terms, with per capita GDP in 2023 still 5 per cent of the US level by current prices or 18 per cent by Purchasing Power Parity, the latter indicating the real gap in living standards.[3]

Crucial to rapid growth was an opening up to export-oriented inward investment, permitted from 1987 and attracted by the country's low wage levels, coastal location and transport infrastructure. Foreign companies were contributing 73 per cent of exports in 2023.[4] Fully 77 per cent of registered capital in 2023 was from Asian countries, led by Korea with 18.4 per cent as they turned Vietnam into an assembly base for exports into high-income countries. The USA was the biggest market, accounting for 27.4 per cent of

2 World Bank Group, *Sustaining Success: Priorities for Sustainable and Inclusive Growth*, (Hanoi, The World Bank in Vietnam, 2016), p. 1.

3 World Bank National Accounts Data, https://data.worldbank.org/indicator/NY.GDP.PCAP.KD.

4 This and subsequent data on Vietnam's economy are from *Statistical Yearbook of Viet Nam 2017* (Hanoi: General Statistics Office, 2018), https://www.gso.gov.vn/en/data-and-statistics/2019/10/7559/ and *Statistical Yearbook of Viet Nam 2023* (Hanoi: General Statistics Office, 2024), https://www.gso.gov.vn/en/default/2024/07/statistical-yearbook-of-2023/.

total exports in 2023, compared with only 2.5 per cent of inward investment, with the EU accounting for another 12.3 per cent of exports. Imports, largely materials and components, came mostly from Asian countries, led by China (33.9 per cent) and South Korea (15.5 per cent). The key sectors at the start were garments and footwear, manufactured by Asian companies to designs from leading world brands and still accounting in 2023 for 15.1 per cent of exports. They were increasingly eclipsed by electronics, boosted when Samsung chose Vietnam as its main assembly base for mobile phones. They alone accounted for 14.8 per cent of Vietnam's exports in 2023, with an increasing share of components produced within the country.

To reach a stated aim of becoming an upper-middle-income country, Vietnam needed good economic relations with its Asian partners and would welcome free-trade agreements, with the USA and the EU, both of which restricted imports especially of garments and footwear. Estimating the gains from trade agreements requires considerable guesswork, not least because they depend on uncertain future trends, on the location decisions of multinational companies and on conditions in customer and likely competitor countries. Nevertheless, substantial gains are very plausible. The European Commission followed a study from 2009, predicting a 35 per cent surge in Vietnam's exports in the event of an agreement removing tariffs to the EU and a resulting 15 per cent increase in GDP. The EU would gain only 0.2 per cent in GDP,[5] but there were prospects of big gains for garment and footwear brands which could import at substantially lower prices. A later Vietnamese belief was of a 44 per cent increase in exports to the EU over ten years.[6] One estimate for the TPP was of an 8.1 per cent increase in Vietnam's GDP over 15 years, much more than for any other participant in the agreement, while the USA's GDP would increase by only 0.5 per cent.[7] A later study for the World Bank showed a 6.6 per cent increase in Vietnam's GDP and then reduced to 3.5 per cent for the CPTPP after the withdrawal of the USA.[8] With the promise of such substantial gains, Viet-

---

5 European Parliament, *EU-Vietnam Free Trade Agreement*, 2018, https://www.europarl.europa.eu/RegData/etudes/BRIE/2018/628248/EPRS_BRI(2018)628248_EN.pdf.

6 Ha Hai Hoang, 'Understanding the EU–Vietnam Free Trade Agreement', *East Asia Forum*, 21 May 2020, https://eastasiaforum.org/2020/05/21/understanding-the-eu-vietnam-free-trade-agreement/.

7 P. A. Petri and M. G. Plummer, *The Economic Effects of the Trans-Pacific Partnership: New Estimates*, Working Paper 16–2, (Washington, DC: Peterson Institute for International Economics, 2016).

8 World Bank Group, *Economic and Distributional Impacts of Comprehensive and Progressive Agreement for Trans-Pacific Partnership: The Case of Vietnam* (Washington, DC: The World Bank, 2018), p. 64.

nam could be expected to be willing to make substantial concessions in return. This could give an opening for pressure on labour standards.

2 The Industrial Relations Background

By 2023, almost 53 per cent of the working population were employees. Most of the rest were self-employed or helping family members who, along with those employed without contracts, were counted as belonging to the informal economy. By 2023, foreign companies were employing 10.3 per cent of the total active labour force, or 34.25 per cent of employees in enterprises. This became the key arena for changes in employment relations, forcing the search for change in the established trade union structure.

The only permitted trade unions were organised in the Vietnam General Confederation of Labour (VGCL) with over 11 million members in 2023, meaning about 40 per cent of employees. Following the model of the former Soviet bloc, it is required to implement the ruling Communist Party's line and policies and to accept that party as the leading force in society, as specified in Article 4 of the country's constitution. In practical terms, that means that the VGCL cannot challenge the party's political authority or present itself as an opposition force, while key appointments within trade unions are subject to party approval. A caveat is that, alongside cases of strong repression, the Vietnamese authorities allow some scope for expression of diverse views, to which they may even listen, as long as they do not challenge the party's monopoly of power. This led one commentator to question the 'authoritarian' label, preferring, perhaps somewhat generously, to characterise Vietnam as a 'responsive-repressive party-state'.[9] Within this, as is shown below, there was scope for worker protests and for debate about reforming trade union practice.

The Soviet model was developed in economies with state ownership of enterprises and wage rates set within a plan, leaving no scope for collective bargaining.[10] Trade unions were expected to promote work effort while retaining employees' loyalty by providing individual support within the law plus a range of social, recreational and welfare services. This model brought almost universal union membership in Soviet bloc countries, but the clearly non-socialist nature of Vietnam's development – the state sector by 2022 accounted

9 B. Kerkvliet, *Speaking Out in Vietnam: Public Political Criticism in a Communist Party-Ruled Nation* (Ithaca and London: Cornell University Press, 2019), p. 6.

10 M. Myant, 'Economies undergoing long transition: employment relations in central and eastern Europe' in A. Wilkinson, G. Wood and R. Deeg (eds) *The Oxford Handbook of Employment Relations* (Oxford: Oxford University Press, 2014), pp. 360–363.

for only 6.6 per cent of employees in enterprises – made that model problematic. Wages were set by individual employers who often ignored labour law and who had no reason to welcome union organisations.

The incompatibility of the Soviet model with Vietnam's economic development was brought home in the 1990s by strikes, covered below. The recognition spread within the VGCL and the government of the need for new approaches to win new members, to retain existing members' loyalty and to pre-empt being outflanked by the emergence of independent worker organisations. Advice on creating a functioning system came from the ILO and from research and projects funded notably by the Friedrich Ebert Stiftung.

Two key problems were identified by critics. The first was that workplace trade union organisations were typically created with the help of management, a responsibility they were given in the 1994 Labour Code,[11] and then frequently headed by the company's HR manager. There was no need for worker involvement while the initiative to set up union organisations in 99 per cent of cases in a VGCL survey in 2012 came from upper levels of the VGCL. It could even use its links to the state to pressure recalcitrant companies.[12] By 2013, aware of the unrepresentativeness of unions, an official emphasis was being put on forming organisations by a bottom-up method, but it made limited headway.[13] Even if there was much interest from ordinary workers, and arguments below suggest that there may not have been, cases were reported of managements blocking any such attempts and victimising their initiators.[14] Moreover, with very limited results from a bottom-up approach, higher levels in the VGCL found it much easier to reach their recruitment targets by their traditional method. One organising official in 2016 also reported preferring union presidents 'to come from the enterprise management' as they could perform union work better with management backing.[15] In one sense this worked. Membership grew from 5.4 million in 2006 to over 11 million in

11 B. van Gramberg, J. Teicher and Tien Nguyen, 'Industrial disputes in Vietnam the tale of the wildcat' *Asia Pacific Journal of Human Resources* (2013) 51, doi:10.1111/j.1744-7941.2012.00062.x. p. 252.

12 Trinh Ly Khanh, 'Trade union organizing free from employers' interference: evidence from Vietnam', *Southeast Asian Studies*, 3 (3) 2014, p. 593.

13 E. Schweisshelm and Do Quynh Chi, 'From harmony to conflict: Vietnamese trade unions on the threshold of reform', in R. Traub-Merz and T. Pringle (eds), *Trade Unions in Transition: From Command to Market Economies* (Berlin: Friedrich-Ebert-Stiftung, 2018), p. 133.

14 Trinh, 'Trade union', pp. 600–2.

15 Do Quynh Chi, *The Missing Link in the Chain: Trade Regimes and Labour Standards in the Garment, Footwear and Electronics Supply Chains in Vietnam*, (Hanoi: Friedrich-Ebert-Stiftung Vietnam, 2017), p. 34.

2023, almost keeping pace with the growth in employment, but the representativeness problem remained unsolved.

The second problem was the absence of genuine collective bargaining. A legal framework for this was created in 1995 and the number of agreements signed at enterprise level increased from 13,429 in 2008 to 28,876 in 2018, with coverage reaching 24.4 per cent of employees. That was still well below the level of union density and covered only 60 per cent of foreign-owned companies. Moreover, the VGCL's first research results from 2015 on the agreements that were signed showed workers' involvement in the bargaining process in only 15 per cent while also only 15 per cent were significantly better than the minimum legal requirements.[16] Agreements, it seemed, were formalities written by HR departments. The VGCL leadership complained of the very weak negotiating skills of union representatives and sought to introduce better training,[17] but the fundamental barrier was the absence of an uninhibited voice of employees in formal negotiations. That could only find expression through strikes.

3 Strikes

Strikes were reaching a significant level in the mid-1990s and were covered for the first time in the 1994 Labour Code, probably reflecting a perceived need to develop an orderly procedure for handling and resolving conflicts.[18] The law was quite restrictive, limiting the right to organise a strike to the VGCL, only within the framework of collective bargaining and only after a complex conciliation process. In practice, no strike was ever organised by the VGCL, but a large number took place without regard to this legal framework, peaking at approaching 1000 in 2011 before declining steadily to 121 in 2019.[19] The exact numbers are unclear as definitions vary slightly between the VGCL, MOLISA (the Ministry of Labour, Invalids and Social Affairs) and local authorities. An action needs to be significant to reach the attention of those organisations and some were very substantial, involving tens of thousands of workers and spreading across enterprises. Nevertheless, they were typically resolved within, at

16 Schweisshelm and Do, 'From harmony', p. 135.

17 'Trade union executive boards to receive training in salary negotiations' *Vietnam Plus*, 11 July 2019, https://en.vietnamplus.vn/trade-union-executive-boards-to-receive-training-in-salary-negotiations-post155917.vnp.

18 J. Buckley, *Vietnamese Labour Militancy: Capital-Labour Antagonisms and Self-Organised Struggles* (Abingdon and New York: Routledge, 2022), p. 84.

19 Buckley, *Vietnamese Labour*, p. 74.

most, a few days. They were widely reported, particularly in media linked to the VGCL, and they have been researched both from newspaper reports and by Vietnamese and foreign researchers speaking to participants.[20]

Strikes were overwhelmingly concentrated into foreign-owned companies, 80 or 90 per cent according to different sources, with disproportionately high numbers in South Korean and Taiwanese firms: half of the former experienced at least one strike in the 2010–2013 period.[21] These workplaces provided the ideal conditions for workers to stage collective actions. Workforces were remarkably homogeneous, created largely from internal migration, estimated in one survey at 70–90 per cent of the labour in industrial parks in 2018.[22] Most of these were young women and they were concentrated into factories that could be enormous, ranging up to 90000 employees.

The main stimuluses for strikes were wages and the firms' authoritarian management style. Average wage levels in foreign-owned companies were consistently slightly above the national average – by 10 per cent in 2022 – but under 80 per cent of the average in the strike-prone garments and footwear (leather) sectors. Apart from the level of wages, managements did not always pay on time and often arbitrarily changed payment systems to the detriment of all, or some, of the workforce.

Managements also alienated workforces by compulsory overtime, imposed often at minimal notice, arbitrary pay deductions, and brutal and degrading treatment of employees. On the first of these, even the ILO's Better Work programme, started in 2009 as a voluntary partnership with companies and covering 426 garment and 44 footwear factories by 2022, including coverage of about half of all employees in garment manufacture, reported 75 per cent in the latter year flouting legal overtime limits.[23] Another survey found overtime averaging 70 hours per month in a sample of electronics firms, ranging up to 100 hours, while the legal maximum at the time was 30 hours.[24] Many enterprises hid the reality of hours worked with a system of double book-keeping, a further clearly illegal activity reported in 35 per cent of Better Work partici-

20 Kerkvliet collated over 900 reports, Kerkvliet, *Speaking Out*, p. 13. Information and summaries of other articles are given in that book, in Buckley, *Vietnamese Labour*, and in other works referred to below.

21 M. Anner, *Wildcat Strikes and Better Work Bipartite Committees in Vietnam: Towards an Elect, Represent, Protect and Empower Framework*, Better Work Discussion Paper 24, (ILO: Geneva, 2017), p. 24.

22 *Industrial Relations Report 2019: Towards Genuine Collective Bargaining* (Geneva: ILO, 2021), p. 3.

23 *Better Work Viet Nam Annual Report 2023* (Geneva: International Labour Office and International Finance Corporation, 2023), p. 15.

24 Do, *The Missing*, p. 29.

pants in 2017–8,[25] albeit somewhat less in later years. Not surprisingly, approaching enterprises not voluntarily involved in state-supported ILO projects could be met with a refusal to answer questions on working hours.[26]

On management brutality, one example from 2012 among many involved a supervisor in a Taiwanese-owned factory supplying shoes for Nike who superglued an employees' hands together. The following strike led to the suspension of the supervisor but he did not face criminal charges.[27] It should be added that in this, as in other cases, the VGCL did not initiate any reaction.

These strikes appeared to start spontaneously, at least without warning to the foreign managements. Once under way, officials from one or all out of the VGCL, MOLISA and the local authority came and mediated a solution. As almost all strikes reportedly end in the workers winning all, or almost all of their demands, mediation probably amounted to telling managements to concede. The law was not used against strikes, which could clearly all be judged illegal, the public media were often supportive and the police, although present, very rarely intervened against strikers, appearing more often to be their protectors. The authorities' behaviour suggested a degree of sympathy for workers rather than foreign companies. A prime minister even indicated that, had he been a worker, he would have been on strike sooner and more often.[28] Whether genuine or not, implying some sympathy might have seemed the best way to head off the danger of independent trade unions, outflanking the VGCL.

Any organisers remained anonymous. Accounts of many strikes suggest that there may have been none. Buckley followed a strike in a footwear factory of 20000 employees in March 2018 and found no identifiable initiators, visible leaders or negotiators with management. The action was provoked by an arbitrary change to the payment system which would have reduced many employees' pay. It started after broad consensus on the Facebook group, with over 10000 members, and ended in the same way when the management was judged to have conceded.[29] However, other researchers have found perma-

25 *Better Work Viet Nam Garment Industry 10th Compliance Synthesis Report* (Geneva: International Labour Office and International Finance Corporation, 2019), p. 27.

26 L. Sreedharan and A. Kapoor, *Sitting on Pins and Needles: A Rapid Assessment Of Vietnam's Garment Sector* (London: Anti-slavery International, 2018).

27 Worker Rights Consortium, *Made in Vietnam: Labor Rights Violations in Vietnam's Export Manufacturing Sector* (Washington, DC: Worker Rights Consortium, 2013), pp. 8–9.

28 W. Däubler, 'Trade union pluralism in Vietnam – coping with informal associations', in R. Traub-Merz and T. Pringle (eds), *Trade Unions in Transition: From Command to Market Economies* (Berlin: Friedrich-Ebert-Stiftung, 2018), p. 161.

29 Buckley, *Vietnamese Labour*, p. 11 and pp. 93–102.

nent activists and loose networks, including experienced workers and even lower managers.[30] Some activists could organise petitions and smaller protest actions and even coordinate actions and demands with the official trade unions, albeit out of view of the top management. A strike was therefore not always the first resort.

Although presumably known to contacts in the media and sometimes to many in their enterprises even including some managers of Vietnamese nationality, the names of activists were not publicised. Being known as a strike leader could provoke arrest by the Vietnamese authorities and dismissal by the foreign company. The small number of activists who have advocated independent unions have suffered long prison sentences.[31] Their involvement in organising strikes has been reported only exceptionally and propagating their aim was clearly an absolute red line for the authorities.[32] Activist networks therefore remain localised and rudimentary.

The implication is that these strikes could not provide a basis for permanent and open worker organisations and ordered employment relations, including open bargaining and dialogue. Nevertheless, they were crucial in encouraging the authorities in Vietnam to seek reform aimed at making the VGCL appear more representative and trustworthy. One tangible result was frequent increases in the minimum wage, peaking at a 29 per cent rise in 2012, alongside a minimal reported increase in the consumer price index. The VGCL could claim some direct credit for later increases which were agreed after, reportedly sometimes tough, negotiation within a tripartite body, the National Wages Council, formed in 2013.

Evidence from ILO projects over the years also points to a general trend towards improvement in the measurable labour conditions that caused discontent, albeit still with some continuing substantial gaps from managements in compliance with basic labour law. The decrease in strike numbers may therefore reflect workers learning how to make their case and foreign managements learning how to react. By 2022 a minimal number of firms involved in the Better Work programme were paying below the legal minimum wage, a result also found in other surveys.[33] Managements were also frequently implementing wage increases won after strike action in other firms, pre-empting similar actions in their own firms, even without genuine collective bargaining

30 Do Quynh Chi, 'The regional coordination of strikes and the challenge for union reform in Vietnam', *Development and Change*, 48(5) (2017): 1052–1068.

31 Kerkvliet, *Speaking out*, pp. 27–8, Buckley, *Vietnamese Labour*, p. 15 and p. 114.

32 J. Buckley, 'Freedom of association in Vietnam: a heretical view', *Global Labour Journal*, 12 (2), (2021), https://doi.org/10.15173/glj.v12i2.4442, p. 89.

33 *Better Work 2023*, p. 17, and *Industrial Relations*, p. 28.

and worker representation. Nevertheless, the employment relations system remained unusual and incomplete, carrying a latent threat for the authorities of the emergence of independent worker organisations. This encouraged the willingness to allow discussion of alternatives and to seek ILO advice, as also appeared desirable in the interests of trade agreements with the USA and EU.

4 The Impact of TPP

The TPP,[34] negotiated between 12 countries, including Vietnam and the USA, was signed on 4 February 2016. Ratification by Vietnam would bring the immediate elimination of most tariffs on exports with effectively all eliminated after 10 years. The agreement was consistently opposed by US trade unions as 'based on the same outdated trade model that has devastated families and communities for decades',[35] and both main candidates in the then forthcoming presidential election joined in expressing their opposition. In January 2017 the newly elected President Donald Trump withdrew his country from TPP which then continued as the CPTPP. This kept the text largely unchanged, apart from the elimination of some points insisted on by the USA alone, such as extended and enhanced patent protection for pharmaceutical products.

Labour provisions, covered in Chapter 19, were essentially a commitment to ensuring that laws and practices were compatible with the ILO declaration of 1998 and the content of the eight fundamental conventions. It appeared weaker than agreements signed by the EU in that it did not require ratification of those conventions, reflecting the fact that, even by 2025, the USA had signed only two of them, Convention 105 on the abolition of forced labour and Convention 182 on the worst forms of child labour. On the other hand, the agreement appeared stronger than EU agreements in giving the power to use the same dispute mechanism as for commercial conflicts. However, this referred to commercial costs as a reason for a dispute (Article 28.3.1(c)) and allowed for redress by suspending equivalent benefits or by a monetary assessment. It would therefore appear that any successful complaint would have to pass the hurdle of demonstrating that a commercial benefit had been gained, an extremely difficult task in relation to violations of trade union and collective bargaining rights.

---

34 Australian Government Department of Foreign Affairs and Trade, *TPP text and associated documents*, 6 October 2015, https://www.dfat.gov.au/trade/agreements/not-yet-in-force/tpp/Pages/tpp-text-and-associated-documents

35 'Trumka outlines a new direction on trade', 28 June 2016, https://aflcio.org/speeches/trumka-outlines-new-direction-trade.

In an effort to limit domestic opposition, the USA insisted on tighter conditions. These became irrelevant after the country's withdrawal. In the United States–Viet Nam Plan for the Enhancement of Trade and Labour Relations, reached also in February 2016,[36] Vietnam agreed to the implementation of legal and institutional changes prior to the entry into force of the TPP Agreement. This included criminal sanctions for forced labour – by then recognised by the Vietnamese authorities in relation to practices in drug rehabilitation centres – and a strategy for its elimination. Discrimination law was to be amended and the labour inspectorate improved, for which the USA offered to help finance ILO technical assistance. Crucially also, the general commitment to allow freedom of association was made explicit in a requirement that laws and regulations should 'permit workers, without distinction, employed by an enterprise to form a grassroots labour union (in Vietnamese *to chuc cua nguoi lao dong*) of their own choosing without prior authorisation'. Such organisations could register with the VGCL or a 'competent government body', to be clarified in further regulations, and would then have 'no lesser rights in law and practice with regard to the labour rights as stated in the ILO Declaration than a grassroots labour union under the VGCL'. The way was thus open for independent unions. Change was also required within the VGCL with the requirement that trade union law was to be amended to ensure that 'all labour union officials on an executive board are elected by that labour union's membership'.

Almost all of this was to be done before any tariff reductions were implemented. An exception was a requirement that grass-roots unions should be able to link up and operate above the single enterprise level. That would be subject to strict review and evaluated from five years after the agreement came into force, while monitoring would continue for 10 years. This would allow for checking whether practice, irrespective of laws, had really changed or whether administrative delays, such as over registration of new unions, were blocking the spirit of the law. Failure on the part of Vietnam could lead the USA to 'withhold or suspend any tariff reductions that are scheduled to come into effect thereafter': there would still be some tariffs on garments and footwear to be eliminated only after 10 years.

This separate US–Vietnam agreement clearly impacted developments within Vietnam, as discussed below. There was a partial follow-up in a side letter agreement between Canada and Vietnam of 8 March 2018 which speci-

---

36 *United States–Viet Nam Plan for the Enhancement of Trade and Labour Relations*, 4 February 2016, https://ustr.gov/sites/default/files/TPP-Final-Text-Labour-US-VN-Plan-for-Enhancement-of-Trade-and-Labor-Relations.pdf.

fied that 'From the date of entry into force of the Agreement for Viet Nam, Viet Nam shall fully implement the obligations of Chapter 19 (Labour)'.[37] In relation to labour rights, Canada could launch a dispute five years after the trade agreement had come into effect, using the established dispute procedure. This lacked the specific detail of the earlier agreement with the USA and, although there was some discussion of using the mechanism in 2024 when the five-year period had elapsed, no action was taken.

The US withdrawal reduced the impact of the TPP which would have been 'a complete labor game-changer in Vietnam'.[38] The course of events, as followed in various sources, shows how TPP provided 'crucial leverage for reformists',[39] who were able to debate amending legislation to allow genuine freedom of association. The party leadership itself, evidently keen to reap the economic and diplomatic benefits of complying with international agreements, indicated their acceptance of the required labour reforms. However, successive amendments to drafts for a proposed new Labour Code showed how reluctant the authorities were to accept the position in the agreement with the USA, despite strong, coherent and open criticism from disappointed reformers.[40] Above all, additional detail ensured that worker organisations were more explicitly limited to a role within one enterprise, not authorised to link up or to establish international contacts, and thereby more clearly prevented from any role in commenting on government policies and from any possible involvement in political activity. It should be added that despite the openness of some discussion, there were still reports of arbitrary detention and beatings of labour activists.

---

37 Government of Canada, *Vietnam – Side Instruments*, 8 March 2018, https://www.international.gc.ca/trade-commerce/trade-agreements-accords-commerciaux/agr-acc/cptpp-ptpgp/text-texte/sl_la-vietnam.aspx?lang=eng#5.

38 Tran Thi Kieu Trang and R. A. Bales, 'On the precipice: prospects for free labor unions in Vietnam', *San Diego International Law Journal*, 19 (71) (2017), p. 74.

39 K. Marslev and C. Staritz, 'Towards a stronger EU approach on the trade-labor nexus? The EU-Vietnam Free Trade Agreement, social struggles and labor reforms in Vietnam', *Review of International Political Economy*, 30 (3), (2023), DOI: 10.1080/09692290.2022.2056903, p. 1139. See also Tran and Bales, 'On the precipice' and Do, *The Missing*.

40 eg 'Experts slam draft law on association', *Viet Nam News*, 24 October 2016, https://vietnamnews.vn/politicslaws/344927/experts-slam-draft-law-on-association.html#UD3k5qqEsr65lz2m.97.

5 EVFTA

The removal of pressure from the USA left the EU to take up the baton, with some accounts judging its role very positively.[41] The EVFTA was negotiated between June 2012 and December 2015 and throughout this period EU negotiators showed minimal interest in labour issues. Of their meetings within the EU 92 per cent were with representatives of business and 2 per cent with labour and social NGOSs.[42] Negotiating the labour side was being left to the USA. Despite claims that labour standards within EVFTA were included in a 'robust, comprehensive and binding chapter on trade and sustainable development',[43] these sections were essentially similar to those in the earlier agreement with Korea. EVFTA similarly included no prior conditions, referring only to the general need to uphold labour standards and to make 'continued and sustained efforts towards ratification' (Article 13.4.3a) of the ILO's Fundamental Conventions.[44]

The EU approach was changed after the signing of the agreement by changes in internal EU politics characterised by greater scepticism towards free trade agreements and even more towards agreements on investment. One detail was to split the agreement into two, one for trade and one for investment. The former, as an all-EU responsibility, did not require unanimity from all member states while the latter could, and this was a realistic possibility, be blocked by one state alone. The fate of the trade agreement was also uncertain as it also needed majority support from the European parliament. The group that would hold the balance and hence determine the outcome were the Socialists and Democrats (S&D), with one quarter of the seats, among whom many were doubting the benefits of trade agreements being proposed at the time.

Having learned from past experience, they used their leverage to insist on changes in Vietnam's laws to bring them into line with ILO conventions before ratification of the agreement. EU negotiators could then inform their Viet-

---

41 Marslev and Staritz, 'Towards a Stronger'; D. Sicurelli, 'The EU as a partner of ILO in trade negotiations. Explaining labour reform in Vietnam', *Journal of Contemporary European Studies*, 30 (3) (2022) https://doi.org/10.1080/14782804.2021.1909544.

42 Marslev and Staritz, 'Towards a Stronger', p. 1134.

43 *Guide to the EU-Vietnam Trade and Investment Agreements*, (Hanoi: Delegation of the European Union to Vietnam, 2019) https://www.eeas.europa.eu/sites/default/files/eu_fta_guide_final.pdf, pp. 6 and 58.

44 'EU-Vietnam: Texts of the agreements', *Official Journal of the European Union*, 12 June 2020, https://policy.trade.ec.europa.eu/eu-trade-relationships-country-and-region/countries-and-regions/vietnam/eu-vietnam-agreement/texts-agreements_en.

namese counterparts that there could be no agreement without such changes. The point was emphasised by Bernd Lange, a prominent MEP representing the S&D group and chair of the parliament's Committee on International Trade, who visited Vietnam in September 2017 to meet with key figures in the parliament, the VGCL and MOLISA. The effect was to revive reformers within Vietnam who could work with ILO advice on the changes needed.

The European parliament ratified both the trade and investment agreements in February 2020 and they were ratified by the Vietnamese parliament on 8 June 2020. The key internal changes that satisfied enough of the S&D group included ratification of ILO Convention 98 on the right to organise and collective bargaining (on 5 July 2019) and imminent ratification of Convention 105 on the abolition of forced labour (achieved on 14 July 2020). Vietnam was also promising ratification of Convention 87 on freedom of association and protection of the right to organise for 2023, the delay being justified by the need for further changes to trade union law. With that Vietnam would have ratified all the eight fundamental conventions at that time.

6 Vietnam's New Labour Code

The Vietnamese parliament also passed the new Labour Code on 20 November 2019,[45] coming into effect in January 2021, albeit on many points requiring details and clarification from further government decrees. This was billed as fulfilling all the obligations included in the CPTPP and EVFTA, doing all that was needed to bring the country into line with the ILO's Fundamental Conventions. As the document stood, this was not yet the case and critics were soon pointing to a number of omissions and problems in the detail.

An example was the definition of forced labour which was limited purely to an employment relationship, as had been the case in the 2012 Labour Code.[46] The possible practical significance of this point emerged when, having ratified Convention 105, Vietnam was subject to ILO monitoring of its laws and that too pointed to the possible transgression of the convention if prison sentences requiring labour could be used to penalise recognised rights to free expres-

45 Ministry of Labour, Invalids and Social Affairs, *Labour Code*, 2019, https://natlex.ilo.org/dyn/natlex2/r/natlex/fe/details?p3_isn=110469.

46 X. T. Nguyen, T. D. Nguyen and X. H. Nguyen, 'Labour commitments in the EVFTA: amendments and supplements to Vietnamese law and recommendations', *Journal of Law, Policy and Globalization*, 125 (2022), p. 79.

sion, free press, free assembly and free association.[47] Nevertheless, there was clear evidence of improvements in laws and practices, with, for example, forced labour hard to find in the Better Work programme surveys.

Reports of child labour had led the USA in 2012 to add garments from Vietnam to its list of products made from forced and child labour,[48] but the latter too was in decline. It was followed in ILO-backed surveys in 2012 and 2018 which showed, respectively, 9.6 per cent and 5.4 per cent of children aged 5 to 17 undertaking work prohibited for that age group by the 2012 Vietnamese Labour Code.[49] Child labour was most common in small family enterprises in the rural, informal economy and part of the decline could therefore have reflected the declining share of that informal sector. However, with the aim of establishing a developed economy and society, the authorities were susceptible to policy and programme suggestions for the elimination of child labour and changes in the new labour code included more specific restrictions for those under 13 years of age and clearer specification on actions and responsibilities for preventing child labour in the informal economy. The free trade agreements were cited by a Deputy Minister at MOLISA as meaning that the 'country must proactively commit to preventing, minimising and moving towards eliminating child labour'.[50]

The most contentious problems related to Convention 87 and the right to organise. On this Vietnamese law remained inadequate, despite this being the area of by far the most substantial change in the new Labour Code with the former section on trade unions substantially reworked in Articles 170–178.

The great novelty was to allow for two kinds of 'representative organizations', defined as 'internal trade unions', established in line with trade union law, meaning that they are affiliated to VGCL, and 'internal employee organizations' (Article 170). Officials of both are protected against employer discrimination, although employers had often circumvented that rule in the past, and both have the right to 'organize and lead strikes', albeit with no change to the restrictive rules for strikes and a unilateral government power

47 https://normlex.ilo.org/dyn/nrmlx_en/f?p=1000:13100:0::NO:13100:P13100_COMMENT_ID,P13100_COUNTRY_ID:4379141,103004.

48 Worker Rights Consortium, *Made in Vietnam*, pp. 11–12.

49 ILO and the Ministry of Labour, Invalids and Social Affairs of Viet Nam, *Viet Nam National Child Labour Survey 2018: Key findings*, Geneva: International Labour Organization, 2020, p.iii and p.ix.

50 Nguyen Thi Ha in Hà Quân 'Tỉ lệ lao động trẻ em ở Việt Nam giảm theo từng năm' (Child labour rate in Vietnam decreases year by year), *Tuổi Trẻ Online*, 27 May 2022, https://tuoitre.vn/ti-le-lao-dong-tre-em-o-viet-nam-giam-theo-tung-nam-20220527142020847.htm.

to ban strikes in workplaces where it decides they could 'threaten national security, national defense, public health or public order' (Article 209.1). Both representative organisations can bargain and sign collective agreements with rules for bargaining in the cases of multiple employee organisations set out in other parts of the labour code. Whether there would be changes in the internal working and role of VGCL organisations remained unclear, depending on anticipated amendments to the trade union law of 2013.

Rules setting out the activities of internal employee organisations suggest a role similar to that of VGCL organisations in heading off worker discontent rather than building from the role of informal activist networks. They are expected to protect 'the lawful rights and interests of the members' and aim for 'progressive, harmonious and stable labour relations' (Article 174.2), with no explicit mention of advancing employees' collective interests. Internal organisations are also expected to 'comply with the constitution' (Article 172.1) which would include recognition of the leading role of the single, ruling party. The details of how 'internal employee organizations' should be established and much on their internal governance were to be set out later by the government. The relevant decree was still awaited in early 2025, despite reported discussions involving ILO representatives. It was made clear that they would have rights only 'after registration is granted by a competent authority' (Article 172.1). Even should that authority ever be specified, there would still be plenty of scope for the authorities to block or delay formation, and then to hamper the activities, of these new organisations, if they so wished. That was presumably recognised by US negotiators with their insistence on continuing monitoring of practices rather than just acceptance of the existence of laws. Finally, there was nothing in the Labour Code's provisions to allow the organisations to link up between workplaces, to create national structures, to receive finance from the government or from abroad, to make contacts internationally or to comment on politics or policies. Vietnam could therefore expect a critical judgement from the ILO if it were to ratify Convention 87 and thereby subject itself to systematic monitoring.

In practice, there has been no sign of Vietnamese workers trying to establish independent organisations. It could be argued that, in view of the results achieved from strike action and clandestine worker organisation, workers may see little gain over the existing form of industrial relations[51] which protects strikers and activists from victimisation. However, the situation could be dra-

51 As discussed in A. Cox and S. Le Queux (2023) 'Towards an independent workers' voice in Vietnam?', *Labour and Industry*, 33 (3) (2023), 385–399, https://doi.org/10.1080/10301763.2023.2244218; and Buckley, 'Freedom'.

matically transformed if genuine freedom from victimisation of independent activists were made more likely. Labour activists could then choose between forming independent organisations and transforming existing VGCL organisations. The independent Solidarity union in Poland claimed, within a year of being allowed to operate legally in 1980, membership equivalent to 80 per cent of the country's employees and quickly became a serious political threat to the regime. Experience of developing independent trade unions in countries of the former Soviet bloc also often followed transformation of inherited organisations. Neither road has, as of early 2025, been possible in Vietnam.

7 After Implementation

Once the EVFTA had been ratified, the EU's leverage diminished rapidly. The EU system depends on dialogue between civil society organisations from the two parties. Each side forms a Domestic Advisory Group (DAG) and the two are expected to meet at prescribed intervals. Complaints from either side can be raised and continuing dispute can lead ultimately to the European Commission, or partner government, starting a dispute procedure. This happened only once, in the case of Korea, and the EU's case was upheld over Korea's failure to 'promote, respect and realise' the ILO's Fundamental Conventions, even though it had ratified only some and even though there was no identifiable impact on trade. A similar judgement in relation to Vietnam would seem likely, although the penalty would again be purely reputational.

Even the first step of establishing a civil society dialogue with Vietnam proved problematic as the government actively restricted participation in the country's DAG, as formed in August 2021, to only three organisations and labour was represented only by the Institute for Workers and Trade Unions (IWTU), a research institute formally subordinated to the VGCL.[52] Complaints from the European side were not assuaged by an expansion to six organisations on 4 January 2022, including no more to represent labour while more independent organisations were ignored. The EU DAG, meeting in November 2023, noted a number of reports of specific repressive acts and, in view of the 'shrinking space for civil society', sought a more assertive approach from

52 K. Marslev and C. Staritz, 'Labor Regimes, Global Production Networks, and State–Society Relations: Assessing the Impact of the EU–Vietnam Free Trade Agreement on Labor in Vietnam', *Economic Geography*, 100 (5–6) 2024, pp. 420–421.

the European Commission in arguing for a broadening of the Vietnamese DAG and for progress on coming into line with ILO conventions.[53]

There was satisfaction with the agreement from the Vietnamese side. Business interests on both sides had every reason to be pleased, pushing concerns over labour issues back down the list of priorities. The official view from Vietnam was that they were improving employment conditions and ensuring stable and harmonious labour relations. A continuing decline in strike numbers, down to 49 recorded in 2024, could support the hope that labour discontent was containable without conceding full freedom of association.[54] At the same time, the party leadership was visibly favouring a more authoritarian approach. The human rights organisation Project88 reproduced a leaked document of July 2023 from the party leadership warning of the need to counter 'hostile and reactionary forces' taking advantage of international integration. Among these were 'civil society alliances' and 'independent trade unions' which could lead to the creation of 'domestic political opposition groups'.[55] This was followed by repressive measures which included the arrests, made public in May 2024, of two figures prominent in efforts to incorporate Convention 87 into Vietnamese law; these were the head of the Legal Affairs Department at MOLISA and the director of IWTU, itself a member of Vietnam's DAG. Both were accused of 'disclosure of classified information' which might mean no more than communicating with the ILO or their European counterparts. The EU DAG, meeting on 26 April 2024, saw these as serious breaches of the terms of EVFTA and called on the European Commission to raise the issue forcefully with the Vietnamese authorities.[56]

This experience supports the general conclusions that labour provisions in trade agreements can make a difference to labour conditions. The effectiveness of pressure depends on relative bargaining strengths and Vietnam was particularly keen to take advantage of the economic benefits offered by agreements first with the USA and then with the EU. The experience also confirms that once an agreement is in force interest in pursuing labour issues rapidly

---

53 *Statement from the European Union Domestic Advisory Group*, 28–29 November 2023, https://www.eesc.europa.eu/sites/default/files/files/eu-vn_dag_-_3rd_dag-to-dag_meeting_2023_-_eu_dag_statement_final.pdf.

54 Diệp, P., 'Tiếp tục hoàn thiện thể chế trong lĩnh vực quan hệ lao động và tiền lương' (Continuing to improve institutions in the field of labour relations and wages), *Lao động thủ đô*, 6 January 2025, https://laodongthudo.vn/tiep-tuc-hoan-thien-the-che-trong-linh-vuc-quan-he-lao-dong-va-tien-luong-182840.html.

55 https://the88project.org/.

56 *Statement from the European Union Domestic Advisory Group of the EU-Viet Nam Free Trade Agreement*, 6 June 2024, https://www.eesc.europa.eu/sites/default/files/2024-06/euvn_dag_statement_final.pdf.

declines. Commercial issues and business interests again become the priority for negotiators while labour has lost its strongest bargaining lever which was the potential ability to block the ratification of the agreement in total.

It remains an open question how far a tougher approach from the USA or the EU could have led to a different outcome. The one-party state regime was not hostile to advice and any associated external pressure in many areas, and nor was it necessarily hostile to Vietnamese workers getting better conditions from foreign employers. The red line remained allowing the possibility of independent trade unions that could lead to a challenge to its monopoly of power.

Acknowledgements

The research for this chapter was helped by funding for an earlier project on labour provisions in trade agreements from the International Labour Organisation's Bureau for Workers' Activities (ACTRAV). The author would also like to acknowledge additional helpful advice for this expanded and updated version from Joe Buckley and from Judith Kirton-Darling (General Secretary, IndustriAll European Trade Union).

Bibliography

Anner, M., Wildcat Strikes and Better Work Bipartite Committees in Vietnam: Towards an Elect, Represent, Protect and Empower Framework, Better Work Discussion Paper 24, (ILO: Geneva, 2017).

Australian Government Department of Foreign Affairs and Trade, *TPP text and associated documents*, 6 October 2015, https://www.dfat.gov.au/trade/agreements/not-yet-in-force/tpp/Pages/tpp-text-and-associated-documents.

Better Work Viet Nam Annual Report 2023 (Geneva: International Labour Office and International Finance Corporation, 2023).

Better Work Viet Nam Garment Industry 10th Compliance Synthesis Report (Geneva: International Labour Office and International Finance Corporation, 2019).

Buckley, J., 'Freedom of association in Vietnam: a heretical view', *Global Labour Journal*, 12 (2), (2021): 79–94, https://doi.org/10.15173/glj.v12i2.4442.

Buckley, J., *Vietnamese Labour Militancy: Capital-Labour Antagonisms and Self-Organised Struggles* (Abingdon and New York: Routledge, 2022).

Cox, A. and Le Queux, S., 'Towards an independent workers' voice in Vietnam?', *Labour and Industry*, 33 (3) (2023): 385–399, https://doi.org/10.1080/10301763.2023.2244218.

Däubler, W. 'Trade union pluralism in vietnam – coping with informal associations', in R. Traub-Merz and T. Pringle (eds), *Trade Unions in Transition: From Command to Market Economies* (Berlin: Friedrich-Ebert-Stiftung, 2018), pp. 149–162.

Diệp, P., 'Tiếp tục hoàn thiện thể chế trong lĩnh vực quan hệ lao động và tiền lương' (Continuing to improve institutions in the field of labour relations and wages), *Lao động thủ đô*, 6 January 2025, https://laodongthudo.vn/tiep-tuc-hoan-thien-the-che-trong-linh-vuc-quan-he-lao-dong-va-tien-luong-182840.html.

Do Quynh Chi, 'The regional coordination of strikes and the challenge for union reform in Vietnam', *Development and Change*, 48(5) (2017): 1052–1068.

Do Quynh Chi, The Missing Link in the Chain: Trade Regimes and Labour Standards in the Garment, Footwear and Electronics Supply Chains in Vietnam, (Hanoi: Friedrich-Ebert-Stiftung Vietnam, 2017).

European Parliament, *EU-Vietnam Free Trade Agreement*, 2018, https://www.europarl.europa.eu/RegData/etudes/BRIE/2018/628248/EPRS_BRI(2018)628248_EN.pdf.

'EU-Vietnam: Texts of the agreements', *Official Journal of the European Union*, 12 June 2020, https://policy.trade.ec.europa.eu/eu-trade-relationships-country-and-region/countries-and-regions/vietnam/eu-vietnam-agreement/texts-agreements_en.

'Experts slam draft law on association', *Viet Nam News*, 24 October 2016, https://vietnamnews.vn/politicslaws/344927/experts-slam-draft-law-on-association.html#UD3k5qqEsr65lz2m.97.

Government of Canada, *Vietnam – Side Instruments*, 8 March 2018, https://www.international.gc.ca/trade-commerce/trade-agreements-accords-commerciaux/agr-acc/cptpp-ptpgp/text-texte/sl_la-vietnam.aspx?lang=eng#5.

Gramberg, B. van, Teicher J. and Tien Nguyen, 'Industrial disputes in Vietnam the tale of the wildcat', *Asia Pacific Journal of Human Resources* (2013) 51, 248–268, doi:10.1111/j.1744-7941.2012.00062.x.

Guide to the EU-Vietnam Trade and Investment Agreements, (Hanoi: Delegation of the European Union to Vietnam, 2019), https://www.eeas.europa.eu/sites/default/files/eu_fta_guide_final.pdf.

Ha Hai Hoang, 'Understanding the EU–Vietnam Free Trade Agreement', *East Asia Forum*, 21 May 2020, https://eastasiaforum.org/2020/05/21/understanding-the-eu-vietnam-free-trade-agreement/.

ILO and the Ministry of Labour, Invalids and Social Affairs of Viet Nam, *Viet Nam National Child Labour Survey 2018: Key findings*, Geneva: International Labour Organization, 2020.

Industrial Relations Report 2019: Towards Genuine Collective Bargaining (Geneva: ILO, 2021).

Kerkvliet, B., Speaking Out in Vietnam: Public Political Criticism in a Communist Party-Ruled Nation (Ithaca and London: Cornell University Press, 2019).

Marslev, K. and Staritz, C., 'Labor regimes, global production networks, and state–society relations: assessing the impact of the EU–Vietnam Free Trade Agreement on labor in Vietnam', *Economic Geography*, 100 (5–6) (2024): 410–436.

Marslev, K. and Staritz, C., 'Towards a stronger EU approach on the trade-labor nexus? The EU-Vietnam Free Trade Agreement, social struggles and labor reforms in Vietnam', *Review of International Political Economy*, 30 (3), (2023): 1125–1150, DOI: 10.1080/09692290.2022.2056903.

Ministry of Labour, Invalids and Social Affairs, *Labour Code*, 2019, https://natlex.ilo.org/dyn/natlex2/r/natlex/fe/details?p3_isn=110469.

Myant, M., 'Economies undergoing long transition: employment relations in Central and Eastern Europe' in A. Wilkinson, G. Wood and R. Deeg (eds) *The Oxford Handbook of Employment Relations* (Oxford: Oxford University Press, 2014), pp. 359–384.

Myant, M., *Labour Rights in Trade Agreements: Five New Stories* (Brussels: ETUI, 2017).

Myant, M., *The Impact of Trade and Investment Agreements on Decent Work and Sustainable Development* (Brussels: ETUI, 2017).

Nguyen Thi Ha, in Hà Quân 'Tỉ lệ lao động trẻ em ở Việt Nam giảm theo từng năm' (Child labour rate in Vietnam decreases year by year), *Tuổi Trẻ Online*, 27 May 2022, https://tuoitre.vn/ti-le-lao-dong-tre-em-o-viet-nam-giam-theo-tung-nam-20220527142020847.htm.

Nguyen, X. T., Nguyen T. D. and Nguyen X. H., 'Labour commitments in the EVFTA: amendments and supplements to Vietnamese law and recommendations', *Journal of Law, Policy and Globalization*, 125 (2022): 76–83.

Petri, P. A. and Plummer, M. G., *The Economic Effects of the Trans-Pacific Partnership: New Estimates*, Working Paper 16–2, (Washington, DC: Peterson Institute for International Economics, 2016).

Schweisshelm E. and Do Quynh Chi, 'From harmony to conflict: Vietnamese trade unions on the threshold of reform', in R. Traub-Merz and T. Pringle (eds), *Trade Unions in Transition: From Command to Market Economies* (Berlin: Friedrich-Ebert-Stiftung, 2018), pp. 109–147.

Sicurelli, D., 'The EU as a partner of ILO in trade negotiations. Explaining labour reform in Vietnam', *Journal of Contemporary European Studies*, 30 (3) (2022): 461–473, https://doi.org/10.1080/14782804.2021.1909544.

Smith, A., Harrison, J., Campling, L., Richardson, B. and Barbu, M., *Free Trade Agreements and Global Labour Governance: The European Union's Trade-Labour Linkage in a Value Chain World* (London: Routledge, 2020).

Sreedharan L. and Kapoor, A., Sitting on Pins and Needles: A Rapid Assessment Of Vietnam's Garment Sector (London: Anti-slavery International, 2018).

Statement from the European Union Domestic Advisory Group of the EU-Viet Nam Free Trade Agreement, 6 June 2024, https://www.eesc.europa.eu/sites/default/files/2024-06/euvn_dag_statement_final.pdf.

Statement from the European Union Domestic Advisory Group, 28–29 November 2023, https://www.eesc.europa.eu/sites/default/files/files/eu-vn_dag_-_3rd_dag-to-dag_meeting_2023_-_eu_dag_statement_final.pdf.

Statistical Yearbook of Viet Nam 2017 (Hanoi: General Statistics Office, 2018), https://www.gso.gov.vn/en/data-and-statistics/2019/10/7559/.

Statistical Yearbook of Viet Nam 2023 (Hanoi: General Statistics Office, 2024), https://www.gso.gov.vn/en/default/2024/07/statistical-yearbook-of-2023/.

Tran Thi Kieu Trang and Bales, R. A., 'On the precipice: prospects for free labor unions in Vietnam', *San Diego International Law Journal*, 19 (71) (2017): 71–93.

Trinh Ly Khanh, 'Trade union organizing free from employers' interference: evidence from Vietnam', *Southeast Asian Studies*, 3 (3) 2014: 589–609.

'Trumka outlines a new direction on trade', 28 June 2016, https://aflcio.org/speeches/trumka-outlines-new-direction-trade.

United States–Viet Nam Plan for the Enhancement of Trade and Labour Relations, 4 February 2016, https://ustr.gov/sites/default/files/TPP-Final-Text-Labour-US-VN-Plan-for-Enhancement-of-Trade-and-Labor-Relations.pdf.

VNA, 'Trade union executive boards to receive training in salary negotiations' *Vietnam Plus*, 11 July 2019, https://en.vietnamplus.vn/trade-union-executive-boards-to-receive-training-in-salary-negotiations-post155917.vnp.

Worker Rights Consortium, *Made in Vietnam: Labor Rights Violations in Vietnam's Export Manufacturing Sector* (Washington, DC: Worker Rights Consortium, 2013).

World Bank Group, *Economic and Distributional Impacts of Comprehensive and Progressive Agreement for Trans-Pacific Partnership: The Case of Vietnam* (Washington, DC: The World Bank, 2018).

World Bank Group, *Sustaining Success: Priorities for Sustainable and Inclusive Growth*, (Hanoi, The World Bank in Vietnam, 2016).

World Bank National Accounts Data, https://data.worldbank.org/indicator/NY.GDP.PCAP.KD.

PART 2

The EU's Approach

CHAPTER 5

Global Trade and Social Fundamental Rights: The Perspective of the European Union

Silvio Bologna

1 The 'Spirit' of Philadelphia: The Historical Linkage between Global Trade and Social Rights

Following the fall of fascisms, with the end of the Second World War, the model of European citizenship was built on the recognition and promotion of social rights. All the constitutional charters coming into force since 1946, like the French or Italian ones, set the principle of substantive equality as a value foundation.[1] This principle was then declined by the same constitutions through the recognition of the rights to work, health care, social security and the freedom of collective action. In other words, the axiology of the European constitutional charters rejected the mere liberal perspective of '*homo oeconomicus*': the 'animal spirits' of capitalism were replaced by the anthropology of '*homo juridicus*', built on the principles of equality, freedom and dignity heritage of the French revolution.[2]

Such a perspective was inscribed in a more general design for the emancipation of Western capitalism from the liberal and authoritarian paradigms, well summarized by the ILO Philadelphia Declaration of 1944, according to

1 Under Art. 3, para. 2 of the Italian Constitution, entered into force on 1 January 1948, 'It is the duty of the Republic to remove those obstacles of an economic or social nature which constrain the freedom and equality of citizens, thereby impeding the full development of the human person and the effective participation of all workers in the political, economic and social organization of the country'. In addition, according to the Preamble to the French Constitution of the Fourth Republic (27 October 1946) 'It shall guarantee to all, notably to children, mothers and elderly workers, protection of their health, material security, rest and leisure. All people who, by virtue of their age, physical or mental condition, or economic situation, are incapable of working, shall have to the right to receive suitable means of existence from society' (para. 11); moreover, 'The Nation guarantees equal access for children and adults to instruction, vocational training and culture' (para 13).

2 A. Supiot, *Homo juridicus. Saggio sulla funzione antropologica del diritto* (Milano: Bruno Mondadori, 1996).

 | HTTPS://DOI.ORG/10.1163/9789004762251-006

which 'labour is not a commodity' (Art. 1).[3] The Declaration, inserted in 1946 in the preamble of the ILO's Constitution, imagined a world built on peace and justice between peoples (the Second World War had not yet ended), to be achieved through the protection of workers:[4] in particular, the Declaration affirmed how all human beings, regardless of race, creed or gender, have the right to pursue their material progress and spiritual development in freedom and dignity and in economic security (Art. 2). Going beyond the mere enunciation of principles, the Declaration held that such a model of development – to be realized – must be the aim of every national and international policy, particularly in the economic and financial fields. In this regard, public action should be able to balance the fight against 'poverty anywhere (which) constitutes a danger to prosperity everywhere' (Art. 1, para. c) and the promotion of 'a high and steady volume of international trade' (Art. 5).

A world without wars was imagined, where trade takes place not only in compliance with the mere economic rationality of States and multinationals corporations but also with the fundamental rights of the person who works under the banner of a reasonable compromise. An enlightened model of capitalism was outlined, in which the free movement of goods, services and capital must not be the result of social dumping and competitive advantages of Ricardian memory; on the contrary, international trade must also be declined according to the metric of social justice. In addition to the original concern for the protection of workers' rights, the environmental issue has been incorporated into the debate on sustainable development and fair trade,[5] with a planet whose survival is threatened by the current capitalist model of production.

The model envisioned by the Philadelphia Declaration is more than ever threatened, if we look at the current geopolitical scenario, characterized by instability due to the proliferation of conflicts, the rise of neoliberalism in the government of labor markets, and protectionist economic policies based on

---

3 ILO Declaration of Philadelphia concerning the aims and purposes of the International Labour Organization, 10 May 1944.

4 A. Perulli, *The Declaration of Philadelphia, WP C.S.D.L.E. 'Massimo D'Antona'.INT -143/2018*, p. 40; J.M. Servais, International Labour Law (The Netherlands: Wolters Kluwer, 2020), p. 50; A. Tyc, 'The linkage between labour standards and international trade: how to offset the global inequality?' (2019) *Wroclaw Review of Law, Administration and Economics*, 9, 1, 62.

5 A. Perulli, 'Towards a Green Labour Law', in A. Perulli and T. Treu (eds.), *Labour Law and Climate Change. Towards a Just Transition* (The Netherlands: Wolters Kluwer, 2023), pp. 17–18.

the 'war of tariffs' between most significant global players, especially after the second mandate of Donald Trump as U.S. President.[6]

The pages which follow will analyse the trade policies of the European Union (henceforth EU) with the rest of the world, with a specific focus on the legal 'tools' to protect fundamental workers' rights. In the second paragraph, the constitutional bases of the external action of the EU that justify a social clause in free trade agreements will be discussed. In the third section, the common features of the treaties signed by the EU with other States will be firstly reconstructed, whose *fil rouge* is the respect of core labor standards enshrined in the International Labour Organization legal framework. Secondly, we will discuss the instruments of workers' protection covered by the treaties, all soft law measures (i.e., consultation of civil society and joint reports). In the fourth paragraph, the description of soft law mechanisms contained in free trade agreements will be accompanied by those more properly sanctioning, such as the generalized preferences systems (GSP, GSP+ and Everything but Arms Arrangement). Finally, from a pro-labor perspective, the essay deals with the Investor–State Dispute Settlement (ISDS) clause, as a mechanism to solve disputes between States and multinational corporations on the application of a free trade agreement, and the efforts made by the EU to reform the system with the aim to minimize its impact on workers' rights.

2 European Union External Action Principles: The Legal Basis of the Social Clause in EU Free Trade Agreements

While the European constitutions were conceived as labor-centred, at the beginning the process of European integration had a purely market-oriented dimension: the then European Coal and Steel Community, later transformed into the European Economic Community, was built on the fundamental freedoms of movement of persons, goods, services and capital, and any intervention in social matters was only instrumental to the proper functioning of the internal market.[7] The so-called 'social frigidity' of Europe[8] has been overcome thanks to the reforms which have taken place in the constitutional architec-

6 For a general framework on the connections among protectionist political economy and international trade law, see A.O. Sykes, 'Regulatory protectionism and the Law of International Trade' (1999) 66 *The University of Chicago of Law Review*, 1, pp. 1–46.

7 S. Giubboni, *Diritti sociali e mercato: la dimensione sociale dell'integrazione europea* (Bologna: il Mulino, 2003), pp. 18–78.

8 G.F. Mancini, 'Intervento', in Vv.A.a., *Atti del convegno di Parma del 30–31 ottobre 1985* (Padova: Cedam, 1988), p. 33.

ture of the Union, especially since the Amsterdam Treaty of 1997 which led, i.e., to the recognition of the principle of non-discrimination and of EU intervention in employment and professional training. Obviously, such principles must be concretized by the ordinary European legislator through the instruments of the treaties (regulations and directives) and, from a historical perspective, they have experienced ups and downs, especially after the global economic and financial crisis of 2010, which brought many States to adopt draconian austerity policies under the aegis of the same European institutions.[9]

In any case, from a dogmatic point of view, the 'birth' of the EU with the Treaty of Lisbon marked the definitive constitutionalizing of fundamental rights in the European legal framework. This positive assessment concerns not only the internal market dimension but also foreign trade and, from an axiological perspective, is linked to the Philadelphia Declaration: the EU cannot act in violation of human rights in any of its areas of competence, which include, *inter alia*, trade and trade policies with third countries.

In particular, since its entry into force in 2009 the Treaty of Lisbon has developed a holistic approach to the EU process of integration:[10] several provisions of the Treaties (Treaty on the Functioning of the European Union and Treaty on European Union, henceforth TFEU and TEU) give shape to a model of society where liberal market principles coexist with the goals of full employment, social progress and cohesion within the broader context of a 'highly competitive social market economy' (Art. 3 TEU).

More precisely, the treaties generalize the fulfilment of social goals in all fields of EU action, conventionally defined as a 'horizontal social clause':[11] such an approach is justified by the systematic interpretation of Arts. 2 and 3 of the TEU and 9 of the TFEU. Indeed, under Art. 9 TFEU, 'In defining and implementing its policies and activities, the Union shall take into account requirements linked to the promotion of a high level of employment, the guarantee of adequate social protection, the fight against social exclusion,

9 R. Erne, S. Stan, I. Szabò, V. Maccarrone, *Politicising Commodification. European Governance and Labour Politics from the Financial Crisis to the Covid Emergency* (Cambridge: Cambridge University Press, 2024), pp. 1–3; A. Seifert, 'European economic governance and Labor Laws of the E.U. Member States' (2014) 35 *Comparative labor law and policy journal*, 3, 311–330.

10 A. Perulli, 'Fundamental Social Rights, Market Regulation and EU External Action' (2014) 30 *International Journal of Comparative Labour Law*, 1, 34; Id., 'Diritti sociali fondamentali e regolazione del mercato nell'azione esterna dell'Unione Europea' (2013) LXIV *Rivista giuridica del lavoro e della previdenza sociale*, I, 328.

11 Perulli, 'Fundamental Social Rights', 33.

and a high level of education, training and protection of human health'. Article 9 is in line with the axiological perspective of Arts. 2 and 3, providing respectively that 'The Union is founded on the values of respect for human dignity, freedom, democracy, equality, the rule of law and respect for human rights, including the rights of persons belonging to minorities' and that 'In its relations with the wider world, the Union shall uphold and promote its values and interests and contribute to the protection of its citizens. It shall contribute to peace, security, the sustainable development of the Earth, solidarity and mutual respect among peoples, free and fair trade, eradication of poverty and the protection of human rights' (para. 5).

The social clause contained in Art. 9 is legally binding on all EU institutions, as it is placed in Title II of the TFEU (*Provisions Having General Application*): in particular, it binds the European Commission, the institutional body responsible for pursuing the general interest of the Union (Art. 17 TFEU) not only as regards the functioning of the internal market but also in connection with the external relations of the Union, which include international trade.

The EU constitutional refusal of social Darwinism in foreign relations and global trade is strengthened by the reference of the same treaties to international human rights law: in fact, under Art. 205 TFEU 'The Union's action on the international scene … shall be guided by the principles, pursue the objectives and be conducted in accordance with the general provisions laid down in Chapter I of Title V of the Treaty on European Union'. More specifically, Art. 205 must be jointly read with Art. 21 contained in Chapter I, establishing that the rationales of each EU intervention are 'democracy, the rule of law, the universality and indivisibility of human rights and fundamental freedoms, respect for human dignity, the principles of equality and solidarity, and respect for the principles of the United Nations Charter and international law'.

Under a pro-labor hermeneutics, this means that the EU must develop trade relationships only with States that have ratified or engaged themselves to ratify or implement the most significant ILO conventions or adhere to the respect of ILO core labor standards.[12] In other words, if a third country wants to negotiate a free trade agreement with the EU, must at least accomplish the ILO Declaration on Social Justice for a Fair Globalization (2008) and the ILO Declaration on Fundamental Principles and Rights at Work (1998, as emended in 2022); or, alternatively, with the ten ILO core conventions on: freedom of association and the effective recognition of the right to collective bargaining;

12 J. Kenner, 'Economic Partnership Agreements: Enhancing the Labour Dimension of Global Governance?', in B. Van Vorren, S. Blovkmans, J. Wouters (eds.), *The EU's role in Global Governance* (Oxford: Oxford University Press, 2013), p. 321.

the elimination of all forms of forced or compulsory labor; the effective abolition of child labor; the elimination of discrimination in respect of employment and occupation; the protection and promotion of a safe and healthy work environment.[13] These are, in short, the constitutional basis of EU external action, which can be defined as 'EU's international social law': indeed, international law is not referred to an *ad hoc* basis but is part of rules remaining international in nature, while at the same time becoming components of EU law for global trade.[14]

3 The EU Free Trade Agreements: A 'Persuasive' Approach to Respect Fundamental Workers' Rights

The EU has currently ratified 41 economic and partnership agreements with 72 third countries all over the world, either with developing States or with peer-to-peer economies (i.e., Canada, Japan and South Korea), and it is currently negotiating other partnerships, especially with Asian countries (India and Indonesia).[15] In the context of the linkage between global trade and fundamental social rights contained in the EU Treaties, all agreements are also characterized by the pursuit of non-trade policies. From a historical perspective, labor provisions have widened and deepened over the past twenty years: in the first period, arising from the Euromed agreements until those signed with

13 For an in-depth analysis of ILO standard-setting instruments and international labour standards, see J.M. Servais, *International labour law*, pp. 80–86 and 100 et seq.

14 S. Robin-Olivier, 'The relationship between international law and European labour legislation and its impact on the development of international and European social law' (2020) 159 *International Labour Review*, 4, 501; T. Novitz, 'The European Union and International Labour Standards: the Dynamics of Dialogue between the EU and the ILO', in P. Alston (ed.), *Labour Rights as Human Rights* (Oxford: Oxford University Press, 2005), p. 216.

15 All free trade agreements negotiated, adopted or ratified by the EU are available at https://policy.trade.ec.europa.eu/eu-trade-relationships-country-and-region/negotiations-and-agreements_en. In particular, most significant categories of EU trade agreements are: free trade agreements (FTAs), enabling mutual market opening with developed countries and emerging economies by granting preferential access to markets; economic partnership agreements (EPAs), a kind of FTAs, tailor-made, and they preferentially deal with development issues (i.e., with Caribbean States); association agreements (AAs), also bolstering political agreements (i.e., with Ukraine and Georgia). For further information, see https://www.consilium.europa.eu/de/global-europe-the-value-of-free-and-fair-trade/#:~:text=The%20EU%20currently%20has%2041,economic%20partnership%20agreements%20(*EPAs*).

Chile (1990–2003), agreements were not numerous, and social provisions essentially referred to technical cooperation or mutual recognition of a same benefit or entitlement.[16]

In addition to technical cooperation, 'second-generation' agreements contain specific provisions on labor issues:[17] in short, there is a specific commitment to respect and promote core labor standards or fundamental ILO conventions deemed as human rights. The first example of the new EU trajectory was the 2008 Cariforum agreement with the Caribbean Community (Caricom): apart from the general commitment to 'facilitate the development of, and compliance with … internationally recognized labour and environmental standards' (Art. 8), the linkage among fair trade and economic growth is highlighted by the provisions under which 'investors act in accordance with core labour standards as required by the International Labour Organization' and 'foreign direct investment is not encouraged by lowering domestic, environmental, labour, occupational safety and health legislation or by relaxing core labour standards or law' (Arts. 72 and 73).

In 2011, the EU–South Korea agreement was the first one to include a specific Trade and Sustainable Development (hereinafter TSD) chapter, which is currently a common practice for all EU free trade agreements: the reasons of distributive justice – not only labor rights but also the quest for environmental protection[18] – falls within the broader notion of sustainable development, instead of being separated.[19] The common features of TSD chapters are

16 L. Van Den Putte and J. Orbie, 'EU Bilateral Trade Agreements and the Surprising Rise of Labour Provisions' (2015) 31 *International Journal of Comparative Labour Law*, 3, 268; M. Oehri, 'Labour Rights Promotion in the Absence of Conditionality? How the EU and the US Engage China and India' (2017) 22 *European Foreign Affairs Review*, 1, 138. I.e., Euromed agreements established that workers from the Southern Mediterranean area would benefit the same social security allowances granted to the citizens of the EU Member States in which they were employed.

17 A. Tyc, 'The European Union and Japan's Economic Partnership Agreement: labour provision under the 'Trade and Sustainable Development Chapter' (2020) 10 *Juridical Tribune*, Special Issue, 21; S. Kuang, 'The European Commission's Discourses on Sustainable Development in 'Trade for All': An argumentative Perspective' (2021) 26 *European Foreign Affairs Review*, 2, 268.

18 T. Novitz, 'Challenges when Combining Labour and Environmental Objectives: Trade and Sustainable Development Chapters and Beyond', in A. Perulli, T. Treu (eds.) *Labour Law and Climate Change*, 98. I.e., the 2021 EU–UK Trade and Cooperation Agreement (TCA) affirms that a breach of TSD provisions, including 'labour and social, environmental or climate protection' may engender 'material impacts on trade and investment between the parties' (Art. 411).

19 I.e., Art. 19.1, para. 2 of Chapter 19 – specifically devoted to TSD – of the FTA between the EU and New Zealand, in force since 2024, affirms that 'The Parties recognise that sus-

the definition of substantive labor standards, the procedural commitments relied upon, the institutional structures created and the way complaints are handled.[20]

It should be highlighted that also trade agreements concluded by the EU with peer-to-peer economies encompass workers' protection:[21] i.e., under the agreements with Singapore and Canada (CETA), signed in 2018 and 2015, social rights are considered part of sustainable development and, in TSD chapters, the parties engage themselves to implement a system of economic partnership on the grounds of ILO Declaration on Social Justice for a Fair Globalization.[22] Moreover, the Economic Partnership Agreement (EPA) between the EU and Japan has a TSD chapter, which forbids at all relaxing or lowering the level of domestic labor legislation to encourage trade and investment (Art. 16.2 para. 3). In addition, the parties refer to the respect of international 'tools', specifically the ILO Declaration on Fundamental Principles and Rights at Work of 1998 and its Follow-up, even if the EPA does not require the ratification of the ILO Conventions to reach an agreement.[23] In a similar vein, in the recent agreement between the EU and the four founding Mercosur countries (Argentina, Brazil, Paraguay and Uruguay), yet to be approved by the EU Parliament and ratified by Member States,[24] the parties engage themselves 'to promote

tainable development encompasses economic development, social development and environmental protection, all three being interdependent and mutually reinforcing'. In a similar vein, the TSD chapter of the new agreement between the EU and Chile (in force since 2025) aims 'to enhance the development of the Parties' trade and investment relationship in a way that contributes to sustainable development, notably its labour and environmental dimensions relevant to trade and investment' (Art. 26.1, para. 3).

20 J. Harrison, M. Barbu, L. Campling, F.C. Ebert, 'Labour Standards Provisions in EU Free Trade Agreements: Reflections on the European Commission's Reform Agenda' (2018) 18 *World Trade Review*, 4, 5.

21 Having regard to peer-to-peer economies, the EU and the USA negotiated the signature of the Transatlantic Trade and Investment Partnership (TTIP): negotiations were launched in 2013 and ended without conclusion in 2016. A Council decision of 15 April 2019 stated that the negotiating directives for the TTIP were obsolete and no longer relevant. For an analysis of the TTIP labor template and related controversial issues, see M. Faioli, 'The Quest for a New Generation of Labor Chapter in the TTIP' (2015) XLIX *Economia e Lavoro*, 2, 103–120.

22 See Chapter 12, Art. 12.1.1 of the FTA between the EU and Singapore; Chapter 22, Art. 22.1.1. of the CETA.

23 Under Art. 16.3, para. 3 'Each party shall make continued and sustained efforts on its own initiative to pursue ratification of the fundamental ILO Conventions and other ILO Conventions which each Party considers appropriate to ratify'.

24 The EU and the four founding Mercosur countries reached a political agreement on 6 December 2024 for a ground-breaking partnership agreement: the EU is the biggest foreign investor in Mercosur with a stock of €340 billion in 2021. For further socio-

and effectively implement the internationally recognised core labour standards, as defined in the fundamental ILO Conventions …'.[25]

What captures the attention, as outlined by scholars,[26] is the lack of effectiveness of TSD chapters, if compared with the other sections of the treaties dealing with the protection of investments and the principle of non-discrimination in trade: in fact, even if labor templates are aligned with the ILO 'constitutional law', effective enforcement mechanisms are absent for disputes concerning workers' rights violations. On the contrary, treaties merely set soft law measures, such as civil society advisory groups and non-arbitral panel recommendations, to back them up. As an example, the agreement with Mercosur has created a Sub-Committee on Trade and Sustainable Development, composed of senior officials, or their delegates, from each party: the Committee may, *inter alia*, monitor the effective implementation of the TSD chapter, including cooperation activities; carry out consultations with the parties on the application of the same chapter, if requested (Art. 16); appoint the list of the 15 individuals who will serve in the Panel of Experts. This other organization is entitled to monitor the provisions of the TSD chapter in accordance with the customary rules of interpretation of public international law and to issue to the parties an *ad interim* report, which will be a basis to discuss appropriate measures to be implemented considering the report and recommendations of the Panel of Experts (Art. 17).

Another criticality of TSD chapters is the role played by civil society (i.e., NGOs) in the monitoring of the related provisions, as its efficacious intervention is hampered by operational failings,[27] including the lack or scarce finan-

---

economic data related to the agreement, see https://policy.trade.ec.europa.eu/eu-trade-relationships-country-and-region/countries-and-regions/mercosur/eu-mercosur-agreement/brief_en.

25 Art. 4.3 Chapter on TSD.

26 L. Compa, 'Labor rights and labor standards in Transatlantic Trade and Investment negotiations: a US perspective' (2015) XLIX *Economia e Lavoro*, 2, 98, who talks about 'soft commitment to international labor standards'; T. Treu, 'Globalization and Human Rights: Social Clauses in Trade Agreements and International Exchanges among Companies', in A. Perulli and T. Treu (eds.), *Sustainable Development, Global Trade and Social Rights* (Wolters Kluwer: the Netherlands, 2018), p. 107; C. Scherrer, 'The Cover Assault on Labor by Mega-Regional Trade Agreements' (2016) 150 *Giornale di diritto del lavoro e di relazioni industriali*, 2, 353.

27 Let's take, as an example, the EU–South Korea agreement: the TSD chapter sets 'a Civil Society Forum in order to conduct a dialogue encompassing sustainable development aspects of trade relations between the Parties' whose functioning is highly bureaucratized and only with an advisory role. Indeed, the Civil Society Forum will meet once a year unless otherwise agreed by the parties; the Domestic Advisory Group(s) will select the representatives from its members in a balanced representation of relevant stake-

cial resources, the inadequateness of relationships with other bodies set in the TSD chapters and difficulties in obtaining representative members for civil society mechanisms.[28]

More in general, it is difficult, if not impossible, that purely promotional tools achieve the objective of ending violations of fundamental workers' rights,[29] which may occur not only in developing countries but also in developed ones: not to go too far, a paradigmatic case is represented by the vast proportions of labor exploitation, especially of workers from non-EU countries, in Italian agriculture, with real forms of reduction into slavery by organized crime.[30]

In any case, within a landscape where light and shadow coexist, the signing of a free trade agreement can lead EU trading partners to increase their standards of protection: indeed, Canada, after the signature of CETA, completed the process of ratification of all fundamental ILO conventions, except for Convention no. 155 on Occupational Safety and Health.[31] On the contrary, in the case of the EPA, Japan has ratified seven of these conventions, lacking Conventions no. 111 concerning Discrimination in respect of Employment and Occupation, no. 155 on Occupational Safety and Health and the 2014 Protocol to the 1930 Forced Labour Convention. It is significant that the Convention against Forced

---

holders (environmental, labor and business organizations as well as other relevant stakeholders). Finally, the parties (EU and South Korea) may only present an update on the implementation of TSD chapter to the Civil Society Forum. The views, opinions or findings of the Civil Society Forum can be submitted to the parties directly or through the Domestic Advisory groups. See Chapter 13, Art. 13.13.

28 Harrison, Barbu, Campling, Ebert, 'Labour Standard Provisions', 10.

29 S. Bologna, 'The Comprehensive Economic and Trade Agreement: What Kind of Space is Given to Fair Trade and Labour Rights?' (2017) 9 *Temilavoro.it*, 1, 4; A. Tyc, 'The European Union and Japan's', 24.

30 According to a survey carried out by FLAI-CGIL, the most representative Italian trade union in agriculture, in Southern Italy there are out of 280,000 illegal workers in all sectors, and almost 62,000 are illegal workers in agriculture; 47,000 of them are Italians and 14,000 foreign. Moreover, labor exploitation, especially in agriculture, is still a widespread phenomenon in Southern Italy. In the South, the highest number of investigations by labor exploitation is registered: 252 cases out of 432 at the national level have been documented between 2011 and 2023. See FLAI-CGIL, *Sicilia, campagna contro sfruttamento e caporalato in agricoltura*, 20 November 2024, www.flai.it.

31 In 2016 Canada ratified ILO Convention no. 138/1973 on Minimum Age; and in 2017 Convention no. 98/1949 on Right to organize and Collective Bargaining: see https://normlex.ilo.org/dyn/nrmlx_en/f?p=NORMLEXPUB:11200:0::NO::P11200_COUNTRY_ID:102582.

Labor was ratified only in 2022, 5 years after the signature of the EPA.[32] The EPA example shows how EU free trade agreements, although formally oriented towards full respect for human rights, cannot ignore political and historical-cultural factors,[33] which often compromise the effectiveness of fundamental workers' rights (at least under a Euro-centric perspective): according to current statistic data, Japan is one of the countries with the highest gender gap among developed economies.[34] Moreover, Japan has been unwilling for a long time to ratify the Convention against forced labor for the risks of claims for compensation from relatives of those, especially from South Korea, who were enslaved in the Second World War to work in heavy industry or were victims of sexual slavery.[35]

4 Workers' Rights and GSP Schemes: A Hard Law Approach (*à la carte*)

As briefly seen, in recent EU trade agreements labor provisions have been deepened, but they seriously risk not being an efficacious remedy in case of violation if we follow the dogmatic perspective of sanctions.[36] A scheme closer to the sphere of the sanction is represented by the Generalized Tariff Preferences (GSP), in force since 1971: the mechanism is not the result of bilateral or

32 The 1957 Convention on Forced Labour is in force in Japan since 22 July 2022: see https://normlex.ilo.org/dyn/nrmlx_en/f?p=1000:11300:0::NO:11300:P11300_INSTRUMENT_ID:312250.

33 F.C. Ebert, 'Labour provisions in EU trade agreements: What potential for channelling labour standards-related capacity building?' (2016) 155 *International Labour Review*, 3, 427; A. Perulli, The perspective of social clauses in international trade, Biblioteca '20 maggio', 2, 2018, 424.

34 According to the 2024 Global Gender Gap report, Japan is 118 of 146 countries studied in terms of gender equality, even up seven places from the previous year, while EU Member States float among the 2nd (Finland) and the 104th position (Czech Republic). See World Economic Forum, *Global Gender gap 2024. Insight report June 2024*, Cologne/Geneva, 2024, p. 32.

35 From 1931 to 1945, between 50,000 and 200,000 girls and young women, euphemistically known as 'comfort women', were forced into sexual servitude in Japanese military bro thels: see Columbia Law School-Center for Korean Legal Studies, *Military Sexual Slavery, 1931–1945*, https://kls.law.columbia.edu/content/military-sexual-slavery-1931-1945. In 2023 the Seoul High Court recognized South Korea's jurisdiction over the Japanese government because the women lived in the country and sought compensation for acts deemed 'unlawful': see https://www.bbc.com/news/world-asia-67512578.

36 A. Perulli, 'The perspective of social clauses in international trade treaties', in A. Perulli and V. Brino (eds.), *A global labour law: towards a new international framework for rights and justice* (Torino-Oxon: Giappichelli-Routledge, 2024), p. 182.

multilateral negotiations like trade agreements, but it represents a unilateral system.

GSP's core idea is to support developing countries through a 'carrot and stick' approach.[37] In short, a developing country may ask for special incentive arrangements by showing the ratification and the implementation of the ten fundamental conventions of the ILO. The EU may temporarily withdraw from the system of preferences of all or certain goods, if it results that the same goods have been made by the resort to slavery and labor prison or if ILO core conventions have been infringed.

The legal basis of the GSP is to be found not only in Arts. 21 TEU and 3 TFEU (see above para. 2) but also in the principles of the TFEU on development cooperation which follow a similar holistic approach: in particular, under Art. 208 'Union development cooperation shall be conducted within the framework of the principles and objectives of the Union's external action'; moreover, according to Art. 209 'The European Parliament and the Council … shall adopt measures necessary for the implementation of development-cooperation policy'.

The current rules on GSP are contained in Regulation no. 978/2012 in force since 1 January 2014, which establishes three different schemes: Standard GSP, GSP+, and Everything but Arms Arrangement (EBA).[38] The first scheme is reserved for the States that have not reached high or upper middle-income status and who agree to abide by ILO core conventions and most significant UN conventions on human rights.[39] GSP+ is devoted to GSP beneficiaries also deemed vulnerable due to the lack of a diversified export base and competitiveness in the EU internal market: the State must ratify and implement 27 international conventions on human rights and good governance.[40] The 2014 GSP+ reform established that countries, part of alternative trade agreements with the EU, would lose their GSP benefits.[41] Finally, the beneficiaries of EBA

37 M. Weiss, 'The EU Generalised Scheme of Preferences and the Special Incentive Arrangement for Sustainable Development and Good Governance', in Perulli and Treu (eds.), 'Sustainable development', p. 122.

38 In November 2023 the application of current GSP regulation was extended until December 2027, pending the approval of a reviewed GSP legal framework by the European Parliament and the Council of the EU: see www.trade.ec.europa.eu.

39 These are the conventions on the prevention and the punishment of genocide; on the elimination of all forms of racial discrimination; on civil and political rights; on the rights of the child; on the elimination of all the forms of discrimination against women.

40 These are the conventions on the fight against corruption and on the control of illegal drugs; the seven UN conventions on human rights; the ten ILO conventions on core labor standards; other UN conventions, most of them on environment protection and sustainability.

41 For instance, in 2016 Costa Rica, Panama, Peru and El Salvador lost their GSP+ benefits.

are least-developed countries with full duty-free and quota-free access, with the sole exception of arms and ammunition.

If we dwell upon the sanction profile, the common feature of the three schemes is that all preferential arrangements may be withdrawn on a temporary basis having regard to all or some categories of goods produced in a beneficiary country for the violations contained in Regulation no. 978/2012 (Arts. 19–21): i.e., the serious and systematic infringement of principles and rights enshrined in core UN and ILO conventions, or the export of goods result of prison labor, or if serious shortcomings in customs controls on transit and export of drugs are observed. In addition, in the case of GSP+, under the Regulation, the Commission is entitled to monitor the situation in the third country having regard to the 'status of ratification of the relevant conventions and shall monitor their effective implementation, as well as cooperation with relevant monitoring bodies …' (Art. 13): this continuous reporting is possible essentially, by drawing on *dossier* produced by relevant international panels of experts (i.e., the ILO Committee of Experts on the Application of Conventions and Recommendations).

At first glance, ordinary EU legislation concretizes treaties' approach to global trade, where the linkage between free competition and social justice has, as criteria of evaluation, international public law standards. However, in terms of effectiveness, the 'carrot and stick' philosophy of GSP schemes is contradictory and presents pros and cons:[42] the measure, animated by the noble intention to implement a model of fair trade, has without a doubt contributed to increase the respect of fundamental labor rights in several developing countries, especially for women, according to the periodical reports of the European Commission and of the ILO.[43] Moreover, the monitoring system is anchored in objective data recognized by the international community, or the 'case law' of the different monitoring bodies of the ILO and the UN, showing the trust of the EU towards a pluralistic approach to human rights which, otherwise, would run the risk to be considered Eurocentric.

In the meantime, all GSP schemes may represent a competitive disadvantage for beneficiaries: indeed, the third country is not obliged to adhere to GSP, by accepting monitoring mechanisms and a possible exclusion from trade benefits. Moreover, in terms of *Law in Action*, the EU has rarely with-

42 A. Tyc, 'The US' and the EU's general system of preferences: a comparison in the context of workers' rights' (2020) 27 *Studies on Labour Law and Social Policy*, 2, 120 et seq.

43 This is the case of Pakistan, country beneficiary of GSP+ scheme: according to an ILO study, child labor has decreased from 4.02 million in 2014 to 3.03 million in 2021. The gender wage gap has reduced from 42 per cent in 2014 to 18 per cent in 2021. See ILO, *GSP+ and compliance. Pakistan's Case (2014–23)*, 2023, VIII, www.ilo.org.

drawn from GSP schemes: i.e., on 12 February 2020, the Commission decided to withdraw part of the tariff preferences granted to Cambodia under the EBA trade arrangement due to serious and systematic violations of the human rights principles enshrined in the International Covenant on Civil and Political Rights.[44] In addition, in 2010, Venezuela was excluded from GSP+ and degraded to GSP due to its failure to ratify the UN Convention against corruption and therefore lost its GSP+ status permanently;[45] finally, in 2007, Belarus was sanctioned for non-compliance with the Convention on freedom of association and collective bargaining.[46]

More broadly, it is not automatic that a withdrawal from the scheme will imply a significant change in human rights standards. Most scholars have highlighted that the EU makes a discretionary resort to GSP schemes, with the aim to pursue political goals instead of the strict promotion of fundamental labor rights in the global economic scenery. The EU should apply negative conditionality on more cases and towards more GSP beneficiaries. Indeed, the EU has applied GSP sanctions only against small developing countries; on the contrary, if violations have taken place in bigger States (i.e., India or Indonesia), which are regional or global geopolitical actors, the EU has not raised tariffs as a form of punishment.

The reasons for the scarce use of GSP sanctions are not only political, but they are also related to general principles of international trade law: multilateral trade rules limit the possibility of the EU punishing developing countries for their lack of engagement in promoting and respecting fundamental labor rights. More precisely, Art. XXIV GATT establishes that trading partners are obliged to 'eliminate duties and other restrictive regulations of commerce with respect to substantially all trade in products originating in the constituents of the agreement'. Even though it is not easy to define 'substantially all' trade barriers, there is a default limitation regarding negative conditionality mechanisms such as GSP.[47]

---

44 See https://circabc.europa.eu/ui/group/f243659e-26f5-44d9-8213-81efa3d92dc7/library/02ab82d2-6152-46f4-9b00-a95c950d386d/details.

45 Commission Decision 2009/454 of 11 June 2009 amending Decision 2008/938 on the list of the beneficiary countries which qualify for the special incentive arrangement for sustainable development and good governance, provided for in Council Regulation (EC) no. 732/2008 applying a scheme of generalized tariff preferences for the period from 1 January 2009 to 31 December 2011 (OJ L 149, 12.6.2009, p. 78).

46 European Parliament Research Service, *Human rights in EU trade policies. Unilateral measures applied by the EU*, 5 May 2018, www.europarl.europa.eu.

47 I. Bochert, P. Conconi, M. Di Ubaldo, C. Herghelegiu, 'The Pursuit of Non-Trade Policy Objectives in EU Trade Policy' (2021) 20 *World Trade Review*, 641.

5 The ISDS Clause and the 'Soft' Version of the Investor Court System: The Persistent Risks for Workers' Rights

In international trade law, one of the most controversial institutions regarding the enforcement of human rights is represented by the Investor–State Dispute Settlement (ISDS) clause. In brief, this mechanism provides foreign investors, essentially multinational corporations, the right to call for arbitration against a State when the company believes that the domestic government (host State) has violated a treaty, complaining about an infringement of international law principles in favour of investments (e.g., the fair and equitable treatment; the put in practice of a legislative or administrative measure representing an indirect expropriation). At the end of the judgement, the arbitral panel may order public compensation mostly on behalf of multinational corporations.[48]

The risk of privatization of the general interest expressed by a political community is maximum: the State (or the EU) – if condemned by the arbitral panel – normally will pay a huge fee for the damage to the interests of the claimant, also including the cost of arbitration swinging among 1,000 $ and 3,000 $ per hour.[49] The functioning of an ISDS complaint is entirely submitted to the logic of private law due to the secrecy of the proceedings, the mutual recognition between the contractors and the recruitment of lawyers and arbitrators from only a few international law firms. In addition, the impartiality of ISDS tribunal decisions is more than dubious: according to the current procedure of annulment of the International Centre for Settlement of Investment Disputes (henceforth ICSID), a review of the merit is not allowed, unless in case of irregular constitution or corruption of the arbitral tribunal, manifest abuse of power, failure to state reasons for the award and serious departure from fundamental procedural rules. Since the 2000s, the number of ISDS complaints has significantly increased and has also interested developed countries:[50] it has been estimated that by the end of 2012 500 of them are pending, with EU and US companies leading such a trend.

48 On the functioning and rationales of ISDS, and on related entrenched barriers for human rights claims, see N.J. Diamond, K.A.N. Duggal, 'Adding New Ingredients to an Old Recipe: do ISDS Reforms and New Investment Treaties Support Human Rights?' (2021) 53 *Case Western Reserve Journal of International Law*, 120–133; B. Pérez de la Heras, 'The European Union in International Investment Governance: a Hybrid Approach to Dispute Settlement' (2019) 18 *Romanian Journal of European Affairs*, 2, 83–84.

49 Scherrer, 'The Cover Assault on Labour', 351; Transnational Institute, *ISDS in numbers. Impact of Investment Arbitration against Latin America and the Caribbean*, October 2024, p. 6, www.tni.org.

50 Unctad, Investor-State Dispute Settlement: Review of Developments in 2017, www.investmentpolicy.unctad.org.

In recent times, there have been at least four cases showing how the ISDS clause could negatively impact workers' rights. The first one is *Veolia Propreté v. Egypt*,[51] which occurred in the wake of the Arab Spring: in 2012 Veolia, a French multinational, contested through the ISDS clause the raise made by Egypt of minimum wage from 400 to 700 liras per month on the basis of the infringement of the private–public agreement between Veolia and Egypt for waste disposal and asked for damage compensation of USD 110 million. Veolia contested that the increase in minimum wage erased its profitability in waste-water services because it could not transfer the unforeseen higher labor cost to consumers.[52]

Mention must also be made of the 2009 case *Centerra v. Kyrgyz Republic*:[53] Centerra, a Canadian company operating in the gold mining sector, claimed that the legislative raise of the salary for high-altitude workers in Kyrgyzstan entailed an unexpected increase in production costs. Eventually, in *Achmea v. Slovakian Republic*[54] the Dutch insurance company Achmea was granted USD 25 million as a compensatory measure for a Slovakian bill limiting the chance for private health companies to distribute their gains. Only in a 2013 ISDS case, labor reasons prevailed over free trade: the same Achmea resorted to international arbitration to stop Slovakian draft legislation introducing a unique universal health insurance scheme. The arbitral panel stated that «the design and implementation of its public health policy is for the State alone to assess».[55]

All these cases clearly show how procedural rules contained in mega-treaties could be easily invoked by foreign investors to change labor law indirectly: States could retrench from an improving intervention in the fields of welfare and social rights,[56] unless they run the risk of having to pay out large amounts of compensation. In addition, they demonstrate how the ISDS model is totally opposite to the paradigm of liberal democracies, which concretizes

---

51 Veolia Propreté v. Arab Republic of Egypt (ICSID Case No. ARB/12/15), www.investmentpolicy.unctad.org.

52 G. Celi, 'How Beneficial is TTIP for EU Countries? Economic Gains and Social Costs of an Ambitious Project' (2015) XLIX *Economia e Lavoro*, 2, 29.

53 Centerra Gold Inc. and Kumtor Gold Company v. Kyrgiz Republic (I), PCA Case No. 2007-01/AA278, www.italaw.com.

54 Achmea B.V. v. Slovak Republic, UNCITRAL, PCA Case No. 2008-13 (formerly Eureko B.V. v. Slovak Republic), www.italaw.com.

55 Achmea B.V. v. The Slovak Republic, UNCITRAL, PCA Case No. 2013-12 (Number 2), www.italaw.com.

56 Faioli, 'The Quest for a New Generation', 108.

general political interests in a transparent way and in compliance with the principles of the rule of law.[57]

In the last decade, the European Union has tried to reform the ISDS mechanism in its free trade agreements, at least on the procedural side. It has introduced numerous corrections in the name of the principles of transparency and impartiality[58] outcome of the post-French Revolution European legal tradition. The model is essentially based on three pillars: independence of the members of the panel, fairness of proceedings and equitable balance among rights and obligations of the parties. Since the failed negotiations of the TTIP with the US administration,[59] the EU has proposed the creation of an International Court System (henceforth ICS) formalized in the treaties signed with Canada (CETA) and Vietnam: in both agreements, ICS is characterized by a two-tier judicial structure (Tribunal of First Instance and Appeal Tribunal), its members are not selected on a case-by-case basis by the signatory parties, but they are chosen within a mandatory roster of ICS adjudicators who will be assigned impartially to disputes.[60] Moreover, the CETA Joint Committee and the EU–Vietnam Trade Committee will fix their fees daily.[61] The strongest procedural guarantees relate to possible grounds for appeal of the decision issued at first instance: as a more favourable provision than those under Art. 52 of the ICSID Convention, a decision of the Tribunal may be appealed even if the same Tribunal has erred in the appreciation of the facts (including EU and domestic legislation and administrative praxis).[62]

The procedural rules seem to follow the same path as the substantial ones: the agreements with Canada and Vietnam emphatically affirm 'the right to regulate' or 'the public interest of the State to legislate'.[63] The reasons for distributive justice would have justified a much less nuanced wording: the Treaties could have provided that the domestic changes to labor, employment and social security law can never represent an indirect expropriation or a discriminatory measure (i.e., the introduction of a basic income, of reinstate-

57 M. Di Pietro, 'Il TTIP (Partenariato Transatlantico per il Commercio e gli Investimenti) e la Cooperazione Normativa' (2015) XLIX *Economia e Lavoro*, 2, 129.

58 V. Cagnin, 'New Generations Treaties and the Attempts for a Renewal of the ISDS', in Perulli and Treu (eds.), 'Sustainable development', p. 153.

59 See above note 18.

60 Arts. 29.8 and 29.7 CETA; Art. 15.23 EU–Vietnam agreement.

61 Art. 12.14 and Art. 13.14 EU–Vietnam agreement; Arts. 8.27.12 and 8.28D CETA.

62 Art. 28.1 EU–Vietnam agreement; Art. 16.2 CETA.

63 Chapter 23, Art. 23.2 – Right to regulate and levels of protection of CETA; Chapter 13, Art. 13.3 of EU–Vietnam FTA.

ment as a general technique of protection against unfair dismissals, and the abolition of the opting-out clause in the architecture of industrial relations). Or, more simply, they could have established that social matters are excluded from the ICS mechanism and are only referred to domestic and regional courts (i.e., the European Court of Justice). In this regard, the most troublesome issue, in compliance with CETA and the EU–Vietnam Agreement, is the interpretation of EU law relevant to solve the dispute: EU law is considered a matter of fact, with serious risks arising from the neo-liberal interpretation of the European Court of Justice (hereinafter ECJ) in some 'sensitive' issues, such as the right to strike[64] or collective dismissals.[65]

Finally, the ICS seems to be in sharp contrast with EU treaties regarding the prerogatives of the same ECJ: under Art. 19 TEU the ECJ is the unique organization institutionally entitled to 'ensure that in the interpretation and application of the Treaties the law is observed'; moreover, under Art. 344 TFEU 'Member States undertake not to submit a dispute concerning the interpretation or application of the Treaties to any method of settlement other than those provided for therein'.

Among the EU Member States a broad consensus on the neoliberal paradigm can be observed, whereby even the matter of fundamental rights can be subject to an arbitration clause, with the sole opposition of Belgium. The State, contrary to the signature of CETA, submitted to the ECJ a request of opinion on the legitimacy of the ICS mechanism with the exclusive competence of the ECJ to provide the definitive interpretation of EU law, the principle of equality and the right to impartially and independently go to courts. The ECJ, by following a favourable opinion of the Advocate General,[66] ruled definitively that ICS contained in CETA is compatible with EU law.[67]

64 This is the case of the so-called 'Laval Quartet'.

65 See, i.e., the AGET Iraklis case: ECJ 21 December 2019, C-201/15, *Anonimi Geneki Etaria Tsimenton Iraklis* (*Aget Iraklis*). In the view of the ECJ, Council Directive 98/59/EC of 20 July 1998 on collective redundancies must be interpreted as not precluding national legislation under which, if there is no agreement with the workers' representatives on projected collective redundancies, an employer can effect such redundancies only if the competent national public authority, which must be notified of the projected collective redundancies, does not adopt, within the period prescribed by that legislation, the situation of the undertaking and the interests of the national economy, a reasoned decision not to authorize some or all of the projected redundancies.

66 Opinion delivered on 29 January 2019.

67 ECJ, 30 April 2019, Opinion 1/17, EU–Canada CETA Agreement.

6 Concluding Remarks: A Contradictory Panorama

Labor provisions in EU free trade agreements have widened and deepened over the past decade for several factors: the stronger influence of the European Parliament, due to its institutional strengthening in development policies since the Treaty on European Union which came into force in 1993; path dependencies stemming from the EU's previous template; the need to gain public support by the EU institutions in the face of criticism of free trade agreements.[68] The EU has signed agreements not only with developing countries but also with peer-to-peer economies such as South Korea, Singapore, Canada and Japan to create a global-level playing field based on the respect of fundamental workers' rights as enshrined in ILO core conventions and Fundamental declarations. All the treaties of the 'new generation' include a TSD chapter, which emphasizes the mutual respect for basic labor rights and establishes cooperative mechanisms of monitoring violations with the intervention of *ad hoc* committees and the involvement of civil society.

In any case, the analysis does not want to overstate the importance of the linkage between fundamental social rights and global trade in the current EU external trade policy: indeed, even in countries considered politically and/or economically more similar to the Member States of the European Union, the investment treaties are not able to ensure that labor rights will be maintained without bottom-down changes, or that there will be an automatic convergence of labor legislations of the involved regional systems, due to their different historical and political patterns. Let's take the Japanese case as an example: EPA TSD chapter states that 'The parties … recognise that the purpose of this Chapter is to strengthen the trade relations and cooperation between the Parties in ways that promote sustainable development, and it is not to harmonise the environment or labour standards of the parties' (Art. 16). Indeed, the Japanese system greatly differs from the European ones in both labor and employment law: industrial relations in the private sector are highly decentralized, as collective bargaining mainly takes place at company level; in addition, under the Japanese civil code the employer may freely dismiss the worker without reasons, even if in practice courts have introduced several limitations on the employers' dismissal rights.[69] We should not confine ourselves to a Eurocentric approach, which claims to easily incorporate the Western theory

68 A. Burni, B. Erforth, N. Keijzeer, 'Global Europe? The new EU external action instrument and the European Parliament' (2021) 7 *Global Affairs*, 4, 472–474.

69 A. Riccobono and S. Bologna, 'Commercio globale e diritto del lavoro: l'accordo di libero scambio UE-Giappone' (2019) 162 *Giornale di diritto del lavoro e di relazioni industriali*, 2, 362; Tyc, 'The European Union and Japan's Partnership Agreement', 23.

and practice of social rights in other domestic realities, with different cultural and anthropological prerequisites.

In wider terms – even if the essay does not underestimate the difficulties along the way ahead and refuses to offer simplifications – contemporary neoliberal tendencies, to deregulate labor law in the interest of market needs, are becoming more and more dominant everywhere.[70] This raises questions about the real scope of the social clause in free trade agreements, especially if we consider the sanction as part of a legal system: this perspective is perhaps more appropriate to the scholar who deals with national labor law but represents a defined criterion to distinguish the legal norm from moral or social ones.[71] For instance, if we consider the CETA, maybe the most advanced in the field of human rights promotion, it is true that the treaty contains additional clauses to monitor workers' rights: there are more detailed provisions on the health and safety of workers, and more analytical requirements for the enforcement of labor rights at national level (labor inspections, judicial interventions). However, such clauses do not deviate from the traditional soft law approach, and their effectiveness is totally dependent on the goodwill of the parties.[72]

The absence of *stricto sensu* sanctioning mechanisms reproposes the historical opposition between 'strong commercial power' and 'poor labor law' in free trade agreements to which the European Union is part and, more generally, in international trade law, similarly to a Grosz cartoon on the dialectic between capital and labor. The maximum contradiction is represented by the ISDS clause: the EU has tried to bypass the criticism towards the arbitral mechanisms with the creation of the ICS in some of its treaties, whose members are more independent and with deeper powers on the appreciation of the concrete circumstances. Unfortunately, complaints on the violation of TSD chapters are excluded from the dispute settlement mechanisms, as the same TSD chapters contain only soft law mechanisms, a hybrid of governmental consultation and the intervention of a panel of experts and civil society. In other words, the treaties do not contemplate the possibility for NGOs or trade unions to bring an action against a multinational corporation or a state infringing core labor standards. The lack of credible enforcement mech-

70 P. Alston, 'Labour Rights as Human Rights: The Not So Happy State of the Art', in Id. (ed.), 'Labour Rights as Human Rights', p. 11; A. Supiot, 'Justice sociale et libéralisation du commerce international' (2009) *Droit social*, 2, 133.

71 N. Bobbio, *Teoria generale del diritto* (Torino: Giappichelli, 1993), p. 128.

72 T. Treu, 'Globalization and Human Rights', p. 105; M. Bronckers, G. Gruni, 'Taking the enforcement of Labour Standards in the EU's Free Trade Agreements Seriously' (2019) 56 *Common Market Law Review*, p. 1592.

anism makes highly difficult, in several cases, compliance with TSD chapter regulations.[73]

The legal framework is not rosier when considering mechanisms out of free trade agreements and reserved only to developing countries: the EU resorts to GSP schemes mainly to reach foreign policy goals, rather than safeguard basic labor rights, and EU withdrawal from preferential benefits covers only small States.

EU strategy does not seem destined to change if we analyse the agreement recently reached between the EU and some Mercosur States: without a doubt, it is positive that the treaty reaffirms the parties' right to fix their own policies deemed appropriate and – especially – it lays down the non-regression clause, since it forbids a reduction in standards with the aim of encouraging trade or investment.[74] However, it is undeniable that labor provisions primarily serve as a moral commitment than a fully enforceable legal one.[75] Also this treaty is perfectly in line with the philosophy of international trade of the European Commission very well embedded in the non-paper[76] presented in 2017 for the reform of TSD chapters:[77] there was a first option in favour of the traditional approach based on dialogue and cooperation contained in agreements in force; and another one aimed to create a TSD section with sanctions, inspired by the US model. In a second non-paper, published in 2018,[78] the EU Commission abandoned any proposal of reform, as it envisaged a set of actions to 'revamp the TSD chapters' such as *inter alia*, the commitment to better dia-

73 A. Marx, F. Ebert, N. Hachez, 'Dispute Settlement for Labour Provisions in EU Free Trade Agreements. Rethinking Current Approaches' (2017) 5 *Politics and Governance*, 4, 50; Harrison, Barbu, Campling, Ebert, 'Labour Standards provisions in EU Free Trade Agreements', 11.

74 See Art. 2 TSD chapter EU-MERCOSUR FTA.

75 L. Pantaleo, F. Seatzu, 'Protecting Workers' Rights and Freedoms Under the EU-MERCOSUR Trade Agreement: a Dream Coming True?' (2023) *Il diritto dell'Unione Europea*, 2–3, 280. I.e., all TSD disputes end with the issue of a non-mandatory dossier with mere recommendations to the parties for the resolution of the matter. Moreover, the Committee will only 'monitor the follow-up of the report' (Art. 17.9 TSD chapter): this means that the follow-up will be based only on mutual political cooperation, and it won't be possible the award of compensatory measures in cases of protracted violations.

76 A non-paper is a document basis for discussion without an automatic commitment to a public position on certain matters: therefore, non-papers do not represent official publications of EU institutions.

77 European Commission, 'Non-paper of the Commission services Trade and Sustainable Development (TSD) Chapters in EU Free Trade Agreements (FTAs)', 11 July 2017, 2.

78 European Commission, 'Feedback and Way Forward on Improving the Implementation and Enforcement of Trade and Sustainable Development Chapters in EU Free Trade Agreements', 26 February 2018.

logue with relevant stakeholders; a closer partnership with the EU institutions, Member States and international organizations; and a 'more assertive enforcement' of obligations contained in TSD chapter, including increased monitoring of commitments.

In 2022 the EU Commission proposed a broad reform of TSD chapters in FTAs, which should include: the extension of the general state-to-state dispute settlement compliance stage to the TSD chapter; and the possibility to apply trade sanctions in cases of failure to comply with obligations that materially defeats the object and purpose of the Paris Agreement on Climate Change or in serious instances of non-compliance with the ILO fundamental principles and rights at work. Moreover, also in 2022 the same EU Commission tried to negotiate with Mercosur an addendum to TSD chapter which also included sanctions.[79] But words have not been yet followed by deeds.[80]

References

Alston, P. 'Labour Rights as Human Rights: the Not so Happy State of the Art', in Id. (ed.), *Labour Rights as Human Rights* (Oxford: Oxford University Press, 2005), pp. 1–24.

Bobbio, N., *Teoria generale del diritto* (Torino: Giappichelli, 1993).

Bochert, I., Conconi, P., Di Ubaldo, M., Herghelegiu, C. 'The Pursuit of Non-Trade Policy Objectives in EU Trade Policy' (2021) 20 *World Trade Review*, pp. 623–647.

Bologna, S. 'The Comprehensive Economic and Trade Agreement: What Kind of Space is Given to Fair Trade and Labour Rights?' (2017), 9 *Temilavoro.it*, 1, pp. 1–12.

Bronckers, M., Gruni, G. 'Taking the enforcement of Labour Standards in the EU's Free Trade Agreements Seriously' (2019) 56 *Common Market Law Review*, pp. 1591–1622.

Burni, A., Erforth, B., Keijzeer, N., 'Global Europe? The new EU external action instrument and the European Parliament' (2021) 7 *Global Affairs*, 4, pp. 471–485.

Cagnin, V. 'New Generations Treaties and the Attempts for a Renewal of the ISDS', in A. Perulli and T. Treu (eds.), *Sustainable development, Global Trade and Social Rights* (Wolters Kluwer: the Netherlands: 2018), pp. 155–168.

Celi, G. 'How Beneficial is TTIP for EU Countries? Economic Gains and Social Costs of an Ambitious Project' (2015) XLIX *Economia e Lavoro*, 2, pp. 11–34.

---

79 The text of the addendum has never been published, though it was admittedly leaked to the press: C. Gijs, S. Lynch, *Von der Leyen Vows to Conclude EU-Mercosur Deal by Year-End*, 12 June 2023, available at www.politico.eu.

80 European Commission, 'The power of trade partnership: together for green and just economic growth', Brussels, 22.6.2022, COM(2022) 409 final, 12.

Columbia Law School-Center for Korean Legal Studies, *Military Sexual Slavery, 1931–1945*, https://kls.law.columbia.edu/content/military-sexual-slavery-1931-1945'.

Compa, L. 'Labor rights and labor standards in Transatlantic Trade and Investment negotiations: a US perspective' (2015) XLIX *Economia e Lavoro*, 2, pp. 87–102.

Diamond, N.J., Duggal, K.A.N. 'Adding New Ingredients to an Old Recipe: do ISDS Reforms and New Investment Treaties Support Human Rights?' (2021) 53 *Case Western Reserve Journal of International Law*, pp. 117–162.

Ebert, F.C. 'Labour provisions in EU trade agreements: What potential for channelling labour standards-related capacity building?' (2016) 155 *International Labour Review*, 3, pp. 407–433.

Erne, R., Stan, S., Szabò, I., Maccarrone, V., *Politicising Commodification. European Governance and Labour Politics from the Financial Crisis to the Covid Emergency* (Cambridge: Cambridge University Press, 2024).

European Commission, 'Feedback and Way Forward on Improving the Implementation and Enforcement of Trade and Sustainable Development Chapters in EU Free Trade Agreements', 26 February 2018.

European Commission, 'The power of trade partnership: together for green and just economic growth', Brussels, 22.6.2022, COM(2022) 409 final.

European Parliament Research Service, *Human rights in EU trade policies. Unilateral measures applied by the EU*, 5 May 2018, www.europarl.europa.eu.

Faioli, M. 'The Quest for a New Generation of Labor Chapter in the TTIP' (2015) XLIX *Economia e Lavoro*, 2, pp. 103–120.

FLAI-CGIL, *Sicilia, campagna contro sfruttamento e caporalato in agricoltura*, 20 November 2024, www.flai.it.

Giubboni, S., *Diritti sociali e mercato: la dimensione sociale dell'integrazione europea* (Bologna: il Mulino, 2003).

C. Gijs, S. Lynch, *Von der Leyen Vows to Conclude EU-Mercosur Deal by Year-End*, 12 June 2023, www.politico.eu.

Harrison, J., Barbu, M., Campling, L., Ebert, F.C. 'Labour Standards Provisions in EU Free Trade Agreements: Reflections on the European Commission's Reform Agenda' (2018) 18 *World Trade Review*, 4, pp. 635–657.

Kenner, J. 'Economic Partnership Agreements: Enhancing the Labour Dimension of Global Governance?', in B. Van Vorren, S. Blovkmans, J. Wouters (eds.), *The EU's role in Global Governance* (Oxford: Oxford University Press, 2013), pp. 306–322.

Kuang, S. 'The European Commission's Discourses on Sustainable Development in 'Trade for All': An argumentative Perspective' (2021) 26 *European Foreign Affairs Review*, 2, pp. 265–288.

ILO, *GSP+ and compliance. Pakistan's Case (2014–23)*, 2023, www.ilo.org.

Mancini, G.F. 'Intervento', in Vv.A.a., *Atti del convegno di Parma del 30–31 ottobre 1985* (Padova: Cedam, 1988), pp. 26–39.

Marx, A., Ebert, F., Hachez, N. 'Dispute Settlement for Labour Provisions in EU Free Trade Agreements. Rethinking Current Approaches' (2017) 5 *Politics and Governance*, 4, pp. 49–59.

Novitz, T. 'The European Union and International Labour Standards: the Dynamics of Dialogue between the EU and the ILO', in P. Alston (ed.), *Labour Rights as Human Rights* (Oxford: Oxford University Press, 2005), pp. 214–242.

Novitz, T. 'Challenges When Combining Labour and Environmental Objectives: Trade and Sustainable Development Chapters and Beyond', in A. Perulli, T. Treu (eds.) *Labour Law and Climate Change* (Wolters Kluwer: The Netherlands, 2023), pp. 87–108.

Oehri, M. 'Labour Rights Promotion in the Absence of Conditionality? How the EU and the US Engage China and India' (2017) 22 *European Foreign Affairs Review*, 1, pp. 137–156.

Pantaleo, L., Seatzu, F. 'Protecting Workers' Rights and Freedoms Under the EU-MERCOSUR Trade Agreement: a Dream Coming True?' (2023) *Il diritto dell'Unione Europea*, 2–3, pp. 278–304.

Pérez de la Heras, B. 'The European Union in International Investment Governance: a Hybrid Approach to Dispute Settlement' (2019) 18 *Romanian Journal of European Affairs*, 2, pp. 77–93.

Perulli, A. 'Diritti sociali fondamentali e regolazione del mercato nell'azione esterna dell'Unione Europea' (2013) LXIV *Rivista giuridica del lavoro e della previdenza sociale*, I, pp. 321–345.

Perulli, A. 'Fundamental Social Rights, Market Regulation and EU External Action' (2014) 30 *International Journal of Comparative Labour Law*, 1, pp. 27–47.

Perulli, A., *The Declaration of Philadelphia, WP C.S.D.L.E. 'Massimo D'Antona'.INT -143/2018*, pp. 39–54.

Perulli, A. 'The perspective of social clauses in international trade', Biblioteca '20 maggio', 2, 2018, pp. 370–440.

Perulli, A. 'Towards a Green Labour Law', in A. Perulli and T. Treu (eds.), *Labour Law and Climate Change. Towards a Just Transition* (The Netherlands: Wolters Kluwer, 2023), pp. 1–23.

Perulli, A. 'the Perspective of Social Clauses in International Trade Treaties', in A. Perulli and V. Brino (eds.), *A global labour law: towards a new international framework for rights and justice* (Torino-Oxon: Giappichelli-Routledge, 2024), pp. 111–190.

Riccobono, A., Bologna, S. 'Commercio globale e diritto del lavoro: l'accordo di libero scambio UE-Giappone' (2019) 162 *Giornale di diritto del lavoro e di relazioni industriali*, 2, pp. 355–383.

Robin-Olivier, S. 'The relationship between international law and European labour legislation and its impact on the development of international and European social law' (2020) 159 *International Labour Review*, 4, pp. 483–503.

Scherrer, C. 'The Cover Assault on Labor by Mega-Regional Trade Agreements' (2016) 150 *Giornale di diritto del lavoro e di relazioni industriali*, 2, pp. 343–363.

Seifert, A. 'European economic governance and Labor Laws of the E.U. Member States' (2014) 35 *Comparative labor law and policy journal*, 3, pp. 311–330.

Servais, J.M., *International Labour Law* (The Netherlands: Wolters Kluwer, 2020).

Supiot, A., *Homo juridicus. Saggio sulla funzione antropologica del diritto* (Milano: Bruno Mondadori, 1996).

Supiot, A. 'Justice sociale et libéralisation du commerce international' (2009) *Droit social*, 2, pp. 131–141.

Sykes A.O., 'Regulatory Protectionism and the Law of International Trade' (1999) 66 *The University of Chicago Law Review*, 1, pp. 1–46". (see footnote no. 6).

Transnational Institute, *ISDS in numbers. Impact of Investment Arbitration against Latin America and the Caribbean*, October 2024, www.tni.org.

Treu, T. 'Globalization and Human Rights: Social Clauses in Trade Agreements and in International Exchanges among Companies', in A. Perulli and T. Treu (eds.), *Sustainable development, Global Trade and Social Rights* (Wolters Kluwer: the Netherlands, 2018), pp. 99–120.

Tyc, A. 'The linkage between labour standards and international trade: how to offset the global inequality?' (2019) *Wroclaw Review of Law, Administration and Economics*, 9, 1, pp. 58–74.

Tyc, A. 'The European Union and Japan's Economic Partnership Agreement: labour provisions under the 'Trade and Sustainable Development Chapter' (2020) 10 *Juridical Tribune*, Special Issue, pp. 20–31.

Tyc, A. 'The US' and the EU's general system of preferences: a comparison in the context of workers' rights' (2020) 27 *Studies on Labour Law and Social Policy*, 2, pp. 115–124.

Van Den Putte, L., Orbie, J. 'EU Bilateral Trade Agreements and the Surprising Rise of Labour Provisions' (2015) 31 *International Journal of Comparative Labour Law*, 3, pp. 263–283.

Weiss, M. 'The EU Generalised Scheme of Preferences and the Special Incentive Arrangement for Sustainable Development and Good Governance', in A. Perulli and T. Treu (eds.), *Sustainable development, Global Trade and Social Rights* (Wolters Kluwer: the Netherlands, 2018), pp. 121–127.

World Economic Forum, *Global Gender gap 2024. Insight report June 2024*, (Cologne/Geneva: 2024).

CHAPTER 6

Strengthening the Implementation and Monitoring of Labour Rights Commitments in EU Free Trade Agreements: What Role for Roadmaps?

Axel Marx and Angela María Vanegas Pérez

1 Introduction

In 2011, the European Union (EU) introduced a new generation of free trade agreements (FTA) with a trade and sustainable development (TSD) chapter whose aim is to ensure a level playing field for social and environmental protection and enhance compliance with international labour standards set by the International Labour Organization (ILO). Research has examined the effectiveness of these chapters and their labour rights provisions, revealing shortcomings in the EU approach in relation to implementation, monitoring, and enforcement. More detailed roadmaps or action plans, to complement existing monitoring instruments, have been proposed as a solution to address these shortcomings. The use of roadmaps should improve the effectiveness of trade and sustainable development chapters by requiring partner countries to submit detailed plans of action regarding ILO conventions, outlining specific measures for implementation, including clear benchmarks and deadlines. The application of the roadmaps approach has already been tested in some cases outside the EU.

This chapter systematically reviews the international experience with roadmaps and similar plans of action for improving compliance by countries with ILO conventions included in EU Free Trade Agreements. Using a comparative case study method, similarities and differences between the roadmaps, as well as possibilities and limitations to the use of roadmaps to strengthen implementation and monitoring, are identified. In total, seven roadmaps (or plans of action) are analysed. On the one hand, the chapter focuses on the cases of Bangladesh and Guatemala for which several action plans or roadmaps related to non-compliance with ILO conventions have been developed. For Bangladesh, three roadmaps have been identified, namely (1) the Sustainability Compact for the Bangladesh Ready Made Garment (RMG) Sector, (2) the roadmap

 | HTTPS://DOI.ORG/10.1163/9789004762251-007

of actions to address all the outstanding issues mentioned in the complaint concerning non-observance by Bangladesh of the Labour Inspection Convention (No. 81), Freedom of Association and Protection of the Right to Organise Convention (No. 87), and the Right to Organise and Collective Bargaining Convention (No. 98), and (3) the National Action Plan on the Labour Sector (2021–2026). For Guatemala, the roadmap adopted with the ILO address violations of Convention No. 87 on Freedom of Association.

On the other hand, three action plans adopted in the context of free trade and bilateral agreements are also assessed. These include (1) the US–Colombia Labour Action Plan (adopted in 2011 to facilitate the adoption by the Congress of the US–Colombia FTA); (2) the Enforcement Plan for Guatemala and the Action Plan for Honduras, both adopted under the US-CAFTA-DR; and (3) the Action Plan under the Canada–Colombia Agreement on Labour Cooperation.

All identified relevant roadmaps and plans of action focus on addressing non-compliance with specific ILO conventions, most notably the Freedom of Association and Protection of the Right to Organise Convention, 1948 (No. 87), and the Right to Organise and Collective Bargaining Convention, 1949 (No. 98). These roadmaps do not follow a fixed template but contain several common elements in relation to the *triggers* for the roadmap, the *provisions contained* in a roadmap, the *structure* in terms of broad goals and concrete actions, timelines, implementation of the roadmap, and support for the implementation of the roadmap. The chapter will provide an overview and discussion of the different approaches and draw implications for the use of roadmaps in the context of EU free trade agreements.

The chapter will be structured as follows. Section 2 will review the literature on the current approach to and effectiveness of labour rights protection in EU trade agreements. This review will identify weaknesses related to implementing and monitoring labour rights commitments in EU free trade agreements and introduce potential solutions to address these weaknesses. Next, the chapter will focus on one of the proposed solutions – roadmaps and action plans – and provide a comparative analysis of existing roadmaps and action plans. First, each of the roadmaps or plans of action is introduced. Second, we compare the different approaches. Based on this analysis, the discussion will explore the possibilities and limitations, as well as the effectiveness and efficiency, of using roadmaps to strengthen the implementation of labour rights commitments in EU free trade agreements.

2 Literature Review on Labour Rights Protection in EU FTAs

The inclusion of Trade and Sustainable Development (TSD) chapters in the European Union's Free Trade Agreements (FTAs) began with its landmark agreement with South Korea in 2011. This innovation set the stage for the 'new generation FTAs,' establishing a 'blueprint' for embedding labour and environmental objectives into the EU's trade relations.[1] TSD chapters rest on three pillars: *substantive standards*, which anchor labour and environmental objectives in international conventions such as the International Labour Organization standards and the Multilateral Environmental Agreements; *procedural commitments*, which foster dialogue and capacity-building as part of the EU's promotional model; and *institutional structures*, which provide mechanisms for monitoring and ensuring compliance.[2] These pillars aim to advance sustainable development and address pressing global challenges.

Over a decade later, challenges in implementing, enforcing, and monitoring TSD provisions have become evident. Scholars have identified weaknesses in the design of TSD chapters, the socio-economic context of partner countries, and governance mechanisms, all of which hinder the operationalization of these commitments.[3] These weaknesses limit the functionality of TSD chapters and the achievement of their intended outcomes. *Design shortcomings* arise from ambiguities and gaps in TSD drafting – how provisions are written and structured, including vague language, lack of binding commitments, and poor integration of labour and environmental goals – limit enforceability.[4] *Contextual shortcomings* reflect disparities in cultural, socio-economic, and

---

1 F.C. Ebert (2016). *Labour provisions in EU trade agreements: What potential for channelling labour standards-related capacity building? International Labour Review*, Vol. 155; J. Harrison, J., Barbu, M., Campling, L., Richardson, B., & Smith, A. (2019a). Governing Labour Standards through Free Trade Agreements: Limits of the European Union's Trade and Sustainable Development Chapters. *Journal of Common Market Studies*, 57(2), 260–277.

2 Harrison, 'Governing Labour Standards through Free Trade Agreements'; van 't Wout, D. (2022). The enforceability of the trade and sustainable development chapters of the European Union's free trade agreements. *Asia Europe Journal*, 20(2), 81–98.

3 Ebert, '*Labour provisions in EU trade agreements*'; Harrison, 'Governing Labour Standards through Free Trade Agreements'; A. Marx, Brando, N., & Lein, B. (2017a). Strengthening Labour Rights Provisions in Bilateral Trade Agreements: Making the Case for Voluntary Sustainability Standards. *Global Policy*, 8, 78–88.

4 Harrison, 'Governing Labour Standards through Free Trade Agreements'; Hoang, H. H., & Sicurelli, D. (2017). The EU's preferential trade agreements with Singapore and Vietnam. Market vs. normative imperatives†. *Contemporary Politics*, 23(4), 369–387; ILO. (2016a). *Assessment of Labour Provisions in Trade and Investment Arrangements*, ILO; Marx, A., Ebert, F., & Hachez, N. (2017b). Dispute settlement for labour provisions in EU free trade agreements: Rethinking current approaches. *Politics and Governance*, 5(4), 49–59.

institutional conditions among trading partners, which hinder compliance.[5] *Governance shortcomings* encompass challenges in coordination, such as fragmented institutional frameworks, as well as weak stakeholder engagement frameworks, and inadequate monitoring systems.[6]

The EU–Korea FTA exemplifies design flaws by relying on aspirational language without providing clear enforcement mechanisms or benchmarks for compliance.[7] This vagueness reduces the enforceability of labour provisions and allows significant leeway in interpretation, undermining their practical impact. Contextual challenges further exacerbate these issues as seen, for example, in Moldova's limited institutional capacity.[8] Weak labour inspection systems and socio-economic constraints, such as the prevalence of informal labour markets, hinder the alignment of national practices with EU-Moldova FTA commitments.[9] Moreover, cultural differences with Asia sometimes frame sustainable development and international labour standards as 'Western values' that may not align with local traditions or priorities, complicating compliance efforts.[10] Similarly, in the EU–Colombia FTA, the socio-political context, including ongoing violence against union leaders, has impeded the effective realization of labour rights, highlighting the interplay between contextual and design-related barriers.[11]

As for governance shortcomings, these are evident in some EU FTAs. In the EU–Korea FTA, difficulties in communication between business representatives and employees as well as the lack of participation of civil society organizations and trade unions in monitoring committees reduced transparency

5 ILO. (2023). *Integrating trade and decent work Volume 1 Has trade led to better jobs?;* Marx, 'Strengthening Labour Rights Provisions in Bilateral Trade Agreements'.

6 L. Campling, Harrison, J., Richardson, B., & Smith, A. (2016). *Can labour provisions work beyond the border? Evaluating the effects of EU free trade agreements. International Labour Review*, Vol. 155; M. Limenta (2022). Toward an ASEAN-EU FTA: Examining the Trade and Sustainable Development Chapter in the Prospective Indonesia-EU CEPA. *Legal Issues of Economic Integration*, 49(2), 191–216; G. Marín Durán (2020). *Sustainable development chapters in EU free trade agreements: Emerging compliance issues*. Retrieved from www.ilo.org/global/research/publications/.

7 van 't Wout, 'The enforceability of the trade and sustainable development chapters'.

8 Harrison, 'Governing Labour Standards through Free Trade Agreements'.

9 J. Orbie, Van den Putte, L., & Martens, D. (2017). The impact of labour rights commitments in EU trade agreements: The case of Peru. *Politics and Governance*, 5(4), 6–18.

10 L. Cuyvers (2014). The Sustainable Development Clauses in Free Trade Agreements of the EU with Asian Countries: Perspectives for ASEAN? *Journal of Contemporary European Studies*, 22(4), 427–449; A. Tyc (2020). The European Union and Japan's Economic Partnership Agreement: labour provisions under the 'Trade and Sustainable Development' Chapter 1. *Juridical Tribune*. doi:10.1007/s.

11 Marx, 'Strengthening Labour Rights Provisions in Bilateral Trade Agreements'.

and accountability, weakening the agreement's oversight framework[12]; in the EU–Peru FTA, insufficient involvement of civil society in the Domestic Advisory Groups (DAGs) has limited the access to information and weaken institutional support for these groups, resulting in ineffective monitoring and follow-up.[13] The EU–Vietnam FTA further illustrates these challenges where state interference delayed the DAG's formation, and its composition remains dominated by state-aligned entities, limiting its capacity to advocate for labour rights, hindering enforcement and accountability, and leaving significant gaps in the operationalization of labour rights commitments.[14]

Scholars and policymakers have proposed several possibilities to address the shortcomings in labour rights protection provisions of TSD chapters and improve their effectiveness. For design-related issues, recommendations include drafting more precise and binding commitments, incorporating enforceable mechanisms such as trade sanctions, and integrating clearer benchmarks to measure compliance.[15] To address contextual shortcomings, capacity-building programmes have been suggested to enhance partner countries' institutional and technical capabilities.[16] Governance shortcomings have prompted calls for enhanced stakeholder engagement, stronger accountability frameworks, and improved monitoring systems, including greater transparency and formalized roles for civil society and trade unions in oversight processes.[17]

Significant shortcomings in the design, contextual relevance, and governance of TSD chapters, particularly in their ability to effectively implement and enforce labour rights commitments, are underscored in the literature. These challenges often leave gaps in monitoring mechanisms, institutional support, and accountability frameworks. Addressing these gaps requires tools that not only enhance compliance but also adapt to the socio-economic and institutional contexts of partner countries. Roadmaps emerge as a practical

12 D. Martens, Potjomkina, D., & Orbie, J. (2020). *Domestic Advisory Groups in EU Trade Agreements: Stuck at the Bottom or Moving up the Ladder?*; van 't Wout, 'The enforceability of the trade and sustainable development chapters'.

13 Martens, *'Domestic Advisory Groups in EU Trade Agreements';* Orbie, 'The impact of labour rights commitments in EU trade agreements'.

14 K. Marslev & Staritz, C. (2023). Towards a stronger EU approach on the trade-labor nexus? The EU-Vietnam Free Trade Agreement, social struggles and labor reforms in Vietnam. *Review of International Political Economy*, 30(3), 1125–1150.

15 van 't Wout, 'The enforceability of the trade and sustainable development chapters'.

16 ILO, *'Assessment of Labour Provisions in Trade and Investment Arrangements'.*

17 K. Hradilová & Svoboda, O. (2018). *Sustainable Development Chapters in the EU Free Trade Agreements: Searching for Effectiveness.* Retrieved from http://www.oecd.org/TAD/events/making-trade-

solution, offering structured frameworks to operationalize commitments and address governance-related barriers. By focusing on concrete actions, measurable timelines, and capacity-building measures, roadmaps bridge the gap between policy intent and actionable outcomes. The following section delves into the concept of roadmaps and their role in improving labour rights compliance.

3 Roadmaps and Action Plans: A Conceptual Reference

Roadmaps are structured frameworks designed to guide countries in implementing and monitoring compliance with international labour and environmental commitments. The concept of 'roadmapping' originates from management literature but has also been used in the context of international organizations and commitments. According to the ILO,[18] 'roadmapping' involves a set of 'activities related to strategic planning and decision-making' and is viewed as 'a project management activity that describes a sequence of processes and their interrelations' over a specified period, typically three to ten years.

In the context of labour rights, roadmaps have played a critical role in bridging the gap between policy and practice. They provide a structured approach to operationalizing commitments, enhancing transparency, accountability, and enforcement mechanisms. By offering clear steps, timelines, and benchmarks, roadmaps help countries address systemic non-compliance while aligning national practices with international conventions.

Broadly, two broad types of roadmaps have emerged from international practice. On one hand, *proactive or ex-ante roadmaps* are developed to fulfil specific commitments in advance of concluding a FTA. These include initiatives such as National Action Plans under the United Nations Guiding Principles on Business and Human Rights or National Adaptation Plans linked to the Paris Agreement. Following the 2010 ILO Global Conference on Child Labour, a global roadmap was adopted to eliminate the worst forms of child labour. In response, countries like Indonesia created tailored plans, such as 'Towards a Child Labour-Free Indonesia in 2022'. These plans identified broad areas for action, including legislative harmonization, education, and social protection, involving multiple stakeholders such as governments, unions, and NGOs. While ambitious, these roadmaps often remain open-ended in their recommendations and lack concrete enforcement mechanisms.

18 ILO. (2016). *Roadmap for fighting undeclared work.*

Conversely, *responsive or ex-post roadmaps* address non-compliance with international conventions. These frameworks are typically adopted to resolve systemic violations, offering specific and actionable solutions tailored to identified deficiencies. For example, the roadmap developed by the ILO and Guatemala to address violations of Convention No. 87 on Freedom of Association exemplifies this approach. Ex-post roadmaps are rooted in accountability and progress, ensuring that commitments are met through concrete actions, timelines, and measurable outcomes. While both types of roadmaps contribute to improving labour rights compliance, ex-post roadmaps are particularly relevant in addressing evidenced shortcomings or weaknesses. By targeting existing violations and fostering accountability, they offer a pathway to overcoming structural and operational barriers, making them indispensable tools for enhancing labour rights protection and sustainable development within international trade frameworks.

Roadmaps have been proposed as a mechanism to enhance the implementation of labour and environmental commitments in the context of EU trade agreements. Scholars and policymakers have suggested that establishing roadmaps for action in key export sectors, with clear monitoring processes, could help improve working conditions and ensure more effective enforcement of labour standards. Structured roadmaps can offer concrete timelines and milestones to track compliance with labour commitments in EU trade agreements, particularly in addressing sector-specific challenges.[19] Similarly, the European Commission has explored the potential of 'implementation roadmaps' as part of a revised approach to Trade and Sustainable Development (TSD) provisions, linking commitments to clear deliverables over time. In the environmental domain, implementation roadmaps have been proposed as part of the EU's efforts to integrate trade policies with sustainability objectives, ensuring that environmental commitments are systematically monitored and enforced.[20] When integrated into trade agreements, these roadmaps could serve as tools for bridging the gap between commitments and enforcement, enhancing accountability, and aligning national practices with international standards. By providing structured approaches with defined actions and oversight mechanisms, roadmaps offer a promising avenue for strengthening the role of trade agreements in advancing sustainable development, improving

19 J. Harrison, Barbu, M., Campling, L., … Smith, A. (2019b). Labour standards provisions in EU free trade agreements: Reflections on the European commission's reform agenda. *World Trade Review*, 18(4), 635–657; A. Smith, Campling, L., Barbu, M., Richardson, B., & Harrison, J. (2017). *Do labour provisions in EU Trade Agreements improve workers' lives and working conditions around the world?* Retrieved from www.researchretold.com.

20 E. Blot (2023). *Reflections on the new approach to the TSD Chapters for greener trade.*

compliance with ILO conventions, providing structured pathways for addressing systemic violations, and aligning national policies with international labour standards.[21]

The various contexts in which roadmaps are developed and implemented emphasize the importance of a structured approach to understanding their effectiveness. While roadmaps generally aim to tackle labour rights and environmental challenges, significant variations arise across different cases. A comparative analysis offers a systematic framework to explore these differences, providing insights into both common elements and unique challenges, helping to distil actionable lessons for enhancing the design and implementation of future roadmaps. The next section elaborates on the methodology employed in this study and the selected cases.

4 Methodology

To gain insights into the possibilities and limitations of roadmaps in the EU context we conduct a comparative case study of existing roadmaps and plans of action which already have been applied. A comparative analysis of case studies provides a systematic framework for examining and contrasting a limited number of cases to identify patterns, understand complex phenomena, and draw actionable conclusions. This method allows researchers to explore both commonalities and differences across cases while accounting for the specific cultural, social, political, and economic contexts in which they operate.[22] As Lijphart[23] notes, the comparative method is particularly effective when applied to a small number of cases, enabling an in-depth understanding of practical challenges and opportunities. Similarly, Yin[24] highlights that a structured comparative approach facilitates the identification of practical strategies for implementation and monitoring, ensuring that lessons learned from one case can be adapted to others. By focusing on the operational aspects of governance and compliance, this method provides policymakers and sta-

21 B. Richardson, Harrison, J., & Campling, L. (2017). *Labour rights in export processing zones with a focus on GSP+ beneficiary countries : study*, European Parliament.

22 A. Marx, Rihoux, B., & Ragin, C. (2014, February). The origins, development, and application of Qualitative Comparative Analysis: The first 25 years. *European Political Science Review*, pp. 115–142.

23 A. Lijphart (1971). Comparative Politics and the Comparative Method. *The American Political Science Review*, 63(3), 682–693.

24 R.K. Yin (2018). Case Study Research and Applications. Design and Methods. 6th Edition. Sage Publishing.

TABLE 6.1 Framework/triggers of roadmaps and action plans analysed (Authors' own elaboration based on reviewed literature)

	Name	Framework/trigger
Roadmap	Sustainability Compact for Bangladesh	Rana Plaza disaster (focus on improving labour rights and factory safety in the RMG sector)
	Bangladesh Roadmap for Labour Inspection Convention, ILO No. 81, 87, 98	ILO Labour Inspection Convention (No. 81), Freedom of Association (No. 87), Right to Organize (No. 98)
	Bangladesh National Action Plan on the Labour Sector (2021–2026)	EU–Bangladesh Joint Commission to align labour sector with ILO and EU requirements
	ILO–Guatemala Roadmap	ILO Article 26 Complaint regarding violations of Freedom of Association (No. 87)
Action plan	US–Colombia Labour Action Plan	Address labour rights issues for FTA adoption
	Enforcement Plans for Guatemala and Honduras under US-CAFTA-DR	Labour enforcement concerns in Guatemala and Honduras
	Canada–Colombia Action Plan under Labour Cooperation Agreement	Enhancing compliance with labour rights

keholders with actionable insights to address systemic shortcomings and improve labour rights protection within the framework of trade agreements.

The case studies selected for the comparative analysis represent a diverse range of roadmaps and action plans addressing labour rights violations in various contexts. These include four (4) roadmaps addressing ILO convention violations and three (3) action plans developed within bilateral trade agreements.

These cases were chosen based on their relevance to the EU's trade and labour rights agenda, detailed documentation availability, and alignment with the objectives of TSD chapters and the GSP+ regulation. The diversity of these cases allows for a comparative understanding of the commonalities and variations in roadmaps and action plan design and implementation across different geopolitical and socio-economic contexts.

5 Comparative Case Analysis

Before we compare the difference roadmaps and plans of action we provide a brief description of the cases based on the original documents outlining the roadmaps and plans of action.

5.1 Sustainability Compact for Bangladesh

The *Sustainability Compact for Bangladesh* emerged in 2013 as a direct response to the tragic Rana Plaza building collapse, which exposed severe deficiencies in workplace safety and labour rights in the Ready-Made Garment (RMG) sector. The Compact was jointly initiated by the European Union, the International Labour Organization, the United States, and Canada to ensure the alignment of Bangladesh's labour laws with ILO conventions, improve workplace safety, and foster freedom of association.[25] A key focus was to address systemic issues in the RMG sector, which had been central to Bangladesh's economic growth but was fraught with labour violations and poor safety standards.

To operationalize its goals, the Compact included several concrete actions and measures. Legislative reforms aimed to align national labour laws with international standards, focusing on improving freedom of association and the right to organize. Capacity-building measures were prioritized, including extensive training for labour inspectors and the development of a centralized safety database to track factory conditions.[26] Other measures involved conducting comprehensive factory safety audits, improving fire safety standards, and enhancing overall working conditions in the RMG sector. These initiatives were supported by the EU, USA, and Canada through technical assistance and funding, ensuring a multi-stakeholder approach to implementation.

Monitoring and evaluation of the Compact were led by the '3+5+1 group', a coalition comprising representatives from Bangladesh, the EU, the USA, Canada, and the ILO, as well as industry and civil society stakeholders. Regular high-level meetings and progress reports assessed the effectiveness of the measures. The Compact achieved significant milestones, including the formation of over 500 trade unions, improved building safety standards, and strengthened institutional mechanisms.[27] However, challenges persisted, particularly in the enforcement of labour laws and the limited capacity of labour inspectors. In 2021, a follow-up roadmap was introduced to address these ongoing issues, highlighting the need for sustained monitoring and commitment to long-term systemic change.

---

25 European Commission, International Labour Organization, & Government of Bangladesh. (2013). Joint Statement Staying engaged: A Sustainability Compact for continuous improvements in labour rights and factory safety in the Ready-Made Garment and Knitwear Industry in Bangladesh. https://www.ilo.org/media/49351/download.

26 European Commission, 'Joint Statement Staying engaged'.

27 European Commission. (2018). Implementation of the Bangladesh Compact – Technical Status Report. https://www.ilo.org/media/10171/download.

5.2 Bangladesh Roadmap for Labour Inspection Convention, ILO No. 81, 87, and 98

The *Bangladesh Roadmap for Labour Inspection Convention, ILO No. 81, 87, and 98* was developed as part of a broader effort to address persistent labour rights violations in the aftermath of the Rana Plaza tragedy. This roadmap was triggered by a formal complaint submitted under the ILO's Article 26 mechanism, highlighting Bangladesh's failure to comply with key conventions on labour inspection, freedom of association, and collective bargaining. The roadmap aimed to address these deficiencies comprehensively, ensuring the establishment of effective labour inspection systems, greater respect for freedom of association, and strengthened mechanisms for collective bargaining.[28]

To meet these objectives, the roadmap included a range of commitments and actions. Legislative measures were a key focus, including amendments to Bangladesh's Labor Act and the adoption of implementing rules to enhance compliance with ILO conventions.[29] Efforts to strengthen institutional capacity featured prominently, with the recruitment and training of labour inspectors, the development of a labour inspection database, and the provision of modern equipment to facilitate workplace inspections. Additional measures targeted the registration and operation of trade unions, aiming to improve workers' ability to organize and engage in collective bargaining. These actions reflected a comprehensive approach, addressing systemic gaps while fostering institutional reform.

The roadmap's implementation and monitoring were overseen by the ILO in collaboration with the Government of Bangladesh and social partners. Regular progress reviews assessed the roadmap's impact, leading to notable improvements, such as the recruitment of additional labour inspectors and enhanced union registration processes. However, significant challenges persisted, including delays in implementing legislative reforms and resistance from certain employers to recognizing trade unions. While progress was achieved in specific areas, the roadmap's overall effectiveness underscored the need for sustained political will, enhanced resources, and stronger monitoring mechanisms to achieve long-term compliance with ILO conventions.

---

28 Governing Body ILO. (2022 March). Report by the Government of Bangladesh on progress made on the implementation of the roadmap taken to address all outstanding issues mentioned in the complaint concerning alleged non-observance of Conventions Nos 81, 87 and 98. https://www.ilo.org/wcmsp5/groups/public/---ed_norm/---relconf/documents/meetingdocument/wcms_837532.pdf.

29 Governing Body ILO, 'Report by the Government of Bangladesh'.

5.3 Bangladesh National Action Plan on the Labour Sector (2021–2026)

The *Bangladesh National Action Plan on the Labour Sector* (*2021–2026*) was developed to build upon earlier initiatives, including the Sustainability Compact and the roadmap addressing ILO conventions.[30] This action plan aimed to address persistent gaps in Bangladesh's labour sector by aligning national labour practices with international standards, particularly those outlined by the International Labour Organization. It was formulated under the guidance of the EU–Bangladesh Joint Commission, ensuring a collaborative framework for improving labour standards and worker protections. The plan focused on achieving long-term systemic change through phased implementation over five years.

The action plan incorporated commitments to strengthen labour rights, workplace safety, and institutional frameworks. Legislative reforms were a central element, focusing on harmonizing labour laws with ILO conventions and enhancing protections for workers in the Ready-Made Garment (RMG) sector and beyond. Capacity-building initiatives included extensive training for labour inspectors, expansion of labour inspection services, and the development of a comprehensive database to monitor compliance. Additional measures targeted gender equality, child labour elimination, and the promotion of social dialogue between workers, employers, and the government. These actions demonstrated a holistic approach to tackling systemic labour issues in Bangladesh.

Implementation and monitoring of the action plan were overseen by Bangladesh's Ministry of Labour, with periodic input from the EU and ILO. Progress reports were mandated to track the plan's effectiveness, enabling adjustments to address emerging challenges. Initial outcomes highlighted improvements in labour inspection infrastructure, increased awareness of workers' rights, and incremental progress in legislative reforms. However, significant obstacles, such as resource constraints and resistance from some employers, continue to limit the plan's full impact. While the National Action Plan represents a comprehensive strategy, achieving its objectives requires sustained commitment, increased funding, and active engagement from all stakeholders.

30 Governing Body ILO, 'Report by the Government of Bangladesh'.

5.4 ILO–Guatemala Roadmap

The *ILO–Guatemala Roadmap* was developed in response to a formal complaint submitted under Article 26 of the International Labour Organization's Constitution. This complaint highlighted Guatemala's failure to comply with Convention No. 87 on Freedom of Association and Protection of the Right to Organise. The roadmap aimed to address systemic labour violations, including restrictions on union activities, violence against trade unionists, and a lack of effective legal protections for workers. It was formulated through collaboration between the ILO and the Government of Guatemala, with input from labour organizations and other stakeholders.[31]

The roadmap included a set of commitments and actions to bring Guatemala into compliance with ILO standards. Key measures included legislative reforms to strengthen protections for union activities, improve labour dispute resolution mechanisms, and enforce penalties for anti-union practices.[32] Efforts to build institutional capacity featured prominently, such as the training of labour inspectors, the establishment of specialized labour courts, and the development of tools to monitor compliance. Additionally, the roadmap emphasized fostering social dialogue between workers, employers, and the government to address labour disputes and promote collective bargaining.

Implementation and monitoring of the roadmap were overseen by the ILO in coordination with the Guatemalan Ministry of Labour. Regular progress assessments were conducted to evaluate the roadmap's impact, revealing mixed results. While improvements were observed in the functioning of labour courts and the resolution of some disputes, challenges persisted, including delays in legislative reforms and ongoing violence against trade unionists. The roadmap underscored the critical need for sustained international support, political will, and robust enforcement mechanisms to achieve meaningful and lasting improvements in labour rights in Guatemala.

---

31 Governing Body ILO. (2013). Complaint concerning non-observance by Guatemala of the Freedom of Association and Protection of the Right to Organise Convention, 1948 (No. 87), made by delegates to the 101st Session (2012) of the International Labour Conference under article 26 of the ILO Constitution. https://www.ilo.org/wcmsp5/groups/public/---ed_norm/---relconf/documents/meetingdocument/wcms_208506.pdf.

32 Governing Body ILO, 'Complaint concerning non-observance by Guatemala'.

5.5 US–Colombia Labour Action Plan

The *US–Colombia Labour Action Plan* was introduced in 2011 to address labour rights concerns and pave the way for the ratification of the US–Colombia Free Trade Agreement (FTA). Triggered by significant violence against trade unionists and weak enforcement of labour rights, the plan sought to improve Colombia's labour conditions and align them with international standards. The action plan outlined commitments such as combating violence against trade unionists, enhancing protections for worker rights, and strengthening labour inspection and dispute resolution mechanisms.[33]

Implementation of the action plan involved establishing specialized labour courts, increasing the number of labour inspectors, and implementing measures to ensure effective enforcement of labour laws. Monitoring was carried out through joint reviews by the United States and Colombia. While the plan achieved progress in reducing violence against union leaders and improving institutional capacity, significant challenges persisted, including delays in fully implementing reforms and ensuring employer compliance with labour laws.

5.6 Enforcement Plans for Guatemala and Honduras

The *Enforcement Plans for Guatemala and Honduras* were developed under the US-CAFTA-DR agreement to address deficiencies in labour law enforcement and ensure compliance with the labour provisions of the FTA. In Guatemala, the plan was initiated following a dispute settlement process under CAFTA-DR's labour chapter, emphasizing issues such as inadequate labour inspections, ineffective prosecution of labour violations, and limited protections for workers.[34] The Honduras plan focused on similar concerns, including strengthening labour institutions and addressing anti-union practices.

Key measures under these plans included legislative changes to strengthen labour protections, increased labour inspections, and enhanced training for enforcement officials. Monitoring involved collaborative efforts between the United States and the respective governments, with regular progress reviews. While both plans resulted in improvements in labour inspection systems and institutional capacity, challenges remained in ensuring sustained compliance and addressing socio-economic factors that undermine worker protections.

---

33 Office of the United States Trade Representative n.d.

34 Government of the United States & Government of Guatemala. (2013). Mutually Agreed Enforcement Action Plan between the Government of the United States and the Government of Guatemala ('Enforcement Plan'). https://www.dol.gov/sites/dolgov/files/ILAB/legacy/files/0413GuatEnforcementPlan.pdf.

5.7 Canada–Colombia Action Plan

The *Canada–Colombia Action Plan* was adopted alongside the Canada–Colombia Free Trade Agreement to enhance compliance with labour rights commitments. Triggered by concerns over labour rights violations and the protection of unionized workers, the action plan aimed to strengthen institutional frameworks, promote social dialogue, and address systemic issues such as anti-union violence.[35]

The plan emphasized capacity-building measures, such as training labour inspectors, improving labour law enforcement, and facilitating the registration of trade unions. Monitoring involved joint oversight by Canada and Colombia, with periodic progress reports assessing implementation. While the action plan led to incremental improvements in labour conditions and institutional capacity, challenges such as insufficient enforcement of labour laws and persistent violence against union leaders highlighted the need for sustained efforts and stronger political will.

5.8 Comparative Analysis

How do these roadmaps compare? Although these roadmaps do not follow a fixed template, they contain several common elements. Table 6.2 compares the different roadmaps on what triggered the elaboration of the roadmap, the focus area, the relevant ILO convention(s), and the measures included in the roadmap (legislative, capacity-building, other measures). We discuss the five most important ones below.

First, all roadmaps and action plans were developed after a clear indication of non-compliance with ILO conventions. Non-compliance can be observed based on regular reporting or, as in the Canada–Colombia Action Plan, on non-compliance in specific cases, which then triggers a broader assessment. This observation of non-compliance determines the scope of the roadmap in terms of the labour rights on which it focuses. All identified relevant roadmaps and plans of action focus on addressing non-compliance with specific ILO conventions, most notably the Freedom of Association and Protection of the Right to Organise Convention, 1948 (No. 87) and the Right to Organise and Collective Bargaining Convention, 1949 (No. 98) (see Table 6.2). Most

35 Government of Canada. (2022). Action Plan under the Canada–Colombia Agreement on Labour Cooperation – 2018–2021. https://www.canada.ca/content/dam/esdc-edsc/documents/services/labour-relations/canada-colombia-action-plan-en.pdf.

TABLE 6.2 Comparative analysis of labour rights roadmaps and action plans

Roadmap/action plan	Trigger of non-compliance	Focus areas	Related ILO conventions	Legislative measures	Capacity-building measures	Other measures
Sustainability Compact for Bangladesh	Observed labour rights violations in the Ready-Made Garment sector after the Rana Plaza disaster.	Workplace safety, freedom of association, and collective bargaining.	ILO Nos. 87 and 98	Strengthening labour law compliance and factory safety standards.	Training for labour inspectors, hiring additional inspectors, capacity-building for factory management.	Creating a public database for factory compliance, fostering multi-stakeholder dialogue.
Bangladesh Roadmap for Labour Inspection	Non-observance of the Labour Inspection Convention and freedom of association as identified by ILO monitoring and complaints	Labour inspection systems, freedom of association, and collective bargaining	ILO Nos. 81, 87, and 98	Amendments to labour laws to align with ILO conventions; revising union registration laws	Recruitment and training of labour inspectors, technical assistance to improve inspection protocols	Strengthening grievance mechanisms, awareness campaigns for workers' rights
Bangladesh National Action Plan	Identified gaps in labour rights enforcement and institutional capacity	Broad labour sector reforms, including workplace safety, gender equality, and child labour elimination	ILO Nos. 87 and 98	New labour legislation focusing on occupational safety and health (OSH) and gender equality	Building capacity in gender-sensitive inspection and workplace safety; upgrading infrastructure	Promoting social dialogue between stakeholders; addressing child labour issues
ILO–Guatemala Roadmap	Violations of ILO Convention No. 87 raised under Article 26 complaint	Freedom of association and strengthening labour courts	ILO No. 87	Revising legal frameworks for union recognition and collective bargaining	Training of labour court judges, support for labour ministry officials	Developing fast-track mechanisms for union cases, awareness-raising among workers and employers

TABLE 6.2 Comparative analysis of labour rights roadmaps and action plans (*cont.*)

Roadmap/action plan	Trigger of non-compliance	Focus areas	Related ILO conventions	Legislative measures	Capacity-building measures	Other measures
US–Colombia Labour Action Plan	Identified issues with anti-union violence and violations of collective bargaining rights	Freedom of association, collective bargaining, and eliminating anti-union violence	ILO Nos. 87 and 98	Reforming criminal law to address anti-union violence; strengthening collective bargaining regulations	Hiring and training of additional labour inspectors, capacity-building for compliance oversight	Establishing a public prosecutor unit for labour-related crimes, addressing informal labour issues
Guatemala Enforcement Plan (CAFTA-DR)	Repeated failures to meet CAFTA-DR labour commitments and non-compliance with ILO labour standards	Freedom of association and enforcement of labour laws	ILO No. 87	Amending labour laws to improve enforcement of freedom of association and collective bargaining	Training labour inspectors and judges on international labour standards	Awareness campaigns for workers and employers; grievance mechanisms for labour violations
Canada–Colombia Action Plan	Specific cases of non-compliance, especially violations of freedom of association and collective bargaining rights	Addressing freedom of association and collective bargaining issues	ILO Nos. 87 and 98	Enhancing legal frameworks for collective bargaining and union recognition	Training programmes for labour inspectors, technical assistance for monitoring labour conditions	Strengthening labour dispute resolution mechanisms, outreach to marginalized worker populations

roadmaps focus on addressing issues related to freedom of association and collective bargaining, which is, from the perspective of a trade agreement, a rather narrow focus.

Second, all roadmaps include broad goals, commitments, or recommendations on one side, and very concrete actions on the other. In terms of a template, the studied roadmaps and plans of action are quite similar, with a strong focus and most attention to the substantive commitments and actions which need to be taken. Often these actions take the form of a long list of precise interventions related to some key aspects of the convention. Some roadmaps feature an extensive list of actions, with more than 50 in some cases.

Table 6.2 maps the different measures and actions proposed in the different roadmaps. Regarding actions, all roadmaps include proposals for legislative changes, whether through the introduction of new laws or the amendment of existing laws related to labour law and other legal areas, including criminal law. They also propose capacity-building and strengthening of enforcement. The latter often takes the form of hiring additional labour inspectors and the training of labour inspectors.

Some roadmaps also strengthen complaint and grievance mechanisms. As summarized in Figure 6.1, together, roadmaps include various actions ranging from initiating legislative change over strengthening monitoring and enforcement instruments to foster compliance to general capacity-building activities such as training. Overall, there is a strong focus on enabling and strengthening the capacity of Ministries of Labour and related (inspection) agencies to perform their duties in implementing international commitments.

Third, roadmaps vary in their execution periods and who needs to implement the roadmaps. One roadmap (Guatemala) had a time horizon of one year, while others extended over multiple years (up to five years). The shorter roadmap was designed as a prerequisite for concluding a trade agreement, thus featuring a more specific focus with tighter deadlines. Additionally, roadmaps specify timeframes by which actions should be completed. In some roadmaps, these timeframes are broad in terms of months, while others specify exact days by which an action or milestone should be reached. Roadmaps also identify government ministries/agencies and the judiciary as the actors responsible for the implementation of the roadmap. Mostly that remains limited to a small number of ministries and agencies due to the often-narrow focus of the roadmap.

Fourth, although there is no systematic evidence, the results of the application and implementation of roadmaps remained mixed. Often, several issues and concerns remain after the official end of a roadmap, triggering further

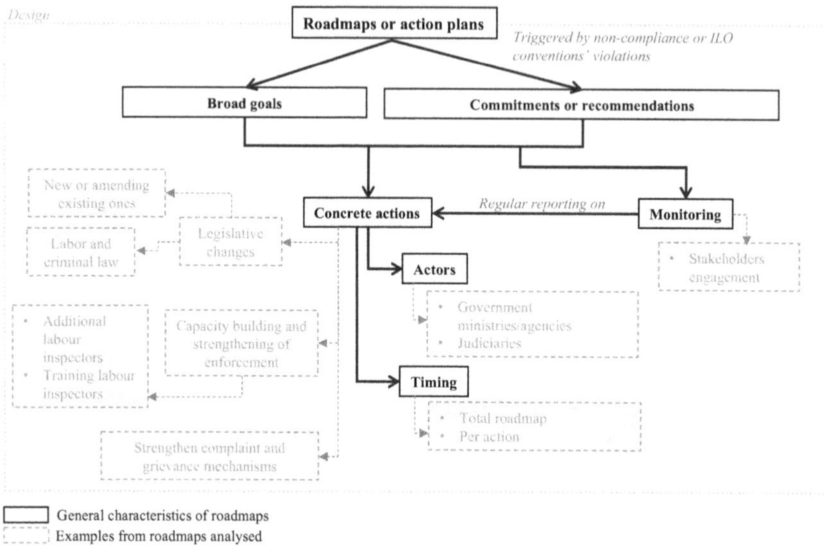

FIGURE 6.1 Common elements of roadmaps and action plans for addressing labour rights and ILO convention violations

dialogue and action. As a result, a roadmap or action plan is never completely finalized and often generates follow-up action, as becomes clear from the Sustainability Compact and the Guatemala case under the US-CAFTA-DR. This is not to argue that roadmaps do not work, but they are also not a silver bullet for quickly addressing systemic non-compliance.

Fifth, implementing roadmaps and plans of action requires additional resources and support, both financially and in terms of capacity-building and technical support. Hence, roadmaps often include commitments to providing technical and financial support, either bilaterally or through multilateral channels, as in the case of the International Labour Organization.

Overall, Figure 6.1 provides a structured visualization of the common elements identified in roadmaps and their operational focus, reflecting both their potential and limitations in addressing systemic labour rights violations.

6 Discussion and Implications

Roadmaps have emerged as a promising tool to address non-compliance or violation of ILO convention challenges and, as such, to manage the critical design, governance, and contextual weaknesses identified for the implementation of TSD chapters of EU FTAs. Indeed, the cases analysed evidence how shortcomings related to some contextual and governance weaknesses have been tackled. For instance, the Bangladesh Roadmap for Labour Inspection incorporated detailed legislative amendments and capacity-building measures, addressing systemic gaps in labour law enforcement. Therefore, roadmaps need to contain, on the one hand, broad goals, commitments, or recommendations and on the other hand very concrete actions that contribute to the goals. These actions should be of different types, ranging from legislative changes to actions to build capacity and strengthen enforcement.

For both the broad goals and the concrete actions, roadmaps need to be time-bound. As illustrated in Figure 6.1, roadmaps incorporate specific timeframes for broad goals and concrete actions, ensuring systematic implementation. The timeframe for the execution of a whole roadmap may range, depending on the complexity of the issues to be addressed, from one year to multiple years. As for when the concrete actions should be completed, roadmaps studied revealed some have broad time indications in terms of months while others indicate dates by when an action or milestone should be achieved. This characteristic represents commendable progress in ensuring systematic implementation. Aligned with these the timeframes, roadmaps should specify the expected outcomes and specific compliance indicators for each concrete action. As depicted in Figure 6.2, establishing compliance indicators tied to these targets would provide a clear benchmark for assessing progress and success. This would enhance transparency and accountability and ensure that roadmaps remain focused on delivering measurable results.

Governance challenges, including fragmented institutional frameworks and inadequate monitoring systems, can be addressed through roadmaps. In fact, roadmaps suggest a multi-stakeholder approach in their monitoring provisions, involving a diverse range of actors to ensure comprehensive oversight, as illustrated in the Sustainability Compact for Bangladesh, which promotes accountability by requiring regular reporting and multi-stakeholder oversight. This approach not only enhances transparency but also builds trust among stakeholders. However, there is an opportunity to expand this participation beyond monitoring. Different actors, including the EU or other international institutions, as well as domestic public and private sector entities, could play a more active role. Figure 6.2 highlights stakeholders' expanded role in monitoring and implementing roadmaps. By leveraging these actors' expertise, resources, and networks, roadmaps can more effectively address complex governance challenges and enhance the likelihood of achieving their goals.

Similarly, roadmaps' emphasis on capacity-building and contextual adaptation addresses disparities in institutional and socio-economic conditions

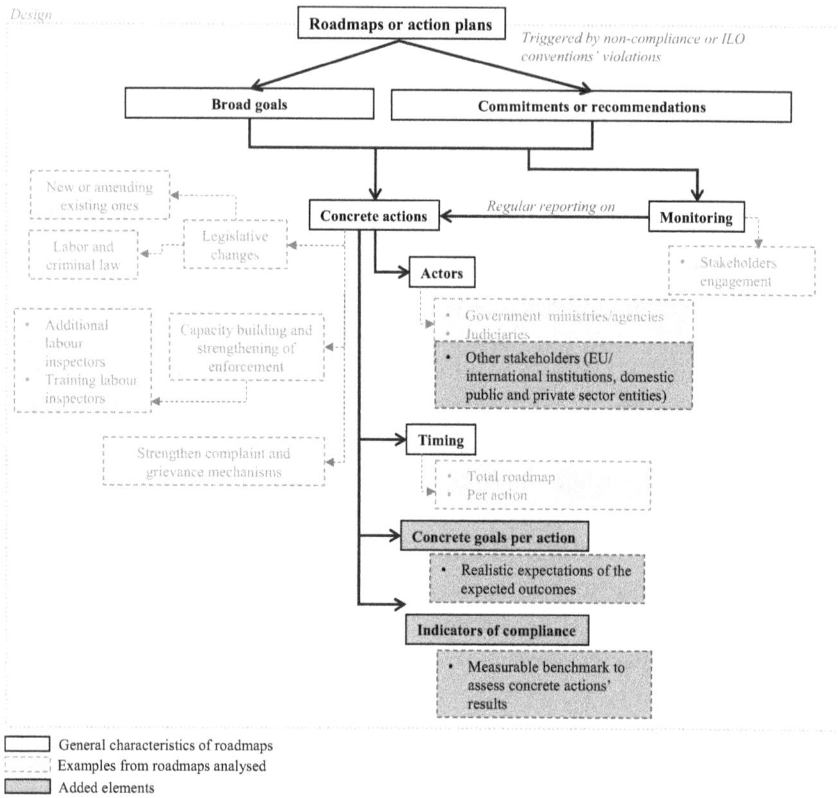

FIGURE 6.2 Enhanced framework: essential elements for roadmaps and action plans

among partner countries. Tailored interventions, such as labour inspector training and grievance mechanism enhancements, align national practices with international standards while considering local constraints. The ILO–Guatemala Roadmap's focus on specialized labour courts is a notable example of addressing specific barriers to effective enforcement.

By combining precise timeframes, multi-stakeholder involvement, and clearly defined targets with compliance indicators, roadmaps can evolve into even more powerful tools for addressing complex challenges and achieving their intended goals.

In sum, Figure 6.2 provides a visual synthesis of the key elements identified in the analysis, offering an enhanced structured framework for designing and implementing effective roadmaps to address labour rights challenges. Nonetheless, despite recognizing that the application of roadmaps might hold the potential to strengthen the implementation of labour rights provisions in EU trade agreements, a few caveats must be mentioned.

First of all, the scope in terms of labour rights covered in roadmaps is limited. As noted above, all identified relevant roadmaps and plans of action focus on addressing non-compliance with specific ILO conventions, most notably the Freedom of Association and Protection of the Right to Organise Convention, 1948 (No. 87) and the Right to Organise and Collective Bargaining Convention, 1949 (No. 98). EU trade agreements include more labour rights conventions, *i.e.* all conventions which are included in the ILO Declaration of Fundamental Rights and Principles at Work which since 2022 includes ten Conventions. Some trade agreements might even include references to more ILO conventions. Applying a roadmap approach to more ILO conventions might become very demanding in terms of commitments by partner countries. As highlighted above, this would require for each Convention specific commitments, benchmarks and investment. The question is whether this is realistic and feasible. This brings us to a second point. For roadmaps to really have an impact there needs to be a significant investment. The question of who carries the burden and what the EU can provide in terms of technical and financial support will need to be addressed. Third, the effective impact of existing roadmaps in terms of improving the protection of labour rights remains unclear, and under-researched. There is no systematic evidence that roadmaps effectively work.

7 Conclusions

The literature on labour rights protection within EU Free FTAs underscores the evolution of TSD chapters since their introduction in the EU–Korea FTA in 2011. While these chapters are designed to embed labour and environmental commitments into trade agreements, significant challenges persist in their implementation, enforcement, and monitoring. Scholars highlight three key shortcomings: design weaknesses, contextual challenges, and governance deficiencies, all of which impede the effectiveness of TSD provisions. Design-related issues stem from vague language and the lack of binding commitments, while contextual disparities in socio-economic and institutional conditions complicate compliance. Governance challenges, including weak stakeholder engagement and ineffective monitoring frameworks, further undermine labour rights protections.

To address these gaps, roadmaps and action plans have emerged as a viable strategy to enhance compliance with international labour standards. Existing roadmaps (or plans of action) include the Sustainability Compact for Bangladesh; Bangladesh Roadmap for Labour Inspection Convention, ILO No. 81, 87, and 98; Bangladesh National Action Plan on the Labour Sector (2021–2026); ILO–Guatemala Roadmap; the Enforcement Plans for Guatemala and Honduras (under the US-CAFTA-DR agreement) and Canada–Colombia Action Plan (linked to the Canada–Colombia Free Trade Agreement). These roadmaps serve as structured frameworks that provide clear timelines, measurable actions, and accountability mechanisms, ensuring a more systematic approach to labour rights enforcement. An analysis of these roadmaps demonstrates the potential of roadmaps to strengthen compliance by incorporating legislative reforms, capacity-building measures, and multi-stakeholder oversight.

Despite their potential, roadmaps are not a panacea for addressing labour rights violations in FTAs. Several limitations must be considered. First, their scope remains narrow, focusing predominantly on Freedom of Association and Collective Bargaining (ILO Conventions No. 87 and No. 98), rather than the full spectrum of labour rights covered under EU trade agreements. Expanding the roadmap approach to additional ILO conventions would require significant commitments from partner countries, raising concerns about feasibility. Second, the successful implementation of roadmaps necessitates substantial financial and technical investment, posing questions about burden-sharing and EU support mechanisms. Third, the effectiveness of roadmaps in practice remains under-researched, with limited systematic evidence on their long-term impact on labour rights protection.

In sum, while roadmaps offer a structured and pragmatic approach to strengthening labour rights compliance in EU FTAs, their design and implementation must be carefully tailored to address governance challenges, contextual barriers, and financial constraints. Future research should focus on evaluating the effectiveness of roadmaps in practice, identifying best practices, and exploring ways to expand their scope to a broader range of labour rights commitments. Addressing these challenges will be crucial to ensuring that EU FTAs genuinely contribute to the promotion and protection of labour rights in global trade relations.

Bibliography

Blot, E. (2023). *Reflections on the new approach to the TSD Chapters for greener trade.*

Campling, L., Harrison, J., Richardson, B., & Smith, A. (2016). *Can labour provisions work beyond the border? Evaluating the effects of EU free trade agreements. International Labour Review*, Vol. 155.

Cuyvers, L. (2014). The Sustainable Development Clauses in Free Trade Agreements of the EU with Asian Countries: Perspectives for ASEAN? *Journal of Contemporary European Studies*, 22(4), 427–449.

European Commission, International Labour Organization, & Government of Bangladesh (2013). Joint Statement Staying engaged: A Sustainability Compact for continuous improvements in labour rights and factory safety in the Ready-Made Garment and Knitwear Industry in Bangladesh. https://www.ilo.org/media/49351/download.

European Commission (2018). Implementation of the Bangladesh Compact – Technical Status Report. https://www.ilo.org/media/10171/download

Ebert, F. C. (2016). *Labour provisions in EU trade agreements: What potential for channelling labour standards-related capacity building? International Labour Review*, Vol. 155.

Governing Body ILO (2013). Complaint concerning non-observance by Guatemala of the Freedom of Association and Protection of the Right to Organise Convention, 1948 (No. 87), made by delegates to the 101st Session (2012) of the International Labour Conference under article 26 of the ILO Constitution. https://www.ilo.org/wcmsp5/groups/public/-ed_norm/-relconf/documents/meetingdocument/wcms_208506.pdf.

Governing Body ILO (2022 March). Report by the Government of Bangladesh on progress made on the implementation of the roadmap taken to address all outstanding issues mentioned in the complaint concerning alleged non-observance of Conventions Nos 81, 87 and 98. https://www.ilo.org/wcmsp5/groups/public/---ed_norm/---relconf/documents/meetingdocument/wcms_837532.pdf

Government of Canada (2022). Action Plan under the Canada–Colombia Agreement on Labour Cooperation – 2018–2021. https://www.canada.ca/content/dam/esdc-edsc/documents/services/labour-relations/canada-colombia-action-plan-en.pdf.

Government of the United States & Government of Guatemala (2013). Mutually Agreed Enforcement Action Plan between the Government of the United States and the Government of Guatemala ('Enforcement Plan'). https://www.dol.gov/sites/dolgov/files/ILAB/legacy/files/0413GuatEnforcementPlan.pdf.

Harrison, J., Barbu, M., Campling, L., Richardson, B., & Smith, A. (2019a). Governing Labour Standards through Free Trade Agreements: Limits of the European Union's Trade and Sustainable Development Chapters. *Journal of Common Market Studies*, 57(2), 260–277.

Harrison, J., Barbu, M., Campling, L., … Smith, A. (2019b). Labour standards provisions in EU free trade agreements: Reflections on the European commission's reform agenda. *World Trade Review*, 18(4), 635–657.

Hoang, H. H., & Sicurelli, D. (2017). The EU's preferential trade agreements with Singapore and Vietnam. Market vs. normative imperatives†. *Contemporary Politics*, 23(4), 369–387.

Hradilová, K., & Svoboda, O. (2018). *Sustainable Development Chapters in the EU Free Trade Agreements: Searching for Effectiveness.* Retrieved from http://www.oecd.org/TAD/events/making-trade-.

ILO (2016a). *Assessment of Labour Provisions in Trade and Investment Arrangements*, ILO.

ILO (2016b). *Roadmap for fighting undeclared work.*

ILO (2023). *Integrating trade and decent work Volume 1 Has trade led to better jobs?.*

Lijphart, A. (1971). Comparative Politics and the Comparative Method. *The American Political Science Review*, 63(3), 682–693.

Limenta, M. (2022). Toward an ASEAN-EU FTA: Examining the Trade and Sustainable Development Chapter in the Prospective Indonesia-EU CEPA. *Legal Issues of Economic Integration*, 49(2), 191–216.

Marín Durán, G. (2020). *Sustainable development chapters in EU free trade agreements: Emerging compliance issues.* Retrieved from www.ilo.org/global/research/publications/.

Marslev, K., & Staritz, C. (2023). Towards a stronger EU approach on the trade-labor nexus? The EU-Vietnam Free Trade Agreement, social struggles and labor reforms in Vietnam. *Review of International Political Economy*, 30(3), 1125–1150.

Martens, D., Potjomkina, D., & Orbie, J. (2020). *Domestic Advisory Groups in EU Trade Agreements: Stuck at the Bottom or Moving up the Ladder?*

Marx, A., Brando, N., & Lein, B. (2017a). Strengthening Labour Rights Provisions in Bilateral Trade Agreements: Making the Case for Voluntary Sustainability Standards. *Global Policy*, 8, 78–88.

Marx, A., Ebert, F., & Hachez, N. (2017b). Dispute settlement for labour provisions in EU free trade agreements: Rethinking current approaches. *Politics and Governance*, 5(4), 49–59.

Marx, A., Rihoux, B., & Ragin, C. (2014, February). The origins, development, and application of Qualitative Comparative Analysis: The first 25 years. *European Political Science Review*, pp. 115–142.

Orbie, J., Van den Putte, L., & Martens, D. (2017). The impact of labour rights commitments in EU trade agreements: The case of Peru. *Politics and Governance*, 5(4), 6–18.

Richardson, B., Harrison, J., & Campling, L. (2017). *Labour rights in export processing zones with a focus on GSP+ beneficiary countries : study*, European Parliament.

Smith, A., Campling, L., Barbu, M., Richardson, B., & Harrison, J. (2017). *Do labour provisions in EU Trade Agreements improve workers' lives and working conditions around the world?* Retrieved from www.researchretold.com.

Tyc, A. (2020). The European Union and Japan's Economic Partnership Agreement: labour provisions under the 'Trade and Sustainable Development' Chapter 1. *Juridical Tribune*. doi:10.1007/s

van 't Wout, D. (2022). The enforceability of the trade and sustainable development chapters of the European Union's free trade agreements. *Asia Europe Journal*, 20(2), 81–98.

Yin, R.K. (2018) Case Study Research and Applications. Design and Methods. 6th Edition. Sage Publishing.

PART 3

The US's and Canada's Approach

CHAPTER 7

Adieu International Labour Rights? US Trade and Labour Linkages in a Post-FTA Era

Jean-Baptiste Velut

1 Introduction

After three decades of policy experiments to expand their scope and reinforce their enforceability, trade and labour linkages in the United States are at a crossroads. Once a central tool to US trade strategy, free trade agreements (FTAs) have been under attack from both progressive and nationalist forces, becoming at best a secondary instrument in trade policy toolboxes, at worst a taboo acronym. The search for a new balance between domestic and international objectives, the geopoliticization of trade and, to a lesser extent, the deepening of trade and sustainability linkages have all converged towards what might be described as a process of "de-FTA-zation" of US trade policy.[1]

First, in the United States (US), the European Union (EU) and elsewhere, governments have been turning away from economic globalization to seek new intermestic compromises that favour industrial or strategic policies challenging the cost-optimization logic of hyperglobalization. The election of Donald Trump for a second term has not only confirmed the resurgence of economic nationalism but legitimized government interventionism in the form of protective measures and industrial policies whose logic, contours and effects are yet to be fully understood.

Second, and in conjunction, the emergence or, more accurately, the *resurgence* of security imperatives has contributed to the diversification of trade policy instruments, as witnessed by renewed government activism in the form of investment and export restrictions, trade and financial sanctions and interference in supply chain management whether in the name of strategic and economic alliances ("friendshoring") or national sovereignty. Many factors have contributed to the changing discourses and policies inherent to the

1 Jean-Baptiste Velut (2022). "Environmental allies and trade competitors: A comparative analysis of US and EU governance models for the trade-and-climate nexus" in Elaine Fahey & Isabella. Mancini (Eds.), *Understanding the EU as a "good" global governance actor* (pp. 74–90). Edward Elgar.

 | HTTPS://DOI.ORG/10.1163/9789004762251-008

"security turn" in trade policies, but the return of great power competition and the supply chain disruptions triggered successively by the pandemic and the Russian invasion of Ukraine both turned the peaceful notion of interdependence into a toxic form of dependence. The advent of this new trade–security nexus is a dual process that entails both the weaponization of economic interdependence[2] and the commodification of security alliances. In the former case, the malleable, if not elusive, notion of "economic security" means that any form of trade dependence can be interpreted as a source of vulnerability: energy security, health security and food security can all be framed as national interests. Likewise, which commodities can be classified as strategic or "critical" becomes a matter of interpretation: if steel, ship-building and auto industries have long made the list of strategic sectors, semiconductors, critical minerals and active pharmaceutical ingredients (APIs) have recently extended it. If trade is "becoming" securitized or, at least, reclaiming its security credentials, US security arrangements are becoming increasingly leveraged for economic purposes. These issue linkages are not new: from the nineteenth-century gunboat diplomacy to the Cold War and the so-called War on Terror, America's military protection has never been disinterested, or dissociated from economic interests. Yet, as witnessed by the tentative US–Ukraine agreement on critical minerals, the second Trump administration has now made this quid pro quo explicit. Whether this "naked transactionalism"[3] survives the Trump administration is beyond the point: economic and security linkages are here to stay. The question here is whether they will shape or overshadow trade–labour linkages.

Third, the contestation and re-embedding of trade policies have paradoxically led to the rise of new forms of trade and regulatory cooperation: first, less visible "mini-deals" such as memoranda of understanding and sectoral agreements;[4] and second, autonomous measures on behalf of labour rights or the environment (e.g. the Uyghur Forced Labor Prevention Act in the US, the

2 Robert Blackwill & Jennifer Harris (2016). *War by Other Means.* Harvard University Press; Henry Farrell & Abraham Newman (2019). "Weaponized inter-dependence: How global economic networks shape state coercion". International Security, 44(1), 42–79; Meunier, Sophie and Kalypso Nicolaidis (2019). The Geopoliticization of European Trade and Investment Policy. *Journal of Common Market* Studies 57, 103–113.

3 Peter D. Feaver (6 November 2024), "How Trump Will Change the World", *Foreign Affairs,* available at: Peter D. Feaver, "How Trump Will Change the World". *Foreign Affairs, available at:* https://www.foreignaffairs.com/united-states/how-trump-will-change-world (last accessed on 2 August 2025).

4 Kathleen Claussen (2022). "Trade's mini-deals". *Virginia Journal of International Law,* 62, 315–382; Lucian Cernat, (2023). "The Art of the Mini-Deals: The Invisible Part of EU Trade Policy". *ECIPE Policy Brief* 11.

Forced Labour Regulation or the regulation on deforestation-free products in the EU). Whether bilateral or unilateral measures, these new trade tools have also contributed to de-FTA-zation. Donald Trump's shift to bilateral sectoral deals in the aftermath of the ill-named "Liberation Day" is likely to reinforce this fragmenting process.

Despite the truculence of Donald Trump's protectionism and its immediate repercussions, these structural forces are long in the making and are likely to have long-lasting effects on the dynamics of trade–labour linkages in the USA and the rest of the world. This chapter takes stock of these trends to discuss the present and future of trade and labour linkages in this new political economic paradigm. It is divided into three parts. The first part goes beyond common criticism on the limitations of labour provisions trade agreement to highlight the imperfect but significant contribution that US FTAs have made to the promotion of international labour rights through multiple channels. The second part explains how the de-FTA-zation of US trade policy threatens the institutionalization of labour rights in trade policymaking. The third part discusses the future forms that trade–labour linkages might take in US trade policy.

2 Beyond the Race to the Bottom: The US Role in Promoting Trade–Labour Linkages

The paradox inherent to US trade policy is that Washington has long been both globalization's loudest cheerleader and its fiercest critic. The dynamics of US trade–labour linkages epitomizes this love-and-hate relationship with trade. While the North American Free Trade Agreement (NAFTA) was a catalyst for globalization critics, it became, as a result of social mobilization, a pioneering agreement connecting trade and workers' rights on the one hand, and trade and environmental standards on the other. Thereafter, NAFTA and subsequent US FTAs served as vehicles for the slow institutionalization of labour rights in trade policy in the USA and beyond. Under sustained pressure from labour advocates and their Democratic supporters, the *scope*, *place* and *enforceability* of labour provisions in US trade agreements incrementally strengthened through "generations" of FTAs.[5] The scope gradually shifted

5 Cathleen D. Cimino-Isaacs & M. Angeles Villarreal (2023), "Worker Rights Provisions in Free Trade Agreements (FTAs)", *Congressional Research Service*, IF10046, October 25; International Labor Organisation (2017). "Handbook on Assessment of Labor Provisions in Trade Arrangements". Geneva: International Labour Office; Sylvain Zini (2016). "Exporter le New Deal - Les normes du travail dans la politique commerciale des Etats-Unis". Québec: Presses de l'Université du Québec.

from the compliance of each trading partners with their domestic labour laws to stricter adherence to internationally recognized workers' rights, including the eight fundamental conventions the ILO 1998 Declaration on Rights at Work, as well as additional labour rights like occupational safety and health, minimum wage, right to strike, labour inspection and the rights of migrant and contingent workers. The place of labour provisions went from NAFTA's side agreements to become core chapters, while their enforcement was initially subject to a separate dispute settlement process before the so-called "May 10 Agreement" of 2007 called for the same dispute settlement procedures to apply to the enforcement of labour provisions. In effect, labour issues shifted from afterthoughts in trade negotiations to pivotal issues to the ratification of trade agreements in Congress – NAFTA, the Dominican Republic–Central American Free Trade Agreement (DR-CAFTA) and the USMCA being only the most prominent examples of the centrality of labour politics in US trade policymaking. Finally, the implementation and enforcement of labour provisions[6] went through a heuristic or learning-by-doing process that began with the lengthy and weak-enforcement model of NAFTA's Labor Secretariat to the ground-breaking work of the USMCA's Rapid Response Labor Mechanism, praised for its ability to solve disputes in a matter of months.[7]

As mentioned previously, Washington's promotion of international labour rights was as conflicted as its relationship with globalization, torn between partisan battles and interest groups clashes. Yet, just as the US government played a key role in shaping the trajectory of trade liberalization, it also considerably shaped both the substance and the process of trade–labour linkages

6 Here, I build on Velut et al.'s distinction between the implementation and enforcement of trade and sustainable development clauses. Implementation can be defined as a set of processes underpinned by specific clauses, institutional mechanisms and administrative rules that allow to put an FTA into practice after its entry into force or as a precondition for ratification. Enforcement refers more specifically to the set of legal provisions and practices designed to prevent or settle disputes between trade partners, either through cooperation (e.g. bilateral consultation) and/or coercion (e.g. threat of suspension of trade benefits or use of trade sanctions). As Velut et al. argue, "there is overlap between these two concepts. For instance, public submission processes are an important lever of enforcement, while they may also be considered as a routine form of civil society participation inherent to implementation mechanisms". Jean-Baptiste Velut et al. (2022). "Comparative Analysis of Trade and Sustainable Development Provisions in Free Trade Agreements", *LSE Consulting*, available at: https://www.lse.ac.uk/business/consulting/assets/documents/TSD-Final-Report-Feb-2022.pdf (last accessed on 2 August 2025), p. 236.

7 For more information on the USMCA's Rapid Response Labor Mechanism, see the contribution of Sandra Polaski in this volume.

in the world. Whether half-hearted or incomplete, the US approach to labour rights in trade policy was never the race to the bottom that trade critics denounced, and made an impact on the rest of the world through multiple channels, all of which are being threatened by the resurgence of US economic nationalism.

The first, and perhaps most obvious impact has to do with the diffusion of labour provisions in trade agreements. As a key architect of the post–World War II international trading system, the US played a central role in the legalization of the international trade[8] (Goldstein & Martin 2000), both through the successive rounds of multilateral trade negotiations and through the proliferation of regional and bilateral levels, to which NAFTA strongly contributed.[9] While the US (and Europe's) attempt to include a "social clause" in multilateral trade negotiations faced fierce resistance from lower-and-middle-income countries, innovations in PTAs allowed US-designed trade-and-labour linkages, as well as trade-and-environment connections to spread from one set of negotiations to another in a common pattern policy transfers.[10] For instance, the recent reform of the EU TSD approach drew considerable attention from both European officials and civil society actors on the design and implementation of the RRLM and the mechanics of public submission processes, as illustrated by the structure and the selection of case

8 Judith Goldstein & Lisa L. Martin (2000). "Legalization, Trade Liberalization, and Domestic Politics: A Cautionary Note". *International Organization*, 54(3), 603–632.

9 Horn, Mavroidis and Sapir once argued that the USA and the EU were behind 80 percent of the rules regulating global markets. Henrik Horn, Petros C. Mavroidis, & André Sapir (2010). "Beyond the WTO? An Anatomy of EU and US Preferential Trade Agreements". *World Economy* 33 (11): 1565–88.

10 On labour provisions, see International Labour Organisation (2017). Handbook on Assessment of Labour Provisions in Trade Arrangements. Geneva: International Labour Office; International Labour Organisation (2019), Labour Provisions in G7 Trade Agreements: A Comparative Perspective. Geneva: International Labour Office. For environmental provisions, see Ida Bastiaens, and Evgeny Postnikov (2017). "Greening Up: The Effects of Environmental Standards in EU and US Trade Agreements", Environmental Politics, vol. 26 (5): 847–869; Jean-Frédéric Morin, Dominique Blümer, Clara Brandi and Axel Berger (2019). "Explaining the Varying Frequency of PTAs' Environmental Provisions", World Economy, vol. 42(9): 2602–2628. For both labour and environmental provisions, see Peter Draper, Nkululeko Khumalo, and Faith Tigere (2017). Sustainability Provisions in Regional Trade Agreements: Can they be Multilateralised? RTA Exchange, International Centre for Trade and Sustainable Development (ICTSD) and Inter-American Development Bank (IDB); Jean-Baptiste Velut et al. (2022). "Comparative Analysis of Trade and Sustainable Development Provisions in Free Trade Agreements", *LSE Consulting*, pp. 206–212 available at: https://www.lse.ac.uk/business/consulting/assets/documents/TSD-Final-Report-Feb-2022.pdf (last accessed on 2 August 2025).

studies in the comparative analysis commissioned by the European Commission.[11]

Second, as the world's leading provider of foreign assistance, the US contributed to the promotion of workers' rights through significant investment in labour-related programmes in lower-income countries through several government agencies, including the Department of Labor's Bureau of International Labor Affairs (ILAB), the State Department and the now-defunct US Agency of International Development (USAID). Thus, between 2009 and 2019, the US government invested, on average, nearly 100 million dollars (99.4) a year on trade-related labour capacity building programme, with ILAB providing two thirds of foreign aid (64%) in 2019, USAID accounting for 29% and the State Department for 7%.[12] According to the Congressional Research Service,[13] this allowed ILAB and its sister agencies to engage with 48 countries through technical assistance and cooperation and to monitor labour conditions in over 150 countries. ILAB's country reports remain a key source of information for the monitoring of labour rights violations across the world.

3 The Power of ex-ante Implementation in US FTAs

A third notable channel through which the United States played an important role in the diffusion of trade–labour linkages is by exerting pressure on labour reforms during trade negotiations. The trade-and-labour literature has shown that Washington has been particularly effective in using the "carrot" of a bilateral trade agreement – whether for economic benefits related to access to the US market or for more geostrategic purposes – to push its trade negotiating partners to adopt legislative reforms protecting workers' rights. Thus, the administration of George W. Bush pushed for labour reforms in Bahrain, Morocco and Oman and strengthened bilateral cooperation on workers' rights before their FTAs went into force.[14] Likewise, the Obama administration lev-

11 Jean-Baptiste Velut et al., "Comparative Analysis of TSD Provisions in Free Trade Agreements," op. cit.

12 USAID (2021), "Trade Capacity Building", available at: https://tcb.usaid.gov/ (accessed on 25 November 2021).

13 Cathleen Cimino-Isaacs & M. Angeles Villarreal, op. cit.

14 Moonhawk Kim (2012). "Ex Ante Due Diligence: Formation of Trade Agreements and Protection of Labour Rights". *International Studies Quarterly* 56 (4): 704–719; James Harrison (2019). "The Labour Rights Agenda in Free Trade Agreements". *The Journal of World Investment & Trade* 20: 705–725; ILO (2013). Social dimensions of free trade agreements. Geneva, ILO.

eraged its bargaining power to extract labour concessions from Panama and Colombia for its bilateral FTAs, before compelling legislative reforms from Brunei, Malaysia and Vietnam during the negotiations of the Transpacific Trade Partnership (TPP). Less known is the fact that TPP negotiations also triggered bilateral discussions on labour reform with Mexico, whose commitment to strengthen freedom of association ultimately served as the basis for the USMCA negotiations under Donald Trump's presidency.[15]

At first sight, these achievements may be interpreted at best as the product of Washington's muscular negotiating style, or at worst, as mere tokenism providing political coverage for vulnerable lawmakers supporting trade liberalization. While there is truth in both arguments, the extraction of labour concessions during US FTA negotiations is underpinned by "ex-ante implementation" processes,[16] a set of institutional mechanisms that have been overshadowed by scholarly and policy debates on the scope and enforceability TPAs' labour provisions. First, the negotiation of labour reforms is codified by a procedure known as "presidential certification of compliance", whereby the executive branch must ensure that the labour commitments (among others, e.g. environmental standards, agriculture, intellectual property etc. provisions) of the US trading partner are translated into legislation after the FTA is signed and ratified but *before* the agreement enters into force. The US Trade Representative and other government agencies like the State, Agriculture and Treasury Departments are to review the relevant laws, regulations and administrative practices of the trading partner, who may be advised of any shortcomings in its legislative and regulatory framework. If requested, the US may provide assistance to help its partner. The President, with a certain degree of discretion, must determine whether the partnering country has taken the measures necessary to comply with the provisions of the FTA, before he can authorize the FTA to enter into force. Presidential certification of compliance had an impact on both the content and timing of Mexico's labour reform on freedom of association and collective bargaining, which the Mexican Congress ratified only a few months before the USMCA entered into force. Conversely, according to a veteran USTR official, the US withdrawal from TPP eliminated the prospect of presidential certification and left the monitoring of Vietnam's labour law reforms uncertain, especially with regard to the right to

15 Sandra Polaski (21 November 2023). "USMCA and the Rapid Response Labor Mechanism: A new approach to cross-border governance of labor rights". Available at SSRN: https://ssrn.com/abstract=4639948 or http://dx.doi.org/10.2139/ssrn.4639948

16 Jean-Baptiste Velut et al, op. cit.

form independent unions.[17] The second way in which this form of ex-ante implementation is codified is through conditional action plans, which can be defined as context-specific implementation roadmaps targeting specific labour rights violations before an agreement enters into force. The first, and most ambitious, ex-ante action plan pertained to environmental protection within the framework of the US–Peru Trade Promotion Agreement (PTPA). It consisted of an Annex on Forest Governance with a detailed list of environmental reforms to be undertaken before the PTPA came into effect in February 2009. In the labour field, the first labour action plan was deployed as part of President Obama's renegotiation of the US–Colombia Trade Promotion Agreement (COTPA) initially signed by George W. Bush.[18] In the face of Colombia's notorious record of union workers' assassinations, Barack Obama was under pressure from organized labour and the progressive wing of the Democratic Party to press for stronger labour rights provisions before submitting the agreement for congressional ratification.[19] In April 2011, after consulting with the US Congress, labour unions and civil society organizations, the White House and the Colombian government of Juan Manuel Santos reached an agreement on a very detailed labour action plan which included:

1) Reforming and converting the Ministry of Social Protection into a Labour Ministry, including, among others, the strengthening of labour inspection and the improvement of the system for citizens to file labour complaints;
2) Reforming the Colombian Criminal Code by establishing criminal penalties for employers violating freedom of association and collective bargaining;
3) Legislating on the protection of labour rights in cooperatives with a detailed plan to address workers' rights violations;
4) Creating an enforcement regime to prevent the use of temporary services agencies and collective pacts to circumvent labour rights;

---

17 Ibid, pp. 148–149.

18 While the US–Cambodia Textile Trade Agreement was an important precedent in trade–labour cooperation, its narrow sectoral scope and its peculiar implementation scheme made it less relevant for future FTAs. For more analysis, see, e.g., Kevin Kolben (2004), "Trade, Monitoring, and the ILO: Working to Improve Conditions in Cambodia's Garment Factories", *Yale Human Rights & Development Law Journal* 7, (3), p. 79; Sandra Polaski (2004). "Cambodia Blazes a New Path to Economic Growth and Job Creation", Carnegie Endowment for International Peace, *Carnegie Papers* 51; Wells, Denis (2006), "Best Practice' in the Regulation of International Labor Standards: Lessons of the U.S.-Cambodia Textile Agreement", Comparative Labor Law & Policy Journal, vol. 27(3).

19 Sylvain Zini, op. cit.

5) Formally requesting technical assistance from the ILO on the implementation of this action plan;
6) Strengthening protection for labour activists and union members through increased funding, streamlining of applications for protection filed by union members and regular assessments of the protection system;
7) Reforming the criminal justice system to protect union members by a) broadening the definition of "illegal threats" to include intimidation against union members and activists seeking to exercise their right to organize and bargain collectively; b) strengthening the penalties for illegal threats to include imprisonment;
8) Organizing bilateral meetings on a regular basis for two years to monitor the progress of the labour action plan.

Like the US–Peru Annex on Forest Governance, the Colombia labour action plan was drafted with minutiae, including numbers of inspectors to be hired ("the hiring of at least 100 new labour inspectors during 2011"), specific deadlines for congressional votes and administrative reforms and precise measures to roll out different schemes (e.g. the creation of a toll-free hotline and a new web-based mechanism to facilitate the filing of workers' complaints), under the tutelage of the US government ("The Colombian Government will share the draft resolution with the U.S. Government and will work with the U.S. Government to ensure that the agreed objectives are addressed").[20] These detailed, if not intrusive, provisions went far beyond any labour chapter hitherto negotiated by Washington. Many of these reforms did take place before the US–Colombia went into force and were monitored on a yearly basis for five years.

Just as significantly, the Colombia labour action plan also created an important precedent for future trade and labour linkages, setting the ground for the "Labor Consistency Plans" (LCP) with Vietnam, Malaysia and Brunei that structured trade–labour linkages during the TPP negotiations. Similarly, these were drawn in accordance with each country's legal and institutional context, respectively focusing on: 1) freedom of association, the right to collective bargaining, protection against employment discrimination and forced labour in Vietnam; 2) freedom of association and the protection of migrant workers in Malaysia; and 3) freedom of association, the eradication of child labour,

20 United States Trade Representative (2011), "Colombian Action Plan Related to Labor Rights", available at https://ustr.gov/sites/default/files/uploads/agreements/morocco/pdfs/Colombian%20Action%20Plan%20Related%20to%20Labor%20Rights.pdf (accessed on 25 June 2025).

migrant workers' rights and the introduction of a minimum wage in Brunei. An analysis of the three cases showed that the LCPs set the ground for labour reforms in these three countries, before the USA withdrew from the TPP on the first day of Donald Trump's presidency. While other countries ratified the newly christened CPTPP (Comprehensive Progressive Transpacific Trade Partnership), Vietnam, Malaysia and Brunei were no longer subject to US presidential certification of compliance, which jeopardized the progress accomplished under LCPs.[21] While the success of labour reforms is shaped by multiple factors, the story of labour action plans in TPP countries tells an important story about the future of trade and labour linkages in a post-FTA context.

4 *Adieu* FTAs, *au revoir* Labour Rights?

For all the imperfections of labour provisions in trade agreements, the consequences of US economic nationalism on labour rights are becoming increasingly clear. To begin with, in the absence of a transparent and accountable trade-negotiating agenda, the underestimated but real benefits of ex-ante implementation under presidential certification of compliance will disappear. The USMCA was the last FTA to deliver substantive results in the labour realm. The absence of a substantive trade-negotiating agenda underpinned by clear rules – other than the "law of the jungle"[22] – means that the US no longer can or wants to leverage its market access on behalf of labour rights.

This new reality goes beyond Trumpian protectionism and has become embedded in Washington's thinking on trade (Hanson 2023). In fact, the Biden administration's aborted negotiations of the Indo-Pacific Economic Framework (IPEF) – designed as an alternative to traditional FTAs – raised a lot of questions about whether US trading partners would ever accept strict enforcement of labour provisions without the quid pro quo of US market access – tariff negotiations being excluded from IPEF negotiations. India's withdrawal from the trade pillar of the negotiations was emblematic of the challenges inherent to this new post-FTA model. From an institutional

---

21 Kevin Kolben (2022). "A merger of TSD approaches? The CPTPP and its consistency plans" in Jean-Baptiste Velut et al. (2022). "Comparative Analysis of Trade and Sustainable Development Provisions in Free Trade Agreements", *LSE Consulting*, pp. 206–212 available at: https://www.lse.ac.uk/business/consulting/assets/documents/TSD-Final-Report-Feb-2022.pdf (accessed on 2 August 2025).

22 Chad P. Bown & Douglas A. Irwin (2019), "Trump's Assault on the Global Trading System". *Foreign Affairs*, August 12. https://www.foreignaffairs.com/china/trumps-assault-global-trading-system-tariff (accessed on 2 August 2025).

standpoint, President Biden's decision to negotiate IPEF as an executive agreement signalled that the White House did not intend to submit this agreement to Congress, and would have eluded presidential certification of compliance, including on labour rights. Paradoxically, by freeing itself of institutional constraints – and expanding Putnam's famous "win-set"[23] – the Biden administration might have reduced its own bargaining power vis-à-vis its trading partners.

As of this writing, the odds of the Trump administration negotiating labour rights provisions as part of his "90 deals in 90 days" are abysmal. This is not just because the rights of foreign workers are not on President Trump's political agenda, but because the personalization of US trade policy precludes any congressional oversight. The fact that Congress has abdicated its constitutional role in trade policymaking means that it can no longer invoke labour rights as "principal trade negotiating objectives" – as codified in US trade law since the 2002 Bipartisan Trade Promotion Authority Act (Sec. 2102b, par. 11) – nor require that the President certifies the situation of workers' rights before Congress can approve a trade agreement. This has two immediate consequences on trade–labour linkages: 1) trade negotiations will no longer be leveraged on behalf of labour rights; 2) the new generation of "mini-deals" will no longer serve as vehicles for the diffusion of policy innovations across the world.

Second, the US role in the promotion trade-and-labour linkages internationally is also likely to take a backseat at the implementation and enforcement stage. This is because the three key US agencies funding international labour rights are currently under assault. Most prominently, USAID, the second contributor to US labour-related foreign assistance programmes (29%) has been shut down, or to be more specific, 99% of its workforce has been eliminated,[24] while its few remaining programmes will be absorbed by the State Department. This marks a radical departure not only from the history of American trade-labour linkages, but, most importantly, from six decades of foreign policy tradition during which the USA became the world's largest provider of foreign assistance. The State Department has not been spared by this anti-government offensive. Data from the President's 2026 Budget show the Trump administration's intent to reduce discretionary spending for the

23 Robert D. Putnam (1988). Diplomacy and domestic politics: The logic of two-level games. *International Organization, 42*(3), 427–460.

24 Both State and labour departments have hitherto been spared by the budget cuts of the Department of Government Efficiency (DOGE) with only 1% of their workforce being affected. For an overview of staff cuts, see Elena Shao and Ashley Wu, (12 May 2025), "The Federal Work Force Cuts So Far, Agency by Agency", The New York Times.

State Department by 83.7%.[25] Nor is the Department of Labor (DOL) – which provides the lion's share (64%) of labour-related foreign aid – immune to this austerity agenda, with the President's 2026 budget requesting a 34.9% reduction of discretionary spending in 2026. Given the administration's contempt for foreign assistance, the DOL's foreign assistance programmes are likely to be the first targets of these budget cuts. Compounding this financial toll, the Trump administration temporarily shut down the website of USAID, thereby erasing the record of on-the-ground efforts to protect workers' rights that served as a benchmark for donor and recipient countries alike. In the next few years, Washington's retreat from trade–labour linkages is likely to apply not just to FTAs but also to other preferential trade agreements like the General System of Preferences, which expired at the end of 2020 and has yet to be renewed, and to the renewal of the African Growth Opportunity Act (AGOA), set to expire in September 2025, which has little chance of being renewed or funded under the current Republican majority in Congress. In short, the main channels through which Washington promoted trade-related labour rights have been severed. In the medium term, the de-FTA-zation of US trade policy will likely jeopardize the promotion of international labour rights at the bilateral, regional or multilateral levels. Does this really mean that the promotion of labour rights in the trade policy sphere is doomed?

5 The Future of US Trade–Labour Linkages

While the rise of US economic nationalism does not bode well for the promotion of international labour rights in the short term, the diversification of trade policy instruments including autonomous or unilateral measures targeting specific sectors or specific labour issues could also lead to new policy experiments. One such experiment that was born before Donald Trump's return to power was the Uyghur Forced Labor Prevention Act (UFLPA), a law signed on 23 December 2021 and which entered into force in June 2022. Born out of the convergence of President Biden's "worker-centered policy" and the securitization of trade, the UFLPA was designed to strengthen the prohibition of imported goods made with forced labour in China's Xinjiang Uyghur Autonomous Region. The UFLPA requires that the U.S. Customs and Border Protection (CBP) apply a presumption that all goods "mined, produced, or manufac-

25 Office of Management and Budget. (2 May 2025). *Budget of the United States Government, fiscal year 2026*. U.S. Government Publishing Office, available at: https://www.govinfo.gov/content/pkg/BUDGET-2026-BUD/pdf/BUDGET-2026-BUD.pdf (accessed on June 15).

tured wholly or in part" in Xinjiang and even those shipped through the region are made with forced labour. The presumption is rebuttable through a long and tedious process whereby importers must respond to all CBP requests for information and demonstrate due diligence following a series of guidelines, including stakeholder engagement, mapping out the supply chain and assessment of risks of forced labour, introduction and monitoring of a code of conduct etc.[26] According to data from CBP, during its first three years, i.e. between June 2022 and May 2025, a total of 16,201 shipments went through detention, 9,739 (60%) of which were denied and 5,738 were released. These shipments represented a total of 3.67 billion dollars, with the automotive, aerospace and electronics sectors experiencing the most cases of detention by CBP.[27] Meanwhile, the DOL's ILAB has recently added new products to the "List of Goods Produced by Child Labor or Forced Labor" in China. This can be interpreted as either a success for the US-attempted crackdown on labour rights violations or a failure to contain Xinjiang imports. Yet, while the jury is still out on the on-the-ground impact of the UFLPA on labour rights in the Xinjiang region, this policy experiment holds three lessons for the future of labour rights in US trade policy and the rest of the world.

First, when it comes to domestic politics, while security and human rights may, at first, seem like strange bedfellows, their linkage under specific unilateral trade initiatives like the UFLPA is more attractive to US lawmakers than FTAs. While the inclusion of labour provisions in trade agreements has long divided political parties, especially in the House of Representatives,[28] the ratification of the UFLPA was notable for the strong bipartisan support enjoyed by the bill, which passed the Senate by unanimous consent, and the House with only one dissenting voice (Thomas Massie, R-KY). Such voting margins are unheard of in contemporary American trade politics and show that supply chain resilience and economic security can be instrumentalized on behalf of workers' and human rights. The broader question is whether and to what extent targeted protective measures – often reduced to the polarizing notion

26 U.S. Customs and Border Protection (CBP). (13 June 2022). *Operational guidance for importers : Uyghur Forced Labor Prevention Act (UFLPA)* [PDF]. U.S. Dept. of Homeland Security. https://www.medey.com/wp-content/uploads/2023/04/CBP_Guidance_for_Importers_for_UFLPA_13_June_2022.pdf (accessed on 25 June 2025), pp. 4, 1–14.

27 U.S. Customs and Border Protection. (17 June 2025). *Uyghur Forced Labor Prevention Act statistics*. U.S. Department of Homeland Security. https://www.cbp.gov/newsroom/stats/trade/uyghur-forced-labor-prevention-act-statistics (accessed on 25 June 2025).

28 James Shoch (2001). *Trading Blows: Party Competition and U.S. Trade Policy in a Globalizing Era*. University of North Carolina Press.

of protectionism – can be leveraged to achieve social objectives. This has arguably been a central question to US trade politics since the American revolution,[29] but it has recently taken a whole new dimension in Donald Trump's second term. Leaving aside the constitutional aspects of the question for a moment, there is evidence that autonomous or unilateral trade measures may become the next generation of trade policy experiments. Restrictions on imports produced with forced labour like the UFLPA in the United States, but also similar measures in Canada and the EU, may herald a "unilateral turn" in trade policymaking[30] that can be instrumentalized for security objectives, but also environmental goals, be they waste management[31] or responsible forest management.[32]

The second and parallel takeaway from the UFLPA that is relevant for the promotion of both labour rights and environmental sustainability is the confirmation of a shift from government-centric approaches to workers' rights protection where governments are liable for the enforcement of labour standards, to a firm-level approach where corporate actors are equally accountable for due diligence and supply chain resilience. While the USMCA's Rapid Response Labor Mechanism has shed light on the shift of enforcement to the facility level,[33] this process was longer in the making than is usually acknowledged. The decentralizing trend in enforcement began with the US–Cambodia Textile Trade Agreement (USCTTA) in 1999 and was renewed under the US–Peru Trade Promotion Agreement's company-level verification mechanism to fight against illegal logging, before being transplanted in the RRLM and strengthened under the UFLPA.

---

29 Susan Aaronson (2001). *Taking Trade to the Streets. The Lost History of Public Efforts to Shape Globalization.* Ann Arbor: The University of Michigan Press; Alfred Eckes (1995). *Opening America's Market. U.S. Foreign Trade Policy Since 1776.* Chapell Hill / London: The University of North Carolina Press; Douglas A. Irwin (2017). *Clashing over commerce: A history of U.S. trade policy.* University of Chicago Press.

30 De Ville, Ferdi, Simon Happersberger, & Harri Kalimo, "The Unilateral Turn in EU Trade Policy? The Origins and Characteristics of the EU's New Trade Instruments", *European Foreign Affairs Review*, vol. 28, 2023, pp. 15–34.

31 Rachel Wellhausen & Jean-Baptiste Velut (forthcoming). "The Green Virtues Of Chinese Protectionism: A Comparative Analysis Of EU and US Responses To The China Garbage Shock", *Papers in Political Economy.*

32 Jean-Baptiste Velut, (forthcoming). "Linking Trade, Illegal Logging and Forest Management: Lessons and Limitations of the US Approach" (under review).

33 See, e.g., Kathleen Claussen & Chad P. Bown (2024). "Corporate Accountability by Treaty: The New North American Rapid Response Labor Mechanism" *American Journal of International Law* 98. Available at SSRN: https://ssrn.com/abstract=4499182; Kevin Kolben (2022), op. cit.

This shift to due diligence dovetails the EU's recent efforts to devolve the liability of enforcing social and environmental standards, an approach epitomized by the series of sustainability autonomous measures, including most emblematically and at the cross-sectoral level, the Corporate Sustainability Due Diligence Directive (adopted in July 2024, but whose implementation has been postponed to July 2027) and the Forced Labor Regulation (adopted in December 2024), as well as sectoral trade initiatives like the Carbon Border Adjustment Mechanism, the Regulation on deforestation-free products, the EU Conflict Minerals Regulation or the EU Batteries Regulation. As the early record of the RRLM shows, this form of labour rights regime can empower labour unions and civil society organizations to monitor corporate practices.

This means that corporations' expanding due diligence obligations, along with the new security imperatives of the current era mean that supply chain resilience could become a strong vehicle for labour rights, not merely under traditional FTAs[34] or new agreements like IPEF (which included provisions on supply chains) but also under new trade policy experiments. Whether the US government mobilizes a new generation of trade policy tools and continues to disseminate its good practices will largely depend on the evolving governance of US trade policy, and whether Congress is willing to continue exercising its constitutional prerogatives on behalf of a broader pool of stakeholders, or if it relinquishes its authority to an omnipotent executive branch with a narrow understanding of US national interests.

Bibliography

Aaronson, Susan (2001). Taking Trade to the Streets. The Lost History of Public Efforts to Shape Globalization. Ann Arbor: The University of Michigan Press.

Bastiaens, Ida and Evgeny Postnikov (2017). "Greening Up: The Effects of Environmental Standards in EU and US Trade Agreements", Environmental Politics, vol. 26 (5): 847–869.

Blackwill, Robert & Jennifer Harris (2016). *War by Other Means*. Harvard University Press.

Bown, Chad P. and Douglas A. Irwin (2019), "Trump's Assault on the Global Trading System". *Foreign Affairs*, August 12. https://www.foreignaffairs.com/china/trumps-assault-global-trading-system-tariff.

34 Kevin Kolben (2024), "Trade, Labor Conditionality, and Supply Chain Resilience, Cornell International Law Journal, Vol. 57, Fall 2024, pp. 73–98.

Cimino-Isaacs, Cathleen & M. Angeles Villarreal (2023), "Worker Rights Provisions in Free Trade Agreements (FTAs)", Congressional Research Service, IF10046, October 25.

Claussen, Kathleen (2022). "Trade's Mini-Deals". *Virginia Journal of International Law, 62*, 315–382; Lucian Cernat, (2023). "The Art of the Mini-Deals: The Invisible Part of EU Trade Policy". *ECIPE Policy Brief* 11.

Claussen, Kathleen and Chad P. Bown (2024). "Corporate Accountability by Treaty: The New North American Rapid Response Labor Mechanism" *American Journal of International Law* 98. Available at SSRN: https://ssrn.com/abstract=4499182.

De Ville, Ferdi, Simon Happersberger, & Harri Kalimo, "The Unilateral Turn in EU Trade Policy? The Origins and Characteristics of the EU's New Trade Instruments", *European Foreign Affairs Review*, vol. 28, 2023, pp. 15–34.

Draper, Peter, Nkululeko Khumalo, and Faith Tigere (2017). Sustainability Provisions in Regional Trade Agreements: Can they be Multilateralised? RTA Exchange, International Centre for Trade and Sustainable Development (ICTSD) and Inter-American Development Bank (IDB).

Eckes, Alfred (1995), Opening America's Market. U.S. Foreign Trade Policy Since 1776. Chapell Hill / London: The University of North Carolina Press.

Farrell, Henry & Abraham Newman (2019). "Weaponized inter-dependence: How global economic networks shape state coercion". International Security, 44(1), 42–79.

Feaver, Peter D. (6 November 2024), "How Trump Will Change the World", Foreign Affairs, available at: https://www.foreignaffairs.com/united-states/how-trump-will-change-world (last accessed on 2 August 2025).

Goldstein, Judith, & Lisa L. Martin (2000). Legalization, Trade Liberalization, and Domestic Politics: A Cautionary Note. International Organization, 54(3), 603–632.

Hanson, G. H. (2023, December 12). *Washington's new trade consensus: And what it gets wrong. Foreign Affairs, 103*(1). Review of *No Trade Is Free: Changing Course, Taking on China, and Helping America's Workers*, by R. Lighthizer.

Harrison, James (2019). The Labour Rights Agenda in Free Trade Agreements. The Journal of World Investment & Trade. 20. 705–725. 10.1163/22119000-12340153.

Horn, Henrik, Petros C. Mavroidis, and André Sapir (2010). "Beyond the WTO? An Anatomy of EU and US Preferential Trade Agreements". World Economy 33 (11): 1565–88.

ILO (2013). Social dimensions of free trade agreements. Geneva, ILO.

ILO (2017). Handbook on Assessment of Labour Provisions in Trade Arrangements. Geneva: International Labour Office.

ILO (2019), Labour Provisions in G7 Trade Agreements: A Comparative Perspective. Geneva: International Labour Office.

Irwin, Douglas A. (2017). *Clashing over commerce: A history of U.S. trade policy*. University of Chicago Press.

Kim, Moonhawk (2012). Ex Ante Due Diligence: Formation of Trade Agreements and Protection of Labour Rights. International Studies Quarterly 56 (4): 704–719.

Kolben, Kevin "a Merger of TSD Approaches? the CPTPP and Its Consistency Plans" in Velut, J.B. et al. (2022). "Comparative Analysis of Trade and Sustainable Development Provisions in Free Trade Agreements", *LSE Consulting*, pp. 206–212 *LSE Consulting*, https://www.lse.ac.uk/business/consulting/assets/documents/TSD-Final-Report-Feb-2022.pdf.

Kolben, Kevin (2024), "Trade, Labor Conditionality, and Supply Chain Resilience, Cornell International Law Journal, Vol. 57, Fall 2024, pp. 73–98.

Kolben, Kevin (2004), "Trade, Monitoring, and the ILO: Working to Improve Conditions in Cambodia's Garment Factories", Yale Human Rights & Development Law Journal, vol. 7, art. 3.

Meunier, Sophie and Kalypso Nicolaidis (2019). The Geopoliticization of European Trade and Investment Policy. *Journal of Common Market* Studies 57, 103–113.

Morin, Jean-Frédéric, Dominique Blümer, Clara Brandi and Axel Berger (2019). "Explaining the Varying Frequency of PTAs' Environmental Provisions", World Economy, vol. 42(9): 2602–2628.

Office of Management and Budget (2 May 2025). *Budget of the United States Government, fiscal year 2026*. U.S. Government Publishing Office, available at: https://www.govinfo.gov/content/pkg/BUDGET-2026-BUD/pdf/BUDGET-2026-BUD.pdf (Accessed June 15).

Polaski, Sandra (2004). "Cambodia Blazes a New Path to Economic Growth and Job Creation", Carnegie Endowment for International Peace, *Carnegie Papers* 51.

Polaski, Sandra (21 November 2023), USMCA and the Rapid Response Labor Mechanism: A new approach to cross-border governance of labor rights. Available at SSRN: https://ssrn.com/abstract=4639948 or http://dx.doi.org/10.2139/ssrn.4639948.

Putnam, R. D. (1988). Diplomacy and domestic politics: The logic of two-level games. *International Organization*, 42(3), 427–460.

Shao Elena and Ashley Wu, (12 May 2025), "The Federal Work Force Cuts So Far, Agency by Agency", The New York Times.

Shoch, J. (2001). *Trading Blows: Party Competition and U.S. Trade Policy in a Globalizing Era*. University of North Carolina Press.

USAID (2021), "Trade Capacity Building", available at: https://tcb.usaid.gov/ (accessed on 25 November 2021).

U.S. Customs and Border Protection (CBP) (13 June 2022). *Operational guidance for importers : Uyghur Forced Labor Prevention Act (UFLPA)* [PDF]. U.S. Dept. of Homeland Security. https://www.medey.com/wp-content/uploads/2023/04/CBP_Guidance_for_Importers_for_UFLPA_13_June_2022.pdf (accessed on 25 June 2025).

U.S. Customs and Border Protection (17 June 2025). *Uyghur Forced Labor Prevention Act statistics*. U.S. Department of Homeland Security. https://www.cbp.gov/newsroom/stats/trade/uyghur-forced-labor-prevention-act-statistics (accessed on 25 June 2025).

United States Trade Representative (2011), "Colombian Action Plan Related to Labor Rights", available at https://ustr.gov/sites/default/files/uploads/agreements/morocco/pdfs/Colombian%20Action%20Plan%20Related%20to%20Labor%20Rights.pdf (accessed on 25 June 2025).

Velut, Jean-Baptiste (2022). "Environmental Allies and Trade Competitors: a Comparative Analysis of US and EU Governance Models for the Trade-and-Climate Nexus" in Elaine Fahey & Isabella Mancini (Eds.), *Understanding the EU as a "good" global governance actor* (pp. 74–90). Edward Elgar.

Velut, Jean-Baptiste (forthcoming). "Linking Trade, Illegal Logging and Forest Management: Lessons and Limitations of the US Approach" (under review).

Wellhausen, Rachel & Jean-Baptiste Velut, J.B. (forthcoming). "The Green Virtues Of Chinese Protectionism: A Comparative Analysis Of EU and US Responses To The China Garbage Shock", *Papers in Political Economy*.

Wells, Denis (2006), "Best Practice' in the Regulation of International Labor Standards: Lessons of the U.S.-Cambodia Textile Agreement", Comparative Labor Law & Policy Journal, vol. 27(3).

Zini, Sylvain. (2016). *Exporter le New Deal – Les normes du travail dans la politique commerciale des Etats-Unis*. Québec: Presses de l'Université du Québec.

CHAPTER 8

The EU–Canada Comprehensive Free Trade Agreement (CETA): An Opportunity for a Fairer Trade Alliance

Vincenzo Ferrante

1 The Provisional Effect of CETA Pending Member-State Ratification

On 30 October 2016 the CETA text was approved for signature by all 28 European Union Member States. Former Prime Minister of Canada Justin Trudeau travelled to Brussels to sign on behalf of Canada, a mark of the importance that the descendants of ancient European settlers from the other side of the Ocean attribute to the agreement. Indeed, the process that led to signature of the treaty was not at all simple, and even today the concerns that accompanied its signature do not appear to have dissipated as CETA has not been ratified by all the signatory states.[1] Currently, it has only come into effect on a provisional basis and limited to those parts that fall within the exclusive competence of the Union.

After introductory talks that began in April 2009, an initial version of the agreement between Canada and the European Union was signed in August 2014. In accordance with the attribution to the Union of new external competences on trade matters set out in the Treaty of Lisbon (art. 218 ff. TFEU), and following the international diplomatic tradition of both parties, the agreement was negotiated exclusively by executive staff and the text only published on the EU's official website for the first time on 26 September 2014. Because the issues included in the initial project had been significantly expanded with respect to the matters traditionally negotiated in a trade agreement, in order to include a regulatory co-operation framework for promoting further bilateral co-operation, the original Trade and Investment Enhancement Agreement

1 The treaty still has to be ratified by Belgium, Bulgaria, Ireland, Cyprus, France, Greece, Hungary, Italy, Poland and Slovenia. An initiative launched in September 2023 by MEP Javier Moreno Sánchez to complete the full ratification process was unsuccessful (see https://www.socialistsanddemocrats.eu/).

 | HTTPS://DOI.ORG/10.1163/9789004762251-009

(TIEA) changed its name to became the Comprehensive Economic and Trade Agreement (CETA).

The long period between the end of negotiations and signature of the treaty (more than two years) has been spent responding to attacks and condemnations from farmers organisations, workers' unions and consumer associations. Due to the concomitant negotiations with the USA for the TTIP, the protests against CETA were unusually strong. European opposition to the two treaties has pointed the finger at the risks of globalisation in the massive abolition of custom barriers, especially the risk that American food, phytosanitary and pharmaceutical products, which currently meet less stringent green standards, could invade Europe to the detriment of local production and people's health.

Another point that has attracted special attention is the binding nature of the treaty provisions and their justiciability being entrusted to private parties (rather than to the national courts) in cases where the interests of foreign companies are involved because of direct investment. This is a standard formula in free trade treaties with emerging countries, but entirely new in bilateral relations with transatlantic partners. Some feared that the CETA provision for an exclusive arbitration system to settle disputes between investors and the state (ISDS) would totally deny national judges the power to rule on any dispute, when a foreign company was involved. On this point it should be pointed out that art. 8.18 ff. of the final version of CETA introduced an innovation to the standard ISDS formula of traditional trade agreements.[2] Instead of an ad hoc arbitration body, it establishes an independent Investment Court System (ICS), composed of a permanent Tribunal and an Appellate Tribunal (art. 8.28) comprising judges appointed by countries with a view to creating an International Multilateral Court.[3]

2 See art. 8, s. f, "Resolution of investment disputes between investors and states" (arts. 8.18–8.45), and see also art. 29 of the treaty. On this point, see L. G. Radicati di Brozolo, *Where is Investor-State Arbitration Heading? Reflections on the Debate over EU Investor Protection Agreements*, in A. Carlevaris, L. Lévy, A. Mourre, E. A. Schwartz (eds.) *International Arbitration Under Review, Essays in honour of John Beechey* (ICC Publishing: Paris, 2015), pp. 319–342.

3 See Council of the European Union, "Negotiating directives for a Convention establishing a multilateral court for the settlement of investment disputes", 20 March 2018, available at data.consilium.europa.eu/doc/document/ST-12981–2017-ADD-1-DCL-1/en/pdf. On this issue, a stakeholders meeting was held by initiative of the European Commission in January 2024 and UNCITRAL, an ad hoc Working Group III, will meet again on April 2025 in New York (uncitral.un.org/en/workinggroups/3/investor-state). See also decision no. 001/2021 of the CETA Joint Committee of 29 January 2021 setting out the administrative and organisational matters regarding the functioning of the Appellate Tribunal, available at https://www.inter

Not surprisingly, the Belgian Government was the last country to come out in favour of signing the treaty, after a previous vote by the Walloon regional Parliament rejecting the move. Its resistance was only overcome thanks to a joint instrument that was signed by all the parties to the agreement[4] which, in accordance with art. 31 of the Vienna Convention on the Law of Treaties (VCLT), sets out an "agreed interpretation" of the "provisions that have been the object of public debate and concerns".

According to this Joint Interpretative Instrument (JII), the parties will "continue to have the ability to achieve the legitimate public policy objectives that their democratic institutions set, such as public health, social services, public education, safety, environment, public morals, privacy and data protection and the promotion and protection of cultural diversity". National "provisions on investment protection and dispute resolution, and on sustainable development, labour rights and environmental protection" will also remain unaffected by the treaty, because the parties undertake to "not lower our respective standards and regulations related to food safety, product safety, consumer protection, health, environment or labour protection. Imported goods, service suppliers and investors must continue to respect domestic requirements, including rules and regulations".

Immediately below, the joint statement adds that: "CETA will not result in foreign investors being treated more favourably than domestic investors. CETA does not privilege recourse to the investment court system set up by the agreement. Investors may choose instead to pursue available recourse in domestic courts" (art. 6(a)).

Art. 6(b) recognises that "CETA clarifies that governments may change their laws, regardless of whether this may negatively affect an investment or investor's expectations of profits. Furthermore, CETA clarifies that any compensation due to an investor will be based on an objective determination by the Tribunal and will not be greater than the loss suffered by the investor". The JII also provides that the parties "are committed to review regularly the content of the obligation to provide fair and equitable treatment" and to prevent "shell" or "mail box" companies established in their territory allowing signatory parties to issue binding notes of interpretation.

national.gc.ca/trade-commerce/trade-agreements-accords-commerciaux/agr-acc/ceta-aecg/appellate-tribunal-dappel.aspx?lang=eng.

4 See document 13541/16 of the General Secretariat of the Council "Joint Interpretative Instrument on the Comprehensive Economic and Trade Agreement (CETA) between Canada and the European Union and its Member States" at http://data.consilium.europa.eu/doc/document/ST-13541-2016-INIT/en/pdf and also in OJEU, 14.1.2017.

Following this feverish mediation, the Kingdom of Belgium finally joined the other Member States of the EU in signing the treaty, nevertheless announcing its intention to apply to the Court of Justice to rule on the legitimacy of the agreement. This resulted in a positive pronouncement recognising that CETA, and in particular the ISDS clause, is compatible with primary EU law, neither violating the autonomy of the EU legal order, or the general principle of equal treatment and the right of access to an independent tribunal.[5]

On this point, it should also be pointed out that the Commission has decided to propose CETA to the Member States as a "mixed" agreement, as in a case examined by the European Court of Justice concerning the trade deal reached between the EU and Singapore.

In that case,[6] Advocate General Sharpston proposed making a distinction between exclusive competence and mixed competence clauses in a trade agreement. The former would be ratified immediately by the Council and could come into force under art. 218(5) TFEU. The latter would then be ratified by the individual national parliaments at a later stage. According to that opinion, provisions setting fundamental labour and environmental standards and falling within the scope of either social or environmental policy require individual state ratification, as do dispute settlement clauses and mediation and transparency mechanisms "in so far as those provisions apply to (and are therefore ancillary to) the parts of [the agreement] for which the EU enjoys shared external competence" (paras. 502 and 562[7]).

In its subsequent decision[8] (properly an opinion), the Court went further, recognising that every issue covered in the agreement falls within the exclusive competence of the European Union (para. 305), with the sole exception of direct investment protection and the Investor–State Dispute Settlement mechanism, which fall within the shared competence of the European Union and the Member States.

When the parties met to sign the treaty, Germany had also overcome the obstacles preventing its Government from signing. The German Constitu-

5 ECJ Opinion 1/17 of 30 April 2019 (ECLI:EU:C:2019:341).

6 Issued on 21 December 2016 (ECLI:EU:C:2016:992).

7 According to para. 502, "The provisions concerning labour protection standards [...] can be regarded as necessary in order to achieve the social policy objectives set out in art. 151 TFEU relating to, in particular, those listed in article 153(1)(a), (b) and (c) TFEU (improvement of the working environment to protect workers' health and safety; working conditions; and social security and social protection of workers). The European Union therefore has shared competence over that component as a result of articles 4(2)(b), 151 and 153(1) TFEU and the second ground under article 216(1) TFEU".

8 No. 2/15 of 16 May 2017 (Full Court) (ECLI:EU:C:2017:376).

tional Court (Betriebsverfassungsgericht) had just rejected the action to obtain an injunction preventing signature of the treaty. However, the Court indicated three conditions that needed to be met for the German Representative to vote in favour of the CETA within the European Council, stressing the possibility of a subsequent different decision in light of the famous *Solange I* case should said conditions not be met.[9]

CETA was signed on October 2016 by a large majority of 408 votes, approved by the European Parliament on 15 February 2017 and provisionally came into force from 21 September 2017.[10] Art. 30.7(3) provides for provisional application of the treaty, pending completion of the procedures for its ratification by each individual national parliament.

Making a distinction between the matters that fall within the shared competence of the European Union from the others over which the European Union enjoys exclusive external competence could be an attractive solution to avoid a diplomatic impasse. Nevertheless, because "trade in goods", "in renewable energy generation" or "foreign direct investment" falls within the scope of the Common Commercial Policy, it would not be not easy, given the provisional effect following the signature and consent expressed by the European Parliament in the light of art. 218 TFEU, to separate the impact that the liberalisation of trade in these areas would produce on working conditions in these sectors due to a reduction in unit price costs.

Following signature of the CETA, the German Court confirmed the legitimacy of the provisions contained therein,[11] as did the French *Conseil Constitu-*

9 See G. Villani, "Considerations on the judgement of the BVerfG on the conclusion of CETA" (2017), *Studi Tributari Europei*, 1, 239 at https:/ste.unibo.it stating that, for example, an inter-institutional agreement could ensure that decisions taken pursuant to article 30(2) of the CETA may only be passed on the basis of a common position unanimously adopted by the Council, and suggesting that a proper interpretation of article 30 (7)(3)(c) CETA should guarantee the possibility for a Member State to unilaterally terminate the provisional application of the agreement by means of written notification in the event of a violation of constitutional identity (§72 of the BVerfG judgment).

10 Council Decision (EU) 2017/38 of 28 October 2016 "on the provisional application of the Comprehensive Economic and Trade Agreement (CETA) between Canada, of the one part, and the European Union and its Member States, of the other part" in OJEU L11, 14.1.2017, pp. 1080–1081; see also Art. 1(1)(d): "the provisional application of Chapters 22, 23 and 24 of the Agreement shall respect the allocation of competences between the Union and the Member States" and Notice "concerning the provisional application of the Comprehensive Economic and Trade Agreement (CETA) between Canada, of the one part, and the European Union and its Member States, of the other part", in OJ L 238, 16.9.2017, pp. 9–19.

11 See Order of 9 February 2022 and the related Press Release no. 22/2022 of 15 March 2022 (in English) on the website of the Court (www.bundesverfassungsgericht.de/).

tionnel which, after examining arguments similar to those put to the German judges, confirmed the legitimacy of the ISDS system, stating that the powers vested in the ad hoc Tribunal constituted under the treaty are limited to payment orders and the restitution of goods and do not override any provisions adopted by individual Member States.[12]

Despite these precautions, the number of Member States that have ratified CETA is still limited, almost nine years after its signature,[13] and it is concerning that the parallel Euro-Canadian cooperation treaty has instead had a much higher number of ratifications.[14]

In the same sense, it is important to point out that on 31 July 2020 the Republic of Cyprus took a formal position against ratification. Because this result was due to the fear that the treaty could be beneficial for Canadian products to the detriment of Halloumi, a traditional local cheese, it was argued that the vote was illegal because the Parliament acted *ultra vires*, it being the competence of the European laws to protect appellation of origin.[15] Of course it may be that, after receiving due guarantees, Cyprus could retrace its steps in the future.

According to an internal Report,[16] in order to avoid exposure to the impossibility of ratifying mixed agreements, the European Parliament's role in conducting trade negotiations and its legitimacy to ratify agreements falling within the exclusive competence of the EU need to be empowered by splitting treaties into two different instruments. This would concentrate into a single agreement the parts of the trade and investment component falling within the exclusive competence of the EU, giving it an interim effect. Conversely, dual ratification insures against the risk of difficulties being caused by the Council or a single Member State, in the event that the Commission proceeds inde-

12 See Decision no. 2017–749 DC of 31 July 2017, *AECG/CETA* and also G. Stegher, "Il Conseil Constitutionnel avalla il CETA: la Francia procede speditamente verso la ratifica?" (2017), *DPCE on line*, 3.

13 See footnote 1.

14 The treaty only remains to be ratified by France, Italy and Ireland.

15 See M. Chamon, T. Verellen, "CETA, Facultative Mixity, Democracy and Halloumi", 7 August 2020, at verfassungsblog.de/whittling-down-the-collective-interest. Also, V. Rubino, "Accordi preferenziali di nuova generazione e fragilità nella cooperazione fra Unione europea e Stati membri: alcune riflessioni sul caso CETA e la tutela delle indicazi oni geografiche dei prodotti alimentari" (2023), *Eurojus*, 1, 122.

16 *Much more than a market – Speed, Security, Solidarity Empowering the Single Market to deliver a sustainable future and prosperity for all EU Citizens*, Enrico Letta's report presented to the European Council on 18 April 2024.

pendently in negotiations. However, it does not provide an adequate solution for the case in which any of the Member States do not ratify the international agreement, claiming to protect the internal market from the risks of competition, as was the case of Cyprus.

The provisional effect that could arise from opening up the market from the very beginning could produce a "conformation" effect on labour-related costs and regulations, and an increase in trade. Nevertheless, the provisional effect relies on the idea that the treaty has not yet come into force, so when it becomes clear that this objective will not be reached, it will be difficult to justify this effect also for the issues that definitely fall within exclusive EU competence.

Obviously, the ISDS clause requires express ratification by the individual Member States to come into force, and special provisions in the treaty and Interpretative Instrument are intended to provide protection to labour issues and avoid a race-to-the-bottom effect. History shows that the removal of customs barriers is ordinarily followed by a convergence in labour market regulation, since the costs of production tend to align. However, Canada has made various efforts to ratify and apply the few ILO conventions that had not yet been ratified (see below), and to date no problems appear to have arisen as a result of the provisional entry into force of the agreement. Meanwhile, the CETA specialised committees have taken action to implement such things as recognition of the professional title of architect, inclusive design for men and women and a common project on due diligence in world value chains in emergent economies.[17] Of course, this convergence effect is part of the history of Canada, which was subject to the influence of the UK until "patriation" was proclaimed in 1982.

2 Protection of Collective Bargaining and the Right to Strike in the Canadian Legal System

It is widely believed that the CETA is a sort of blueprint for the final conclusion of next generation of FTAs, a testbed to establish whether the expansion of the common market has led to a lowering of European standards and reduction in traditional social protections (it was originally planned to adopt the same solutions in the TTIP, before it was dropped by President Trump).

17 For these activities and agreements, see the website https://www.international.gc.ca/trade-commerce/trade-agreements-accords-commerciaux/agr-acc/ceta-aecg/ceta_governance_committees-gouvernance_aecg_comit. See also footnote 23.

Although the level of worker protection guaranteed by Canadian law is commonly considered higher than in the USA, because of the influence exercised over the country by the UK until a few decades ago, on closer analysis the Canadian worker protection system does not appear to be that strongly influenced by European legislation. This can be demonstrated by, among other things, the high level of integration between the Canadian and American unions due to the historical relationship between AFL-CIO and the Canadian Labour Congress (CLC). Indeed, to European eyes, the comparable legal approach and workforce mobility between Ontario and New England mean these bonds are closer than those between unions of different traditions within the ETUC (although the latter now has years of common history).

It is difficult to give even a brief description of the Canadian labour law system. The absence of linguistic homogeneity, very small number of inhabitants (only 30 million in one of the largest countries in the world) and independence trends in Quebec culminating in twice-held separatist referendums which have both failed, make Canadian law more sensitive to autonomous local institutions than in the USA, where the "commerce clause" guarantees a certain homogeneity to the regulatory employment model. Federal powers are therefore limited to public sector employees (including telecommunications, chartered banks, postal services, airports and all kinds of transportation services), so that, for the rest, reference is made to the legislation of each province (or territory).

The Canadian legal model is a compound system because (similarly to Lousiana) in Quebec the 1804 French Civil Code is a source of law, while the other states apply British common law. The influence of the French regulatory tradition has also penetrated Canadian public law, as well as the tendency to *clarité*, resulting in the enactment of a Labour Code, which is simply an Act of Parliament that consolidates certain statutes governing industrial relations. Specifically, the code concerns occupational health and safety, certain employment standards (such as working hours, wages, leave, holidays, sexual harassment and termination of employment), strikes and lockouts. The code also applies to some Crown corporations (the British monarch is still the Head of State) and to the Royal Canadian Mounted Police (RCMP), whose union has instigated important judgments in recent years (see below).

As far as federal legislation is concerned, the industrial relations system is modelled on US law, with the adoption of a Wagner model. Under this, a workers' or employers' trade union recognised by the Canada Labour Relations Board has a duty to meet the other side and negotiate "in good faith and make every reasonable effort to enter into a collective agreement". Naturally, the provision of a right to collective bargaining means the overall picture of the rules that apply to private companies is particularly fragmented.

A more in-depth look at the provisions of the law shows that the biggest difference between Canada and the EU is constitutional, because the Canadian Charter of Rights and Freedoms is almost entirely concentrated on the problem of the definition of legislative powers vested in the states and territories. The issue is, to a certain extent, unknown to European constitutionalism, which never fails to include provisions that emphasise the social nature of the state. Even the most reticent constitutions recognise the traditional rights of workers.[18]

The history of the Canadian constitution is completely different. because it does not derive from an original people's declaration of rights following the founding of a new state after the end of a war or the fall of a dictatorship. On the contrary, when the independence process had been fully accomplished ("patriation"), the Charter was originally approved by a law of the British Parliament in 1982 and was subject to change only at the initiative of the Canadian Parliament. It simply recognised the fundamental right of freedom of association under section 2(d) of the Charter.

However, analysis of Canadian case law shows how the differences with respect to Europe should not be over-emphasised. Indeed, the Canadian Charter of Rights and Freedoms is essentially a tool designed to distribute power between the various states and territories, and in it the part dedicated to the recognition of rights is even more concise. Thus, the Supreme Court's interpretation plays an essential role in specifying the rights of individuals and collective subjects and has developed the only provision that appears to refer to labour law, while the Charter provides for the right of association.[19]

Although in the past, the Canadian Supreme Court has adopted a strictly literal approach, the recognition of union rights has recently been reinforced by three important decisions of the Court, which complete the meagre provisions of the Canadian Constitution. In three sentences issued in a very short period of time since January 2015, the Court overturned previous case law, which had denied constitutional protection for the right to collective bargaining and to strike, for the first time acknowledging that a meaningful process of

18 The German Basic Law (GG) shows a certain reluctance in giving detailed provisions on social matters. In any case, as in Canada more recently, the Constitutional Court of Karlsruhe has played an important role in developing freedom of association as recognised in art. 9(3) GG.

19 J. Webber, *The Constitution of Canada, A contextual analysis*, Hart, Oxford and Portland, 2015. In Italian jurisprudence, see G. Rolla (ed.), *Lo sviluppo dei diritti fondamentali in Canada* (Milano: Giuffrè, 2000).

collective bargaining provides employees with a degree of choice and independence sufficient to enable them to determine and pursue their collective interests.

In *Saskatchewan Federation of Labour v. Saskatchewan* [2015 SCC 4], the Supreme Court recognised by a majority of 5 to 2 that workers' right to strike is an essential part of a meaningful collective bargaining process.[20] It has to be emphasised that this essential target was reached by referring to international labour standards, and that its decision was heavily influenced by comparison of the Canadian constitutional charter with the decisions of the ILO's Committee on Freedom of Association and the provisions of some European constitutions (the charters of France, Italy, Germany and Spain were specifically referred to).

As has been pointed out by an academic observer,[21] "Not so very long ago, when Canadian labour lawyers thought about international labour law – that is, when they thought about it at all – they imagined a distant and lighter-than -air body of vague rules and soft law that had nothing to do with their daily legal practice. And they were right". Conversely, the decision of January 2015 "has provided a full-blooded endorsement of international labour law as a seminal source for the protection and evolution of fundamental rights at work in Canada".

In *Mounted Police Association of Ontario v. Canada*, the Court found that s. 2 (d) guarantees the right of employees to meaningfully associate in the pursuit of collective workplace goals, including the right to collectively bargain, and that the government cannot enact laws or impose a labour relations process that substantially interferes with those rights. In this way the Court rejected the notion that collective bargaining is merely a "derivative" right, that lies outside the core of freedom of association under s. 2(d), as had been argued by various governments. Rather, the Court held that collective bargaining is a necessary precondition to the meaningful exercise of the constitutional guarantee of freedom of association.

Also in *Meredith v. Canada,* the Supreme Court, whose members are appointed not for life, as in the USA, but until they are 75 years old, recognised the right to collective bargaining, defending unions' right in a case in which for

20 The Court ruled that "[a]long with their right to associate, speak through a bargaining representative of their choice, and bargain collectively with their employer through that representative, the right of employees to strike is vital to protecting the meaningful process of collective bargaining within s. 2(d)" of the Charter.

21 M. Lynk, *The fall and rise of a good idea: the use of international labour law in the interpretation of the Charter of Rights and Freedoms*, in *2015* New Labour Trilogy, CFLR Report (labourrights.ca/research-publications/2015-new-labour-trilogy-cflr-forum.pdf).

budgetary reasons salary was cut by legislative intervention (ERA). The Court concluded by a 6 – 1 majority that the federal legislation did not violate section 2(d) of the *Charter* because a process of consultation between RCMP members and management regarding compensation continued after the ERA was enacted, so that the salary cap provided by law had not "substantially impaired the collective pursuit of the workplace goals of RCMP members". The Court stated that the right to free collective bargaining has been not infringed for the following reasons. First, the level at which the Act capped wage increases was consistent with the going rate reached in agreements concluded with bargaining agents inside and outside of the core public administration. Second, the salary limit applied for a limited three-year period. Third, the Act did not preclude consultation on other compensation-related issues and indeed permitted the negotiation of additional allowances for workers.

Also in this latter case the Canadian Supreme Court tackled issues well known to European constitutionalism that have affected the European Court of Justice and in particular the European Court of Human Rights, as well as the national courts of Spain, Portugal, Greece and Italy. These include restrictions on rights to social benefits and collective bargaining as a result of the crisis of 2008. In recent years, European democracies appear to have discovered their social fragility, finding that constitutional provisions are inadequate for providing protection from the changes resulting from a new approach to the issue of a balanced budget.

The reference to international standards has revealed a clear trend not only in Europe towards deconstruction of the deep-rooted system protecting workers' rights. At the end of the process, international standards have taken on the role of workers' human rights. Awareness of the phenomenon should make Europeans more aware of the international movement towards deregulation and, perhaps, less hostile to the processes of economic globalisation and the spread of free trade treaties.

In conclusion, neither the adoption of a US Wagner Act model of industrial relations nor the absence of constitutional provisions on social rights appears to lead the Canadian system far astray from the individual and collective protection of labour rights of European countries, which should prompt researchers to make a more in-depth comparative study of the legislation.

3 CETA Provisions on the Free Movement of Workers and Mutual Recognition of Professional Qualifications

CETA[22] retains the form and provisions of an international free trade agreement, not unlike the 1957 Treaty of Rome. It includes 30 chapters dedicated to the discipline governing the goods to be exchanged and the services to be provided across borders. Special measures are applied, for instance, to food safety and animal and plant health (chapter 5), investment (chapter 8), financial or maritime transport services (chapters 13 and 14), telecommunications (chapter 15), e-commerce (chapter 16), government procurement (chapter 19), fair competition policies (chapters 2, 3, 4 etc.), and so on.

An important part of CETA is dedicated to the freedom of movement of European citizens to North America and vice versa. Here it can be said that although the EU has lost the UK due to Brexit, it has won Canada, whose citizens are to be treated from now on as European "Unionists", as regards the freedom of movement required to accept jobs and orders for goods and services. Chapter 10 of the agreement (Temporary Entry and Stay of Natural Persons for Business Purposes) provides special status for trained workers temporarily entering the EU or Canada to work for a foreign-owned overseas companies or to provide a service.

The treaty contains an innovative prediction compared with the TFEU, with distinct special categories of migrant workers, giving them different status and referring to contractual services suppliers (natural persons employed by an enterprise that has no establishment in the territory and that has concluded a bona fide contract to supply a service); independent professionals (natural persons engaged in the supply of a service) and key personnel (business visitors for investment purposes or natural persons who establish, develop or administer the operation of an investment in a capacity that is supervisory or executive).

Particular importance has to be paid to the notion of "intra-corporate transferees", which refers to natural persons who have been employed by an enterprise in one of the following categories: (i) senior personnel; (ii) specialists (persons who possess uncommon knowledge of the enterprise's products or services and its application or an advanced level of expertise or knowledge of the enterprise's processes); (iii) graduate trainees with a university degree;

---

22 Two different websites are devoted to it. See: http://ec.europa.eu/trade/policy/in-focus/ceta/ceta-chapter-by-chapter/, with a useful chapter-by-chapter guide, and the official website: http://www.consilium.europa.eu/en/press/press-releases/2016/10/28-eu-canada-trade-agreement/.

and – finally – key personnel, contractual services suppliers, independent professionals and short-term business visitors who are citizens of a Party to the treaty. Art. 10.7 CETA also regulates the maximum length of their stay on an equal-treatment basis (from a minimum of 90 days within any six-month period for business visitors for investment purposes to three years, with a possible extension of up to 18 months, for intra-corporate transferees, specialists or senior personnel).

Here the treaty's provisions move away from those of the TFEU (and from directives 96/71/EC and 2014/67/EU governing the posting of workers within the framework of the provision of services), since there is not a general provision for freedom of movement that would equate Canada to a full member of the Union, but CETA imposes limits on citizens' stays on the territory of the other Party, thus overlapping with the competencies of each Member State of the EU.

Chapter 11 (Mutual Recognition of Professional Qualifications) establishes a framework that would allow one Party to recognise professional qualifications earned in the other, to allow professionals on both sides of the Atlantic to practice in each other's countries. The treaty leaves it to the relevant authorities or professional bodies in both the EU and Canada to negotiate a proposal on so-called mutual recognition that can then be integrated into CETA.[23]

4 CETA Provisions on Labour Items and Enforcement Procedures

To understand the other provisions of Chapter 23 of the CETA, it is worth referring to the content of art. 8 of the Joint Interpretative Instrument (mentioned above), in which the parties open-mindedly send a clear signal of appeasement, stating in para. a that "CETA commits Canada and the European Union and its Member States to improving their laws and policies with the goal of providing high levels of labour protection. CETA provides that they cannot relax their labour laws in order to encourage trade or attract investment and, in case of any violation of this commitment, governments can remedy such violations regardless of whether these negatively affect an investment or investor's expectations of profit. CETA does not change the rights of

23 On this issue, further steps need to be taken. It should be noted that the fourth CETA Joint Committee meeting held in Brussels on February 2024 discussed progress towards the adoption of a Mutual Recognition Agreement on the professional qualifications of architects: see https://www.international.gc.ca/trade-commerce/trade-agreements-accords-commerciaux/agr-acc/ceta-aecg/2024-02-09-agenda-odre-jour.aspx?lang=eng.

workers to negotiate, conclude and enforce collective agreements and to take collective action".

This is an important statement if opponents had considered this the main risk, committing both sides to avoid starting a race to the bottom to make their economies more competitive. The treaty also states in art. 8(c) that: "CETA also creates a framework for Canada and the European Union and its Member States to cooperate on trade-related labour issues of common interest, including through involvement of the ILO and a sustained dialogue with civil society, to ensure that CETA encourages trade in a way that benefits workers and in a manner supportive of labour protection measures".

This is the spirit that must drive everyone reading and interpreting the treaty, which in Chapter 23 on Trade and Labour, sets out the provisions strictly related to social matters, laying down a bilateral duty to respect the standards set by the ILO, and to ratify and implement their fundamental conventions (art. 23.3), which constitutes a social clause in the strict sense.[24]

In art. 23.1 CETA, after formally recalling the social values shared by the signatory parties, the parties recognise "the beneficial role" that "policy coherence in decent work, encompassing core labour standards, and high levels of labour protection coupled with their effective enforcement" can have on "economic efficiency, innovation and productivity". The role that social dialogue between workers and employers, and their respective organisations is also recognised, committing the parties "to the promotion of such dialogue" (art. 23.1(2)).

Article 23.2 CETA reads as follows, "recognising the right of each Party to set its labour priorities, to establish its levels of labour protection and to adopt or modify its laws and policies accordingly in a manner consistent with its inter-

---

24 The topic has now acquired extensive literature, see A. Perulli and V. Brino, *A Global Labour Law: Towards a new International Framework for Rughts and Justice* (Torino: Giappichelli-Routledge, 2024); K. A. Elliott (ed.), *The Handbook of Globalisation and Labour Standards* (Cheltenham: Edward Elgar, 2022; A. Tyc, *Global trade, labour rights, and international law: a multilevel approach* (N.Y.: Routledge, 2021); J.L. Gil y Gil, T. Ushakova (eds.), *Comercio y justicia social en un mundo globalizado*, (Modena: ADAPT e-Book series) at https://www.adaptuniversitypress.it/prodotto/comercio-y-justicia-social-en-un-mundo-globalizado/; T. Treu, *Globalizzazione e diritti umani. Le clausole sociali dei trattati commerciali*, 2017, 133 available at https://csdle.lex.unict.it/working-papers/wp-csdle-m-dantona-int/globalizzazione-e-diritti-umani-le-clausole-sociali-dei; ILO, *International Institute for Labor Studies, Social dimension of free trade agreements* (Geneva, 2013); A. Blankett, A. Trebilcock (eds.), *Research Handbook on Transnational Labour Law* (Cheltenham: Edward Elgar, 2015); A. Vandaele, *International Labour Rights and the Social Clause: Friends or Foes* (London: Cameron May, 2005); G. Van Roozendaal, *Trade Unions and Global Governance. The Debate on a Social Clause*, (London and N.Y.: Continuum, 2002).

national labour commitments, including those in this Chapter, each Party shall seek to ensure those laws and policies provide for and encourage high levels of labour protection and shall strive to continue to improve such laws and policies with the goal of providing high levels of labour protection". On the other hand, in art. 23.4(1), "the Parties recognise that it is inappropriate to encourage trade or investment by weakening or reducing the levels of protection afforded in their labour law and standards".

Despite their vocational language, the two clauses make an important commitment. Having established that it is prohibited to reduce the level of protection in the initial solemn declaration, both clauses indicate that the objective of the treaty is to develop competitiveness while ensuring a mutual, albeit not absolute, commitment to the promotion of working conditions, in language that does not stray too far from the provisions of the TFEU. Of course, the experience gained over years of implementation of European directives means it is important to remain vigilant so that legislators do not reduce protections through a process of downwards alignment.

The ILO is recognised as having a special role. According to art. 23.3(4) of the treaty, "each Party reaffirms its commitment to effectively implement in its law and practices in its whole territory the fundamental ILO Conventions that Canada and the Member States of the European Union have ratified respectively. The Parties shall make continued and sustained efforts to ratify the fundamental ILO Conventions if they have not yet done so. The Parties shall exchange information on their respective situations and advances regarding the ratification of the fundamental as well as priority and other ILO Conventions that are classified as up to date by the ILO".[25]

In art. 23.3(2), each party undertakes to "ensure that its labour law and practices promote the [...] objectives included in the ILO Decent Work Agenda, and in accordance with the ILO Declaration on Social Justice for a Fair Globalization of 2008 adopted by the International Labour Conference at its 97th Session, and other international commitments".

The Treaty pays special attention to the establishment of acceptable minimum employment standards for wage earners, including those not covered by a collective agreement; and to the non-discrimination principle in respect of

25 Unlike the USA (which has only ratified Conventions 105 and 182 on child labour), all the fundamental conventions were only recently ratified by Canada (C138/1973 came into force for Canada on 8 Jun 2017 with the minimum age specified as 16 years). The 1949 Right to Organise and Collective Bargaining Convention no. 98 was only ratified on 14 June 2017. However, on a general basis, only 22 ILO conventions are in force in Canada, with a very low uptake compared with Europe (e.g. Spain, which can boast 87 ratifications).

working conditions, including for migrant workers (23.3(2)(a) and (b)). Health and safety obligations at work are also reaffirmed in "the prevention of occupational injury or illness and compensation in cases of such injury or illness". In full awareness of the human and environmental disaster that has sadly marked the exploitation of the earth's resources in recent decades, the treaty requires that the legislation of each country "shall take into account existing relevant scientific and technical information and related international standards, guidelines or recommendations" (art. 23.3(3)).

Sub-para. 3 also includes an important projection covering the care required in of sectors where technology is developing: "The Parties acknowledge that in case of existing or potential hazards or conditions that could reasonably be expected to cause injury or illness to a natural person, a Party shall not use the lack of full scientific certainty as a reason to postpone cost-effective protective measures".

This formula, which is repeated in the chapter devoted to sustainability (see art. 24.8), seems to derive from the Canadian failure to ratify ILO Convention C155 (1981) on Occupational Safety and Health, so the parties have deemed it useful to underline that it is not necessary to reach a certain degree of scientific certainty for the binding adoption of rules of conduct inspired by a precautionary principle.

A bilateral mechanism of enforcement is also established, ensuring both sides put the "Trade and Labour" chapter's provisions into practice (Art. 23.5 ff.). Without wishing to enter into a detailed analysis of the provisions, it should be noted that particular attention is paid to "enforcement procedures, administrative proceedings and review of administrative action", in order to insure effectiveness and compliance with all the standards set up in the treaty. This is achieved by maintaining a labour inspection system (art. 23.5.1(a)) and by "ensuring that administrative and judicial proceedings are available to persons with a legally recognised interest in a particular matter who maintain that a right is infringed under its law, in order to permit effective action against infringements of its labour law, including appropriate remedies for violations of such law" (Art. 23.5.1(b)).

This special attention to administrative procedures and independent tribunals is a direct consequence of the fear of seeing the rules applied differently so as to favour national institutions or commercial companies. This focus is particularly the case within the administrative apparatus, which is directly controlled by the government of each state. It must also be remembered that, at the time CETA was signed, the ILO C081 Labour Inspection Convention had not yet been ratified by Canada.[26]

In article 23.6 the parties undertake "to encourage public debate with and among non-state actors as regards the development and definition of policies that may lead to the adoption of labour law and standards by its public authorities", while art. 23.7 covers cooperative activities to achieve the goals of this chapter. An "institutional mechanism" to resolve problems that could arise from the interpretation of the treaty is set out in art. 23.8, giving the Committee on Trade and Sustainable Development established under article 26.2(1)(g) a mandate to oversee the implementation of the social Chapter also by means of a special procedure (art. 23.10) designed to find mutually satisfactory solutions to prevent disputes in the matters regulated by the treaty (art. 23.11.2).

5 Conclusions

After more than seven years, it is not a straightforward matter to assess the provisional application of the treaty. What is certain[27] is that transatlantic trade has increased at pace (except during the years of COVID quarantine), without any real impact on the protection of intellectual property or geographic identifications in the area of high-quality foods.[28] As regards labour, there has been convergence mainly in the North American side of the agreement, without the risk having emerged of a weakening of European labour protection standards. Nevertheless, widespread fears remain, primarily on the part of Europeans; fears not that different from those that led to the US neo-protectionist issues with the TTIP referred to above, and which meant that the issue of ratification of CETA by every single state was set aside.

The fact that trade treaties, such as those at issue here, do not have a guaranteed predictable outcome with respect to the benefits that each party will acquire is not surprising, because the CETA (and *a fortiori* the TTIP, should it ever be signed and ratified) bring about a truly unpredictable expansion of the market, triggering a process in which it is not easy to identify which

26 And was only done so in June 2019. The C129 Labour Inspection (Agriculture) Convention has still not been ratified.

27 For an evidence-based analysis of the impacts of CETA, see the preliminary reports provided by a multidisciplinary team of experts on behalf of DG Trade at. https://www.ceta-evaluation.eu/.The final report is expected for March 2025.

28 From an Italian point of view, specific questions have only arisen in limited areas, like milk production and wheat exports, for which solutions have been easily found. On this point, see the data at www.centrostudi-italiacanada.it/.

areas will ultimately achieve the most in terms of the increased exports. This should confirm that trade agreements are a challenge for the economic systems of both sides and not necessarily an imperialistic, commercial event.

However, such effects are temporary and cannot be considered to have been permanently integrated into the system, given what has been said about the mixed nature of CETA and the need for all the signatory countries to ratify it. In this sense, the changes in the political and economic conditions that are a consequence of the war in Ukraine and the re-election of President Trump now mean that it is even more urgent for the countries still so unsure about the merit of the treaty that they have delayed its ratification to make a choice. The recent resignation of President Trudeau shows that Canada seems to find itself in an uncomfortable position, in which it is overly dependent on goods and services produced in the USA.

When she resigned from the Canadian cabinet in December 2024, Finance Minister Chrystia Freeland wrote that her country was facing "a grave challenge" because "the incoming administration in the United States is pursuing a policy of aggressive economic nationalism".[29]

This is no bolt from the blue, but the logical consequence of the change in American trade policy after the first Trump presidency, which also led to the WTO crisis. And it is no coincidence that it was Canada, which shares its only very long border exclusively with the USA, which promoted a multilateral group for the reform of the WTO.

Since 2018, Canada has been leading a group of 14 like-minded WTO Members, known as the Ottawa Group,[30] to contribute ideas and analysis towards achieving meaningful, realistic and pragmatic reforms to the WTO over the short, medium and long term, reinvigorating the negotiating function and strengthening the deliberative function and dispute-settlement mechanism of the WTO.

These premises make it clear the role that a free trade agreement with Europe can play for the Northernmost part of America in developing its economy. The provisions represent the realisation that international standards aim to complement and support trade liberalisation and the reduction of customs duties, not only constituting a common standard to all countries, but also ensuring their political independence (although such a statement would have seemed ridiculous just a few years ago).

---

29 See the complete text of the letter at https://www.cbc.ca/news/politics/chrystia-freeland-resignation-letter-1.7411607.

30 Australia, Brazil, Canada, Chile, European Union, Japan, Kenya, South Korea, Mexico, New Zealand, Norway, Singapore, Switzerland and the United Kingdom.

In carrying out my research, I can directly verify that the Canadian public and academic debate has paid more attention to the CETA than the Europeans have, and perhaps the time has come for fears to be publicly addressed in order to avoid that the lack of public debate leads to decisions that Europeans may come to regret in the future.

Bibliography

Adinolfi G.; (ed.), *Gli Accordi preferenziali di nuova generazione dell'Unione europea* (Torino: Giappichelli, 2021).

Baroncini E., F.P. Cunsolo (eds.), *L'accordo CETA tra UE e Canada: sostenibilità e partecipazione* (Bologna: Dipartimento di scienze giuridiche, 2021) (http://amsacta.unibo.it/id/eprint/6732/).

Blankett A., A., Trebilcock (eds.), *Research Handbuch on transnational labor law* (Cheltenham: Edward Elgar Pub., 2015).

Burkett B., "Globalization in Transition: The Canadian Perspective" (2018), *Canadian Labour & Employment Law Journal*, vol. 21, 2, 399–432.

Cagnin V., "Investor-State Dispute Settlement (ISDS) from a Labour Law Perspective" (2017), *European Labour Law Journal*, 8, 217.

Canadian master labour guide, 38th edition, Toronoto, Ontario, LexisNexis, 2023.

Calamita M.R., "Sulla competenza dell'Unione europea a stipulare accordi di libero scambio. Il caso dell'EU-Singapore Free Trade Agreement" (2017), *DPCE online*, 3.

Deblock C., J. Lebullenger, S. Paquin, *Un nouveau pont sur l'Atlantique: l'Accord économique et commercial global entre l'Union européenne et le Canada* (Québec: Pressese l'Université du Québec, 2015).

Elliott K.A., "Hard and Soft Law Approaches to Protecting Workers Rights", K. A. Elliott (ed.), *The Handbook of Globalisation and Labour Standards* (Cheltenham, UK, Northampton, MA, USA: Edward Elgar Publishing, 2022), 326–338.

Fahey E., "CETA and Global Governance Law: What Kind of Model Agreement Is It Really in Law?" (2017) *European Papers*, 293 (https://www.europeanpapers.eu/en/europeanforum/ceta-and-global-governance-law-what-kind-of-model-agreement-is-it-really-in-law).

Giunta A. et AA., *Gli Accordi di libero scambio. Opportunità per le imprese italiane. Casi studio: Corea del Sud e Canada* (Roma: ICE, 2018) (https://www.ice.it/it/sites/default/files/inline-files/Studio%20ICE%20CRES_CoreaSud%20e%20Canada.pdf).

Gil y Gil J.L. (dir.), T. Ushakova (coord.), Comercio y justicia social en un mundo globalizado, (Modena: ADAPT Labour Studies e-Book series, 2016) (https://www.adaptuniversitypress.it/prodotto/comercio-y-justicia-social-en-un-mundo-globalizado/).

Griller S. et AA., *Mega-Regional Trade Agreements: CETA, TTIP, and TiSA: New Orientations for EU External Economic Relations* (Oxford: OUP, 2017).

Hübner K., *Europe, Canada and the Comprehensive Economic and Trade Agreement* (London: Routledge, 2011).

International Labour Organization; International Institute for Labour Studies, *Social dimensions of free trade agreements* (Geneva: ILO, 2013. Revised edition 2015) https://www.ilo.org/wcmsp5/groups/public/---dgreports/---inst/documents/publication/wcms_228965.pdf.

Klemen D.D., E. Beaulieu, *Trade Policy Trends: CETA Ratification* (Calgary, University of Calgary, 2019).

Larik J., "Prêt-à-ratifier: the CETA decision of the French Conseil constitutionnel of 31 July 2017" (2017) *European constitutional law review*, 759.

Lynk M., *The fall and rise of a good idea: the use of international labour law in the interpretation of the Charter of Rights and Freedoms*, in *2015 New Labour Trilogy*, CFLR Report labourrights.ca/research-publications/2015-new-labour-trilogy-cflr-forum.pdf.

Manfredi M., *La promozione e la tutela dei diritti economici e sociali nell'Unione Europea* (Bari: Cacucci, 2022).

Perulli A. and V. Brino, *A Global Labour Law: Towards a new International Framework for Rughts and Justice* (Torino, Giappichelli-Routledge, 2024).

Radicati di Brozolo L.G., "Where Is Investor-State Arbitration Heading? Reflections on the Debate over EU Investor Protection Agreements", in A. Carlevaris, L. Lévy, A. Mourre, E. A. Schwartz (eds.), *International Arbitration Under Review, Essays in honour of John Beechey*, (CC Publishing: Paris, 2015) 319–342.

Rolla G. (ed.), *Lo sviluppo dei diritti fondamentali in Canada* (Milano: Giuffrè, 2000).

Rubino V., Accordi preferenziali di nuova generazione e fragilità nella cooperazione fra Unione europea e Stati membri: alcune riflessioni sul caso "CETA" e la tutela delle indicazioni geografiche dei prodotti alimentari, Eurojus, 2023, 1, 106–133 https://rivista.eurojus.it/archivio-rivista/2023-1/.

Stegher G., "Il "Conseil Constitutionnel" avalla il CETA: la Francia procede speditamente verso la ratifica?" (Nota a Consiglio costituzionale 31 luglio 2017, n. 749) (2017), *DPCE online*, 3.

Tyc A., *Global trade, labour rights, and international law: a multilevel approach* (Milton Park, Abingdon, Oxon; New York, NY, Routledge, 2021).

Vandaele A., International Labour Rights and the Social Clause: Friends or Foes (London: Cameron May, 2005).

Van Roozendaal G., *Trade Unions and Global Governance. The Debate on a Social Clause*, (London and N.Y.: Continuum, 2002).

Treu T., *Globalizzazione e diritti umani. Le clausole sociali dei trattati commerciali*, 2017, WP CSDLE "M. D'Antona", 133https://csdle.lex.unict.it/working-papers/wp-csdle-m-dantona-int/globalizzazione-e-diritti-umani-le-clausole-sociali-dei.

Webber J., *The Constitution of Canada, A contextual analysis* (Oxford and Portland: Hart, 2015).

CHAPTER 9

Trying to Build a Better Future: The Modernised 2023 Canada–Ukraine Free Trade Agreement and Labour Rights

Jo Carby-Hall and Aneta Tyc

1 Introduction

In order to maintain a high standard of living, Canada puts efforts into trade diversification and tries to enhance access to international markets through negotiating and concluding free trade agreements (FTAs). Its first FTAs, namely the Canada–US Free Trade Agreement (CUSFTA) and the North American Free Trade Agreement (NAFTA), dated back to 1989 and 1994, respectively.[1] Currently, Canada has 15 FTAs in force covering 63% of the world's GDP and opening markets to 1.5 billion consumers.[2] Ukraine is one of the countries with which Canada has concluded a FTA.

Signed on 11 July 2016, the free trade agreement between Canada and Ukraine (CUFTA) entered into force on 1 August 2017. However, over four years later in January 2022, Canadian Minister of Export Promotion, International Trade and Economic Development Mary Ng and Ukraine's First Deputy Prime Minister and Minister of Economy Yulia Svyrydenko launched modernisation negotiations which were disrupted by the outbreak of war in Ukraine in February 2022 and re-launched in June 2022. Fortunately, both countries were finally able to conclude the negotiations, and on 22 September 2023, Ukraine's President Volodymyr Zelenskyy and Canadian Prime Minister Justin Trudeau signed the modernised agreement in Ottawa. Bill C-57, namely an Act to implement the 2023 Free Trade Agreement between Canada and Ukraine,

1 Marie-France Paquet and Georgina Wainwright-Kemdirim, "Crafting Canada's gender-responsive trade policy", in Amrita Bahri, Dorotea López and Jan Yves Remy (eds.), *Trade policy and gender equality* (Cambridge: Cambridge University Press, 2023), pp. 312–313.

2 These numbers do not include Ecuador for FTA negotiations between Canada and Ecuador were concluded only on 4 February 2025. See: https://www.canada.ca/en/global-affairs/news/2025/02/minister-ng-welcomes-the-successful-conclusion-of-free-trade-agreement-negotiations-between-canada-and-ecuador.html, FTAs: https://international.canada.ca/en/global-affairs/services/trade/agreements-negotiations/investment-agreements.

 | HTTPS://DOI.ORG/10.1163/9789004762251-010

received Royal Assent[3] on 19 March 2024. Chrystia Freeland, Deputy Prime Minister and Minister of Finance, has argued that "Canada's modernized free trade agreement with Ukraine will create new jobs for workers and new opportunities for businesses in both of our countries – while also supporting Ukraine's economic recovery, national security, and stability. Canada will continue to do everything we can to support Ukraine through to victory and into the reconstruction of a free and prosperous Ukraine".[4] The modernised CUFTA officially entered into force on 1 July 2024.

The aim of this chapter is to focus on the development of Ukrainian trade relations with Canada, paying particular attention to the modernised 2023 CUFTA and assessing its labour and temporary entry for business persons' provisions, as well as chapters on Indigenous Peoples and gender through the prism of labour and employment laws in Ukraine. In the final part, the authors try to answer the questions whether the modernised CUFTA may contribute to the development of Ukraine after the war with Russia in order to expand businesses, create jobs, improve working and wage conditions and protect employment.

2 Historical Background Seen through the Prism of Ukraine

In 1991, when the Soviet Union collapsed, Ukraine declared its independence from Russia. Its first post-Soviet president Leonid Kravchuk adopted a pro-European stance and the Partnership and Cooperation Agreement between the European Communities and their Member States, and Ukraine was signed in Luxembourg on 14 June 1994. It entered into force on 1 March 1998, and constituted the legal basis for EU–Ukraine relations until 31 August 2017.[5] In the meantime, namely between 2007 and 2011, the EU and Ukraine negotiated

3 Canada has to have the Royal Assent for its legislation because it is a constitutional monarchy which means that the Crown forms part of the Canadian Parliament. For a Bill to become law, it must receive the assent from the British Crown whose representative is the Governor General. The Royal Assent serves as a symbolic and constitutional requirement which signifies the culmination of the Canadian legislative process. Once the Canadian House of Commons and Senate pass a Bill in both the French and English languages, the Governor General grants the Royal Assent on behalf of the Monarch. The Bill then becomes an Act of Parliament, in other words a law.

4 https://www.canada.ca/en/global-affairs/news/2023/10/minister-ng-introduces-modernized-canada-ukraine-free-trade-agreement-legislation-in-the-house-of-commons.html.

5 https://eur-lex.europa.eu/legal-content/EN/TXT/?uri=oj:JOL_1998_049_R_0003_002, https://www.consilium.europa.eu/pl/documents-publications/treaties-agreements/agreement/?id=1994019.

the Association Agreement (AA), including a Deep and Comprehensive Free Trade Area (DCFTA). Signed on 21 March and 27 June 2014, the EU–Ukraine AA entered fully into force on 1 September 2017 after a long period of ratification, while the DCFTA has provisionally applied since 1 January 2016. Upon the Russian invasion in 2022, in order to support Ukraine's economy, the EU adopted the Autonomous Trade Measures Regulation and established temporary measures in the form of full trade liberalisation and suspension of import duties, quotas and trade defence measures for imports from Ukraine.[6]

The year 2008 was also important in terms of Ukraine's participation in international trade. It not only became the member of the World Trade Organization (WTO), but also signed a Trade and Investment Cooperation Agreement (TICA) with the USA, which established the US–Ukraine Council on Trade and Investment aiming at covering a broad spectrum of trade and investment issues, such as labour, environment, intellectual property or market access.[7]

Ukraine has so far concluded trade agreements with Armenia, Azerbaijan, Belarus, Canada, Georgia, United Kingdom, Iceland, Israel, Kazakhstan, Kyrgyzstan, Liechtenstein, Macedonia, Moldova, Montenegro, Norway, Russia, Switzerland, Turkmenistan, Tajikistan, Turkey and Uzbekistan.[8] It should, however, be noted that in May 2025, the Cabinet of Ministers of Ukraine – not surprisingly – approved the termination of many agreements with Russia, Belarus and the Commonwealth of Independent States,[9] including agreements on free trade.[10]

Historically, there are strong ties between Ukraine and Canada. The first wave of Ukrainian labour immigrants settled in Canada between 1897 and 1914.[11] From 1920 until today, there have been five more flows of immigration:

6 https://policy.trade.ec.europa.eu/eu-trade-relationships-country-and-region/countries-and-regions/ukraine_en.

7 https://www.trade.gov/country-commercial-guides/ukraine-trade-agreements.

8 https://www.trade.gov/country-commercial-guides/ukraine-trade-agreements.

9 More on the Commonwealth of Independent States, see: https://ec.europa.eu/eurostat/statistics-explained/index.php?title=Glossary:Commonwealth_of_Independent_States_(CIS).

10 https://unn.ua/en/news/ukraine-terminates-a-number-of-agreements-with-the-russian-federation-belarus-and-the-cis-details-of-cabinet-decisions.

11 During World War I, some 5,000 Ukrainian Canadians were interned in fear of ethnic persecution, were forced to hard labour and had their properties confiscated. Former Prime Minister Paul Martin acknowledged that it was a "dark day in Canada's history", expressed his formal apology and granted the Ukrainians and other groups funds for educational exhibitions and memorials. Wayne C. Thompson, *Canada. The World Today Series 2016–2017* (Lanham: Rowman & Littlefield, 2016), 32nd edition, p. 28. See also: Iryna

the interwar immigration (1920–1939), the political immigration (1945–1990), the economic immigration (1991–2011), the fifth wave of immigration (2014–2018) after the Revolution of Dignity (2013–2014)[12] and the war immigration (2022–).[13]

On 2 December 1991, Canada and Poland were the first two countries to recognise Ukraine's independence[14] and a new chapter in history of bilateral cooperation between Ukraine and Canada was opened.[15] In terms of the approach to trade, the 20th Prime Minister of Canada Jean Chrétien and his government drew conclusions from Canada's failure to take advantage of the emerging markets of Eastern Central Europe after the fall of the Berlin Wall.[16] It was trade, in particular, that constituted "a touchstone of the Chrétien government's foreign policy, reflecting neoliberal beliefs and perspectives".[17] What mattered the most from the point of view the Canada–Ukraine relationship and the Ukrainian success and prosperity after the transitional period, was not only economic reform in the latter, but also the agreements signed with the Leonid Kuchma government, which represented a considerable role that trade and economic development had to play. These mainly included declaration on economic cooperation of July 1992, Agreement between the Government of Canada and the Government of Ukraine on Trade and Commerce of March 1994 and, in particular, the Agreement between Ukraine and Canada on Economic Cooperation of October 1994.[18]

Bogdanova, "Turning Crisis into Opportunity: Unfolding Ukraine's Trade Potential with the Canada-Ukraine Free Trade Agreement" (2021) 8, 2 *East/West: Journal of Ukrainian Studies* 151–191 at 161.

12 More on the Revolution of Dignity, see: https://war.ukraine.ua/faq/revolution-of-dignity-ukraine/.

13 Ukrainian World Congress, "Ukrainians in Canada: from the first wave of immigration to now", 1 July 2022, https://www.ukrainianworldcongress.org/ukrainians-in-canada-from-the-first-wave-of-immigration-to-now/ Mykhaĭlo Petrivs'kyĭ, *Oĭ, Kanado, Kanadon'ko ... = O Canada, Dear Canada: Opovidannia Z Pobutovoho Z HYttia UkraïNs'kykh Poselentsiv V Kanadi* (Vinnipeg: Petrivs'kyĭ, 1974), p. 8. More: Orest T. Martynowych, *Ukrainians in Canada: The Formative Years 1891–1924* (Edmonton: Canadian Institute of Ukrainian Studies, University of Alberta Press, 1991); Orest T. Martynowych, *Ukrainians in Canada: The Interwar Years* (Toronto: CIUS Press, 2016).

14 Marta Dyczok, *Ukraine: Movement without change, change without movement* (Amsterdam: Harwood Academic Publishers, 2000), p. x.

15 Bogdanova, "Turning", 162.

16 Bohdan S. Kordan, *Strategic Friends. Canada-Ukraine Relations from Independence to the Euromaidan* (Montreal & Kingston-London-Chicago: McGill-Queen's University Press, 2018), p. 44.

17 Kordan, Strategic Friends, p. 43.

18 Kordan, Strategic Friends, p. 43. For the Agreement between Ukraine and Canada on Economic Cooperation, see: United Nations Conference on Trade and Development,

Since the Russian aggression against Ukraine in 2014, the Stephen Harper government, as well as the public opinion, has supported democracy and the rule of law, realising the importance of the stability of a rules-based order.[19] Canada has helped Ukraine on many levels. Suffice to say, a 5-year (2016–2021) Canadian development assistance initiative – namely the Canada–Ukraine Trade and Investment Support (CUTIS) Project – was established in order to lower poverty in Ukraine via investment from Canada to Ukraine and increasing exports from Ukraine to Canada.[20] Focusing on small and medium enterprises, the CUTIS programme funded by Global Affairs Canada has not only made an important contribution to Ukraine's economic growth and employment, but also has supported the CUFTA.[21]

3 Labour and Employment Laws in Ukraine

In Ukraine, unfortunately, there is a noticeable erosion of fundamental labour rights. As reported by Jozef Niemec and Anton Leppik, since 2019, attempts have been made to push through reforms that would limit trade union freedoms and would simplify in an alarming way hiring and dismissal procedures. Initially, these proposals did not enter into force because they were fiercely criticised for being incompatible with the International Labour Organization (ILO) conventions ratified by Ukraine, the European Social Charter (revised) and obligations under Association Agreement (AA) and Deep Comprehensive Free Trade Agreement (DCFTA) between Ukraine and the EU. However, as the authors further point out that, in 2021, the same ideas were adopted by the parliament and, to top it all off, in March 2022, namely shortly after the outbreak of the war, the Law on the Organisation of Labour Relations Under Martial Law[22] (hereinafter referred to as the "martial law regime") was adopted.

International Investment Instruments: A Compendium, UNCTAD/DITE/3 (New York and Geneva: United Nations, 2002), vol. X, pp. 103–107, https://unctad.org/system/files/official-document/dite3vol10_en.pdf and for the Agreement between the Government of Canada and the Government of Ukraine on Trade and Commerce: https://gac.canadiana.ca/view/ooe.b3001192/1.

19 Bohdan S. Kordan and Mitchell C.G. Dowie, *Canada and the Ukrainian crisis* (Montreal: McGill-Queen's University Press, 2020), p. 23.

20 https://www.cucc.ca/cutis-stories-of-change/.

21 https://www.globenewswire.com/news-release/2017/08/21/1090590/0/en/CUTIS-launches-CUFTA-Opening-Doors.html. For interesting "success stories" resulting from the project, see: https://www.cucc.ca/activities/publication/.

22 No. 2136-IX of 18 March 2022 (draft law No. 7160 of 14 March 2022), https://zakon.rada.gov.ua/laws/show/2136-20#Text.

Jozef Niemec and Anton Leppik highlight that the latter reform has been introduced under short procedures, without any consultation with employers or workers' organisations, and has imposed serious restrictions on workers' rights. Special employment provisions have been promulgated regarding, *inter alia*, remuneration, leaves, the conclusion and termination of an employment contract, a decrease in weekly rest time and an increase in working hours, transferring to another job (not determined by an employment contract and without the employee's consent) and changes in essential working conditions (the right of the employer not to notify the employee two months in advance of a change in essential working conditions). Jozef Niemec and Anton Leppik argue that "several provisions that narrow the rights of employees and are not fully justified by the conditions of martial law". For example, according to the "martial law regime", "the employer may, on its own initiative, suspend certain provisions of the collective agreement" (Article 11). Such suspension takes place without consultation with trade unions. Moreover, the employer is allowed to dismiss the employee during his/her temporary incapacity for work or during his/her leave, except for maternity leave and leave to care for a child. The employer specifies the date of dismissal, which is the first working day, the next after the end of temporary incapacity for work specified in the document on temporary incapacity for work, or on the first working day after the end of the leave. As indicated by Monika Smusz-Kulesza *et al.*, the reform also covered remuneration: Employers are exempted from the liability for the "violation of payment terms as a result of hostilities or other force majeure circumstances". Finally, the same authors highlight "restrictions on the activities of trade unions" and "banning of strikes". As an example, they give the suspension of a provision on the minimum deduction of 0.3% of the wage fund for the benefit of trade unions for cultural and mass, health work.[23] Volodymyr O. Havrylyuk *et al.* add that the working week has been increased to 60 hours and the rest time has been reduced to 24 hours per week. It is possible under the "martial law regime" that the working day lasts 10 hours, 6 days a week, with only one day off. The authors also highlight that the simplification of conclusion by the employer of fixed-term labour contracts with new employees for the period of martial law or for the period of substitution of a tem-

23 Jozef Niemec and Anton Leppik, "Labour legislation reforms in Ukraine during war time. A trade union reading" (2022) 176, 4 *Giornale di diritto del lavoro e di relazioni industriali* 697–704, at 697–699. Monika Smusz-Kulesza, Alla Fedorova and Bogdan Moysa, *Social Rights in Ukraine in Times of War. Report on the needs assessment,* (Strasbourg: Council of Europe, 2022), pp. 46–52, https://rm.coe.int/needs-assessment-eng-2/1680a9b407. For developments in Ukrainian law, see: https://www.lexology.com/library/detail.aspx?g=6462728e-f59b-4b93-9023-2a359eb848ab.

porarily absent employee has been adopted.[24] Volodymyr O. Havrylyuk *et al.* conclude, however, that: "…all changes (…) are aimed at ensuring the functioning of the country's economy in conditions of war, state defence, ensuring the operation of critical infrastructure, protecting the lives of citizens by simplifying bureaucratic procedures. On this basis it can be argued that although the rights have been limited in one way or another, on the other hand these restrictions lead to the protection of other important human rights and the protection of the state".[25] Although the attempt at justification for some may be acceptable in times of war, one needs to think about providing better labour and employment laws for times of peace.

4 "Labour" Chapter in the Modernised CUFTA

There is no doubt that a well-designed FTA, together with its labour provisions, can exert a positive influence on workers. Since the modernised CUFTA includes a new chapter – no. 14 entitled "Labour" – the purpose of this paper is to assess its shape and demonstrate its potential to other countries that would like to follow Canada's footsteps and conclude a FTA with Ukraine.

The analysis contained in this work thus covers in particular key features of the modernised CUFTA and its updated labour chapter subject to the dispute settlement mechanism. Special attention should be paid to: the new and broader (compared to the 2017 Canada–Ukraine Free Trade Agreement) definition of "labour laws" which now means a measure of a party that implements or otherwise relates to the commitments and rights set out in Section B entitled "Obligations" (it encompasses both general and special obligations), new provisions on fair and balanced labour laws (explained below), a clause prohibiting parties to weaken or reduce the protections afforded in their labour laws (Article 14.5), a new clause prohibiting the importation of goods produced in whole or in part by forced or compulsory labour, including forced or compulsory child labour (Article 14.7), and a new article on violence against workers[26] (Article 14.8), according to which the parties recognise that workers and labour organisations must be able to exercise the rights set out in

---

24 Volodymyr O. Havrylyuk, Nataliya V. Rybak, Volodymyr V. Kuzmenko, Olha V. Lets and Oleh P. Deneha, "The influence of martial law on labour relations in Ukraine" (2023) No. Especial 2023 Mecanismos de Proteção Jurídica no Direito Civil, *Revista Jurídica Portucalense* 276–294 at 282 and 286.

25 Havrylyuk, Rybak, Kuzmenko, Lets and Deneha, "The influence", 292.

26 The authors use the terminology "employee", "worker" and "worker organization" based on the modernised CUFTA itself.

Article 14.3[27] in a climate that is free from violence, threats and intimidation, and the imperative of governments to effectively address incidents of violence, threats and intimidation against workers.[28]

The parties to the CUFTA affirm their obligations as members of the ILO including those stated in the ILO Declaration on Fundamental Principles and Rights at Work (as amended in 2022) and undertake (in the framework of "General Obligations") to adopt and maintain in their labour laws the following "internationally recognized labour principles and rights", taking into account their commitments, where applicable, under the ILO 1998 Declaration:

- freedom of association and the effective recognition of the right to collective bargaining, given that, for greater certainty, the right to freedom of association includes protection of the right to organise and the right to strike;
- the elimination of all forms of forced or compulsory labour;
- the effective abolition of child labour and a prohibition on the worst forms of child labour;
- the elimination of discrimination in respect of employment and occupation;
- a safe and healthy working environment;
- acceptable minimum employment standards such as minimum wage, hours of work and overtime pay for wage earners, including those not covered by collective agreements; and
- non-discrimination in respect of working conditions for migrant workers (Article 14.3.1). The parties add that for greater certainty, non-discrimina-

27 Entitled "General Obligations" with a reference to the ILO Declaration on Rights at Work and the core ILO conventions. It should be recalled that the ILO core labour instruments are as follows: Forced Labour Convention, 1930 (No. 29); Protocol of 2014 to the Forced Labour Convention, 1930; Freedom of Association and Protection of the Right to Organise Convention, 1948 (No. 87); Right to Organise and Collective Bargaining Convention, 1949 (No. 98); Equal Remuneration Convention, 1951 (No. 100); Abolition of Forced Labour Convention, 1957 (No. 105); Discrimination (Employment and Occupation) Convention, 1958 (No. 111); Minimum Age Convention, 1973 (No. 138); Occupational Safety and Health Convention, 1981 (No. 155); Worst Forms of Child Labour Convention, 1999 (No. 182); Promotional Framework for Occupational Safety and Health Convention, 2006 (No. 187).

28 Accordingly, a party shall not fail to address violence or threats of violence against workers, directly related to exercising or attempting to exercise the rights set out in Article 14.3, in a matter related to trade or investment. The parties add that for purposes of dispute settlement, a panel shall presume that a failure is in a matter related to trade or investment, unless the responding party demonstrates otherwise.

tion in respect of working conditions for migrant workers means providing migrant workers in a party's territory with the same legal protection as the party's nationals in respect of working conditions.

As mentioned above, special attention should be bestowed on new and important provisions on fair and balanced labour laws (Article 14.4), in particular because they specify "particular grey zone situations that may undermine the rights to freedom of association and collective bargaining".[29] Thus, apart from the provision according to which Canada and Ukraine shall ensure that their labour laws provide for high labour standards and "shall endeavour to continue to improve those standards", both countries shall also ensure that their labour laws:

- promote best practices in labour relations (they shall endeavour to improve those practices);
- do not undermine or erode the ability of employers and workers to meaningfully bargain collectively;
- do not prevent workers' organisations from negotiating collective agreements that include a requirement for workers covered by the collective agreement to pay a reasonable fee to the workers' organisation.

Moreover, the parties to the CUFTA shall adopt and maintain measures to prohibit and effectively deter employer interference with the organisation of workers, including any exercise of undue influence, coercion or intimidation by employers and any form of retaliation against a person involved in the organisation of workers. For greater certainty, in footnote 5 the parties have clarified that such measures shall ensure that employees are not required, as a condition of employment or in order to avoid any employment sanction, to listen or otherwise attend to communications by the employer intended to persuade the employee not to be represented by a workers' organisation.

As stipulated by the parties to the CUFTA, Canada and Ukraine shall in addition establish a legislative framework enabling the adoption and maintenance of measures to ensure that workers' organisations are representative of, and accountable to, their members, as well as independent of the employer and the party to the CUFTA.[30]

---

29 https://www.international.gc.ca/trade-commerce/trade-agreements-accords-commerciaux/agr-acc/ukraine/modernized-canada-ukraine-moderniser.aspx?lang=eng.

30 With further conditions that:
- leaders of workers' organisations are duly elected by the worker members they represent;
- workers vote to approve any collective agreement applicable to them;

Finally, there is also a negative obligation, according to which a party shall not provide special legal recognition to collective agreements between employers and workers unless such agreements are negotiated through workers' organisations that are representative of, and accountable to, their members; as well as independent of the employer and the party to the CUFTA.

It must be stressed that the chapter on "Labour" is subject to the dispute settlement provisions of the CUFTA embracing even a possibility of suspension of benefits to the party complained against (Article 28.13), which reflects a "sanctions-based" approach favoured by Canada.[31] This is one of the strongest solutions existing in FTAs and should undoubtedly be assessed positively for the deterrent effect of sanctions can increase the effectiveness of the rights included in a FTA. Before the final – sanctioning – step, however, as it is often regulated in diverse FTAs, labour consultations (Article 14.15) are organised to address any matter that may arise between the parties: "A Party may request consultations (requesting Party) with the other Party regarding any matter under this Chapter by delivering a written request to the National Administrative Office of the other Party". A National Administrative Office is designated by each party within its ministry responsible for labour issues, or an equivalent entity, as a contact point to address matters related to the "Labour" Chapter. If the parties still fail to resolve the matter, in the second step, a party may request that the Labour Council representatives of the other party[32] convene to consider the matter at issue by delivering a written request to the other party through its National Administrative Office. If the parties fail to resolve the matter within a specified period of time, the requesting party may request the establishment of a panel under Article 28.7, as provided in Chapter 28 (Dispute Settlement). A party shall not have recourse to dispute settlement under Chapter 28 (Dispute Settlement) for a matter arising under the "Labour" Chapter without first seeking to resolve the matter in accordance with Articles 14.15 and 14.16.

- workers have timely access to by-laws of the workers' organisations representing them and to collective agreements applicable to them; and
- workers' organisations have a duty to represent their members.

31 Marco Bronckers and Giovanni Gruni, "Retooling the Sustainability Standards in EU Free Trade Agreements" (2021) 24 *Journal of International Economic Law* 25–51 at 25.

32 Both parties establish a Labour Council composed of senior governmental representatives at the ministerial or other level from the ministries responsible for labour issues.

5 Temporary Entry for Business Persons

As explained at the Government of Canada's website,[33] since the CUFTA is an international agreement, any work permit applications are assessed under paragraph 204(a) of the Immigration and Refugee Protection Regulations (IRPR), which falls under the "International Mobility Program". Chapter 21 entitled "Temporary Entry for Business Persons"[34] of the CUFTA facilitates temporary entry to Canada for certain categories of business persons who hold citizenship or are permanent residents in Ukraine.[35] More specifically, four categories of business persons are covered by the provisions in question: business visitors, intra-corporate transferees, investors, and professionals.

The CUFTA business visitors category is open to citizens and permanent residents of Ukraine, namely business visitors who are seeking to engage in one of the following business activities: meetings and consultations, research and design, manufacturing and production, marketing, sales, distribution, after-sales or after-lease services, and general services. Importantly, business visitors are business persons for whom the primary source of remuneration for the proposed business activity is outside Canada and the principal place of business and the predominant place of accrual of profits remain outside Canada. The maximum initial length of stay is 6 months, but extensions are possible.

The intra-corporate transferees category is comprised of citizens and permanent residents of Ukraine who are employed by an enterprise in Ukraine and who are seeking to render services to an enterprise in Canada that is the parent entity, a subsidiary, an affiliate. The business person must belong to one of the following occupational categories: executives, managers or specialists. At the time of submitting their application, all intra-corporate transferees must also meet further requirements: be a citizen or permanent resident of Ukraine, have been continuously employed by the transferring company for at least one year within the previous three years, show that their employment or partnership was in an enterprise in Ukraine, be transferred to a qualifying enterprise in Canada. The length of stay is up to 3 years for initial applications,

33 https://www.canada.ca/en/immigration-refugees-citizenship/corporate/publications-manuals/operational-bulletins-manuals/temporary-residents/foreign-workers/international-free-trade-agreements/cufta.html.

34 https://www.international.gc.ca/trade-commerce/trade-agreements-accords-commerciaux/agr-acc/ukraine/text-texte/2023/21.aspx?lang=eng.

35 One of the benefits is that there is no need to obtain a Labour Market Impact Assessment to work in Canada. See: https://canadaopen.org/en/news/gfxhjfhjxdhxth.html.

with possible extensions. However, the total period of stay may not exceed 7 years for executives and managers or 5 years for specialists.

The CUFTA contains provisions for the temporary entry of investors. To be eligible as an investor under the CUFTA, applicants must: be a citizen or permanent resident of Ukraine; establish, develop or administer an investment to which a substantial amount of capital was committed or is in the process of being committed; be in a supervisory or executive role or a role that involves essential skills (for example, setting up a specific franchise or a laboratory). The initial length of stay is one year, but further extensions of stay are allowed.

Finally, the CUFTA contains provisions for the temporary entry of professionals. To qualify as a professional the applicant must: have an International Mobility Program (IMP) offer of employment in an eligible Training, Education, Experience and Responsibilities (TEER) 0 or 1 occupation;[36] have a post-secondary credential of three or more years of study and any additional educational requirements as per their specific occupation in the NOC (the NOC code is auto-populated from the IMP offer of employment); have two years of paid work experience in the sector of activity of the contract; be remunerated at a level commensurate with other similarly qualified professionals in the industry and region where the work is performed. Such remuneration should not include non-monetary elements, such as housing costs and travel expenses. The assessment of the level of remuneration should be based on the prevailing wage. The initial length of stay is one year, but extensions by one-year increments are allowed.

Work authorisation for accompanying spouses is also facilitated, with the exception of business visitors. For spouses, the length of stay, including extensions, should be the same as the principal applicant.

A general positive assessment is given to encouraging easier movement for the above-discussed groups under the CUFTA. It is often highlighted that it enhances international cooperation, business operations, job creation and "stimulates economic growth through increased investment and collaboration". Investors looking for new opportunities in the two countries will find these processes "more accessible, promoting economic diversification and innovation". By developing investment opportunities and facilitating the mov-

36 All TEER 0 and 1 occupations are permitted, except the following:
- health, education and social services occupations and related occupations;
- judges, lawyers and notaries except for foreign legal consultants;
- managers in postal and courier services;
- managers of telecommunications carriers;
- occupations related to cultural industries;
- recreation, sports and fitness programme and service directors.

ement of skilled professionals, the CUFTA contributes to enhancing economic links between Canada and Ukraine and "aims to create a more dynamic and interconnected economic landscape", which benefits "industries across the board, from technology and healthcare to manufacturing and agriculture.[37] Undoubtedly, activities like these are and will be a key factor in the reconstruction and recovery of Ukraine devastated during the Russian aggression.

6 Indigenous Peoples and Gender in the Modernised CUFTA

A comprehensive evaluation of the modernised CUFTA, conducted from the perspective of labour lawyers, requires an examination of its new chapters entitled "Trade and Gender" (Chapter 23) and "Trade and Indigenous Peoples" (Chapter 25). The latter is the first and the only one of its kind chapter that Ukraine or Canada has ever negotiated and included in their trade agreement. The term "Indigenous Peoples" means for Canada "Aboriginal peoples (including First Nations, Inuit, and Métis peoples) as defined in subsection 35(2) of the Constitution Act, 1982 of Canada", and for Ukraine "Karaite, Crimean Tatar, and Krymchak, including those based on the Crimean Peninsula". The authors of this chapter argue that the opportunities created by the modernised CUFTA, *inter alia*, programmes designed in order to encourage capacity building and skills enhancement, such as digital skills, as well as other ways to facilitate the engagement of Indigenous Peoples in international trade and investment, are important instruments that may help support these groups and promote inclusive work environments. As pointed out by José-Antonio Monteiro, over the years, regional trade agreements "have often been dubbed as laboratories in which some countries establish new types of provisions in order to address recent trade-related issues and challenges". For example, "Provisions mentioning explicitly gender have been incorporated into an increasing number of RTAs".[38] It is certainly worth proposing that future FTAs partners follow the CUFTA model and add chapters on trade and Indigenous Peoples. When designing the provisions, care should be always taken to ensure that they duly take into account the economic and social interests of

37 Eivy Joy Quito, "Canada-Ukraine Free Trade Agreement – A New Era of Economic Collaboration", 11 July 2024, https://immigcanada.com/canada-ukraine-free-trade-agreement-a-new-era-of-economic-collaboration/.

38 José-Antonio Monteiro, "Gender-Related Provisions in Regional Trade Agreements", World Trade Organization Economic Research and Statistics Division, Staff Working Paper ERSD-2018–15, 18 December 2018, p. 32, https://www.wto.org/english/res_e/reser_e/ersd201815_e.pdf.

Indigenous Peoples so that they could really contribute not only to improving employment opportunities of that group, but also improving market access (also in the context of better paid jobs), and guaranteeing better working conditions, as well as better business opportunities.

The same remarks apply to women in the context of the chapter entitled "Trade and Gender", which is generally intended to promote gender equality and improve the situation of women, and to give them access to opportunities created by the modernised CUFTA. As in the case of Indigenous Peoples, these opportunities include programmes that encourage capacity-building and skills enhancement of women at work or programmes to improve women's digital skills.

As it has been highlighted by José-Antonio Monteiro: "Over the years, the number of RTAs with explicit gender-related provisions has increased slowly but relatively steadily".[39] The aim of gender-related provisions is to "create a level playing field for women and distribute the benefits of free trade equally among men and women".[40] Seungbin Park and Mi Jeong Shin have pointed out that "[t]he number of the type of gender-related provisions in RTAs differs across agreements, ranging from 1 (e.g. Australia–Indonesia RTA) to 13 (Canada–Chile RTA)".[41]

As mentioned above, in their modernised CUFTA, Ukraine and Canada have included the whole chapter on "Trade and Gender". Pursuant to its content, the parties, *inter alia*, affirm their commitment to implement their obligations under the Convention on the Elimination of All Forms of Discrimination Against Women of 1979, as well as to implement the obligations addressing gender equality or women's rights under any other international agreement to which it is a party. It is worth mentioning here that Ukraine has ratified 9 out of 11 fundamental ILO instruments and Canada has ratified 10 out of 11 fundamental ILO instruments, with the remark that both countries have ratified both Equal Remuneration Convention, 1951 (No. 100), as well as Discrimination (Employment and Occupation) Convention, 1958 (No. 111).[42]

---

39 Monteiro, "Gender-Related Provisions", p. 4.

40 International Trade Centre, *From Europe to the World: Understanding Challenges for European Businesswomen* (Geneva: International Trade Centre, 2019). Quotation from: Seungbin Park and Mi Jeong Shin, "Women's descriptive representation and support for the inclusion of gender-related provisions in trade agreements" (2023) January–March, *Research and Politics* 1–12 at 1. See the cited literature.

41 Park and Shin, "Women's descriptive representation", 1. See the cited literature.

42 Only Promotional Framework for Occupational Safety and Health Convention, 2006 (No. 187) and Protocol of 2014 to the Forced Labour Convention, 1930, have not been ratified yet by Ukraine. As for Canada only Occupational Safety and Health Convention, 1981 (No. 155) has not been ratified yet. See: https://normlex.ilo.org/.

Moreover, in the modernised CUFTA the parties affirm their commitment to implement the "Joint Declaration on Trade and Women's Economic Empowerment". Adopted in 2017, on the Occasion of the Eleventh WTO Ministerial Conference in Buenos Aires, this document acknowledged "the importance of incorporating a gender perspective into the promotion of inclusive economic growth, and the key role that gender-responsive policies can play in achieving sustainable socioeconomic development", as well as "that inclusive trade policies can contribute to advancing gender equality and women's economic empowerment, which has a positive impact on economic growth and helps to reduce poverty". The document also acknowledged "that international trade and investment are engines of economic growth for both developing and developed countries, and that improving women's access to opportunities and removing barriers to their participation in national and international economies contributes to sustainable economic development".[43] So far, 127 WTO members and observers, including both Canada and Ukraine, have endorsed the 2017 Declaration.[44]

Currently, Global Affairs Canada is adopting a new analytical approach to help create a coherent gender-responsive and inclusive trade policy.[45] Importantly, Canada has sought to mainstream gender issues throughout its FTAs (so-called "gender-mainstreaming approach in FTAs"). In view of the Office of the Special Advisor on Gender to the United Nations' words, "[Gender] [m]ainstreaming is not an end in itself but a strategy, an approach, a means to achieve the goal of gender equality. Mainstreaming involves ensuring that gender perspectives and attention to the goal of gender equality are central to all activities". These include activities related to the development, implementation and monitoring of government policies, programmes and projects.[46]

The modernised CUFTA is only one example of a FTA in which Canada has included a chapter on gender. The others include the Canada–Israel Free Trade Agreement (CIFTA) and the Canada–Chile Free Trade Agreement (CCFTA) with their "Trade and Gender" chapters. In addition, "comprehensive, binding, and enforceable commitments in its labour chapters related to gen-

43 Joint Declaration on Trade and Women's Economic Empowerment on the Occasion of the WTO Ministerial Conference in Buenos Aires in December 2017, https://www.wto.org/english/thewto_e/minist_e/mc11_e/genderdeclarationmc11_e.pdf.

44 https://www.wto.org/english/tratop_e/womenandtrade_e/buenos_aires_declaration_e.htm.

45 More: Paquet and Wainwright-Kemdirim, "Crafting Canada's gender-responsive trade policy", p. 311.

46 See: https://international.canada.ca/en/services/business/trade/policy/inclusive/gender/agreements.

der" has been included in other agreements, e.g. the Comprehensive and Progressive Agreement for Trans-Pacific Partnership (CPTPP) or the United States–Mexico–Canada Agreement (USMCA).

"Global Trade and Gender Arrangement" signed by Canada in August 2020 and some other countries[47] also reflects their approach towards promoting "mutually supportive trade and gender policies in order to improve women's participation in trade and investment and in the furtherance of women's economic empowerment and sustainable development".[48]

The literature indicates that the establishment of explicit links between trade policies and broader objectives such as gender equality and women's economic empowerment could help trade to become a means of long-term inclusive development. According to Amrita Bahri and Renata Amaral, there are at least two arguments in support of this position. Firstly, FTAs can help countries "encourage their trade partners to reduce trade barriers and create a business- and employment-conducive environment for women as entrepreneurs and employees". Secondly, by increasing trade flows FTAs can "lead to an increase in economic opportunities for all, including women". However, the authors are concerned about the current split between the content of these provisions and the distributional impact of trade liberalisation, on the one hand, and the barriers which women confront in trade, on the other hand. In this context they argue that gender provisions should "relate to both the economical and social roles of women, the challenges that women face, and the need to expand opportunities in lucrative industries for women".[49]

---

47 Chile (August 2020), New Zealand (August 2020), Mexico (October 2021), Colombia (June 2022), Peru (June 2022), Ecuador (May 2023), Costa Rica (May 2023), Argentina (October 2023), Australia (February 2024) and Brazil (February 2024).

48 https://international.canada.ca/en/services/business/trade/policy/inclusive/action-group/arrangement.

49 Amrita Bahri and Renata Amaral, "Gender Equality Provisions in Trade and Investment Agreements: Are They Widening the Negotiation Capacity Gap?" (2024) 23, 1 *World Trade Review* 47–71 at 52–53. See the cited literature. According to Yiagadeesen Samy *et al.*, international trade can provide greater employment opportunities for women and can stimulate productivity and economic growth, which translates into empowering women and improving gender equality. The authors examine the relationship between trade and women's economic empowerment; in particular, they research the relationship between trade and job creation for women, and the extent to which these jobs contribute to women's economic empowerment. For more information, see: Yiagadeesen Samy, Adeniran Adedeji, Augustine Iraoya, Madhurjya Kumar Dutta, Jasmine Lal Fakmawii and Wen Hao, *Trade and Women's Economic Empowerment. Evidence from Small and Medium-Sized Enterprises* (Cham: Palgrave Macmillan, 2023), pp. 2 and 146.

7 Conclusions and Postulates

Ukrainian employment law (*trudove pravo*) was already weak before the war,[50] but – as it has been proved in this chapter – the war weakened it even more.[51] A new labour chapter in the modernised CUFTA, subject to the dispute settlement provisions, is designed so that it could "improve labour standards and working conditions in the two countries by building on international labour principles and rights".[52] The authors of this chapter argue that a new labour chapter alone cannot guarantee the introduction of high labour standards in Ukraine (or standards such as those in force in Canada), but is a good step forward and in conjunction with other chapters discussed in the present contribution may be beneficial to workers, including women and Indigenous Peoples, as well as enterprises. The fact that "Labour" chapter is subject to the dispute settlement mechanism and reflects a "sanctions-based" approach shall be assessed positively as having potential to contribute to the effectiveness of the rights provided for in the CUFTA. Moreover, the authors hold the opinion that the modernised CUFTA with its crucial solutions such as the provisions on "temporary entry for business persons" can exert a major impact on fostering the future participation of Canadian businesses in the process of the recovery – including the economic recovery – of Ukraine after the war. The authors argue that what Ukraine will need after the war is activating business there, attracting investors, creating labour intensive infrastructure construction programmes, constructing of industrial enterprises, expanding the services sector, etc. Such actions should translate into job creation, employment protection and improvement in pay and working conditions. Hopefully the modernised CUFTA will encourage other countries to conclude FTAs with Ukraine that will help business invest there and create decent jobs.

---

50 Havrylyuk, Rybak, Kuzmenko, Lets and Deneha, "The influence", 277–278.

51 For example, in the light of the European Commission's "Ukraine 2024 Report", Ukraine remains at an early stage of preparation (we shall just remind the reader that the country applied for EU membership on 28 February 2022) in the field of social policy and employment. The European Commission's recommendations embrace, *inter alia*, adopting new framework legislation for labour relations and occupational safety and health in compliance with the EU acquis, ensuring an enabling environment for bipartite and tripartite social dialogue, as well as strengthening the capacities of social partners. European Commission, "Ukraine 2024 Report, Accompanying the document Communication from the Commission to the European Parliament, the Council, the European Economic and Social Committee and the Committee of Regions", Commission staff working document, Brussels, 30 October 2024, SWD(2024) 699 final, p. 15.

52 https://www.international.gc.ca/trade-commerce/trade-agreements-accords-commerciaux/agr-acc/ukraine/summary-negotiated-resume-negocies.aspx?lang=eng.

The expansion of FTAs is indeed one of key recommendations for a strategic investment policy of Ukraine proposed by Dmytro Riznyk. The author also highlights the urgent need of reforms regarding the rule of law and property rights protection, for this is a sine qua non condition for attracting investment both in the short term and from the perspective of the country's long-term growth. Apart from recommendations relating to rebuilding and developing the quality infrastructure, improving logistics and transport links between Ukraine and the EU, eradicating corruption, establishing a modern, effective system of governance and providing tax incentives for investors, the author points out that it is essential to introduce new insurance schemes for risks for foreign investments.[53] As matter of fact, according to the European Commission's "Ukraine 2024 Report", the first steps have already been taken in what amounts to an insurance of direct investments in Ukraine, namely in November 2023, amendments to the Law on financial mechanisms for stimulating exports concerning insurance of investments in Ukraine against war risks were adopted. This reform has expanded the activities of the Export Credit Agency in the area of insurance and reinsurance and has introduced insurance and reinsurance of direct investments in Ukraine against political, as well as war risks.[54]

Given that the future debate shall be focused on matters relevant to the investment activity in Ukraine, which "plays a crucial role in the recovery of the economy and ensuring its sustainable development",[55] Dmytro Riznyk identifies priority and promising sectors attractive from the point of view of foreign investors in the future. These are as follows: the energy sector with emphasis on green energy; the engineering industry and various equipment, including military equipment; information, communication and technology sector; the construction industry and building materials; food industry and agriculture; the metallurgical industry; the pharmaceutical market and the medical industry.[56] Without a doubt, the instruments in the modernised CUFTA can help find investors and can set an example for other countries which could conclude a FTA with Ukraine. It is worth stressing that in the current world of US tariffs and the still unresolved WTO crisis, FTAs may become a key mechanism to guarantee free trade for many countries.

---

53 Dmytro Riznyk, "Priorities and Mechanisms for Enhancing Ukraine's Investment Strategy in the Post-War Reconstruction Period" (2023) 8, 4 *Economics & Education*, 49–53 at 49–52.

54 European Commission, "Ukraine 2024 Report", p. 70.

55 Riznyk, "Priorities", 50.

56 Riznyk, "Priorities", 51. See the cited literature.

Finally, the authors should like to point out that this chapter and recommendations are based on the optimistic scenario for Ukraine regarding the war with Russia and their deep hope that such an expectation will come true.

Bibliography

Bahri, Amrita and Amaral, Renata, "Gender Equality Provisions in Trade and Investment Agreements: Are They Widening the Negotiation Capacity Gap?" (2024) 23, 1 *World Trade Review* 47–71.

Bogdanova, Iryna, "Turning Crisis into Opportunity: Unfolding Ukraine's Trade Potential with the Canada-Ukraine Free Trade Agreement" (2021) 8, 2 *East/West: Journal of Ukrainian Studies* 151–191.

Bronckers, Marco and Gruni, Giovanni, "Retooling the Sustainability Standards in EU Free Trade Agreements" (2021) 24 *Journal of International Economic Law* 25–51.

Dyczok, Marta, *Ukraine: Movement without change, change without movement* (Amsterdam: Harwood Academic Publishers, 2000).

European Commission, "Ukraine 2024 Report, Accompanying the document Communication from the Commission to the European Parliament, the Council, the European Economic and Social Committee and the Committee of Regions", Commission staff working document, Brussels, 30 October 2024, SWD(2024) 699 final.

Havrylyuk, Volodymyr O., Rybak, Nataliya V., Kuzmenko, Volodymyr V., Lets, Olha V. and Deneha, Oleh P., "The influence of martial law on labour relations in Ukraine" (2023) No. Especial 2023 Mecanismos de Proteção Jurídica no Direito Civil, *Revista Jurídica Portucalense* 276–294.

Kordan, Bohdan S., *Strategic Friends. Canada-Ukraine Relations from Independence to the Euromaidan* (Montreal & Kingston-London-Chicago: McGill-Queen's University Press, 2018).

Kordan, Bohdan S. and Dowie, Mitchell C.G., *Canada and the Ukrainian crisis* (Montreal: McGill-Queen's University Press, 2020).

Martynowych, Orest T., *Ukrainians in Canada: The Formative Years 1891–1924* (Edmonton: Canadian Institute of Ukrainian Studies, University of Alberta Press, 1991).

Martynowych, Orest T., *Ukrainians in Canada: The Interwar Years* (Toronto: CIUS Press, 2016).

Monteiro, José-Antonio, "Gender-Related Provisions in Regional Trade Agreements", World Trade Organization Economic Research and Statistics Division, Staff Working Paper ERSD-2018–15, 18 December 2018, https://www.wto.org/english/res_e/reser_e/ersd201815_e.pdf.

Niemec, Jozef and Leppik, Anton, "Labour legislation reforms in Ukraine during war time. A trade union reading" (2022) 176, 4 *Giornale di diritto del lavoro e di relazioni industriali* 697–704.

Paquet, Marie-France and Wainwright-Kemdirim, Georgina, "Crafting Canada's Gender-Responsive Trade Policy", in Amrita Bahri, Dorotea López and Jan Yves Remy (eds.), *Trade policy and gender equality* (Cambridge: Cambridge University Press, 2023).

Park, Seungbin and Shin, Mi Jeong, "Women's descriptive representation and support for the inclusion of gender-related provisions in trade agreements" (2023) January–March, *Research and Politics* 1–12.

Petrivs'kyĭ, Mykhaĭlo, *Oĭ, Kanado, Kanadon'ko ... = O Canada, Dear Canada: Opovidanna Z Pobutovoho ZHYtta UkraïNs'kykh Poselentsiv V Kanadi* (Vinnipeg: Petrivs'kyĭ, 1974).

Quito, Eivy Joy, "Canada-Ukraine Free Trade Agreement – A New Era of Economic Collaboration", 11 July 2024, https://immigcanada.com/canada-ukraine-free-trade-agreement-a-new-era-of-economic-collaboration/.

Riznyk, Dmytro, "Priorities and Mechanisms for Enhancing Ukraine's Investment Strategy in the Post-War Reconstruction Period" (2023) 8, 4 *Economics & Education*, 49–53.

Samy, Yiagadeesen, Adedeji, Adeniran, Iraoya, Augustine, Kumar Dutta, Madhurjya, Lal Fakmawii, Jasmine and Hao, Wen, *Trade and Women's Economic Empowerment. Evidence from Small and Medium-Sized Enterprises* (Cham: Palgrave Macmillan, 2023).

Smusz-Kulesza, Monika, Fedorova, Alla and Moysa, Bogdan, *Social Rights in Ukraine in Times of War. Report on the needs assessment*, (Strasbourg: Council of Europe, 2022) https://rm.coe.int/needs-assessment-eng-2/1680a9b407.

Ukrainian World Congress, "Ukrainians in Canada: from the first wave of immigration to now", 1 July 2022, https://www.ukrainianworldcongress.org/ukrainians-in-canada-from-the-first-wave-of-immigration-to-now/.

United Nations Conference on Trade and Development, *International Investment Instruments: A Compendium*, UNCTAD/DITE/3 (New York and Geneva: United Nations, 2002), vol. X, https://unctad.org/system/files/official-document/dite3vol10_en.pdf.

Thompson, Wayne C., *Canada. The World Today Series 2016–2017* (Lanham: Rowman & Littlefield, 2016), 32nd edition.

PART 4

Australia and New Zealand's Approach

CHAPTER 10

Labour Provisions in Trade Agreements: The Curious Case of Australia

Joo-Cheong Tham

1 Introduction

In a 'somewhat surprising and largely unexpected' development,[1] there has been a proliferation of labour provisions in trade agreements, to the extent that some commentators have characterised these provisions as a 'global norm'.[2]

This development is indeed surprising, given the failure to include a 'social clause' in the rules of the World Trade Organization (**WTO**), with its first Ministerial Conference rejecting such clauses, and declaring that '[t]he International Labour Organization (**ILO**) is the competent body to set and deal with [internationally recognized core labour standards], and we affirm our support for its work in promoting them'.[3] The development is even more surprising, given the ILO's 'customary hesitance to engage with and comment on issues of trade and investment, *even when affecting labour standards*'.[4]

The spread of labour provisions in trade agreements is clearly not due to a concerted push by multilateral organisations such as the WTO and ILO. The explanation lies more in the approaches taken at national and regional levels. These approaches have been a central focus of the voluminous scholarship on

1 International Institute for Labour Studies, *Social Dimensions of Free Trade Agreements* (Geneva: International Labour Organization, rev. ed., 2015), p. v.

2 Evgeny Postnikov and Lachlan McKenzie, 'Resisting issue-linkage: Social standards and Australian trade agreements' (2022) 25 *Journal of International Relations and Development* 1079, 1082.

3 World Trade Organization, Singapore Ministerial Declaration, adopted 13 December 1996, WT/MIN(96)/DEC (18 December 1996), para. 4, https://www.wto.org/english/thewto_e/minist_e/min96_e/wtodec_e.htm. See Sandra Polaski, 'The strategy and politics of linking trade and labor standards: An overview of issues and approaches', in Kimberly Elliott (ed.), *Handbook on Globalisation and Labour Standards* (Cheltenham: Edward Elgar Publishing, 2022), pp. 203–25.

4 Tonia Novitz, *Trade, Labour and Sustainable Development: Leaving No One in the World of Work Behind* (Cheltenham: Edward Elgar Publishing, 2024), p. 148 (emphasis added).

 | HTTPS://DOI.ORG/10.1163/9789004762251-011

this subject[5] with a predominant emphasis on studying the approaches taken by the European Union and the United States[6] and, to a far lesser extent, the approach adopted by China.[7]

---

5 Key monographs include: Olivier de Schutter, *Trade in the Service of Sustainable Development: Linking Trade to Labour Rights and Environmental Standards* (Oxford: Hart Publishing, 2017); Evgeny Postnikov and Lachlan McKenzie, *Social Standards in EU and US Trade Agreements* (Abingdon: Routledge, 2020); Aneta Tyc, *Global Trade, Labour Rights and International Law: A Multilevel Approach* (Abingdon: Routledge, 2021); Novitz, *Trade, Labour and Sustainable Development.*

6 This extensive literature includes: Francesco Giumelli and Gerda van Roozendaal, 'Trade agreements and labour standards clauses: Explaining labour standards developments through a qualitative comparative analysis of US Free Trade Agreements' (2017) 17(1) *Global Social Policy* 38; Billy Melo Araujo, 'Labour provisions in EU and US mega-regional trade agreements: Rhetoric and reality' (2018) 67(1) *International and Comparative Law Quarterly* 233–54; Maria Garcia, 'Building global governance one treaty at a time? A comparison of the US and EU approaches to preferential trade agreements and the challenge of TTIP', in Elaine Fahey (ed.), *Institutionalisation beyond the Nation State: Transatlantic Relations – Data, Privacy, and Trade Law* (Cham: Springer, 2018), pp. 213–42; Katerina Hradilová and Ondrej Svoboda, 'Sustainable development chapters in the EU Free Trade Agreements: Searching for effectiveness' (2018) 52(6) *Journal of World Trade* 1019; Alessia Vatta, 'The social clauses in EU trade agreements: Contents and prospects' [2018] (2) *Poliarchie/Polyarchies* 286; Austin Chad Cohen, 'Trading places: With the United States in retreat, who writes the international rules for trade' (2019) 47(2) *Georgia Journal of International and Comparative Law* 539; James Harrison et al., 'Labour standards provisions in EU Free Trade Agreements: Reflections on the European Commission's reform agenda' (2019) 18(4) *World Trade Review* 635; Postnikov and McKenzie, *Social Standards*; Christoph Scherrer, 'Novel labour-related clauses in a trade agreement: From NAFTA to USMCA' (2020) 11(3) *Global Labour Journal* 291; Isabella Mancini, 'Labour rights protection in EU trade agreements: Can trade agreements "only do so much"?' in Federico Casolari and Lucia Serena Rossi (eds), *Integrating EU Free Trade Agreements into the EU Legal Order* (Cheltenham: Edward Elgar Publishing, 2022 forthcoming), https://ssrn.com/abstract=4130430; Evgeny Postnikov, 'Labor standards in EU and US preferential trade agreements: Mainstreaming the trade-labor linkage', in Kimberly A. Elliott (ed.), *Handbook on Globalisation and Labour Standards* (Cheltenham: Edward Elgar Publishing, 2022), pp. 244–57.

7 Ronald C. Brown, 'Asian and US perspectives on labor rights under international trade agreements compared', in Axel Marx et al. (eds), *Global Governance of Labour Rights: Assessing the Effectiveness of Transnational Public and Private Policy Initiatives* (Cheltenham: Edward Elgar Publishing, 2015) ch. 5; Jadranka Petrovic and Benjamin Grunberg, 'Intersecting trade, politics and human rights: The negotiation phase of the Australia-China Free Trade Agreement' (2017) 51(1) *Journal of World Trade* 67–104; Wei Yin, 'Challenges, issues in China-EU investment agreement and the implication on China's domestic reform' (2018) 26(2) *Asia Pacific Law Review* 170; Xianbai Ji, 'China's cautious approach to labour provisions in Free Trade Agreements', in Soon Beng Chew, Lingli Huang and Kai Xiang Kwa (eds), *Political, Economic and Social Dimensions of Labour Markets: A Global Insight* (World Scientific, 2022) ch. 16; Yueming Yan, 'A new chapter in China's stance on labour protection? An assessment of the China–EU CAI' (2022) 25(3) *Journal of International Economic Law*

This chapter contributes to such work by analysing Australia's approach to labour provisions in trade agreements. At the heart of this chapter is the puzzling stance taken by Australia to the linking of trade and labour standards. At the first Ministerial Conference of the WTO, the push by the United States, France and other developed countries to include such a linkage in the WTO rules was successfully opposed by a substantial number of developing countries, the United Kingdom *and* Australia.[8] Yet, Australia has accepted such a linkage through labour provisions in key trade agreements.

This chapter seeks to understand the puzzle of Australia's stance via three steps. First, it draws out the mixed picture of the inclusion of labour provisions in Australia's trade agreements. It then analyses the labour provisions in Australian trade agreements, distinguishing between provisions that include insubstantial obligations and others that are more substantial, being largely based on the United States' approach. Finally, the chapter attempts to make sense of Australia's approach to labour provisions which can be summed up as labour provisions being viewed as both protectionist and protection-lite.

2 A Mixed Picture: Australia's Trade Agreements and Labour Provisions

Table 10.1 maps out the presence and absence of labour provisions in Australia's trade agreements. It shows no singular pattern of Australia being for or against labour provisions. Neither is there any evident pattern from a chronological or geopolitical perspective: Australia's trade agreements with labour provisions are not clustered in any particular time period; nor have they been reached principally with Global North or Global South countries.

Table 10.2 compares Australia's record with a sample of other countries (with the denominators and numerators of the fractions respectively indicating the total number of trade agreements, and the trade agreements with labour provisions based on agreements in force from 2010). It clearly shows Canada, the European Union, New Zealand, and the United States as being in favour of labour provisions in trade agreements, whilst a contrary approach is

464–83; Zhao Zhujun, 'China's legal countermeasures to CPTPP labour provisions' (2022) 5(4) *Pacific International Journal* 38–44; Yueming Yan, 'Labour and trade in Asia Pacific: Origin, development, and prospects' (2023) 31(2) *Asia Pacific Law Review* 576–95.

8 See, e.g., Tim Fischer, 'Australia', WTO Ministerial Conference, Singapore, 9 December 1996, WT/MIN(96)/ST/26, https://www.wto.org/english/thewto_e/minist_e/min96_e/st26.htm; Ian Lang, 'United Kingdom', WTO Ministerial Conference, Singapore, 9 December 1996, WT/MIN(96)/ST/9, https://www.wto.org/english/thewto_e/minist_e/min96_e/st9.htm.

TABLE 10.1 The inclusion of labour provisions in Australia's trade agreements

Trade agreement	Year of entry into force	Trade partner	RTA composition	Labour provisions
United Kingdom–Australia	2023	United Kingdom of Great Britain and Northern Ireland; Australia	Bilateral	Yes
India–Australia	2022	Australia; India	Bilateral	No
Hong Kong, China–Australia	2020	Hong Kong, China; Australia	Bilateral	No
Pacific Agreement on Closer Economic Relations Plus (PACER Plus)	2020	Tonga; Solomon Islands; Australia; Tuvalu; Nauru; Niue; New Zealand; Samoa; Cook Islands; Kiribati; Vanuatu	Plurilateral	Yes
Indonesia–Australia	2020	Indonesia; Australia	Bilateral	No
Peru–Australia	2020	Australia; Peru	Bilateral	Yes
Comprehensive and Progressive Agreement for Trans-Pacific Partnership (CPTPP)	2018	Brunei Darussalam; Canada; United Kingdom of Great Britain and Northern Ireland; Japan; Mexico; Australia; New Zealand; Chile; Malaysia; Vietnam; Peru; Singapore	Plurilateral	Yes
Australia–China	2015	China; Australia	Bilateral	No
Japan–Australia	2015	Japan; Australia	Bilateral	No
Republic of Korea–Australia	2014	Republic of Korea; Australia	Bilateral	Yes
Malaysia–Australia	2013	Malaysia; Australia	Bilateral	Yes
ASEAN–Australia–New Zealand	2010	Association of Southeast Asian Nations (ASEAN); Australia; New Zealand	Plurilateral; One Party is an RTA	No[a]
Australia–Chile	2009	Chile; Australia	Bilateral	Yes
Thailand–Australia	2005	Thailand; Australia	Bilateral	No
United States–Australia	2005	United States of America; Australia	Bilateral	Yes
Singapore–Australia	2003	Australia; Singapore	Bilateral	No
Australia–New Zealand Closer Economic Relations Trade Agreement (ANZCERTA)	1983	New Zealand; Australia	Bilateral	No
South Pacific Regional Trade and Economic Cooperation Agreement (SPARTECA)	1981	Australia; Kiribati; Vanuatu; Nauru; Tuvalu; New Zealand; Marshall Islands; Solomon Islands; Micronesia (Federated States of); Tonga; Fiji; Niue; Samoa; Cook Islands; Papua New Guinea	Plurilateral	No
Australia–Papua New Guinea (PATCRA)	1977	Papua New Guinea; Australia	Bilateral	No

Source: ILO, *Labour Provisions in Trade Agreements Hub*, https://webapps.ilo.org/LPhub/
a Labour provisions are only present in the New Zealand–Philippines MoA on Labour Cooperation.

TABLE 10.2 Examples of national approaches to labour provisions in trade agreements based on trade agreements in force from 2010

Countries for labour provisions	Countries against labour provisions	Countries with a mixed record
Canada (11/11)	Brazil (0/2)	Australia (6/12)
European Union (16/20)	China (3/12)	Chile (6/11)
New Zealand (8/8)	India (0/7)	Japan (4/7)
United States (4/4)	Indonesia (0/10)	South Korea (10/17)

Source: ILO, *Labour Provisions in Trade Agreements Hub*, https://webapps.ilo.org/LPhub/

evident in relation to Brazil, China, India, and Indonesia. Australia sits in between these two categories, in an intermediate category that includes Chile, Japan, and South Korea. Since 2010, half of the Australian trade agreements that have come into force include labour provisions with labour provisions absent from the rest.

This chapter now turns to the detail of the labour provisions found in Australia's trade agreements.

3 Labour Provisions in Australia's Trade Agreements

Drawing upon the ILO's *Labour Provisions in Trade Agreements Hub* and the typology it employs,[9] Table 10.3 provides details of the labour provisions in Australia's trade agreements. It enables us to distinguish between labour provisions in Australia's trade agreements that impose insubstantial obligations, and those that impose more substantial ones. The first category includes labour provisions in the Australia–Chile FTA, which lists labour as one of the *possible* areas for cooperation between the Parties; and that such cooperation (if undertaken) 'will be based on the concept of decent work, including the principles embodied in the ILO Declaration on Fundamental Principles and Rights at Work and its Follow-up (1998)'.[10]

9 Marva Corley-Coulibaly, Ira Postolachi and Netsanet Tesfay, 'A multi-faceted typology of labour provisions in trade agreements: Overview, methodology and trends', *International Labour Organization*, 24 November 2021, https://www.ilo.org/resource/multi-faceted-typology-labour-provisions-trade-agreements-overview.

10 ILO Declaration on Fundamental Principles and Rights at Work and its Follow-Up, adopted 1998, amended 2022, art. 18.2, paras (3)–(4).

The other two of Australia's trade agreements that impose insubstantial obligations are the Pacific Agreement on Closer Economic Relations Plus (PACER Plus) and the Malaysia–Australia FTA; both of which reflect an approach based on affirmation and recognition, with no substantive obligation to act. The labour provisions in PACER Plus include a preambular statement that the Parties '[share] a common aspiration to promote high standards of environmental and labour protection and, to uphold these in the context of sustainable development'; and Article 19, which provides as follows:[11]

> *Article 19: Investment and Environment, Health and Other Regulatory Objectives*
> 1. Parties *recognise* that it is inappropriate to encourage investment by investors of another Party and of non-Parties by not enforcing their own environmental, health, labour, safety or other regulatory standards. (emphasis added)

This approach of affirmation and recognition is also reflected in the side-letters of the Malaysia–Australia FTA, although their effect is even more diluted as they do not form part of the main agreement. The side-letters provide as follows:[12]

> In the course of exploring the inclusion of appropriate labour provisions in the Agreement, we have *affirmed* our commitments as members of the International Labour Organisation and under the Declaration on Fundamental Principles and Rights at Work and its Follow-up (1998). We have also *affirmed* our interest in facilitating cooperation and consultation on labour issues of mutual interest. Malaysia and Australia have also *recognised* each Party's responsibility to adopt, administer and enforce its own labour laws, regulations and practices and both are committed to ensuring that such labour laws, regulations and practices are not used for trade protectionist purposes or labour standards weakened to gain a trade advantage. (emphasis added)

The five remaining agreements (US–Australia FTA; Korea–Australia FTA; CPTPP; Peru–Australia FTA; Australia–UK FTA) are broadly similar and impose more substantial obligations based on the United States' approach to

---

11 Pacific Agreement on Closer Economic Relations Plus (PACER Plus), *ILO Labour Provisions in Trade Agreements Hub*, https://webapps.ilo.org/LPhub/#.

12 Malaysia–Australia, *ILO Labour Provisions in Trade Agreements Hub*, https://webapps.ilo.org/LPhub/#; 'Side letter labour: Australia to Malaysia', *Department of Foreign Affairs and Trade*, 11 January 2018, https://www.dfat.gov.au/trade/agreements/in-force/mafta/Pages/side-letter-labour-australia-malaysia.

labour provisions.[13] As Table 10.3 shows, they all impose obligations to adopt, establish, maintain, and/or modify labour laws; to enforce labour laws and to not derogate, waive, lower labour laws or act in a protectionist manner; and to lay down commitments regarding access to courts and tribunals, access to remedies and transparency, and public awareness of labour laws. They also establish monitoring and cooperation mechanisms in relation to these obligations. In addition, they provide recourse for labour disputes under either the labour chapter and/or general dispute settlement provisions, with remedies available for non-compliance (except for the labour provisions in the Korea–Australia FTA).

The obligations to adopt, establish, maintain, and/or modify labour laws are heavily based on the ILO's 1998 Declaration on Fundamental Principles and Rights at Work and its Follow-up (**1998 Declaration**) – and not the relevant ILO Conventions. Article 19.3 of the CPTPP is illustrative:[14]

> Article 19.3: Labour Rights.
> 1. Each Party shall adopt and maintain in its statutes and regulations, and practices thereunder, the following rights as stated in the ILO Declaration:[3] [4]
> (a) freedom of association and the effective recognition of the right to collective bargaining;
> (b) the elimination of all forms of forced or compulsory labour;
> (c) the effective abolition of child labour and, for the purposes of this Agreement, a prohibition on the worst forms of child labour; and
> (d) the elimination of discrimination in respect of employment and occupation.
>
> [3] The obligations set out in Article 19.3 (Labour Rights), as they relate to the ILO, refer only to the ILO Declaration.
> [4] To establish a violation of an obligation under Article 19.3.1 (Labour Rights) or Article 19.3.2, a Party must demonstrate that the other Party has failed to adopt or

13 Notably, the labour provisions in the CPTPP were 'Made in America': see Rodrigo Polanco Lazo and Sebastián Gómez Fielder, 'A requiem for the Trans-Pacific Partnership: Something new, something old and something borrowed?' (2017) 18(2) *Melbourne Journal of International Law* 298–348.

14 Comprehensive and Progressive Agreement for Trans-Pacific Partnership (CPTPP), *ILO Labour Provisions in Trade Agreements Hub*, https://webapps.ilo.org/LPhub/#. See also, United States–Australia FTA, *ILO Labour Provisions in Trade Agreements Hub*, art. 18.1, paras (1)–(2), https://webapps.ilo.org/LPhub/#.

TABLE 10.3 Labour provisions in Australia's trade agreements

	US–Australia FTA (2005)	Australia–Chile FTA (2009)	Side-letter to Malaysia–Australia FTA (2013)	Korea–Australia FTA (2014)
DOMESTIC LABOUR LAWS				
Adopt, establish, maintain, and/or modify labour laws	Yes	No	No	Yes
Enforce labour laws	Yes	No	Yes	Yes
Commitment to not derogate, waive, lower labour laws, or act in a protectionist manner	Yes	No	No	Yes
Access to courts and tribunals	Yes	No	No	Yes
Access to remedies	Yes	No	No	No
Transparency and public awareness of labour laws	Yes	No	Yes	Yes
MONITORING AND COOPERATION				
Cooperation activities	Yes	Yes	Yes	Yes
Institutional mechanisms	Yes	Yes	No	Yes
DISPUTE SETTLEMENT MECHANISMS				
Recourse for labour disputes under labour/specialised chapter	Yes	No	No	Yes
Recourse for labour disputes under general dispute settlement chapter with conditions	Yes	No	No	No
Remedies for non-compliance	Yes	No	No	No

	Comprehensive Progressive Agreement for Trans-Pacific Partnership (CPTPP) (2018)	Peru–Australia FTA (2020)	Pacific Agreement on Closer Economic Relations Plus (PACER Plus) (2020)	Australia–United Kingdom FTA (2023)
DOMESTIC LABOUR LAWS				
Adopt, establish, maintain, and/or modify labour laws	Yes	Yes	No	Yes
Enforce labour laws	Yes	Yes	No	Yes
Commitment to not derogate, waive, lower labour laws, or act in a protectionist manner	Yes	Yes	Yes	Yes
Access to courts and tribunals	Yes	Yes	No	Yes

TABLE 10.3 Labour provisions in Australia's trade agreements (*cont.*)

	Comprehensive Progressive Agreement for Trans-Pacific Partnership (CPTPP) (2018)	Peru–Australia FTA (2020)	Pacific Agreement on Closer Economic Relations Plus (PACER Plus) (2020)	Australia–United Kingdom FTA (2023)
Access to remedies	Yes	Yes	No	Yes
Transparency and public awareness of labour laws	Yes	Yes	No	Yes
MONITORING AND COOPERATION				
Cooperation activities	Yes	Yes	No	Yes
Institutional mechanisms	Yes	Yes	No	Yes
DISPUTE SETTLEMENT MECHANISMS				
Recourse for labour disputes under labour/specialised chapter	Yes	No	No	Yes
Recourse for labour disputes under general dispute settlement chapter	Yes	Yes	Yes	Yes
Remedies for non-compliance	Yes	Yes	Yes	Yes

maintain a statute, regulation or practice in a manner affecting trade or investment between the Parties.

2. Each Party shall adopt and maintain statutes and regulations, and practices thereunder, governing acceptable conditions of work with respect to minimum wages, hours of work, and occupational safety and health.[5]

[5] For greater certainty, this obligation relates to the establishment by a Party in its statutes, regulations and practices thereunder, of acceptable conditions of work as determined by that Party.

The obligations relating to the 1998 Declaration, however, differ in two key respects: the stringency of the obligation and whether breach of the obligation is conditioned upon an impact on trade or investment (see Table 10.4).

TABLE 10.4 Key differences in Australian labour provisions of obligations relating to ILO 1998 Declaration

	Stringency of obligation	Impact on trade requirement
US–Australia FTA: art. 18.1, paras (1)–(2)	'shall strive to ensure'	No
Korea–Australia FTA: art. 17.1, para. (1)	'shall endeavour to adopt or maintain'	No
CPTPP: art. 19.3	'shall adopt and maintain'	Breach 'in a manner affecting trade or investment between the Parties'
Peru–Australia: art. 18.3	'shall endeavour to adopt and maintain'	No
Australia–UK: art. 21.4	'shall adopt and maintain'	Breach 'to encourage trade or investment'

4 Making Sense of Australia's Approach to Labour Provisions in Trade Agreements

4.1 Labour Provisions as Protectionism

The preceding analysis has drawn out a complicated picture of Australia's approach to labour provisions in trade agreements: it is mixed, both in relation to whether its agreements contain labour provisions and also the content of the labour provisions. How do we make sense of this?

In a comprehensive study, Postnikov and McKenzie have sought to explain Australia's resistance to incorporating social standards in trade agreements, including labour standards. Their explanation consists of two related arguments. First, using public opinion data, they demonstrate the broad public support in Australia for trade openness and globalisation. They argue that this makes linking social standards with trade challenging and results in a low level of political contestation regarding the advantages and detriments of free trade.[15]

Second, in the context of low levels of political contestation regarding free trade, Postnikov and McKenzie foreground the framing of social standards as damaging to the national interest by key policy-makers, particularly officials in the Australian Department of Foreign Affairs and Trade (DFAT), with social standards in trade agreements variously portrayed as protectionism, 'un-pragmatic', and harmful to economic growth and prosperity. Drawing upon interviews with key actors involved in the making and negotiation of Australian trade agreements (including policy-makers and civil society organisations), they trace the origin of DFAT's resistance to social standards in trade agreements to the position that Australia took in the multilateral trade liberalisation rounds of the late 1980s and 1990s; a policy orientation that has persisted, prompting one interviewee to describe DFAT officials as 'neoliberals to the bootstrap'.[16] Postnikov and McKenzie also highlight how inadequate cross-government (department) coordination, and DFAT's limited resources for dealing with the diverse and complex challenges arising from globalisation, resulted in 'a fairly narrow conception of the purpose and role of FTAs'.[17]

The analysis by Postnikov and McKenzie provides a cogent explanation for Australia's approach to labour provisions, and a convincing explanation for the trade agreements that do not have labour provisions. Yet, their explanation is somewhat incomplete, as it does not fully account for the mixed picture of labour provisions in Australia's trade agreements. For Postnikov and McKenzie, these agreements (including the CPTPP) 'are rather exceptions, as the inclusion of social standards were demanded by the partner'.[18] This characterisation of the Australian agreements containing labour provisions is problematic. It is debatable whether, at the time of Postnikov and McKenzie's analysis in 2022, these provisions were exceptions, as six out of Australia's 15 trade agreements (signed and/or ratified) had labour provisions.[19] In 2025, it is certainly not the case that these provisions are exceptions, when half of Australia's trade agreements have labour provisions (see Table 10.1).

This chapter suggests two reasons underlying the labour provisions in Australia's trade agreements, both of which complement the analysis by Postnikov and McKenzie: (i) the labour provisions are *minimalist in terms of the*

15 Postnikov and McKenzie, 'Resisting issue-linkage', 1090–92.
16 Ibid, 1093.
17 Ibid, 1094.
18 Ibid, 1080.
19 Ibid, 1082.

substance of their obligations, and (ii) Australia has *a lacklustre commitment to the ILO Conventions on freedom of association*. Both mean that the labour provisions in Australia's trade agreements have not significantly altered the status quo in terms of labour standards in Australia. Combining the analysis of Postnikov and McKenzie with these arguments, we can better understand Australia's approach towards labour provisions through the framing of these provisions as both protectionism and protection-lite.

4.2 Labour Provisions as Protection-Lite

4.2.1 The Minimalism of Australia's Labour Provisions

The claim of minimalism is evident in the insubstantial obligations of the labour provisions in the Australia–Chile FTA, PACER Plus, and the side-letters to the Malaysia–Australia FTA (see Section 3: Labour provisions in Australia's trade agreements).

Australia's labour provisions exhibit 'different shades of minimalism'.[20] Although less obvious, minimalism is also apparent in the more demanding labour provisions of US–Australia FTA, Korea–Australia FTA, CPTPP, Peru–Australia FTA, and Australia–UK FTA. This point is illustrated by the core obligation built into the labour provisions in these agreements; namely, the obligation relating to the ILO's Declaration on Fundamental Principles and Rights at Work. In three of the five agreements, the obligation is to 'strive to ensure' (US–Australia FTA) and to 'endeavour to adopt and maintain' (Korea–Australia FTA; Peru–Australia FTA) (see Table 10.4). Such effort-based obligations will be easily satisfied or, more accurately, it will be exceedingly difficult to demonstrate breaches.

In the CPTPP and Australia–UK FTA, more stringent language is used ('shall adopt and maintain'); however, the difficulty here is in the way that obligations are tethered to the ILO's 1998 Declaration on Fundamental Principles and Rights at Work, which results in flexible standards. By 'flexible standards', it is not simply a reference to flexibility in the application of labour regulation, as labour regulation will invariably have such flexibility, especially at the international level. What is conveyed by this phrase are situations where the flexibility is so significant as to call into question whether a standard is being laid

20 This phrase is borrowed from Katsaroumpas who coined it to refer to the approach of the United Kingdom: Ioannis Katsaroumpas, 'Different shades of minimalism: The multilateral construction of labour clauses in the UK–Australian and UK–New Zealand FTAs' (2023) 34(1) *King's Law Journal* 71–104.

down at all; where the flexibility is so considerable, that it is tempting to say there is no legal norm.

An example of this flexibility is found in the centrepiece of the CPTPP's 'Labour' chapter, which is Article 19.3 (extracted in Section 3. Labour provisions in Australia's trade agreements).[21] Both paragraphs in Article 19.3 provide for flexible standards (as understood in this chapter). In the first paragraph, there is flexibility stemming from the reliance on 'rights as stated in the ILO Declaration'. Given that there are no rights stated in the ILO Declaration – only principles informed by rights in the ILO Conventions, which the CPTPP effectively excludes from the agreement in footnote 3[22] of Article 19.3 – this is a poor piece of drafting, at best.

Footnote 3 points to a further source of flexibility. Two significant implications of this footnote are illustrated by reference to freedom of association.

1. First, as already pointed out, the obligations under art. 19.3, para. (1), do not incorporate the relevant Conventions and Recommendations relating to these rights. This means that art. 19.3, para. (1) will not necessarily benefit from the greater degree of specificity found in the relevant Conventions. For instance, the two ILO Conventions on freedom of association, although cast at a high level of generality, provide more detailed obligations relating to the establishment of trade unions;[23] their right to constitute the rules of their organisations, and organise their activities; their autonomy from employers;[24] anti-union discrimination;[25] and the prohibition of employer-dominated worker organisations.[26]
2. Second, it is unclear whether the meaning of rights referred to in art. 19.3, para. (1) will be influenced by the jurisprudence of ILO supervisory bodies. The critically important question with freedom of association is whether art. 19.3, para. (1), in providing for 'freedom of association and the effective recognition of the right to collective bargaining' includes the right to strike. This right, whilst not explicitly mentioned in ILO Conventions 87 and 98, has been held by the ILO Committee on Free-

21 This analysis draws on Joo-Cheong Tham and KD Ewing, 'Labour provisions in trade agreements: Neoliberal regulation at work?' (2020) 17 *International Organizations Law Review* 153–77.

22 'The obligations set out in Article 19.3 (Labour Rights), as they relate to the ILO, refer only to the ILO Declaration'.

23 Freedom of Association and Protection of the Right to Organise Convention (No. 87), San Francisco, 17 June 1948, in force 4 July 1950, 96 UNTS 257, art. 2 (**ILO Convention No. 87**).

24 Right to Organise and to Collective Bargaining Convention (No. 98), Geneva, 8 June 1949, in force 18 July 1951, 96 UNTS 257, arts 2(2), 3 (**ILO Convention No. 98**).

25 Ibid, arts 1, 3.

26 Ibid, arts 2, 3.

> dom of Association and the ILO Committee of Experts on the Application of Conventions and Recommendations to be implied by arts 3 and 10 of ILO Convention 87.[27]

It should be noted, however, that the Expert Panel's decision in relation to the EU–South Korea FTA[28] suggests that there are ways to harden obligations in the ILO's 1998 Declaration, as it relates to freedom of association.[29] The following section takes up this decision.

The flexible standards in art. 19.3 are further qualified by the impact of trade requirements under footnote 4,[30] which contrasts with the more demanding 'impact on trade' requirement under the Australia–UK FTA.[31] The requirement in footnote 4 has the potential to render the obligations under art. 19.3 nugatory. This risk is highlighted by the unsuccessful complaint of the US against Guatemala, under the CAFTA–DR 2017 Arbitral Panel Decision; the first ever arbitration relating to labour provisions under a trade agreement, where an analogue of this requirement proved fatal to the complaint. The latter was initiated by the AFL–CIO, and six Guatemalan trade unions, alleging that Guatemala was failing to effectively enforce its labour laws as required under Chapter 16 of the Dominican Republic–Central America–United States Free Trade Agreement (CAFTA–DR). The reason for its rejection by the Arbitral Panel is summed up in the following paragraph:

> The United States has proven that at eight worksites and with respect to 74 workers Guatemala failed to effectively enforce its labor laws by failing to

---

27 ILO Convention No. 87.

28 Yoo-Duk Kang, 'EU–Korea FTA (2011–2020): First experience of implementing the Trade and Sustainable Development Chapter under the FTA', in Nicola Casarini et al. (eds), *The Routledge Handbook of Europe–Korea Relations* (Abingdon: Routledge, 2021) ch. 11.

29 *Panel of Experts Proceeding Constituted Under Article 13.15 of the EU–Korea Free Trade* Agreement, Report of the Panel of Experts, 20 January 2021, pp. 78–9, https://www.worldtradelaw.net/document.php?id=fta/panel/korea-labourlawsandpractices(ftapanel).pdf (**Panel of Experts, 2021 EU–Korea FTA report**).

30 'To establish a violation of an obligation under Article 19.3.1 (Labour Rights) or Article 19.3.2, a Party must demonstrate that the other Party has failed to adopt or maintain a statute, regulation or practice in a manner affecting trade or investment between the Parties'.

31 Footnote 2 to art. 21.4 (Labour Rights) of the Australia–UK FTA states: 'To establish a violation of an obligation under paragraph 1 of Article 21.4 (Labour Rights) a Party shall demonstrate that the other Party has failed to adopt or maintain a law, regulation or practice to encourage trade or investment'. See Australia–UK FTA, *ILO Labour Provisions in Trade Agreements Hub*, https://webapps.ilo.org/LPhub/#.

secure compliance with court orders, but not that these instances constitute a course of inaction that was *in a manner affecting trade*.[32] (emphasis added)

Key to the decision of the panel was its interpretation of 'in a manner affecting trade' to require the conferral of 'some competitive advantage on an employer or employers engaged in trade between the Parties'.[33] Thus, in that case, it was not sufficient for a failure to effectively enforce a Party's labor laws, through a sustained or recurring course of action or inaction, to affect trade between the Parties. To do so, it would need to reach the threshold of 'confer[ring] some competitive advantage on an employer or employers engaged in trade between the Parties'.[34] In considering whether such a conferral had taken place, the Panel focused on, inter alia, 'whether these effects are sufficient to confer some competitive advantage on such an enterprise or such enterprises'.[35]

The difficulties with the Panel's analysis and conclusion are highlighted in an abridged and annotated version of the ruling by the International Labor Rights Forum (**ILRF**).[36] The Panel's analysis makes clear the evidential challenges resulting from the ruling. These stem, first, from the type of information necessary to demonstrate a competitive advantage. As the ILRF states, the Panel's decision on labour costs[37] 'requires showing that an employer gained

---

32 *Arbitral Panel Established Pursuant to Chapter Twenty of the Dominican Republic–Central America–United States Free Trade Agreement*, Final Report of the Panel, 14 June 2017, para. 594, available at https://ustr.gov/issue-areas/enforcement/dispute-settlement-proceedings/fta-dispute-settlement/cafta-dr/matter-guatemala-issues-relating-obligations-under-article-1621a-cafta-dr (**Arbitral Panel, 2017 CAFTA–DR final report**).

33 Ibid, para. 190.

34 Ibid, para. 190.

35 Ibid, para. 196. The 'effects' referred to concerned 'whether the enterprise or enterprises in question export to CAFTA–DR Parties in competitive markets or compete with imports from CAFTA–DR Parties', and identification of 'the effects of a failure to enforce'.

36 International Labor Rights Forum (**ILRF**), 'Wrong turn for workers' rights: The US–Guatemala CAFTA labor arbitration ruling – and what to do about it' (March 2018), https://usw.org/wp-content/uploads/2019/06/Wrong20Turn20for20Workers20Rights20-20March202018-4.pdf. See also, Tequila J. Brooks, 'US–Guatemala Arbitration Panel clarifies effective enforcement under labor provisions of Free Trade Agreement' (2018) 4(1) *International Labor Rights Case Law* 45–51.

37 Here, the ILRF is referring to the Panel's finding that: 'In light of this determination, it does not follow that any failure to enforce labor laws that affects in any way the labor costs of an employer engaged in trade will thereby be in a manner affecting trade. A complainant must demonstrate that labor cost effects reasonably expected in light of the record evidence are sufficient to confer some competitive advantage …': Arbitral Panel, 2017 CAFTA–DR final report, para. 480, quoted in ILRF, 'Wrong turn for workers' rights', p. 20.

a competitive advantage, with sufficient financial evidence and analysis to prove it'.[38] It pointedly observes that, 'only the most intimate cost/sales/profits information in the hands of that employer alone could support such a showing'.[39] Second, the specificity required by the Panel's decision sets up formidable evidentiary hurdles, with the impact on particular firms needing to be demonstrated. As the ILRF analysis cogently notes, in one case, the required specificity necessitated 'a nearly impossible research job in practical terms';[40] and in another, threw up 'impossible logistical hurdles'.[41]

4.2.2 A Lacklustre Commitment to the ILO Conventions on Freedom of Association

As noted earlier, the decision of the EU–South Korea Expert Panel points to meaningful obligations relating to the 1998 ILO Declaration when it comes to freedom of association. On 20 January 2021, contrary to expectations, the Panel of Experts adjudicating this dispute released a decision that offered a hitherto unexpected degree of potential cogency to FTA clauses, such as the one contained in art. 13.4.3 of the EU–Korea FTA. The latter provision is common to many FTAs signed by the EU and the EU–Korea FTA; it obliged the Parties to 'commit to respecting, promoting and realising' fundamental labour rights, including the freedom of association 'in accordance with the obligations deriving from membership of the ILO'. The Panel concluded that this kind of provision can produce 'a legally binding commitment on both Parties in relation to respecting, promoting and realizing the principles … as they are understood in the context of the ILO Constitution'.[42]

This is clearly a positive finding. However, it is important to note that – strictly speaking – a panel decision does not amount to a binding precedent on other trade agreements (including Australia's trade agreements). As the

38 ILRF, 'Wrong Turn for Workers' Rights', p. 20.
39 Ibid.
40 Ibid, p. 25.
41 Ibid, p. 26.
42 Panel of Experts, 2021 EU–Korea FTA report, para. 107. For discussion, see June Namgoong, 'Two sides of one coin: The US–Guatemala arbitration and the dual structure of labour provisions in the CPTPP' (2019) 35(4) *International Journal of Comparative Labour Law and Industrial Relations* 483–510; Tonia Novitz, 'Enforceable social clauses in trade agreements with "bite"? Implications of the EU-South Korea Panel of Experts Report of 20 January 2021', *ETUI Policy Brief* (June 2021), https://www.etui.org/publications/enforceable-social-clauses-trade-agreements-bite; Aleydis Nissen, 'Not that assertive: The EU's take on enforcement of labour obligations in its Free Trade Agreement with South Korea' (2022) 33(2) *European Journal of International Law* 607–30.

Panel's decision was made in the context of labour provisions based on the EU approach, it is unlikely to apply to labour provisions in Australia's trade agreements, which are based on the United States' approach.

Even if the Panel's reasoning is fully applied to labour provisions in Australia's trade agreements, the effective implementation of obligations faces a formidable hurdle: Australia's lacklustre commitment to the ILO Conventions on freedom of association. This diluted commitment assists in the understanding of Australia's approach towards labour provisions in trade agreements. Saying 'no' to such provisions is explained by Australia's view that they are a form of protectionism; saying 'yes' to these provisions is explained as Australia assuming minimal obligations *and* not honouring key obligations it has assumed.

The ILO's Committee on Freedom of Association, and its Committee of Experts, have repeatedly found the provisions of Australia's principal industrial statute – the Fair Work Act 2009 (Cth) (**Fair Work Act**) – which relate to collective bargaining and industrial action to have breached the ILO Conventions on freedom of association and collective bargaining (ILO Conventions 87 and 98).[43] The breaches relate to (i) the level of bargaining, (ii) the subject matter of bargaining, and (iii) the ability to take industrial action.

The Fair Work Act's restrictions on the *level of bargaining* stem from the structural bias of the Act towards bargaining at the enterprise level. This bias is explicit, with the main object of the Act's bargaining provisions being 'to provide a simple, flexible and fair framework that enables collective bargaining in good faith, particularly at *the enterprise level,* for *enterprise agreements* that deliver productivity benefits'.[44] Good faith bargaining obligations are unenforceable;[45] and the ability to take protected industrial action is generally not available with multi-employer bargaining.[46] The Fair Work Act also limits the *content of enterprise agreements* to 'permitted matters', with terms that are

43 ILO Convention No. 87; ILO Convention No. 98. See Gudrun Biffl and Joe Isaac, 'Globalisation and core labour standards: Compliance problems with ILO Conventions 87 and 98. Comparing Australia and other English-speaking countries with EU Member States' (2005) 21(3) *International Journal of Comparative Labour Law and Industrial Relations* 405–44; Zoe Hutchinson, 'The right to freedom of association in the workplace: Australia's compliance with international human rights law' (2010) 27(2) *UCLA Pacific Basin Law Journal* 119–52; Renee Burns, 'Australia: Free to associate?' (2019) 26(2) *International Union Rights* 20–21; Renee Burns, 'Freedom of association and collectivity in Australia' (2019) 44(2) *New Zealand Journal of Employment Relations* 20–34.

44 Fair Work Act 2009 (Cth), s. 171, para. (1)(a) (emphasis added) (**Fair Work Act**).

45 Ibid, s. 229, para. (2).

46 Ibid, s. 413, para. (2).

not about 'permitted matters' having 'no effect'.[47] The concept of 'permitted matters' also shapes the lawfulness of industrial action, as discussed below.

Restrictions on the *ability to take industrial action* result from the implacable hostility of the common law to industrial action, and the limited immunity provided by the Fair Work Act to common law actions against industrial action. At common law, industrial action is invariably a fundamental breach of the contract of employment, enabling employers to lawfully dismiss striking workers; persons organising industrial action can also be committing various torts. In the context of such common law liability, the Act provides for immunity against common law actions through a complicated regime of 'protected industrial action'.[48] Amongst others, this regime ties the immunity for 'protected industrial action' to 'permitted matters'; a requirement for 'protected industrial action' by employees is that it is 'organised or engaged in for the purpose of supporting or advancing claims in relation to the agreement that are only about, or are reasonably believed to only be about, permitted matters'.[49] The immunity is also generally unavailable with industrial action taken in relation to multi-employer bargaining.[50]

As noted earlier, the ILO Committee on Freedom of Association has found these restrictions to be in breach of the ILO Conventions on freedom of association. The restrictions on the level and subject matter of bargaining undermine the autonomy of collective bargaining; specifically, 'the principle of free and voluntary collective bargaining embodied in Article 4 of Convention No. 98'.[51] The restrictions on the ability to take industrial action violate the right to strike, which 'not only concern better working conditions or collective claims of an occupational nature, but also the seeking of solutions

---

47 Ibid, s. 253, para. (1)(a).

48 Shae McCrystal, *The Right to Strike in Australia* (Annandale: Federation Press, 2010).

49 Fair Work Act, s. 409, para. (1)(a).

50 Ibid, s. 413, para. (2). The limited exceptions to the enforceability of good faith bargaining obligations, and the availability of protected industrial action in respect of multi-employer bargaining, are the supported bargaining and single-interest employer bargaining streams enacted by the Fair Work Legislation Amendment (Secure Jobs, Better Pay) Act 2022 (Cth).

51 Case No. 2698: *Complaint against the Government of Australia presented by the Communications, Electrical, Electronic, Energy, Information, Postal, Plumbing and Allied Services Union of Australia (CEPU)*, International Labour Office, 357th Report of the Committee on Freedom of Association (Geneva, June 2010), para. 220 (**Case No. 2698**). For analysis, see Shae McCrystal, 'Fair Work in the international spotlight: The CEPU complaint to the ILO's Committee on Freedom of Association' (2011) 24(2) *Australian Journal of Labour Law* 163–72.

to economic and social policy questions and problems facing the undertaking which are of direct concern to the workers'.[52]

It is not the fact of these breaches that is of salience; rather, it is that the breaches – together with the absence of any real attempt to address them – reflect a lacklustre commitment to the ILO Conventions on freedom of association. The legislative opportunities to address this deficit have not been wanting. Since enactment of the Fair Work Act in 2009, there have been several major rounds of amendments.[53] If the ILO is 'the social conscience of world development', as former Australian Prime Minister Bob Hawke once put it,[54] then it is a conscience that Australia in a Pinocchio-like fashion seems willing to ignore.

5 Concluding Thoughts

At the time of writing, global trade is being profoundly affected by the decisions of the second Trump Administration; a presidency that is amplifying the approach of the first Trump Administration towards international trade, with a heightened emphasis on nationalism ('Make America Great Again'), unilateralism, and protectionism.[55]

52 Case No. 2698, para. 224.

53 Notably, the Fair Work Legislation Amendment (Secure Jobs, Better Pay) Act 2022 (Cth); Fair Work Legislation Amendment (Closing Loopholes) Act 2023 (Cth); Fair Work Legislation Amendment (Closing Loopholes No. 2) Act 2024 (Cth).

54 Quoted in CE Landau, 'The influence of ILO standards on Australian labour law and practice' (1987) 126(6) *International Labour Review* 669, 670.

55 For analysis of the first Trump Administration's approach towards global trade, see Rachel Brewster, 'The Trump Administration and the future of the WTO' (2018) 44 *Yale Journal of International Law Online* 6–15; Steve Charnovitz, 'How American rejectionism undermines international economic law' (2018) 10(2) *Trade, Law and Development* 226–69; Rachel Brewster, 'Analyzing the Trump Administration's international trade strategy' (2019) 42(5) *Fordham International Law Journal* 1419–30; Daniel CK Chow, 'United States unilateralism and the World Trade Organization' (2019) 37(1) *Boston University International Law Journal* 1–34; Geneviève Dufour and Delphine Ducasse, '"America First" and the return of economic isolationism and nationalism to the United States: A historic turning point for international trade law' (2019) 57 *Canadian Yearbook of International Law* 223–55; Harold Hongju Koh, 'Trump change: Unilateralism and the "disruption myth" in international trade' (2019) 44 *Yale Journal of International Law Online* 96–103; Nancy Williams, 'The resilience of protectionism in US trade policy' (2019) 99(2) *Boston University Law Review* 683–720; Daniel CK Chow, 'US trade infallibility and the crisis of the World Trade Organization' [2020] (3) *Michigan State Law Review* 599–642; Virdzhiniya Petrova Georgieva, 'Trump's foreign policy and international trade law' (2020) 20 *Anuario Mexicano de derecho internacional* 687–721; Uchechukwu Nwoke,

There has been a dialectical impact on Australia. At time of writing, the United States has imposed a 10 per cent baseline tariff on most goods imported from Australia, with higher tariffs on certain goods (including Australian steel, aluminium, and automobiles).[56] Apart from seeking to be exempt or lowering these tariffs, Australia has responded by renewing its efforts to reach new trade agreements,[57] including the resumption of negotiations with the European Union for a broad-based Australia–EU trade agreement.[58] Also in the negotiation phase is the Australia–India Comprehensive Economic Cooperation Agreement to build upon the countries' Economic Cooperation and Trade Agreement.[59]

How will Australia's approach to labour provisions play out in these Trump-era negotiations? If agreements are reached with the European Union and India, it is likely that the Australia–EU agreement will have labour provisions, whilst the opposite will be true of the Australia–India Comprehensive Economic Cooperation Agreement.

'Imposition of trade tariffs by the USA on China: Implications for the WTO and international trade law' (2020) 19(2) *Journal of International Trade Law and Policy* 69–84; Kenneth Holland, 'The Trump Administration's critique of the World Trade Organization and its implications for the international trading system' (2021) 13 *The Indian Journal of International Economic Law* 154–78; Kristen Hopewell, 'Trump & Trade: The crisis in the multilateral trading system' (2021) 26(2) *New Political Economy* 271–82; Nerina Boschiero, *US Trade Policy, China and the World Trade Organisation* (London: Routledge, 2023).

56 'Latest on US tariffs', *Australian Government, Department of Foreign Affairs and Trade*, https://www.dfat.gov.au/trade/trade-and-investment/latest-us-tariffs.

57 Agence France-Presse, 'Angered by Trump's "unjustified" tariffs, Australia chases new trade deals', *South China Morning Post*, 8 June 2025, https://www.scmp.com/news/asia/australasia/article/3313526/angered-trumps-unjustified-tariffs-australia-chases-new-trade-deals.

58 'Australia and the European Union determined to seal trade deal as talks revived', *ABC News*, 5 June 2025, https://www.abc.net.au/news/2025-06-05/australia-and-eu-trade-deal/105378252. See Lachlan McKenzie, 'Overcoming legacies of foreign policy (dis)interests in the negotiation of the European Union–Australia Free Trade Agreement' (2018) 72(3) *Australian Journal of International Affairs* 255–71; Lachlan McKenzie and Evgeny Postnikov, 'The EU's and Australia's approaches to trade bilateralism: Discrepancies and synergies' (2019) 5(4–5) *Global Affairs* 523–30; Aneta Tyc, 'Free Trade Agreements between the EU and New Zealand and the EU and Australia: An assessment of labour law provisions' (2024) 107 *Acta Universitatis Lodziensis Folia Iuridica* 119–26.

59 'Australia–India Comprehensive Economic Cooperation Agreement (CECA)', *Australian Government, Department of Foreign Affairs and Trade*, https://www.dfat.gov.au/trade/agreements/negotiations/aifta/australia-india-comprehensive-economic-cooperation-agreement.

Bibliography

Agence France-Presse, 'Angered by Trump's "unjustified" tariffs, Australia chases new trade deals', *South China Morning Post*, 8 June 2025, https://www.scmp.com/news/asia/australasia/article/3313526/angered-trumps-unjustified-tariffs-australia-chases-new-trade-deals.

Araujo, Billy Melo, 'Labour provisions in EU and US mega-regional trade agreements: Rhetoric and reality' (2018) 67(1) *International and Comparative Law Quarterly* 233–54.

Arbitral Panel Established Pursuant to Chapter Twenty of the Dominican Republic–Central America–United States Free Trade Agreement, Final Report of the Panel, 14 June 2017, available at https://ustr.gov/issue-areas/enforcement/dispute-settlement-proceedings/fta-dispute-settlement/cafta-dr/matter-guatemala-issues-relating-obligations-under-article-1621a-cafta-dr.

'Australia and the European Union determined to seal trade deal as talks revived', *ABC News*, 5 June 2025, https://www.abc.net.au/news/2025-06-05/australia-and-eu-trade-deal/105378252.

'Australia–India Comprehensive Economic Cooperation Agreement (CECA)', *Australian Government, Department of Foreign Affairs and Trade*, https://www.dfat.gov.au/trade/agreements/negotiations/aifta/australia-india-comprehensive-economic-cooperation-agreement.

Australia–UK FTA, *ILO Labour Provisions in Trade Agreements Hub*, https://webapps.ilo.org/LPhub/#.

Biffl, Gudrun and Joe Isaac, 'Globalisation and core labour standards: Compliance problems with ILO Conventions 87 and 98. Comparing Australia and other English-speaking countries with EU Member States' (2005) 21(3) *International Journal of Comparative Labour Law and Industrial Relations* 405–44.

Boschiero, Nerina, *US Trade Policy, China and the World Trade Organisation* (London: Routledge, 2023).

Brewster, Rachel, 'The Trump Administration and the future of the WTO' (2018) 44 *Yale Journal of International Law Online* 6–15.

Brewster, Rachel, 'Analyzing the Trump Administration's international trade strategy' (2019) 42(5) *Fordham International Law Journal* 1419–30.

Brooks, Tequila J., 'US–Guatemala Arbitration Panel clarifies effective enforcement under labor provisions of Free Trade Agreement' (2018) 4(1) *International Labor Rights Case Law* 45–51.

Brown, Ronald C., 'Asian and US Perspectives on Labor Rights under International Trade Agreements Compared', in Axel Marx et al. (eds), *Global Governance of Labour Rights: Assessing the Effectiveness of Transnational Public and Private Policy Initiatives* (Cheltenham: Edward Elgar Publishing, 2015) ch. 5.

Burns, Renee, 'Australia: Free to associate? (2019) 26(2) *International Union Rights* 20–21.
Burns, Renee, 'Freedom of association and collectivity in Australia' (2019) 44(2) *New Zealand Journal of Employment Relations* 20–34.
Case No. 2698: *Complaint against the Government of Australia presented by the Communications, Electrical, Electronic, Energy, Information, Postal, Plumbing and Allied Services Union of Australia (CEPU)*, International Labour Office, 357th Report of the Committee on Freedom of Association (Geneva, June 2010).
Charnovitz, Steve, 'How American rejectionism undermines international economic law' (2018) 10(2) *Trade, Law and Development* 226–69.
Chow, Daniel CK, 'United States unilateralism and the World Trade Organization' (2019) 37(1) *Boston University International Law Journal* 1–34.
Chow, Daniel CK, 'US trade infallibility and the crisis of the World Trade Organization' [2020] (3) *Michigan State Law Review* 599–642.
Cohen, Austin Chad, 'Trading places: With the United States in retreat, who writes the international rules for trade' (2019) 47(2) *Georgia Journal of International and Comparative Law* 539–574.
Comprehensive and Progressive Agreement for Trans-Pacific Partnership (CPTPP), *ILO Labour Provisions in Trade Agreements Hub*, https://webapps.ilo.org/LPhub/#.
Corley-Coulibaly, Marva, Ira Postolachi and Netsanet Tesfay, 'A multi-faceted typology of labour provisions in trade agreements: Overview, methodology and trends', *International Labour Organization*, 24 November 2021, https://www.ilo.org/resource/multi-faceted-typology-labour-provisions-trade-agreements-overview.
de Schutter, Olivier, *Trade in the Service of Sustainable Development: Linking Trade to Labour Rights and Environmental Standards* (Oxford: Hart Publishing, 2017).
Dufour, Geneviève and Delphine Ducasse, '"America First" and the return of economic isolationism and nationalism to the United States: A historic turning point for international trade law' (2019) 57 *Canadian Yearbook of International Law* 223–255.
Fair Work Act 2009 (Cth).
Fair Work Legislation Amendment (Secure Jobs, Better Pay) Act 2022 (Cth).
Fischer, Tim, 'Australia', WTO Ministerial Conference, Singapore, 9 December 1996, WT/MIN(96)/ST/26, https://www.wto.org/english/thewto_e/minist_e/min96_e/st26.htm.
Freedom of Association and Protection of the Right to Organise Convention (No. 87), San Francisco, 17 June 1948, in force 4 July 1950, 96 UNTS 257.
Garcia, Maria, 'Building Global Governance One Treaty at a Time? A Comparison of the US and EU Approaches to Preferential Trade Agreements and the Challenge of TTIP', in Elaine Fahey (ed.), *Institutionalisation beyond the Nation State: Transatlantic Relations – Data, Privacy and Trade Law* (Cham: Springer, 2018), pp. 213–242.

Georgieva, Virdzhiniya Petrova, 'Trump's foreign policy and international trade law' (2020) 20 *Anuario Mexicano de derecho internacional* 687–721.

Giumelli, Francesco and Gerda van Roozendaal, 'Trade agreements and labour standards clauses: Explaining labour standards developments through a qualitative comparative analysis of US Free Trade Agreements' (2017) 17(1) *Global Social Policy* 38–61.

Gött, Henner, 'Linkages of Trade, Investment and Labour in Preferential Trade Agreements: between Untapped Potential and Structural Insufficiencies', in Marc Bungenberg et al. (eds), *European Yearbook of International Economic Law 2019* (Cham: Springer, 2019), pp. 133–165.

Harrison, James et al., 'Labour standards provisions in EU Free Trade Agreements: Reflections on the European Commission's reform agenda' (2019) 18(4) *World Trade Review* 635–658.

Hradilová, Katerina and Ondrej Svoboda, 'Sustainable development chapters in the EU Free Trade Agreements: Searching for effectiveness' (2018) 52(6) *Journal of World Trade* 1019–1042.

Holland, Kenneth, 'The Trump Administration's critique of the World Trade Organization and its implications for the international trading system' (2021) 13 *The Indian Journal of International Economic Law* 154–178.

Hopewell, Kristen, 'Trump & Trade: The crisis in the multilateral trading system' (2021) 26(2) *New Political Economy* 271–282.

Hutchinson, Zoe, 'The right to freedom of association in the workplace: Australia's compliance with international human rights law' (2010) 27(2) *UCLA Pacific Basin Law Journal* 119–152.

ILO Declaration on Fundamental Principles and Rights at Work and its Follow-Up, adopted 1998, amended 2022.

International Institute for Labour Studies, *Social Dimensions of Free Trade Agreements* (Geneva: International Labour Organization, rev. ed., 2015).

International Labor Rights Forum (ILRF), 'Wrong turn for workers' rights: The US–Guatemala CAFTA labor arbitration ruling – and what to do about it' (March 2018), https://usw.org/wp-content/uploads/2019/06/Wrong20Turn20for20Workers20Rights20-20March202018-4.pdf.

Ji, Xianbai, 'China's Cautious Approach to Labour Provisions in Free Trade Agreements', in Soon Beng Chew, Lingli Huang and Kai Xiang Kwa (eds), *Political, Economic and Social Dimensions of Labour Markets: A Global Insight* (World Scientific, 2022) ch. 16.

Kang, Yoo-Duk, 'EU–Korea FTA (2011–2020): First Experience of Implementing the Trade and Sustainable Development Chapter under the FTA', in Nicola Casarini et al. (eds), *The Routledge Handbook of Europe–Korea Relations* (Abingdon: Routledge, 2021) ch. 11.

Katsaroumpas, Ioannis, 'Different shades of minimalism: The multilateral construction of labour clauses in the UK–Australian and UK–New Zealand FTAs' (2023) 34(1) *King's Law Journal* 71–104.

Koh, Harold Hongju, 'Trump change: Unilateralism and the "disruption myth" in international trade' (2019) 44 *Yale Journal of International Law Online* 96–103.

Lang, Ian, 'United Kingdom', WTO Ministerial Conference, Singapore, 9 December 1996, WT/MIN(96)/ST/9, https://www.wto.org/english/thewto_e/minist_e/min96_e/st9.htm.

Landau, CE, 'The influence of ILO standards on Australian labour law and practice' (1987) 126(6) *International Labour Review* 669–690.

'Latest on US tariffs', *Australian Government, Department of Foreign Affairs and Trade*, https://www.dfat.gov.au/trade/trade-and-investment/latest-us-tariffs.

Lazo, Rodrigo Polanco and Sebastián Gómez Fielder, 'A requiem for the Trans-Pacific Partnership: Something new, something old and something borrowed?' (2017) 18(2) *Melbourne Journal of International Law* 298–348.

Malaysia–Australia, *ILO Labour Provisions in Trade Agreements Hub*, https://webapps.ilo.org/LPhub/#.

Mancini, Isabella, 'Labour Rights Protection in EU Trade Agreements: Can Trade Agreements "Only Do so Much"?' in Federico Casolari and Lucia Serena Rossi (eds), *Integrating EU Free Trade Agreements into the EU Legal Order* (Cheltenham: Edward Elgar Publishing, 2022 forthcoming), https://ssrn.com/abstract=4130430.

McCrystal, Shae, *The Right to Strike in Australia* (Annandale: Federation Press, 2010).

McCrystal, Shae, 'Fair Work in the international spotlight: The CEPU complaint to the ILO's Committee on Freedom of Association' (2011) 24(2) *Australian Journal of Labour Law* 163–172.

McKenzie, Lachlan, 'Overcoming legacies of foreign policy (dis)interests in the negotiation of the European Union–Australia Free Trade Agreement' (2018) 72(3) *Australian Journal of International Affairs* 255–271.

McKenzie, Lachlan and Evgeny Postnikov, 'The EU's and Australia's approaches to trade bilateralism: Discrepancies and synergies' (2019) 5(4–5) *Global Affairs* 523–530.

Namgoong, June, 'Two sides of one coin: The US–Guatemala arbitration and the dual structure of labour provisions in the CPTPP' (2019) 35(4) *International Journal of Comparative Labour Law and Industrial Relations* 483–510.

Nissen, Aleydis, 'Not that assertive: The EU's take on enforcement of labour obligations in its Free Trade Agreement with South Korea' (2022) 33(2) *European Journal of International Law* 607–630.

Novitz, Tonia, 'Enforceable social clauses in trade agreements with "bite"? Implications of the EU-South Korea Panel of Experts Report of 20 January 2021', *ETUI*

Policy Brief (June 2021), https://www.etui.org/publications/enforceable-social-clauses-trade-agreements-bite.

Novitz, Tonia, *Trade, Labour and Sustainable Development: Leaving No One in the World of Work Behind* (Cheltenham: Edward Elgar Publishing, 2024).

Nwoke, Uchechukwu, 'Imposition of trade tariffs by the USA on China: Implications for the WTO and international trade law' (2020) 19(2) *Journal of International Trade Law and Policy* 69–84.

Pacific Agreement on Closer Economic Relations Plus (PACER Plus), *ILO Labour Provisions in Trade Agreements Hub*, https://webapps.ilo.org/LPhub/#.

Panel of Experts Proceeding Constituted Under Article 13.15 of the EU–Korea Free Trade Agreement, Report of the Panel of Experts, 20 January 2021, https://www.worldtradelaw.net/static.php?type=public&page=ftapanels

Petrovic, Jadranka and Benjamin Grunberg, 'Intersecting trade, politics and human rights: The negotiation phase of the Australia-China Free Trade Agreement' (2017) 51(1) *Journal of World Trade* 67–104.

Polaski, Sandra, 'The Strategy and Politics of Linking Trade and Labor Standards: An Overview of Issues and Approaches', in Kimberly Elliott (ed.), *Handbook on Globalisation and Labour Standards* (Cheltenham: Edward Elgar Publishing, 2022), pp. 203–225.

Postnikov, Evgeny, 'Labor Standards in EU and US Preferential Trade Agreements: Mainstreaming the Trade-Labor Linkage', in Kimberly A. Elliott (ed.), *Handbook on Globalisation and Labour Standards* (Cheltenham: Edward Elgar Publishing, 2022), pp. 244–257.

Postnikov, Evgeny and Lachlan McKenzie, *Social Standards in EU and US Trade Agreements* (Abingdon: Routledge, 2020).

Postnikov, Evgeny and Lachlan McKenzie, 'Resisting issue-linkage: Social standards and Australian trade agreements' (2022) 25 *Journal of International Relations and Development* 1079–1100.

Right to Organise and to Collective Bargaining Convention (No. 98), Geneva, 8 June 1949, in force 18 July 1951, 96 UNTS 257.

Scherrer, Christoph, 'Novel labour-related clauses in a trade agreement: From NAFTA to USMCA' (2020) 11(3) *Global Labour Journal* 291–306.

'Side letter labour: Australia to Malaysia', *Department of Foreign Affairs and Trade*, 11 January 2018, https://www.dfat.gov.au/trade/agreements/in-force/mafta/Pages/side-letter-labour-australia-malaysia.

Tham, Joo-Cheong and KD Ewing, 'Labour provisions in trade agreements: Neoliberal regulation at work?' (2020) 17 *International Organizations Law Review* 153–177.

Tyc, Aneta, *Global Trade, Labour Rights and International Law: A Multilevel Approach* (Abingdon: Routledge, 2021).

Tyc, Aneta, 'Free Trade Agreements between the EU and New Zealand and the EU and Australia: An assessment of labour law provisions' (2024) 107 *Acta Universitatis Lodziensis Folia Iuridica* 119–126.

United States–Australia FTA, *ILO Labour Provisions in Trade Agreements Hub*, https://webapps.ilo.org/LPhub/#.

Vatta, Alessia, 'The social clauses in EU trade agreements: Contents and prospects' [2018] (2) *Poliarchie/Polyarchies* 286–306.

Williams, Nancy, 'The resilience of protectionism in US trade policy' (2019) 99(2) *Boston University Law Review* 683–720.

World Trade Organization, Singapore Ministerial Declaration, adopted 13 December 1996, WT/MIN(96)/DEC (18 December 1996), https://www.wto.org/english/thewto_e/minist_e/min96_e/wtodec_e.htm.

Yan, Yueming, 'A new chapter in China's stance on labour protection? An assessment of the China–EU CAI' (2022) 25(3) *Journal of International Economic Law* 464–83.

Yan, Yueming, 'Labour and trade in Asia Pacific: Origin, development, and prospects' (2023) 31(2) *Asia Pacific Law Review* 576–595.

Yin, Wei, 'Challenges, issues in China-EU investment agreement and the implication on China's domestic reform' (2018) 26(2) *Asia Pacific Law Review* 170–202.

Zhujun, Zhao, 'China's legal countermeasures to CPTPP labour provisions' (2022) 5(4) *Pacific International Journal* 38–44.

CHAPTER 11

New Zealand's Trade Agreements and Labour Rights

Stephen Hoadley

1 Introduction

Trade agreements are more than officially negotiated economic frameworks. In their modern form, they embody also a variety of socio-political and cultural values and aims of the partner governments. Protecting labour rights is one of those values, albeit one explicitly manifested only recently, and one incorporated mainly in agreements among liberal democratic states. New Zealand is a liberal democratic state that since 1983 has negotiated a series of increasingly progressive free trade agreements with three dozen partners. But labour rights appeared explicitly only in 2005 in the free trade agreement with Thailand. This chapter traces New Zealand's labour history, then New Zealand's trade history, and then brings the two together to show how the assertion of labour rights became a fixture in New Zealand's trade agreements and policies.

2 Labour Rights in New Zealand History

The acknowledgement of labour rights has been implicit in the unique trading history of New Zealand since the early 1800s.[1] When British settlers began arriving in Aotearoa, Land of the Long White Cloud, as the island nation was known by the indigenous Māori, they survived by trading with their hosts, exchanging manufactured goods for food and land. Proliferation of guns and liquor led to disorder and subsequently to conflict, land confiscation, and legal trickery, all contributing to a decline in Māori population relative to Europeans and the loss of 90 per cent of their land to the Government and European firms and individuals. By the end of the nineteenth century, Māori were

1 Brian Easton (2020). *Not in Narrow Seas: The Economic History of Aotearoa New Zealand. Wellington*: Victoria University of Wellington Press. See especially Chapter 25 'The Rise of Labour' pp. 262–282.

 | HTTPS://DOI.ORG/10.1163/9789004762251-012

reduced to rural small-holders or urban service workers in European enterprises.[2]

Anglican missionaries ministering to the spiritual and social needs of the settlers were aware of deepening injustices, and they decried this immiseration of the indigenous people. Their pleas for equity were buttressed by progressive voices in the United Kingdom, where social reform movements were emerging to deal with the deleterious social effects of the industrial revolution. England passed the Factory Act in 1802 and the New Poor Law in 1834.[3] These statutes and other reform policies were adapted by New Zealand in 1846 and reflected in the Destitute Persons' Ordinance.[4]

As well, New Zealand's founding document, the Treaty of Waitangi of 1840, expressed a partnership between the Crown (Queen Victoria at that time) and the Māori chiefs. Whereas the Crown asserted sovereignty, the Māori were granted rights over their tribal institutions, customs, lands, and natural resources. Although violated in practice, this partnership remained an ideal of equity between the races, and was often cited to legitimise reforms in inter-ethnic relations.[5]

With regard to settler (British, non-Māori) labour, New Zealand's economic growth had been retarded by a persistent shortage of workers. Those who migrated tended to be lower-middle-class Britons seeking economic autonomy by breaking in new farms or founding new enterprises. A labouring underclass as emerged in the mines and factories of Britain never developed in New Zealand. Scarcity enhanced the value of each worker and contributed to the national ethos of egalitarianism. The idea of workers' value, and then of workers' rights, was a logical corollary.

The effect on workers' rights of social legislation and charitable initiatives, underpinned by New Zealand's founding document, was positive. Whereas earlier governments dealt with pockets of unemployment by encouraging rural development (at the expense of Māori land ownership[6]), the Government near the turn of the century addressed workers' rights head-on by establishing a Ministry of Labour in 1891 and passing the Industrial Conciliation and

2 Simon Winchester (2021). *Land: How the Hunger for Ownership Shaped the Modern World.* London: Harper-Collins. See especially Part V, Chapter 1, 'Māori in Arcady', pp. 323–342.

3 Lindsay J. Benstead (2006). 'Labour Rights and Standards'. Ashish K. Vaida, ed., *Globalization: Encyclopedia of Trade, Labour and Politics.* Santa Barbara: ABC CLIO. p, 810.

4 Easton, p. 274.

5 Matthew Wright (2019). *Waitangi: a Living Treaty.* Auckland: David Bateman Ltd.

6 Winchester, pp. 335–337.

Arbitration Act of 1894.[7] This was followed the Workers' Compensation Act of 1900, the Widows' Benefit in 1911, and the Family Allowances Act of 1926. In 1919 New Zealand became a founder member of the nascent International Labour Organization and reaffirmed its commitment when the ILO became a specialised agency of the United Nations.[8] The Labour Government elected in 1935 responded to the Great Depression with a plethora of legislation and policies that brought New Zealand to maturity as a welfare state, with attendant benefits for workers and their families.

Parallel to government reforms, workers were active in asserting their rights. The on-shore labour force was dispersed in small towns and farms, or in small guild-like craft unions, so it was maritime workers, and miners, who first organised and mobilised. The Great Maritime Strike of 1890, led by the General Labourers Union, may be taken as the start of the organised labour movement. The Blackball strike followed in 1908 and led to establishment of the Federation of Miners. These, joined by others such as the Tramway Workers Union and the Amalgamated Searers and Labourers Union, merged into an omnibus Federation of Labour, and a series of strikes inspired by the International Workers of the World (IWW), followed in the early 1900s. Worker energy coalesced into the foundation of the Labour Party which led New Zealand through the Great Depression and World War II, and which has governed intermittently to the present.[9]

3 International Standards of Labour Rights

In a burst of post–World War II idealism, the United Nations Commission on Human Rights drafted a series of international human rights declarations, covenants, and treaties. Each proclaimed fundamental labour rights including the right to organise and strike and to enjoy choice of employment, safe working conditions, and fair remuneration. New Zealand, with its history of labour reform and social welfare legislation, had no hesitation in endorsing these instruments and incorporating into statutes and policies their attendant standards and prescriptions. They included the following human rights con-

7 Said to be the world's first legislative implementation of labour's right to arbitration. See Easton, p. 215. It is ironic that the Act made strikes illegal. This was remedied later.

8 https://www.ilo.org/new-zealand#:~:text=A%20founding%20member%20of%20the,New%20Zealand%20%2D%20ILO%20partnership%20page.

9 Easton, pp. 224–225. Also see James Belich (2001). Paradise Reforged: A History of New Zealanders from the 1880s to the Year 2000. Auckland: Allan Lane The Penguin Press, pp. 133–146.

ventions, the articles relevant to labour rights, and New Zealand's year of accession.[10]

Universal Declaration of Human Rights, Article 23. NZ ratified in 1949.
International Covenant on Economic, Social and Cultural Rights, Articles 6, 7 and 8. NZ ratified in 1978.
International Covenant on Political and Civil Rights, Article 22. NZ ratified in 1978.
International Convention on the Elimination of All Forms of Racial Discrimination, Article 5. NZ ratified in 1972.
Convention on the Elimination of All Forms of Discrimination Against Women, Article 11. NZ ratified in 1982.
Convention on the Rights of the Child, Article 32. NZ ratified in 1993.
Convention on the Rights of Persons with Disabilities, Article 27. NZ signed in 2007.

In the period 1938 to 2003 New Zealand ratified six fundamental ILO conventions and one declaration. They include, with New Zealand's year of accession, the following:[11]

ILO Convention 29, on forced labour. NZ acceded in 1938.
ILO Convention 105, on abolition of forced labour. NZ acceded in 1968.
ILO Convention 100, on equal remuneration. NZ acceded in 1983.
ILO Declaration on Fundamental Principles and Rights of Work. NZ acceded in 1998.
ILO Convention 182, on the worst forms of child labour. NZ acceded in 2001.
ILO Convention 98, on the right to organized and collective bargaining. NZ acceded in 2003.

4 New Zealand's Trade and Labour Context

New Zealand's trade in the 1800s was conducted by local enterprises with British, Australian, American partners with minimal government regulation, in accordance with Adam Smith's free market doctrine. The 'most favoured

10 New Zealand Handbook on International Human Rights (3rd ed 2008). Wellington: New Zealand Ministry of Foreign Affairs and Trade.

11 New Zealand declined to ratify ILO Convention 87, on freedom of association and protection of the right to organise, and ILO Convention 138, on minimum age, on the grounds that its laws and practices were already in compliance with their principles,

nation' precedent set by the Cobden-Chevalier Treaty of 1860 guided Britain's, and therefore New Zealand's, international trade relations. New Zealand's principal trade partners were predominantly Great Britain, followed by Australia and the United States, and their legislation and practices were adopted by New Zealand governments and private sector traders. While labour rights were not explicit in these trading arrangements, they were implicit, inasmuch as all four democratic governments had acknowledged the legitimacy of labour unions and had legislated labour reforms. Implementation was reluctant, intermittent and incomplete under conservative governments, but these were temporary exceptions.[12]

Therefore, when the victors of World War II met to negotiate the still-born International Trade Organization (the predecessor of the General Agreement on Tariffs and Trade (GATT) and the World Trade Organization (WTO)), the principle of fairness to all stakeholders, including labour, in the enterprises of domestic production for international trade was on negotiators' minds. The examples of how worker poverty led to populism-fuelled fascism in Germany and Italy motivated negotiation of an international trade regime (and corresponding domestic economic regimes) that incorporated notions of equity to workers, even though labour rights were rarely at the centre of discussions. The leading states of the post–World War period addressed issues of international economic stability by establishing the World Bank and the International Monetary Fund. Negotiations to establish a parallel trade institution, the International Trade Organization, culminated in the Havana Charter, which the New Zealand delegation endorsed. The Charter addressed labour rights explicitly, as follows.[13]

> Havana Charter, Article 7, Fair Labour Standards.
> 1. The Members recognize that measures relating to employment must take fully into account the rights of workers under inter-governmental declarations, conventions and agreements. They recognize that all countries have a common interest in the achievement and maintenance of fair labour standards related to productivity, and thus in the improvement of wages and working conditions as productivity may permit. The Members recognize that unfair labour conditions, particularly in product for export, create difficulties In international trade, and,

12 Brian Easton discusses resistance to labour reforms by farmer-dominated centre-right leaders and parties. See his Chapter 21, 'Class War, Great War, Post War'.

13 UNITED NATIONS CONFERENCE ON TRADE AND EMPLOYMENT HELD AT HAVANA, CUBA FROM NOVEMBER 21, 1947, TO MARCH 24, 1948 FINAL ACT AND RELATED DOCUMENTS https://www.wto.org/english/docs_e/legal_e/havana_e.pdf.

> accordingly, each Member shall take whatever action may be appropriate and feasible to eliminate such conditions within its territory.

Opposition by protectionist US senators made Charter adoption unviable, and negotiators attempted to salvage some international consensus on trade stabilisation and liberalisation issues. The outcome was the General Agreement on Tariffs and Trade (GATT), which guided international trade negotiations until the establishment of the World Trade Organization (WTO) in 1995.[14]

However, gone from the GATT text was any explicit reference to labour rights. GATT's Article XX makes only oblique references to labour rights in phrases protecting public morals, human health, and prison labour.

> ...nothing in this Agreement shall be construed to prevent the adoption or enforcement by any contracting party of measures: (a) necessary to protect public morals; (b) necessary to protect human, animal or plant life or health; ... (e) relating to the products of prison labour...[15]

Labour advocates assert that these phrases can be interpreted to support workers' rights in trade agreements. But most GATT member governments adopted a minimalist economic neo-liberal interpretation and resisted the injection of rights and justice language into the agreement. Repeated attempts by reform governments, including New Zealand's, to incorporate ILO standards, wholly or in part, into the GATT were rejected by a majority of member governments. Instead, the majority focussed on preventing the alleged 'race to the bottom' by poor countries, that is, the exploitation of a cheap labour force to reduce production costs and unfairly (in the view of the developed countries) undercut competition by high-wage economies, sometimes conflated with 'dumping'.[16] Members reluctant to impede trade declined to use economic sanctions against alleged offenders but rather obliged trade partner governments to pledge not to use cheap labour to gain a trade advantage. Hence the members, including New Zealand, adopted, and adapted, the fol-

---

14 See the WTO homepage at https://www.wto.org/.

15 General Agreement on Tariffs and Trade. Text of the General Agreement. Geneva, July 1986. https://www.wto.org/english/docs_e/legal_e/gatt47_e.pdf.

16 Maria Artuso and Carolan McLarney (2015). 'A Race to the Top: Should Labour Standards be Included in Trade Agreements?' VIKALPA The Journal for Decision Makers 40(1) 1–14. https://journals.sagepub.com/doi/pdf/10.1177/0256090915573610.

lowing (or similar) formula in trade agreements, that, as exemplified in the NZ–Thailand FTA, the negotiating parties undertake…[17]

> a political commitment not to weaken or derogate from labour or environment laws or standards to gain an unfair trade advantage.

5 New Zealand's Trade Agreements

This chapter has argued that New Zealand has been a pioneer in promoting and protecting labour rights domestically. Labour scarcity, strong unions, progressive law and courts, and Labour Party-led governments have assured protection of labour rights for over a century. Abroad, New Zealand has joined and implemented the standards of international human rights institutions and the ILO, and in international fora has consistently argued the case for adopting labour standards in the GATT and WTO. The question to be addressed now is the extent to which New Zealand has reflected these ideals in its post–World War II trade agreements.

In 1983 New Zealand completed one of the world's first, and most comprehensive, free trade agreements, with Australia, called Closer Economic Relations, or CER.[18] It was followed by an equally high-quality FTA with Singapore in 2000.[19] This agreement was broadened to include Chile and Brunei in 2004, called P-4.[20] None of these three early agreements contained a labour protection chapter or even a clause. In the case of CER, the labour standards of New Zealand and Australia were already progressive. And they were similar inasmuch as Australia and New Zealand adhered to the same international human rights and labour rights instruments. Thus, their negotiators felt no need for an explicit labour protection section.

Furthermore, the two governments had negotiated a TransTasman Travel Arrangement that allowed free movement of persons between the two econo-

17 New Zealand Ministry of Foreign Affairs and Trade. New Zealand Thailand Closer Economic Partnership. National Interest Analysis. March 2005. p. 56 https://www.mfat.govt.nz/assets/Trade-agreements/Thailand-NZ-CEP/nz-tha-icep-nationalinterestanalysis.pdf.

18 Stephen Hoadley (2006) 'Australia New Zealand Closer Economic Trade Agreement (ANZCERTA). Ashish K. Vaida, ed., *Globalization: Encyclopedia of Trade, Labour and Politics.* Santa Barbara: ABC CLIO. pp, 471–478.

19 Stephen Hoadley (2002). *Negotiating Free Trade: The New Zealand-Singapore CEP Agreement.* Wellington: New Zealand Institute of International Affairs.

20 https://www.mfat.govt.nz/en/trade/free-trade-agreements/free-trade-agreements-in-force/trans-pacific-strategic-economic-partnership-p4.

mies, ideally creating a single labour market.[21] But in the 1990s Australian politicians complained that New Zealand workers collectively were enjoying greater welfare privileges in Australia than Australian workers were in New Zealand, and demanded payment to equalise the expenses to Canberra. To avoid punishing costs, New Zealand's prime minister compromised by acceding to Australia's denial of unemployment benefits and other government privileges to resident non-citizens, must of whom were New Zealanders, while New Zealand continued to extend all domestic labour protections and privileges to resident Australians.[22] The issue of unequal treatment irritates Wellington to the present day and remains a rare disagreement marring an otherwise close trans-Tasman Sea relationship. But it does not jeopardise the protection of workers' rights in either economy.

The conclusion of the FTA with Singapore in 2000 without explicit labour protection clauses has other explanations, those embedded in the politics of negotiation. Projection of one's labour standards into another economy entails crossing sovereign boundaries and is liable to objection by sensitive governments. Singapore's government was not only sensitive but also disciplined, and its restrictions of civil liberties and labour protections have been widely noted.[23] New Zealand's early broaching of a labour protection element in the negotiations, prodded by New Zealand's unions, was firmly rejected at the outset by the Singapore negotiators. New Zealand was faced with a choice familiar to all small countries dealing with powerful partners: compromise or exit. Given convergence of economic interests and a long history of diplomatic and security cooperation with Singapore, New Zealand compromised. The outcome was a model trade liberalisation agreement, but one silent on worker protections. But this was to be the last such omission.

---

21 Australia. Department of Home Affairs. Fact Sheet: New Zealanders in Australia. https://www.homeaffairs.gov.au/foi/files/2021/fa-210301073-document-released.PDF.

22 Stephen Hoadley (2002). 'Trans-Tasman Migration: Issues and Politics' Bob Catley, ed. *NZ-Australia Relations: Moving Together or Drifting Apart?* Wellington: Dark Horse Publishing.

23 See reports by US Department of Labor https://www.dol.gov/agencies/ilab/labor-rights-report-singapore and the Office of the US Trade Representative https://ustr.gov/archive/assets/Trade_Agreements/Bilateral/Singapore_FTA/Reports/asset_upload_file891_3211.pdf.

6 The New Zealand Thailand Closer Economic Partnership 2005

Nevertheless, the domestic debate following that agreement, provoked by the Confederation of Trade Unions, stimulated Government leaders to reflect on how New Zealand's labour protection ideals, history, and domestic practices could be manifested in trade agreements. New Zealand's uniquely transparent trade agreement process assured that public and group interests were taken into account. The New Zealand trade negotiation process traverses eight phases: 1) problem identification, 2) prescription, 3) pre-negotiation, 4) negotiation, 5) legitimation, 6) ratification, 7) implementation, and 8) adjustment.[24] At each phase the Government is sensitive to public and interest group views. While the earlier phases are technical, and the negotiation phase is confidential, the legitimation phase is deliberately public, entailing publication of a National Interest Analysis of pros and cons, and presentations by trade officials to all significant interest groups and population centres. And the ratification phase facilitates public and group submissions to the Parliamentary Select Committee on Foreign Affairs, Trade, and Defence, scheduled hearings, and subsequent debate in the House of Representatives. And the adjustment phase corrects anomalies pointed out by trade-oriented groups affected by the FTA.

One of the outcomes of this process, accelerated by controversy between the Government's free-trade commitment and a protectionist anti-globalisation movement, was the Government's 2001 Framework for Integrating Labour Issues into Free Trade Agreements.[25] The standards enunciated in this Framework then guided New Zealand's ministers and officials as they initiated and negotiated further FTAs. This paradigm shift, amplified by election of a Labour Government, and coupled with evolving liberal international economic circumstances, resulted in New Zealand's first trade agreement explicitly protecting labour rights: the Arrangements to the FTA with Thailand in 2005. During the Parliamentary phase of the draft agreement, the Ministry of Foreign Affairs

24 Stephen Hoadley (2017). *New Zealand Trade Negotiations*. Wellington: New Zealand Institute of International Affairs. Chapter 1 outlining the trade negotiating process is followed by bilateral and multilateral case studies.

25 New Zealand Ministry of Foreign Affairs and Trade (2005). 'Arrangements on Labour and Environment' Wellington. http://www.mft.govt.nz/foreign/tnd/newissues/labour/labourframework.html.

and Trade engaged intensely with domestic stakeholders, including unions. The Ministry's National Interest Analysis named the most prominent stakeholders in the engagements as follows.[26]

> Business New Zealand, the Council of Trade Unions, the Federation of Māori Authorities, the Employers and Manufacturers' Association (Northern), Canterbury Manufacturers' Association, Local Government New Zealand, the ASEAN/ New Zealand Business Council, Chambers of Commerce, the Council for International Development, and the Royal Forest and Bird Protection Society of New Zealand....

Furthermore, Parliament's Foreign Affairs, Trade, and Defence Select Committee invited submissions from the public. According the National Interest Assessment,[27]

> Among submissions critical of the CEP, most cited among their reasons 'unfair' competition stemming from Thailand's labour conditions and environmental regulation, plus concerns about the risks of 'dumped' Thai products undercutting New Zealand domestic producers.

Several submissions explicitly recommended insertion of ILO core labour standards in the Thailand CEP. Critical of the fact that Thailand had ratified only four of eight core ILO conventions, they insisted also on measures to inspect and verify suitable conditions of work in Thailand, not only to achieve social justice but also to prevent 'unfair' competition arising from depressed labour wage rates. However, other submissions and representations, notably from Business NZ and the Trade Liberalisation Network, opposed inclusion of labour (or environmental) provisions as potentially hampering trade liberalisation. This contrast echoed the wide, deep and enduring political divide between the advocates of international commerce and trade on the one hand and those prioritising human rights and social justice on the other. But fortuitously the two sides converged on raising labour protection standards, the one to prevent unfair competition from a low-wage economy, the other to promote social justice. Thus, New Zealand's policy of inclusion of labour rights in subsequent FTAs was legitimised in the domestic political arena despite the

26 New Zealand Ministry of Foreign Affairs and Trade. New Zealand Thailand Closer Economic Partnership. National Interest Analysis. March 2005. p. 56 https://www.mfat.govt.nz/assets/Trade-agreements/Thailand-NZ-CEP/nz-tha-icep-nationalinterestanalysis.pdf.

27 National Interest Analysis, p. 57.

ongoing clash of ideologies. It should be noted also that the gap was bridged pragmatically by negotiators adopting the tactic of moving the assertion of labour rights out of the parent FTA into a 'side agreement'. This technique is often employed by trade negotiators to acknowledge but ringfence disagreements so as to progress the core FTA.[28] In 2005 the side agreement ploy was sufficient to satisfy critics, and negotiators were able to progress the parent Agreement to signature.

The outcome was a compromise. Labour rights were not included in the Agreement's text except to repeat the GATT formula regarding exceptions for public order and morals and human health. But the two governments negotiated a significant side agreement: 'Arrangements on Labour and Environment'. It was summarised by the National Interest Assessment as follows.[29]

> These [Arrangements] reinforce both countries' commitment to maintaining sound labour policies and practices and high levels of environmental protection, in harmony respectively with International Labour Organisation labour principles and rights and international environmental obligations. The Arrangements entail a political commitment not to weaken or derogate from labour or environment laws or standards to gain an unfair trade advantage.

7 Subsequent FTAs

As indicated above, this progressive augmentation was precipitated by political pressure by New Zealand's Confederation of Trade Unions during the negotiation of the NZ–Singapore FTA five years previously. New Zealand's newly elected Labour Party-led government responded to the CTU's demands by drafting and adopting a policy document entitled *'Frameworks for Integrating Labour and Environment Standards in Trade Agreements'* in 2001.[30] This document incorporated and applied to New Zealand's trade negotiation process the aims and standards of the several ILO conventions and recommendations that the Government had adopted over the years since 1919. Subsequently it guided the drafting of explicit chapters on labour rights embedded in FTAs with Thailand in 2005, China in 2008, Philippines in 2009, Korea in

28 Hoadley (2017). See Chapter 11 on 'Lessons Learned' for an inventory of this and other tactics used to advance trade negotiations to agreement despite national differences.

29 National Interest Analysis, p. 4.

30 New Zealand Ministry of Foreign Affairs and Trade (2001). 'Frameworks for Integrating Labour and Environment Standards in Trade Agreements'. Wellington. http://www.mft.govt.nz/foreign/tnd/newissues/labour/labourframework.html.

2015, the United Kingdom in 2023 and the European Union in 2024, and plurilateral agreements such as the Comprehensive and Progressive Trans Pacific Partnership (CPTPP) in 2018.[31] Other bilateral and plurilateral FTAs such as those with Hong Kong, Taiwan, and Pacific island and Southeast Asian partners, dealt with labour protection by means of either side agreements or joint declarations. In all cases New Zealand negotiators were able to secure acknowledgement of labour rights in one format or another, often in the face of initial scepticism.

On 26 September 2024 New Zealand concluded negotiations with United Arab Emirates for the New Zealand–United Arab Emirates Comprehensive Economic Partnership Agreement (CEPA). This agreement does not include a specific chapter on labour rights. It is no secret that international human rights watchdogs have been critical of UAE's poor protection of workers, particularly migrant workers, for some years.[32] New Zealand negotiators would have been aware of these adverse reports, but proceeded with negotiations anyway. This author surmises that the UAE negotiators made it clear to their New Zealand counterparts at the outset that labour rights were not to be highlighted; otherwise, progress to speedy completion in an otherwise high-quality FTA greatly desired by New Zealand would be delayed. In the event, negotiations reportedly were completed in a record four-month period. Negotiators were doubtless assisted by borrowing prior experience, detail work and preliminary drafting from the documentation regarding the yet-to-be-concluded FTA with the Gulf Cooperation Council, of which UAE is a member. Nevertheless, New Zealand was able to secure from the UAE an indirect acknowledgement of labour rights in their joint statement, which reads as follows.[33]

> On labour rights, the CEPA recognises the importance of adopting and maintaining the ILO Fundamental Principles and Rights at Work. It facilitates cooperation on eliminating all forms of forced or compulsory labour, and steps to encourage enterprises to adopt responsible business conduct policies.

---

31 For summaries of each completed FTA, and several pending FTAs, see the Ministry of Foreign Affairs and Trade FTA page at https://www.mfat.govt.nz/en/trade/free-trade-agreements.

32 See for example the report on the UAE by Human Rights Watch at https://www.hrw.org/world-report/2019/country-chapters/united-arab-emirates. Note parallel reports by the US State Department and Department of Labor, cited above.

33 https://www.mfat.govt.nz/en/trade/free-trade-agreements/free-trade-agreements-concluded-but-not-in-force/new-zealand-united-arab-emirates-free-trade-agreement/overview-of-cepa-chapters.

A core provision linking all these agreements was a prohibition of the abuse of labour standards to constrain or distort trade. This applied not only to depressing labour wages and conditions, the alleged unfair advantage of Global South economies, but also the Global North's elevation of health, safety and bio-security standards to unreasonably high thresholds (as Japan and the EU were alleged to do) to create import barriers constituting hidden protectionism. For example, the labour protection agreement with Thailand includes 'a political commitment not to weaken or derogate from labour or environment laws or standards to gain an unfair trade advantage, or use them for protectionist purposes'.[34]

To meet the criticism that globalisation and FTAs have advantaged larger highly capitalised exporters at the expense of small and medium enterprises that employ the greatest numbers of workers, thus exacerbating inequality, New Zealand's Labour-led government in 2021 instituted a policy of 'Trade for All' to encourage wider distribution of the benefits of trade liberalisation.[35] This was elaborated in 2023 as the Aotearoa New Zealand Trade and Labour Framework.[36] The aim of the revised Framework is as follows.

> ...a coherent and coordinated approach to ensure that trade agreements are crafted and implemented in ways that reinforce, and do not undermine, full and productive employment based on respect for international labour rights and standards and the promotion of decent work for all people.

8 Remedies

Progressive governments can choose from a variety of procedures to enhance labour rights protections in their trade negotiations with partners. This author suggests the following spectrum of initiatives, ranging from least controversial to most confrontational, that might be incorporated in a trade agreement negotiating process in the pursuit of labour rights.

Unilateral announcement of commitment to labour rights
Joint communique commitment to labour rights

---

34 National Interest Analysis, p. 4.

35 New Zealand (2021). Broad Perspectives to Inform Trade For All Agenda. https://www.beehive.govt.nz/release/broad-perspectives-inform-trade-all-agenda.

36 New Zealand (September 2023). Ministry of Foreign Affairs and Trade. Aotearoa New Zealand Trade and Labour Framework found at https://www.mfat.govt.nz/assets/Trade-General/Trade-policy/Aotearoa-New-Zealands-Trade-and-Labour-Framework.pdf.

- Side agreement on labour rights
- Treaty chapter devoted to labour rights
- Establishment of a joint labour rights monitoring committee
- Establishment of labour rights inspection institutions and procedures
- Institution of regular public reporting on trade effects on specific labour rights
- Appeals for compliance at top political leadership level
- Public accusations of nonfeasance with threats to suspend the FTA
- Appeals to human rights Institutions and NGOs of gross violations
  - International Labour Organization commissions of inquiry under Art 26–33.
  - Human Rights Committee of the ICCPR
  - UN Human Rights Council
  - Human Rights Watch
  - Lawyers Committee for Human Rights
  - Campaign for the Abolition of Sweatshops and Child Labor
  - International Labor Rights Fund
- Refusal to import those products made with noncompliant labour
- Threat to suspend the FTA

9 Criticism and Challenges

Less positive than the progressive rhetoric and available options of FTAs cited above is the reality that most trading governments are unable to monitor and enforce labour rights outside their own borders, that is, within the borders of their trade partners. New Zealand is no exception, and as a small and distant country is less able than most. The principles of sovereignty and non-intervention prevail, either legitimately or as a pretext. As a recourse, negotiating officials including New Zealand's attempt to secure agreements for joint liaison committees, periodic reports on labour conditions in partner countries, and dispute resolution procedures. But often to respect the sensitivities of Global South partners, these monitoring devices are couched in vague terms of reference, rely on voluntary reporting, and specify no enforcement remedies. More often, negotiators are obliged to be satisfied with unilateral or joint statements referencing ILO standards, relying on trust without verification. For example, New Zealand's most recent FTA, the CEPA, specifies only in a unilateral statement that the agreement 'recognises the importance of' and 'facilitates cooperation on' and 'steps to encourage enterprises to adopt' labour protections consistent with ILO principles.[37] Public accusations of noncompliance and ban of noncomplying products risk diplomatic enmity

37 See the full statement above.

and countermeasures. The final recourse, a threat to terminate an FTA, is counterproductive for a vulnerable trading state such as New Zealand and almost never used. As a generalisation, the worse the reputation of a partner country for abuse of workers the milder the requirement for labour rights protection will be written into the trade agreement, and vice versa.

If circumstances are favourable, progressive pro-labour groups such as New Zealand's Confederation of Trade Unions can exert pressure on their trade officials to monitor and protect labour rights, that is, to adopt more proactive policies further down the list of options displayed above. But in practice information on labour conditions in partner countries abroad is not readily available to the public, or even to diplomats or labour specialists on the ground, and if locally available it may not be up to date or reliable regarding the whole country. And establishing the specific effects of the new FTA in the context of historic abusive labour conditions can be problematic. Consequently, labour reformers lack systematic and definitive evaluations of the efficacy of labour rights prescriptions as applied to a specific FTA at a specific time and place. Their reliance on anecdotal media exposés and international agency and NGO assessments are vulnerable to rebuttal on methodological and empirical grounds, and they must rely on political assertion, mobilisation, and pressure, with uncertain results.

In conclusion, this author believes that providing greater transparency by partner governments into the effects of trade liberalisation on labour rights should remain prominent on the agendas of labour advocates and researchers in New Zealand and in all developed trading states. How to devise effective policies of post-FTA monitoring and enforcement of labour rights in economies of the Global South will remain a steep challenge to labour rights reformers. It is hoped that this account of New Zealand's experience, added to the other essays of successes and best practices included in this book, will inspire and equip trade reformers, official negotiators, and progressive governments to incorporate effective labour rights protections into their trade agreements in future.

Bibliography

General Trade and Labour

Alvarez-Jimenez, A. (2018). 'The international law gaze: protection of labour rights in free trade agreements: mission impossible?' New Zealand Law Journal, 9, 287–297.

Araujo Melo (January 2018) 'Labour Provisions in EU and US Mega-regional Trade Agreements: Rhetoric and Reality'. International & Comparative Law Quarterly, 67 (1), 233–253. DOI: https://doi.org/10.1017/S0020589317000422.

Artuso, Mario and Carolan McLarney (2015). 'A Race to the Top: Should Labour Standards be Included in Trade Agreements' SAGE. www.vik.sagepub.

Benstead, Lindsay J. (2006). 'Labour Rights and Standards'. Ashish K. Vaida, ed., *Globalization: Encyclopedia of Trade, Labour and Politics*. Santa Barbara: ABC CLIO.

Burtless, Gary (September 1, 2001). 'Workers' Rights: Labor standards and global trade'. Washington: Brookings. https://www.brookings.edu/articles/workers-rights-labor-standards-and-global-trade/.

Carrere, Céline, Marcelo Olarreaga and Damian Raess (2017) 'Labor Clauses in Trade Agreements: worker protection or protectionism?' IDEAS www.ideas.repec.org/p/fdi/wpaper/3959.html.

Centre for Labour Research (2022) 'Labour Rights Index: New Zealand'. Amsterdam. https://labourrightsindex.org/heatmap-2022.

Corley-Coulibaly, Marva, Ira Postolachi, and Netsanet Tesfay ILO. A Multi-faceted Typology of Labour Provisions in Trade Agreements: Overview, Methodology and Trends. Geneva: ILO. https://www.ilo.org/wcmsp5/groups/public/---dgreports/---inst/documents/genericdocument/wcms_829644.pdf comprehensive summary of issues and statistics, extensive bibliography.

Harrison, James (2019). 'The Labour Rights Agenda in Free Trade Agreements' 20 *Journal of World Investment & Trade* 705 https://hdl.handle.net/10289/12428.

ILO (n.d.). *Introduction to International Labour Standards*. International Labour Organization. https://www.ilo.org/global/standards/introduction-to-international-labour-standards/lang–en/index.htm.

ILO (2017). Handbook on Assessment of Labour Provisions in Trade and Investment Arrangements www.ilo.org.

ILO (2019). ILO Centenary Declaration for the Future of Work. International Labour Organisation. www.ilo.org.

ILO (2019) Rules of the Game: An introduction to the standards-related work of the International Labour Organization (Centenary edition 2019) https://www.ilo.org/global/standards/information-resources-and-publications/publications/WCMS_672549/lang–en/index.htm.

Ionel, Zamfir (January 2022). Labour rights in EU trade agreements Towards stronger enforcement. European Parliamentary Research Service Author: Members' Research Service PE 698.800 https://www.europarl.europa.eu/RegData/etudes/BRIE/2022/698800/EPRS_BRI(2022)698800_EN.pdf.

Polaski, Sandra (2004) 'Protecting Labor Rights through Trade Agreements: An Analytical Guide' Washington D.C.: Carnegie Endowment www.carnegieendowment.org/pdf/files/2004-07-polaski-JILP.pdf.

Siroën, Jean Marc and David Andrade (2016). 'Trade Agreements and Core Labour Standards' Researchgate. www.researchgate.net/publication/310621600.

Siroën, Jean-Marc (2008). 'The use, scope and effectiveness of labour and social provisions and sustainable development aspects in bilateral and regional free trade agreements' EC ec.europa.eu https://www.academia.edu/86563107/The_Use_Scope_and_Effectiveness_of_Labour_and_Social_Provisions_and_Sustainable_Development_Aspects_in_Bilateral_and_Regional_Free_Trade_Agreements_.

Stern, Robert M. (2003). 'Labor Standards and Trade Agreements' *IDEAS* ideas.repec.org/p/mie/wpaper/496.html.

Tsogas, George (1999). 'Labour standards in international trade, workers' rights, social clause in trade'. The International Journal of Human Resource Management 10:2 April 1999 351–375.

Tyc, Aneta (2021). Global trade, labour rights and international law – a multilevel approach. London: Routledge.

United States. Congressional Research Service (2023). 'Worker Rights Provisions in Free Trade Agreements (FTAs)' Washington D.C. https://crsreports.congress.gov/product/pdf/IF/IF10046.

Vaidya, Ashish K, (2006). Globalization: Encyclopedia of Trade, Labour, and Politics. Santa Barbara CA: ABC-CLIO. See entries on 'Human Rights and Globalization', 'Labour Markets and Wage Effects', and 'Social Policy'.

New Zealand Trade and Labour Policies

Belich, James (2001), Paradise Reforged: A History of New Zealanders from the 1880s to the Year 2000. Auckland: Allan Lane The Penguin Press.

Easton, Brian (2020). *Not in Narrow Seas: The Economic History of Aotearoa New Zealand.* Wellington: Victoria University of Wellington Press. Chapter 25 'The Rise of Labour' 262–282.

European Commission (n.d.). 'How will the agreement uphold workers' rights in both the EU and New Zealand?' in *The EU-New Zealand agreement explained. Brussels.* https://policy.trade.ec.europa.eu/eu-trade-relationships-country-and-region/countries-and-regions/new-zealand/eu-new-zealand-agreement/agreement-explained_en#workers-rights.

Hoadley, Stephen (2017). *New Zealand Trade Negotiations.* Wellington: New Zealand Institute of International Affairs.

Hoadley, Stephen (2006) 'Australia New Zealand Closer Economic Trade Agreement (Anzcerta). Ashish K. Vaida, ed., *Globalization: Encyclopedia of Trade, Labour and Politics*. Santa Barbara: ABC CLIO.

Hoadley, Stephen (2002). *Negotiating Free Trade: The New Zealand-Singapore CEP Agreement.* Wellington: New Zealand Institute of International Affairs.

Hoadley, Stephen (2002). 'Trans-Tasman Migration: Issues and Politics' Bob Catley, ed. *NZ-Australia Relations: Moving Together or Drifting Apart?* Wellington: Dark Horse Publishing.

ILO (n.d.). ILO in the Asia Pacific: New Zealand. Geneva: ILO. https://www.ilo.org/asia/countries/WCMS_DOC_ASI_CNT_NZL_EN/lang–en/index.htm#:~:text=As%20well%20as%20being%20a,of%20labour%20and%20social%20justice.

Malik, Abdul (2020). 'The Use of Labour Clauses in Free Trade Agreements' Unpublished essay in course LAWS533: ST: Regulating Labour, Faculty of Law, Victoria University, Wellington, New Zealand. https://ir.wgtn.ac.nz/bitstream/handle/123456789/30395/paper_access.pdf?sequence=1.

New Zealand (2021). Broad Perspectives to Inform Trade For All Agenda. https://www.beehive.govt.nz/release/broad-perspectives-inform-trade-all-agenda.

New Zealand Confederation of Trade Unions (10 July 2023). 'NZCTU welcomes commitment to labour standards within the NZ/EU Free Trade Agreement' https://union.org.nz/nzctu-welcomes-commitment-to-labour-standards-within-the-nz-eu-free-trade-agreement/.

New Zealand International Business Forum: Trade Works (2022). Submission to the Ministry of Foreign Affairs and Trade: Re-Development of the Framework for Integrating Labour Standards and Trade Agreements. https://www.tradeworks.org.nz/submission-to-mfat-re-development-of-the-framework-for-integrating-labour-standards-and-trade-agreements/.

New Zealand Ministry of Business, Innovation, and Employment (n.d.). 'Trade and Labour'. Wellington. https://www.mbie.govt.nz/business-and-employment/employment-and-skills/our-international-labour-relations/trade-and-labour/.

New Zealand Ministry of Business, Innovation, and Employment (n.d.). Employment Standards Legislation Act. Wellington. https://www.mbie.govt.nz/business-and-employment/employment-and-skills/employment-legislation-reviews/employment-standards-legislation-act/.

New Zealand Ministry of Foreign Affairs and Trade (2008). New Zealand Handbook on International Human Rights. Wellington: New Zealand Ministry of Foreign Affairs.

New Zealand Ministry of Foreign Affairs and Trade (2005). 'Arrangements on Labour and Environment' Wellington. http://www.mft.govt.nz/foreign/tnd/newissues/labour/labourframework.html.

New Zealand Ministry of Foreign Affairs and Trade (2001). 'Frameworks for Integrating Labour and Environment Standards in Trade Agreements'. Wellington. http://www.mft.govt.nz/foreign/tnd/newissues/labour/labourframework.html.

New Zealand Ministry of Foreign Affairs and Trade (2023). Aotearoa New Zealand Trade and Labour Framework. Wellington. https://www.mfat.govt.nz/assets/Tra

de-General/Trade-policy/Aotearoa-New-Zealands-Trade-and-Labour-Framework.pdf.

New Zealand Ministry of Foreign Affairs and Trade (n.d.). 'Memorandum of Understanding on Labour Cooperation'. Wellington. https://www.mfat.govt.nz/assets/Trade-agreements/China-NZ-FTA/NZ-China-FTA-Labour-MOU.pdf.

Winchester, Simon (2021). *Land: How the Hunger for Ownership Shaped the Modern World*. London: Harper-Collins.

Wright, Matthew (2019). *Waitangi: a Living Treaty*. Auckland: David Bateman Ltd.

CHAPTER 12

A Recapitulation: Lessons Learnt and Recommendations Made for the Future

Jo Carby-Hall and Aneta Tyc

In late July 2025, Ursula von der Leyen and Donald Trump concluded an agreement on tariffs and trade[1] establishing a US tariff of 15% for EU goods (except for steel, aluminium and copper for which a 50% tariff remains in place). The agreement has been presented by the European Commission as a guarantee of "stability and predictability for citizens and businesses on both sides of the Atlantic",[2] even though it be a non-binding instrument and only the first step in the process of negotiations. Moreover, given that before Donald Trump's second presidency the average tariff rate in the USA was around 1.5%, the new rate of 15% will lead to a reduction in the competitiveness of EU enterprises.[3] It is therefore understandable and praiseworthy that the European Commission searches for new trading partners and enters into negotiations with a view to concluding free trade agreements (FTAs). Additionally, the crisis of the World Trade Organization[4] is a kind of a support for such an approach.

In this context, the EU is currently negotiating FTAs, e.g. with India, Indonesia, Malaysia, Philippines and United Arab Emirates.[5] The fundamental question therefore arises as to what approach to labour standards in future

1 Followed by a Joint Statement on transatlantic trade and investment published on 21 August 2025, https://ec.europa.eu/commission/presscorner/detail/en/ip_25_1973.

2 https://ec.europa.eu/commission/presscorner/detail/en/qanda_25_1930.

3 https://pism.pl/publications/eu-us-agree-framework-of-new-trade-deal.

4 The WTO crisis is due to the collapse of the dispute settlement system which is unable to hear appeals when the United States blocked in 2019 the appointments to the appellate body, namely the highest court for global trade disputes. This had the effect of affecting the enforcement of trade rules leading to increased unilateral trade measures and questioning the WTO's ability to adapt to new global economic and geopolitical challenges. The WTO is currently attempting to find solutions including the establishment of a multi-party interim appeal Arbitration Arrangement (MPIA) by a group of countries. However, little progress has been made.

5 https://policy.trade.ec.europa.eu/eu-trade-relationships-country-and-region/negotiations-and-agreements_en.

 | HTTPS://DOI.ORG/10.1163/9789004762251-013

FTAs the EU should adopt: promotional or sanction-based, in other words, managerial or enforcement.[6] Just for the record, promotional approach – as defined by the ILO – means that labour provisions included in FTAs "do not link compliance to economic consequences but provide a framework for dialogue, cooperation, and/or monitoring". A conditional approach comes down to the fact that FTAs contain labour provisions that make the conclusion of a trade agreement conditional upon respect for particular labour standards (pre-ratification conditionality) and/or provisions in the concluded trade agreements that authorise sanctions if labour standards are infringed (post-ratification conditionality).[7] Such a question as above is justified, in particular, in the light of the violation of human labour rights in future partner countries. All of the countries mentioned above, namely India, Indonesia, Malaysia, Philippines and United Arab Emirates, received "Rating 5, no guarantee of rights" in a scale from 1 (sporadic violations of rights) to 5+ (no guarantee of rights due to the breakdown of the law) according to the 2025 ITUC Global Rights Index.[8] By way of illustration, only recently in 2024, in India more than 900 workers were detained after organising a street protest as a strike against their employer.[9] In 2024, in Malaysia, a global packaging company Amcor unfairly dismissed a union secretary in relation to its union-busting strategy aimed at preventing workers from organising. Shortly before, other disciplinary measures were taken against her, *inter alia* "a unilateral and unjustified 50 per cent wage cut for 19 days". Moreover, Amcor organised a secret ballot during which workers, in particular migrant workers, were sent home early to deprive them of the right to vote.[10] In 2025, the Philippines are among ten worst countries in the world for workers' rights.[11] This is a country in which employers routinely

6 Some authors divide the approaches into two "schools of thought" and call them: "enforcement" or "managerial". Gregory Felder, Kirthana Ganeson, Martin Jehli, Patrick Wagner, The Trade and Labour Nexus. Envisioning the Design and Implementation of Future Labour Chapters in Preferential Trade Agreements. In: The Concept Design of a Twenty-First Century Preferential Trade Agreement. Trends and Future Innovations, Kathleen Claussen, Manfred Elsig, Rodrigo Polanco (eds.), Cambridge University Press 2025, 291–315, p. 297.

7 ILO, Social Dimensions of Free Trade Agreements: Studies on Growth with Equity (Geneva: ILO 2013) 1.

8 International Trade Union Confederation, 2025 ITUC Global Rights Index, Brussels 2025, https://www.ituc-csi.org/global-rights-index, p. 20.

9 Ibidem, p. 49. More: https://www.reuters.com/world/india/india-police-detains-600-workers-union-members-samsung-protests-escalate-2024-10-01/.

10 International Trade Union Confederation, 2025 ITUC..., pp. 6, 31 and 54.

11 The other are as follows: Bangladesh, Belarus, Ecuador, Egypt, Eswatini, Myanmar, Nigeria, Tunisia and Türkiye.

refuse to apply or breach collective bargaining agreements. The practice of maintaining charges against trade unionists related to their trade union duties "with the threat of re-arrest" is commonplace.[12] In the UAE, there are severe restrictions on the rights to free association and assembly, and situations "that may amount to forced labour" of migrant workers.[13] In fact, according to the Global Slavery Index, the UAE has one of the highest prevalence of modern slavery in the world, with 13,4 out of every 1,000 people affected by this pathology.[14] Finally, despite recent multifaceted efforts to improve workers' rights in Indonesia, including the Constitutional Court ruling of 2024 with significant implications for labour law,[15] violations of human labour rights still exist. This pertains, for example, to commercial fishers who are at risk of forced labour mainly due to "the informal nature of their employment, reluctance of the government to inspect working conditions on fishing vessels and the absence of a formal mechanism to record cases of forced labour in the sector".[16] Exploring our future trading partners' approach to labour rights, we shall also pose questions about their ratifications of core ILO conventions. At the time of writing, namely on 23 August 2025, India and UAE ratified only 6 out of 10 fundamental conventions, Malaysia 8 out of 10, and Indonesia and Philippines 9 out of 10.[17] And yet, we are all aware of the fact that there is often a great gap between formal ratification and compliance. Taken together, all these reasons more than justify the search for the most effective approach to protecting workers' rights, and FTAs are currently one of the areas where such protection is possible.

The authors of this book do not neglect to mention other avenues of protection of workers' rights in the context of global trade, including the history of the labour and trade linkage. The latter issue is raised by Sandra Polaski who reminds us of the US' McKinley Tariff Act dating back to 1890 with a ban of imports of products made by convicts, the 1919 Treaty of Versailles establishing the International Labour Organisation (ILO), the ILO's Constitution with its famous words: "the failure of any nation to adopt humane conditions of

---

12 France Castro and the "Talaingod 18" group, Anne Krueger and Danny Tabura are examples of such practice. Ibidem, pp. 6, 51 and 55.

13 Human Rights Watch, United Arab Emirates. Events of 2024, https://www.hrw.org/world-report/2025/country-chapters/united-arab-emirates.

14 https://www.walkfree.org/global-slavery-index/.

15 International Trade Union Confederation, 2025 ITUC…, p. 31.

16 Wayne Palmer, Michele Ford, Benni Yusriza Hasbiyalloh, The alignment of Indonesian laws, policies and their enforcement with the ILO international labour standards on forced labour: Situation and gap analysis, ILO 2024, passim.

17 https://normlex.ilo.org/.

labour is an obstacle in the way of other nations which desire to improve the conditions in their own countries", the creation of the General Agreement on Tariffs and Trade (GATT) in 1948 (with only one labour provision) and World Trade Organization (WTO) in 1995, and finally a permanent discharge from the WTO agenda of a labour–trade nexus initiated in the WTO Ministerial Meeting in Singapore in 1996. Silvio Bologna mentions the Generalised Systems of Preferences (GSP, GSP+ and Everything But Arms Arrangement) as a protection area with a sanctioning potential. He also adds an important analysis of the EU Treaties from which we can derive a "horizontal social clause", namely the "fulfilment of social goals in all fields of EU action", in particular under the systemic interpretation of Article 9 TFEU and Articles 2 and 3 TEU. The author highlights that such a clause is legally binding in all EU institutions and "[u]nder a pro-labor hermeneutics, this means that the EU must develop trade relationships only with States that have ratified or engaged themselves to ratify or implement the most significant ILO conventions or adhere to the respect of ILO core labor standards".

Jean-Baptiste Velut and Sandra Polaski have signalled new paths for the trade and labour linkage and new tools of diversification of trade policy, including those related to supply chains such as the EU Corporate Sustainability Due Diligence Directive, the EU Regulation on prohibiting products made with forced labour on the Union market or the Uyghur Forced Labor Prevention Act adopted in the USA. Jean-Baptiste Velut has concluded pointing to "a shift from government-centric approaches to workers' rights protection where governments are liable for the enforcement of labor standards, to a firm-level approach where corporate actors are equally accountable for due diligence and supply chain resilience". In a similar vein, Sandra Polaski has written about the modification of the EU's and the US's approaches to cross-border labour policy and a shift of focus "from the level of the state to the level of the firm and supply chain". Undoubtedly, unilateral instruments are already a serious component of trade policy and – in the context of the protection of labour rights – must be taken into consideration alongside with the FTAs discussed in this book.

So, returning to the main topic and drawing out lessons from the previous chapters on FTAs, we shall first pay attention to Christoph Scherrer's contribution in order to understand better whether or not FTAs are suitable for raising labour standards and ensuring their enforcement internationally, in particular in the light of divergent positions in economics on the impact of a labour clause included in them. According to the author's findings, a sanctionable labour clause in multilateral trade agreements is an appropriate instrument of enforcement of core labour rights on a binding basis at the international level. Rather than fretting over whether compliance with these rights will provoke competitive disadvantage, individual competitors "can assume that their competitors are competing on a level playing field". Moreover, neo-institutionalism advocates that compliance with labour rights "secures a country's industrial development in the long run: development of human capital and more efficient use of workers". On the other hand, in the short run, non-compliance "promises competitive advantages, so that in addition to power-political motives, economic calculations lead to their violation". The scholar has pointed out that if one country gains a comparative advantage as a result of violating workers' rights, other countries will not be willing to raise labour standards due to fear of losing market share and employment opportunities. Such conclusions fully confirm the above-mentioned wording contained in the ILO's Constitution.

Focusing on the policy-relevant insights, in the next step we should highlight the main findings from the chapter co-authored by Axel Marx and Angela María Vanegas Pérez who have conducted a comparative analysis of existing roadmaps and plans of action in order to offer a wise lesson for the future of the EU FTAs. After a systematic and thorough discussion of seven selected instruments adopted for Bangladesh, Guatemala, Colombia and Honduras, the contributors have assessed that roadmaps and plans of action might have "the potential to strengthen the implementation of labour rights provisions" in the EU FTAs. In particular, they might enhance compliance "by incorporating legislative reforms, capacity-building measures, and multi-stakeholder oversight". However, the authors have also noticed three limitations of these tools. Firstly, they have determined that the scope of the covered rights does not include all ten fundamental conventions of the ILO (as often is the case in FTAs), but is rather limited chiefly to the Freedom of Association and Protection of the Right to Organise Convention, 1948 (No. 87) and the Right to Organise and Collective Bargaining Convention, 1949 (No. 98). Axel Marx and Angela María Vanegas Pérez have reminded the reader that sometimes FTAs include references to more (than ten core) ILO conventions, and this could be a real challenge because there "would require for each Convention specific commitments, benchmarks and investment" from the partner countries. Shortly speaking, the authors doubt in the feasibility of such a scenario. Secondly, they have concluded that effective implementation of roadmaps requires substantial investment, both technical and financial. The questions are who should bear these costs and what would be the EU's role in this? Thirdly, Axel Marx and Angela María Vanegas Pérez have also accentuated the "under-researched" and "unclear" long-term impact of roadmaps on strengthening labour rights. Thus, the authors have concluded that further research might embrace the evaluation of the effectiveness of existing roadmaps in practice. Moreover, they emphasise that "identifying best practices, and exploring ways to expand their scope to a broader range of labour rights commitments" may turn out to be fruitful in the context of "ensuring that EU FTAs genuinely contribute to the promotion and protection of labour rights in global trade relations".

Roadmaps and plans of action have also been under the scrutiny of Jean-Baptiste Velut who has focused on them in the context of a significant impact of ex-ante implementation (pre-ratification conditionality) on targeted countries. The author has mentioned the first labour action plan established "as part of President Obama's renegotiation of the US-Colombia Trade Promotion Agreement (COTPA) initially signed by George W. Bush" and finally agreed in April 2011. Interestingly, the author has pointed out that it was a very detailed labour action plan, which "went far beyond any labor chapter hitherto negotiated by Washington". The resulting reforms had taken place even before the agreement went into force and "were monitored on a yearly basis for five years". Jean-Baptiste Velut has diagnosed the Colombia labour action plan as an important precedent for the future "Labour Consistency Plans" (LCPs) with countries like Malaysia, Vietnam and Brunei created in the framework of the Trans-Pacific Partnership (TPP) negotiations. The analysis of the situation in those countries has helped the scholar to demonstrate that the LCPs constituted the basis for labour reforms before the US's withdrawal from the TPP. However, the subsequent Comprehensive and Progressive Agreement for Trans-Pacific Partnership between twelve economies and without the USA reduced the pressure put on Malaysia, Vietnam and Brunei, and they "were no longer subject to US presidential certification of compliance, which jeopardized the progress accomplished under LCPs".[18]

Drawing together the key themes the authors have identified that we should further pay closer attention to the case of Vietnam, which became the subject of consideration in the chapter by Martin Myant. The author has ascertained that labour provisions in FTAs can make a difference to labour conditions. He has examined the impact of both the TPP and the EU–Vietnam Free Trade Agreement (EVFTA) on labour rights in Vietnam and has inferred that the level of pressure exerted on this country depends on "relative bargaining strengths" and that Vietnam was particularly interested in becoming an upper middle income country, thus in taking advantage of the economic benefits resulting from FTAs with the USA and the EU. Martin Myant's research has discovered that "once an agreement is in force interest in

18 See also the cited literature.

pursuing labour issues rapidly declines" and commercial and business matters prevail. In the case of Vietnam, the entry into force of a FTA meant for negotiators that labour issues have lost their "strongest bargaining lever which was the potential ability to block the ratification of the agreement in total". Trying to highlight the main findings from the chapter in question, we shall indicate the potential of the separate US–Vietnam Plan for the Enhancement of Trade and Labour Relations reached in February 2016, namely before the US withdrawal from the TPP in January 2017. The above-mentioned agreement required Vietnam to adopt labour commitments (before the entry into force of the TPP), e.g. related to forced labour, discrimination and freedom of association, and indeed impacted developments. Unfortunately, its positive influence obviously declined in January 2017. On the other hand, in examining the case of the EVFTA, Martin Myant noticed the minimal interest of negotiators in the topic of labour rights. As was the case with the EU–South Korea FTA, the EVFTA did not include pre-ratification conditionality. However, the contributor has pointed out that the split of the initial agreement into two (for trade and for investment) and the subsequent pressure form the Socialists and Democrats on Vietnam to comply with the ILO core conventions (before ratification of the agreement) contributed to ratification by Vietnam of the Right to Organise and Collective Bargaining Convention, 1949 (No. 98) and the Abolition of Forced Labour Convention, 1957 (No. 105). Despite the promises that it would be done in 2023, as of the end of August 2025, Vietnam has not yet ratified Freedom of Association and Protection of the Right to Organise Convention, 1948 (No. 87).

Exploring the theme of pre-ratification conditionality, in particular in the US FTAs, the authors contributing to this book have given other examples of its successful use. Jean-Baptiste Velut has mentioned, e.g. Bahrain, Morocco, Oman and Panama as countries that succumbed to US pressure and changed their labour laws in the FTAs negotiation process. Sandra Polaski has reminded us about the labour law reform, which took place in Mexico before the entry into force of the US–Mexico–Canada Agreement (USMCA). But this is only one part of the story of the conditional approach. The other part, as mentioned before, concerns the so-called post-ratification conditionality with sanctions for non-compliance with labour standards envisaged by the FTA. For instance, Sandra Polaski has systematically and meticulously presented – not only from a theoretical point of view, but from a practical one as well – the Facility-Specific Rapid Response Labor Mechanism (RRM) included in the USMCA. Although in 2026 this agreement will undergo a joint review with possible subsequent amendments, the author has pointed out the lessons derived from its relatively short but intense history. Thus, underlining that the governments of the three trading partners have assessed the RRM as successful, Sandra Polaski has admitted that (at the time of writing) "[w]ith respect to deterrence, twenty-three of the firms in resolved RRM cases were deterred from continued violations. In those cases the violations of victims' rights were directly remedied through the new trade union elections, reinstatement with back pay, pledges of future neutrality by the firms and other measures". However, the contributor remains more sceptical about what she calls "broader deterrence" and convinces that "a continued sense of impunity among many firms" is connected with the poor enforcement by the Mexican government of labour reforms. In her opinion "The thirty-eight RRM cases to date are not yet enough to meaningfully deter the thousands of firms covered by the USMCA".

Much like the USA, Canada prefers a sanction-based approach towards labour provisions in FTAs and that is exactly the one adopted in the modernised 2023 Canada–Ukraine FTA (CUFTA). Jo Carby-Hall and Aneta Tyc consider such a solution as having greater potential to ensure effectiveness of labour standards included in FTAs than a promotional approach. The modernised CUFTA embraces an updated labour chapter subject to the dispute settlement mechanism and even allows for suspension of benefits to the party complained against, which is perceived by the authors as a significant deterrent. However, this is not the only advantage of the new version of the agreement between Canada and Ukraine. The other positive aspect of CUFTA is that it creates a basis for easier temporary entry to Canada of certain business persons who hold citizenship or are permanent residents in Ukraine. These are: business visitors who are seeking to engage in specified business activities, investors, professionals, as well as people employed by an enterprise in Ukraine and who are seeking to render services to an enterprise in Canada which is the parent entity, a subsidiary, an affiliate. Such provisions may prove very helpful, including in the context of the need to rebuild Ukraine after the war. They may contribute to fostering the future participation of Canadian businesses in the process of its partner's recovery. They have the potential to develop international cooperation, stimulate investment and contribute to job creation, gradual improvement of working conditions and economic growth. Business persons have the opportunity to gain new contacts, partners, investors, experience, etc.; in other words, they receive a tool, the use of which may directly translate into future changes in Ukraine. The authors highlight that Ukraine will need, *inter alia*, activating business after the war, attracting investors, creating labour intensive infrastructure construction programmes, constructing of industrial enterprises and expanding the services sector. The modernised CUFTA may serve as a formula for other countries should they wish to conclude a FTA with Ukraine. Apart from that, Aneta Tyc and Jo Carby-Hall have pointed out an important role of the chapters entitled "Trade and Gender" and "Trade and Indigenous Peoples" in the modernised CUFTA. Although Canada has already before sought to mainstream gender issues throughout its FTAs, "Trade and Indigenous Peoples" chapter is the first of its kind that Ukraine or Canada have ever negotiated and included in their FTA. Given that both chapters offer interesting opportunities and support for the groups covered by them, as well as favourable solutions promoting inclusive work environments, the authors propose that future FTAs partners follow the modernised CUFTA example and include chapters related to gender and Indigenous Peoples in their newly negotiated agreements.

Weaving together the various strands of research included in this book, we shall indicate that – when discussing CETA – Vincenzo Ferrante has also highlighted the freedom of movement of people between both partners. He has mentioned special categories of migrant workers with different status, *inter alia* contractual services suppliers, independent professionals, the so-called "key personnel" or "intra-corporate transferees" (also known from the CUFTA). A wide range of development opportunities given in this treaty seems to make the contributor take the view that it is an urgent matter to take final decisions regarding the ratification of CETA by hesitant EU countries. He calls for it all the more in the light of the war in Ukraine and the re-election of President Donald Trump. Organising a public debate and addressing the concerns of states opposing ratification could be crucial given that according to the author's findings, up to now "the Canadian public and academic debate has paid more attention to the CETA than the Europeans have". Finally, Vincenzo Ferrante pays attention to another key characteristic of CETA, namely the resolution of investment disputes between investors and states, which should be mentioned here. Due to the fact that the traditional ISDS (Investor–State Dispute Settlement) shape has always caused a number of objections, the author has stressed an innovation in CETA consisting of the fact that instead of an *ad hoc* arbitration body, there is an independent Investment Court System (ICS). It is composed of a permanent Tribunal with fifteen members (five of which shall be nationals of a Member State of the EU, five shall be nationals of Canada and five shall be nationals of third countries, according to the general, from which there are exceptions; Article 8.27) and an Appellate Tribunal (Article 8.28). Vincenzo Ferrante has pointed to the idea of the establishment of a multilateral investment tribunal and appellate mechanism, namely that "[t]he Parties shall pursue with other trading partners the establishment of a multilateral investment tribunal and appellate mechanism for the resolution of investment disputes. Upon establishment of such a multilateral mechanism, the CETA Joint Committee shall adopt a decision providing that investment disputes under this Section will be decided pursuant to the multilateral mechanism and make appropriate transitional arrangements" (Article 8.29). This has responded to concerns "that the CETA provision for an exclusive arbitration system to settle disputes between investors and the state (ISDS) would totally deny national judges the power to rule on any dispute, when a foreign company was involved".

Looking back on the most important findings in the book and examining experience around the world, the editors should also focus on insights from Australia and New Zealand. Joo-Cheong Tham has found that there is "no singular pattern of Australia being for or against labour provisions, and also appears to lack any evident pattern from a chronological or geopolitical perspective". The author has conducted an analysis of diverse countries and noticed that on the one hand there is a group of actors, more specifically Canada, the EU, New Zealand and the USA that are favourable towards labour provisions in FTAs, and on the other hand there are countries presenting a completely different approach. He has classified Brazil, China, India and Indonesia to the latter group. Interestingly, Joo-Cheong Tham has distinguished the third intermediate category to include Australia alongside other countries like Chile, Japan and South Korea. Thus, according to his findings, Australia has adopted a "mixed" approach to labour provisions in FTAs, "both in relation to whether its agreements contain labour provisions, and also the content of the labour provisions". Trying to explain this phenomenon, the contributor has complemented previous research conducted by Postnikov and McKenzie and has argued that "the labour provisions are minimalist in terms of the substance of their obligations" and "Australia has a lacklustre commitment to the ILO Conventions on freedom of association". Thus, in the opinion of Joo-Cheong Tham, these arguments determine that the labour provisions in Australia's FTAs have not changed in a momentous way "the status quo in terms of labour standards" in this country. The author brings together his results and the analysis of Postnikov and McKenzie in order to "better understand Australia's approach towards labour provisions through the framing of these provisions as both protectionism and protection-lite". Beyond that, in his engaging chapter the author has expressed concern about the second Trump Administration policy geared towards nationalism, unilateralism and protectionism. He has highlighted that the USA has imposed a 10 per cent baseline tariff on most imports from Australia, with higher tariffs on selected goods. The two-pronged action by Australia has embraced not only seeking to be exempt or lowering these tariffs, but also renewing efforts to conclude new FTAs. The latter refers to both the EU–Australia FTA and Australia–India Comprehensive

Economic Cooperation Agreement. Joo-Cheong Tham has predicted that should these agreements be concluded, it is likely that the EU–Australia FTA will contain labour provisions, but the opposite scenario will be true for the Australia–India Comprehensive Economic Cooperation Agreement.

Reflecting upon the preceding parts of the book and trying to synthesise some key perspectives that run throughout the volume, the editors would wish to attract the reader's attention to the chapter by Stephen Hoadley because New Zealand's FTAs constitute one of the core themes explored. The author has pointed out that there is a whole array of procedures at the disposal of progressive governments in order to strengthen the protection of workers' rights in their negotiations with trade partners. He has enumerated and has arranged the tools from least controversial (such as a unilateral announcement of commitment to labour rights) to most confrontational (such as a threat to suspend the FTA) that might be taken in consideration in the framework of the negotiation process. However, the contributor has also warned us against the "the reality" that the majority of trading governments, including "a small and distant" New Zealand, do not have the capability to monitor and enforce labour standards outside their own border, i.e. within the borders of their trade partners. At the same time, recourse to other means such as securing agreements for joint liaison committees, periodic reports on labour conditions in partner countries, as well as dispute resolution procedures is ineffective and does not produce the desired results. This is mainly due to the fact that these tools are formulated in a vague frame of reference, are based on voluntary reporting and do not prescribe any enforcement measures. It is very common that some unverifiable unilateral or joint statements making references to the ILO standards must satisfy the negotiators of FTAs. The contributor has stressed that public accusations about non-compliance, as well as ban on non-compliant products "risk diplomatic enmity and countermeasures". The author is also lukewarm towards the last resort, namely the threat of termination of the agreement, perceiving it as "counterproductive for a vulnerable trading state such as New Zealand and almost never used". Generalising, he has concluded that "the worse the reputation of a partner country for abuse of workers the milder the requirement for labour rights protection will be written into the trade agreement, and vice versa". Stephen Hoadley has added that sometimes "progressive pro-labour groups such as New Zealand's Confederation of Trade Unions" are able to apply leverage on their trade officials in order to monitor and protect labour rights. This could even mean the adoption of more confrontational tools, but from a practical point of view labour reformers for various reasons have very limited access to the information on labour conditions in partner countries abroad, as well as to the systematic and definitive assessments of the effectiveness of labour rights provisions in a specific FTA. The author very aptly has crowned his work by stating that ensuring increased transparency from partner governments regarding the impact of trade liberalisation on labour rights should continue to be a key priority for labour advocates and researchers not only in New Zealand, but also in other developed trading nations. Designing effective strategies for monitoring and enforcing labour rights after the implementation of FTAs in Global South economies will continue to pose a significant challenge for labour rights reformers.

Seeking to draw key lessons from the chapters of this volume, the editors suggest that the EU has used the pre-ratification and post-ratification conditionality too seldom. Both Silvio Bologna and Vincenzo Ferrante refer to the same example of Canada, which made efforts to ratify the ILO outstanding fundamental conventions, thus fulfilling commitments under the CETA's Trade and Labour Chapter. It is worth noting, however, that this took place not in the framework of some EU's broader pre-ratification strategy, but rather as a result of Canada's serious approach to the EU's non-serious (and very common) soft formulation, according to which: "The Parties shall make continued and sustained efforts to ratify the fundamental ILO Conventions if they have not yet done so". It is worth recalling that against the background of the same formula, the EU has waited for so many years for ratifications by Korea, given that the EU–Korea FTA was provisionally applied from 2011, and that the Forced Labour Convention, 1930 (No. 29), the Freedom of Association and Protection of the Right to Organise Convention, 1948 (No. 87), as well as the Right to Organise and Collective Bargaining Convention, 1949 (No. 98), were ratified by Korea only in 2021, and after a formal dispute. The Abolition of Forced Labour Convention, 1957 (No. 105) has not been ratified yet. Pre-ratification conditionality, despite all its imperfections enumerated by the authors of the chapters to this book, is something the EU should pay more attention to when shaping FTAs with new partners. Obviously, the same applies to the concept of post-ratification conditionality. The EU–New Zealand FTA concluded in 2022 is the only one including on the one hand Chapter 19 entitled "Trade and Sustainable Development", and on the other hand Chapter 26 entitled "Dispute Settlement", which provides for the possibility of imposing sanctions in the event of a serious violation of fundamental labour rights. It introduces temporary remedies, according to which if non-respect of core labour rights is found by the panel, a "mutually acceptable compensation" may be developed by the parties. Moreover, the suspension of "the application of obligations under the covered provisions" has been envisaged. This was a very welcome step towards achieving better effectiveness of labour rights and instilled hopes for a lasting change. However, the European Commission was unable to continue this hard policy and did not have the clout to introduce sanctions to subsequent FTAs. For example, the proposal of the European Commission for introducing sanctions for violating fundamental labour standards met with the following response from the Mercosur countries, namely Argentina, Brazil, Paraguay and Uruguay: "There should be no sanctions (or even a hint of sanctions) incorporated into the document and parties should avoid using measures designed to achieve sustainable development as an unjustified or unnecessary obstacle to trade. The instrument needs to be based on a cooperative approach".[19]

More studies should be carried out which aim to analyse, on an ongoing basis, newly concluded FTAs. Future work might, in particular, focus on developing more advanced tools for the enforcement of labour rights included in the FTAs, both in the context of pre-ratification and post-ratification conditionality. The examples of the EU future trade partners mentioned at the beginning of this chapter clearly confirm the need for such research.

Bibliography

Felder Gregory, Kirthana Ganeson, Martin Jehli, Patrick Wagner, the Trade and Labour Nexus. Envisioning the Design and Implementation of Future Labour Chapters in Preferential Trade Agreements. In: The Concept Design of a Twenty-First Century Preferential Trade Agreement. Trends and Future Innovations, Kathleen Claussen, Manfred Elsig, Rodrigo Polanco (eds.), Cambridge University Press 2025, 291–315.

ILO, Social Dimensions of Free Trade Agreements: Studies on Growth with Equity (Geneva: ILO 2013).

International Trade Union Confederation, 2025 ITUC Global Rights Index, Brussels 2025.

Palmer Wayne, Michele Ford, Benni Yusriza Hasbiyalloh, The alignment of Indonesian laws, policies and their enforcement with the ILO international labour standards on forced labour: Situation and gap analysis, ILO 2024.

19 https://www.whitecase.com/insight-alert/mercosur-trade-alert.

Index

www.ingramcontent.com/pod-product-compliance
Lightning Source LLC
LaVergne TN
LVHW011215150926
848065LV00003B/26